GENERATING GENEROS...

Using an innovative methodological approach combining field experiments, case studies, and statistical analyses, this book explores how the religious beliefs and institutions of Catholics and Muslims prompt them to be generous with their time and resources. Drawing upon research involving more than 1,000 Catholics and Muslims in France, Ireland, Italy, and Turkey, the authors examine Catholicism and Islam in majority and minority contexts, discerning the specific factors that lead adherents to help others and contribute to social welfare projects. Based on theories from political science, economics, religious studies, and social psychology, this approach uncovers the causal connections between religious community dynamics, religious beliefs and institutions, and sociopolitical contexts that promote or hinder the generosity of Muslims and Catholics. The study also provides insight into what different religious beliefs mean to Muslims and Catholics, and how they understand those concepts.

Carolyn M. Warner is Professor of Political Science in the School of Politics and Global Studies at Arizona State University. She is the author of *Confessions of an Interest Group: The Catholic Church and Political Parties in Post-War Europe* (2000), *The Best System Money Can Buy* (2007), and articles in *Perspectives on Politics* and *Psychological Science,* among other journals.

Ramazan Kılınç is Associate Professor of Political Science and Co-Director of the Islamic Studies Program at the University of Nebraska at Omaha. He has published articles in *Comparative Politics, Political Science Quarterly, Politics and Religion,* and *Studies in Conflict and Terrorism,* among other journals.

Christopher W. Hale is Assistant Professor of Political Science at the University of Alabama. He has published in outlets such as the *American Journal of Political Science* and *Comparative Politics.*

Adam B. Cohen is Professor of Psychology at Arizona State University, and is an associate editor of the *Journal of Personality and Social Psychology.* He is the author of numerous articles, book chapters, and essays, and editor of the book *Culture Reexamined* (2014).

CAMBRIDGE STUDIES IN ECONOMICS, CHOICE, AND SOCIETY

Founding Editors

Timur Kuran, *Duke University*
Peter J. Boettke, *George Mason University*

This interdisciplinary series promotes original theoretical and empirical research as well as integrative syntheses involving links between individual choice, institutions, and social outcomes. Contributions are welcome from across the social sciences, particularly in the areas where economic analysis is joined with other disciplines such as comparative political economy, new institutional economics, and behavioral economics.

Generating Generosity in Catholicism and Islam

Beliefs, Institutions, and Public Goods Provision

CAROLYN M. WARNER

Arizona State University

RAMAZAN KILINÇ

University of Nebraska, Omaha

CHRISTOPHER W. HALE

University of Alabama

ADAM B. COHEN

Arizona State University

CAMBRIDGE
UNIVERSITY PRESS

CAMBRIDGE
UNIVERSITY PRESS

University Printing House, Cambridge CB2 8BS, United Kingdom

One Liberty Plaza, 20th Floor, New York, NY 10006, USA

477 Williamstown Road, Port Melbourne, VIC 3207, Australia

314–321, 3rd Floor, Plot 3, Splendor Forum, Jasola District Centre, New Delhi – 110025, India

79 Anson Road, #06–04/06, Singapore 079906

Cambridge University Press is part of the University of Cambridge.

It furthers the University's mission by disseminating knowledge in the pursuit of education, learning, and research at the highest international levels of excellence.

www.cambridge.org
Information on this title: www.cambridge.org/9781107135512
DOI: 10.1017/9781316471722

© Carolyn M. Warner, Ramazan Kılınç, Christopher W. Hale and Adam B. Cohen 2018

First published 2018

Printed in the United Kingdom by Clays, St Ives plc

A catalogue record for this publication is available from the British Library.

Library of Congress Cataloging-in-Publication Data
Names: Warner, Carolyn M., 1961– author. | Kılınç, Ramazan, 1977– author. | Hale, Christopher W., 1980– author.
Title: Generating generosity in Catholicism and Islam : beliefs, institutions, and public goods provision / Carolyn M. Warner, Ramazan Kılınç, Christopher W. Hale, and Adam B. Cohen.
Description: New York : Cambridge University Press, 2018. | Series: Cambridge studies in economics, choice, and society | Includes bibliographical references and index.
Identifiers: LCCN 2017055506 | ISBN 9781107135512 (hardback : alk. paper) | ISBN 9781316501320 (pbk. : alk. paper)
Subjects: LCSH: Generosity–Religious aspects–Christianity. | Catholic Church. | Generosity–Religious aspects–Islam. | Islam.
Classification: LCC BV4647.G45 G46 2018 | DDC 241/.4–dc23
LC record available at https://lccn.loc.gov/2017055506

ISBN 978-1-107-13551-2 Hardback
ISBN 978-1-316-50132-0 Paperback

To G. J. Lilly Cohen, Erica Hale, Halide Görgün Kılınç,
and Robert Warner

Contents

Figures

Tables

Acknowledgments

This book's proximal origins lie in a "request for proposals" notification that one of the authors received from the University of Notre Dame's Science of Generosity Program, funded by the Templeton Foundation. We thank the Science of Generosity Program, as well as the Templeton Foundation, for research funding, and Christian Smith for his role in creating and leading the program. The project benefited from the skillful work of helpful research assistants. We thank Sevde Arpacı, Matthew E. Bergman, Sherman Duckworth, Kathryn A. Johnson, Jenna A. Mudrick, Angela Pirlott, Dimitri Sementchoukov, Nick Sobecki, Scott Swagerty, and Chloe Westlund for research assistance. We are very grateful for the helpful comments and critiques of Lenka Bustikova, Paul Djupe, Richard Fording, Abdullahi Gallab, Tony Gill, Ahmet Kuru, Larry Iannaccone, Jared Rubin, Bernhard Reinsberg, David Siroky, Joseph Smith, several anonymous reviewers, and participants at seminars at Arizona State University, Chapman University, Duke University, AALIMS-Princeton University, and Yale University, on earlier papers that became part of this book. We regret if we did not or could not successfully take and implement all of their advice. Notably, we thank Timur Kuran for his initial and continuing interest in the project and book manuscript, and his insightful critiques and suggestions to improve the book. All interpretations, arguments, and any errors are our responsibility.

We also thank the Institute for Social Science Research at Arizona State University for its financial contribution to the project. We note with appreciation the contributions of Carolyn Forbes and Maureen Olmsted, of Arizona State University's Center for the Study of Religion and Conflict. Their good-spirited, competent assistance was invaluable in all aspects of the logistics of the project, including dealing with the human subjects review boards of four different universities (two overseas) and the sponsored projects offices of two universities. Carolyn Warner thanks Pat Kenney, who facilitated release time for her field research, and, especially, her co-authors, who have been wonderful, indeed, generous, collaborators on all aspects of research and writing for this project.

This work could not have been done without the assistance and cooperation of the religious officials who allowed access to their religious communities, and we thank them sincerely for their openness and assistance. Professors David Farrell and Christopher Whelan at University College Dublin and Professors Ali Tekcan and Kutlu Ülgen at Boğaziçi University provided crucial assistance in facilitating the conduct of experiments with students at their universities. We appreciate the assistance of Noel Barber, S.J., and Guido Formigoni in facilitating contacts with Catholic entities in Dublin and Milan, respectively. We especially thank the interviewees and experiment participants for their willingness to take part in this project.

Parts of this book are drawn, in revised form, from "Micro-Foundations of Religion and Public Goods Provision: Belief, Belonging and Giving in Catholicism and Islam," *Politics and Religion*, 8/4 (2015): 718–744; "Religion and Public Goods Provision: Experimental and Interview Evidence from Catholicism and Islam in Europe," *Comparative Politics* 47/2 (Jan. 2015): 189–209; and "Charitable Giving Model or Muddle?," *The Review of Faith and International Affairs* 11/4 (Winter 2013): 32–36. The revised material is presented here with permission from Cambridge University Press, City University of New York, and Taylor & Francis, respectively. We thank the anonymous reviewers and the journal editors for helpful comments on the articles.

A project like this one also benefits immensely from the generosity of loved ones. Chris Hale expresses his profound gratitude to his wife, Erica Hale, who never ceases to be an inspiration and whose love, support, and sacrifice are deeply appreciated. Ramazan Kılınç's deepest gratitude goes to his beloved wife Halide Görgün Kılınç. She is certainly the person who deserves the biggest acknowledgment, not only for her support, love, and belief in him but also for making his life a happy one. Carolyn Warner thanks her husband, Joe Cutter, for his long-standing support and love, not to mention good humor about the work, and for holding down the fort while she conducted field research. She takes this opportunity to dedicate the book to her father, Robert Warner, whose love and support have been unflagging.

Abbreviations

AKP	Adalet ve Kalkınma Partisi (Justice and Development Party)
CCFD	*Comité catholique contre la faim et pour le développement-Terre Solidaire* (Catholic Committee against Hunger and for Development-Solidarity of the Earth)
DC	Dublin Catholic interviewee
DM	Dublin Muslim interviewee
EP	experiment participant
IC	Istanbul Catholic interviewee
IM	Istanbul Muslim interviewee
KYM	Kimse Yok Mu (Is Anybody Listening?)
MC	Milan Catholic interviewee
MM	Milan Muslim interviewee
PC	Paris Catholic interviewee
PM	Paris Muslim interviewee
SVdP	Société Saint Vincent-de-Paul, Società San Vincenzo de Paoli, Society of St. Vincent de Paul
TIECS	Turkish-Irish Educational and Cultural Society
UCD	University College Dublin
UNICEF	United Nations Children's Fund

Introduction

What We Do and Don't Know about Religious-Based Generosity

On July 7, 2009, Pope Benedict XVI issued an Encyclical Letter, "Charity in Truth," exhorting Christians to understand charity as an expression of God's gift of love and as the foundation of human development. That same year, in late September, Muslims around the world celebrated the religious holiday of Eid al-Fitr, which marks the end of Ramadan and highlights giving money or food to the poor and needy.[1] Even though religions have charity and giving as virtues and obligations, how religions affect the generosity and public goods provision of their adherents and organizations has not been well understood. There are many questions of theoretical and practical importance. What specific religious beliefs and institutions promote generosity? Do these vary across religious traditions? Do religions promote generosity toward their own members as well as others, or do religions tend to favor their own? How, if at all, do taxation, social welfare arrangements, and religion–state regulations affect the public goods provision of adherents of different religions?

From Indonesian tsunami relief efforts to health clinics in the Gaza Strip to promoting civic culture in America, organized religions have been credited with providing social services. How they do so is not yet well understood. What motivates their adherents to expend time and other resources helping others? Why do religious adherents help in their own organization, when they could simply coast on the labor of others? The intuitive answer may be "their faith," but faith has many dimensions. What aspects of their faith motivate such behavior? Do these individuals help because of a sense of duty to God? Divine inspiration? Love of others? Do they help due to religious commandments, membership requirements, or

---

[1] Ramadan is the ninth month of the Islamic calendar. During the month, Muslims fast from sunrise to sunset and put more emphasis on charity.

group expectations? Is this generosity an effect of socializing with other adherents? With a wide range of practices and beliefs among religions, do the reasons for prosocial behavior vary across religious traditions?

Additionally, it is not altogether clear why religious adherents make the effort to help others where the state already provides social welfare resources. Conversely, if the state reduces its welfare provision, do organized religions, among other organizations, have the capacity to fill the gap? Furthermore, are the motivations of adherents of minority religions within a particular country different from those of religious majorities? Finally, religious traditions with strict membership requirements and expulsion threats often have extensive social services for their members precisely because of their strictness (Berman 2009; Cammett and Issar 2010; Iannaccone 1992; McBride 2007). How, then, do we explain the large charitable operations of mainstream religious institutions?

This book seeks to answer these questions through a study of Muslims and Catholics in Western Europe and Turkey. It investigates the forces within Catholicism and Islam that lead Catholics and Muslims to provide public goods such as social services and to provide the resources that help sustain their own religious organizations.[2] We have too easily assumed that "the Golden Rule" explains the helping behavior of the religious without pausing to consider whether various religious traditions interpret that rule differently, practice it differently, or even share it at all. Given the prevalence of religion in human society, and given that Islam and Catholicism claim over 2.5 billion followers combined, the subject has broad implications. Worldwide charitable giving is heavily dependent upon the generosity of the major world religions. Even though religions commonly focus on charity and giving as virtues and obligations, the causal mechanisms of the generosity of their adherents and organizations are not well understood. Why are the religious generous?

We think the answer lies in the impact of *religious beliefs* and *religious institutions* on prompting and channeling the generous and helping behavior of religious adherents. We call this behavior "prosocial." First, *beliefs* have a role in generating prosocial behavior and in overcoming collective action barriers. Contributions of time, effort, and other resources to the collective good need not rely on secular or temporal punitive monitoring and sanctioning arrangements but may be instead prompted by faith. Yet these effects could vary across Catholics and Muslims.

---

[2] "Islam" throughout refers to Sunni Islam, the major branch to which about 80 percent of the world's Muslims adhere. The Shia branch of Islam is more centralized and is far less present in Europe and Turkey (Navaro-Yashin 2002, 46–51; Roy 2005).

Catholics may respond to love of others; Muslims may respond to duty to God. But it is not even as simple as that. The very meaning of these religious concepts varies across religions; we show how it does and what impact that variation has on the generosity of Catholics and Muslims. Second, *religious institutions* create communities (parishes and associations, for example) that in turn engender a sense of solidarity. These communities inspire generosity not through fear but through the positive emotions and sense of solidarity that are produced by social interaction. We see differences between Catholic and Muslim communities as well, and we explore the sources and consequences of those variations.

Clearly, these questions are situated within the ongoing debates about why people help other people, and if, when they are helping others, they really are just helping themselves. Sociobiologists, evolutionary anthropologists, and psychologists tend to argue that we help each other in order to help ourselves (Wilson 2015). It comes down to evolutionary fitness and perpetuating one's genes. In other words, generosity and altruism, as commonly understood, do not exist; instead, those are labels we give to behavior that is promoting individual and group fitness. As Richard Dawkins theorized, helping, at any cost to oneself, is a matter of perpetuating the genes one is carrying by creating an environment that will help them survive (Dawkins 1976/2006). This argument, amid much debate, has been extended to explain multilevel selection: that groups that foster altruism "beat selfish groups," even though within a group, "Selfishness beats altruism" (Wilson and Wilson 2007, 345). When there is "fitness interdependence," with individuals' survival mutually dependent on each other, there may be need-based transfers between members of a group (Aktipis 2016, 22–26). Economists such as Gary Becker of the Chicago School have argued that helping others, or altruism, is merely selfishness in disguise, as helping others creates conditions from which the helper profits (1976).

The philosopher Ayn Rand argued that selfishness is just "concern with one's own interests" and that the concept is not in itself moral or amoral. Rather, for Rand, the immoral is altruism, which she held promoted the idea that anything done to benefit others is good; anything done to benefit the self is "evil" (1961/1964, xii; Den Uyl and Rasmussen 1984). While not carrying this view quite as far as Rand did, evolutionary biologists, social psychologists, and observers of international aid efforts have noted, to put it bluntly, that "[t]here is no reason to assume that altruistic motivation will always be accompanied by wisdom" (Batson, Lishner, and Stocks 2015, 17; Dawkins 1976/2006; Hancock 1989). The question remains, though: why do people help others, if, as Rand asserts, doing so is usually deleterious to the self and potentially to others?

These perspectives may be challenged by some examples of altruism, such as rescuing Holocaust victims (Monroe 1996) or donating time and money to help complete strangers in other countries belonging to very different ethnic or racial groups. Humans' capacity for making sacrifices for those not closely genetically related (outside the "kin" group) is perhaps greater than sociobiologists and economists would expect. This leaves the question of how such sacrifices are prompted. There is some research that indicates that feeling empathy for another individual can do so (Batson, Lishner, and Stocks 2015); other research places helping behavior, as a subcategory of cooperative behavior, as due to effective quid pro quo strategies and enforcement mechanisms (Aktipis 2016). To explain altruism, or at least prosocial helping behavior in larger group contexts, some scholars turn to religion, conceptualizing it as a phenomenon with some functional features that are useful for creating ingroup cooperation, which helps the group survive.

Within this functionalist paradigm, religion enters as something that prompts helping behavior. Humans have evolved an adaptation, religion, that enhances group fitness (Wilson 2002). Evolutionary anthropologists and psychologists have speculated and found evidence that religion promotes individual helping behavior on behalf of the group by creating norms of reciprocity and helping that are enforced by a third-party observer (a deity or deities) and by signaling commitment to the group. In other words, religion is a means of improving group fitness, of making large-scale cooperation possible (Atran and Heinrich 2010). We note, however, that helping others is a characteristic of most nonsociopaths, not just the religious, and that the functionalist approach based on evolution still does not explain outgroup helping. That said, our work is not meant to weigh in on the merits of an evolutionary approach to religion. Our question is not whether religion, by prompting helping behavior, serves some evolutionary function; it is what specific aspects of religion elicit that behavior.

We also are not asking whether people who are "religious" help others more than those who are not. Setting aside the charged nature of the question (Hitchens 2007), the evidence on this question is mixed, with a number of findings showing that the religious are less altruistic, and others that the religious are more helpful or compassionate (Blouin, Robinson, and Starks 2013; Decety et al. 2015; Putnam and Campbell 2010). We are not aware of studies that make comparisons specifically between the areligious, or "less" religious, and Catholics or Muslims.[3] In Chapter 3,

---

[3] One problem with much of the research is that studies often include religious institutions, such as churches, synagogues, and mosques, in their definition of a charity. Because many

we analyze our demographic data to assess the impact of religiosity based on a commonly used scale, and in Chapter 8 we analyze demographic data from the European Values Survey to assess the relative imperviousness of religiosity to expansive welfare states. We cannot say, however, that there are not secular mechanisms and beliefs that prompt giving as well, with empathy, responsibility, and a "feel good" factor often said to play a role (Andreoni 1990; Singer 2015b). As a number of our interviewees, including religious officials, noted, one does not have to be religious to be generous. They saw helping others as integral to their experience and expression of their faith, but did not view it as something on which religion had a monopoly (MC6, PC7, DC15, PC16, PC26).[4] The questions we focus on primarily in this book are: in what ways do various religions prompt helping behavior, and which aspects of those religions do so? What are the meanings and interpretations adherents give to their generosity? Even if altruism were harmful, or even if religion had evolved as a behavioral and cognitive adaptation that leads people to help each other, significant questions remain about how religions actually foster helping behavior. How do specific religious beliefs and institutions prompt generosity?

What We Already Know and What We Need to Know

We know surprisingly little about the role of religion in prosocial behavior. One noted study on "why people cooperate" didn't mention religion at all (Tyler 2011), while another, on the "social and evolutionary roots of cooperation," devoted only 2 of 246 pages to the impact of religion (Cronk and Leech 2012). The conventional wisdom in political science, economics, and to some extent psychology sees prosocial behavior as a quid pro quo in disguise, or as a public good beset with collective action problems that can only be solved with monitoring and sanctioning mechanisms (Boix and

---

"religious" people donate to their religious institutions, it appears that the religious give more to charity, which in turn is interpreted as the religious helping others more than do the nonreligiously observant. The latter may belong to secular organizations to which they pay membership fees rather than make donations, while the former's donations mostly are going to the institutions' operating costs (in essence, both are helping to provide club goods). In our study, we do consider adherents' donating to and helping their own religious institution as a form of generosity, or at least helping behavior, but we are also not trying to establish whether religious adherents are more generous than those who are not religious.

[4] We assign each interviewee a code to preserve the anonymity of our interviewees. In coding the interviews, we use the initial of the city, religious affiliation of the interviewee, and a number. For example, the first Catholic interviewee in Milan is coded as MC1; the third Muslim interviewee in Dublin is coded as DM3.

Posner 1998; Edlin, Gelman, and Kaplan 2007; Leeson 2014; Luttmer 2001; Ostrom 1990; Shayo 2009; Smith 2006). These disciplines also, by and large, view religious beliefs per se as epiphenomenal and inconsequential – what matters is some underlying desire to attain power, resources, and better life chances. Others suggest that prosociality is largely the result of circumstance and context, with beliefs too inconsistent and ephemeral to have a role in behavior (Chaves 2010). Yet it would be odd, given all the intellectual, emotional, and cognitive energy that human beings put into formulating, promulgating, and adhering to religious beliefs, if those beliefs had no impact on people's prosocial behavior (Boyer 1994; Prothero 2010; Wuthnow 2011).

The disregard for the impact of beliefs has been accompanied by an emphasis on the capacity of formal and informal institutions to prompt prosocial behavior. Economists and political scientists argue that strict religious sects, terrorist groups, and ethnoreligious groups provide public goods because such groups rigorously monitor and punish (sanction) their members. Evolutionary anthropologists and some economists view religion as a means by which individuals signal to others that they are members of the same group and willing to cooperate with each other (Berman 2009; Bulbulia 2004; Cohen et al. 2015; Hall et al. 2015; Iannaccone 1988; Power 2017; Roes and Raymond 2003; Sosis 2003; 2005; 2006). Extreme sacrificial rites such as "distinctive diet, dress, or speech" demonstrate the willingness of individuals to help others in the group (Iannaccone 1994, 1182). Yet this raises a question: how do mainstream religions, often lacking in effective monitoring and sanctioning structures or extreme sacrifice requirements, create collective goods? Why are the adherents of mainstream religions prosocial despite the absence of demonstrated self-sacrifice and punishment mechanisms?

One answer might be that people internalize the monitoring and sanctioning mechanisms through belief in a punitive deity (Norenzayan 2013) or by internalizing group norms of generosity and reciprocity (Ostrom 2007, 196–197). Another perspective holds that believing in a benevolent God is just as effective (Johnson, Cohen, and Okun 2016). While college students, mostly in North America, have exhibited such behavior in experiments, we do not know if these effects obtain specifically with Muslims or Catholics, and outside the United States and Canada.

Another answer might be that people gain "warm glow" rewards from helping others; generous activity is intrinsically rewarding (Andreoni 1990; Hungerman 2009). There is an accumulating amount of evidence that sanctions and incentives are not the only or even necessary factors to bring about generous, helping behavior in individuals (Jaeggi, Burkart, and Van Schaik 2010, 2725; Tyler 2011; Warneken 2013). As many have noted, religious teachings typically instruct the faithful to help others. Religions are also organized around communities of the faithful. Both these theological and community mechanisms could have a big role in turning "on" and channeling the prosocial nature of individuals. What we need is an account of the types and content of religious beliefs and religious communities that activate prosocial tendencies and how they do so. Social psychology tells us that the faithful should be generous partly because religious communities have behavioral norms about helping others and because (many) religions create perceptions of someone watching each individual's behavior. Social psychologists have found that individuals tend to be more generous to their ingroup rather than to the general public (outgroup), and have some evidence that this is the case for religious individuals as well (Preston, Ritter, and Hernandez 2010; Tajfel and Turner 1979). However, the field, with a few exceptions (Ritter and Preston 2013), treats "religion" as a unitary concept, thus associating the multiple meanings and aspects of religion with one outcome. The field also has not paid sufficient attention to the impact of different contexts or different religions (but see Cohen et al. 2005; Cohen and Hill 2007). Largely for these reasons, findings have been contradictory and variable (Galen 2012). Social psychologists are only beginning to study the "psychology of Islam" and, prior to our study, had not directly assessed the role of Islam in prompting prosocial behavior (El Azayem and Hedayat-Diba 1994; Ji and Ibrahaim 2007; Raiya et al. 2008; Saroglou and Galand 2004). Mainstream Catholicism, also, has not received the sustained attention with regard to prosociality that other Christian denominations have.

We need to find out if Catholics and Muslims perceive expectations from their religious communities, if the communities are structured to monitor compliance with those expectations and punish deviance from them, and, of course, what those expectations are about helping the group (or others not necessarily in the group). In addition, we then need to see if those expectations create or lead to generous behavior.

We need to examine the kinds of organizations Catholics and Muslims volunteer in and contribute to, assess whether Catholics and Muslims are cognizant of ingroup/outgroup distinctions, and assess whether these group distinctions make any difference to generous behavior. This inquiry is complementary to research on the historical and sociopolitical origins of Catholic and Muslim charitable foundations and activities (Bonner, Ener, and Singer 2003; Brown and McKeown 2009; Clark 2004; Kozlowski

1998; Kuran 2001; 2003; Mollat 1986, 39–53). Catholic and Muslim charitable institutions have developed as vehicles for the expression of religiously inspired or, at least, religiously organized generosity and as religious-based responses to perceived social needs (Flynn 1989; Singer 2002). That development has sometimes been prompted or inhibited by political figures. At the risk of oversimplifying, we know from earlier research that Christian and Islamic benevolent activities developed quickly after the birth of each religion, and, with considerable geographic variation, Christians and Muslims created institutions, some more permanent than others, such as the Islamic *waqf* systems, to produce activities intended to benefit the community (Arjomand 1998; Diefendorf 2004; Misner 1991). How do the contemporary structures of Catholic parishes and Islamic associations affect the generosity of their members, and how are charitable religious institutions sustained in secularizing societies? Religious-based charities are sometimes analyzed as tools for members' sociopolitical advancement (Cammett and Issar 2010; Clark 2004; Davis and Robinson 2012). How do the members themselves understand the organizations' activities and why they contribute time and other resources to them? It is clear from research on religions in the United States that, as one study put it, people of faith give "spiritual meanings" to their social volunteerism and work in charitable organizations (Cherry 2014; Cnaan 2002; Kniss and Numrich 2007; Unruh and Sider 2005, 67). We ask, in a non-US context, what are the meanings and motivations of Catholics and Muslims, and do they vary by religion?

Finally, we have some evidence that as the welfare state expands, religiosity, typically measured as attendance at religious services, declines because the marginally faithful can get social services from the state instead of a religious organization (Gill and Lundsgaarde 2004). For Christian denominations, the findings on the relationship between religious generosity, defined as adherents' donations of time and material resources to their own religion, and the extent of the welfare state, are contradictory (Franck and Iannaccone 2014; Traunmüller and Freitag 2011; Van Oorschot and Arts 2005). We know that *zakat* and *waqf* giving systems of Islam were not capable, for various reasons, of providing comprehensive, long-term public welfare in the states that tried to rely on them (Kuran 2001; 2003; Rubin 2017).[5] Whatever the impact of the welfare state on generosity, we nevertheless do not know why the faithful in welfare states give generously of their time and other resources.

---

[5] Zakat, or obligatory giving based on a percentage of one's wealth, is discussed in Chapter 2, and waqf, a type of charitable foundation, in Chapters 2 and 8.

Puzzles of Catholic and Muslim Prosocial Behavior

What do we know of the faithful themselves? What aspects of their religious community and faith do Catholics and Muslims think matter in generosity? Nearly twenty years ago, Robert Wuthnow asked whether "different religious traditions encourage different kinds (or levels) of charitable involvement" (1991, 124), and our study is situated within the scholarship that has responded to his question. While social scientists debate the impact of religion on generosity, do the faithful themselves think their generous actions have their religion as the source? How do believers understand and think of their motivations for generosity? Learning the ways people describe their actions provides a window on how, if at all, their religious beliefs and institutions have affected their understanding of their generosity. As Wuthnow notes, "having a language to describe our motives for caring is one of the ways in which we make compassion possible in the individualistic society in which we live" (1991, 49–50).

We know Catholicism as a formally practiced religion in Europe has been in decline. If, as many say, the pews are empty at mass, who is contributing and why? We do not know the pathways that lead practicing Catholics to contribute to collective goods. If we examine the extensive descriptive research by sociologists on religion and charity in (mostly) Protestant denominations and (mostly) in the United States, we would speculate that it is from some combination of belief and a desire to evangelize (Davis and Robinson 2012; Smith and Emerson 2008; Tropman 2002; Wuthnow and Evans 2002). However, we do not have systematic data on which beliefs, motivations, or organizational structures foster or inhibit adherents' helping behaviors. There are hundreds of Catholic charities in France, Italy, and Ireland alone, not to mention the constrained set in Turkey; how is it that parishes sustain their charitable activities? How do they meet the expenses of their parish church? Numerous parishes in Europe, as elsewhere, have had to turn to the laity to do tasks that used to be done by priests; how do parishes meet those needs?

We also know Islam is spreading in Western Europe and has been reinvigorated in Turkey and elsewhere, but we have limited knowledge of generosity and public goods provision in the widely practiced nonextremist variants of Islam. The extant literature has focused on the *waqf* system's impact on economic development (e.g., Kuran 2001) and on zakat obligations (Utvik 2006). It has also focused on particular charitable organizations or political groups such as the Red Crescent (e.g., Benthall and Bellion-Jourdan 2003) and the Muslim Brotherhood (e.g., Davis and

Robinson 2012), on trends in Middle Eastern countries (Atia 2013; Bonner, Ener, and Singer 2003; Cammett 2014; Clark 2004), or on the broad history of philanthropy in Islam (e.g., Kozlowski 1998). What we don't (yet) have is a targeted assessment of the impact of Islamic beliefs and institutions on individual Muslims' generosity or prosocial behavior. The conventional wisdom is that the zakat obligation is what is behind any generosity by Muslims, yet there have not been empirical studies that support this understanding.

As mentioned earlier, most of our knowledge of public goods provision and Islam stems from studies of groups such as Hamas and Hezbollah. Passing under the radar screen of scholars and policymakers are mainstream groups. Given that the vast majority of Muslims adhere to mainstream versions of Islam and associate with mainstream mosques and cultural centers (Esposito and Mogahed 2008; Fish 2011), any further understanding of contemporary Islam and generosity depends on some examination of nonextremist groups.

Our Approach

The goal of this volume is to illuminate which aspects of Catholicism and Islam lead to adherents' generosity. In the remainder of this chapter, we first present key concepts and terms. We then introduce our theoretical framework and focus on two main areas that may influence the prosocial behavior of religious adherents. These are the impacts of (1) religious institutions and their communities and (2) religious beliefs. We pay attention to how these factors are affected by sociopolitical contexts such as whether a religious group is a majority or minority, the character of religion–state relations, and the extent of state-provided social welfare. Following this discussion, we review our research strategy and methodology while elaborating on our research sites. In this chapter, we explain our use of experimental and case study research.

To preview the findings of our analyses, some, but not all, religious beliefs we typically associate with generosity do motivate prosocial behavior in Catholics and Muslims, and they are not the same in both religions. Second, some aspects of religious institutions prompt prosocial behavior, but they are not the ones expected by those who focus on monitoring and sanctioning mechanisms. Instead, they are the aspects that create positive feelings about the religious communities and that enhance adherents' sense of responsibility to sustain the organization. This "responsibility" effect is, as one would expect, more pronounced in the communities of religious minorities. Finally, we think our evidence shows that while Muslims and Catholics are more generous than political scientists and economists might expect, their capacity for generosity is not sufficient to substitute for state-extracted and redistributed resources.

Key Definitions and Terms

We need to explain our use of terms, both those that are seemingly intuitive and others that may require additional explanation. We start with the one for which most people have an intuitive understanding: *generosity.* We define generosity as the giving freely of one's resources, including funds, time, skills, and effort, to other individuals and organizations. "Freely" means that the actions are done largely without an expectation of reciprocity or reward, something that flies in the face of the conventional wisdom in political science, economics, anthropology, and social psychology: people are theorized to nearly always do something with an expectation of a payback or a payoff (even if that payoff is just a warm glow). Some scholars argue that helping others, when boiled down to its essentials, is an act that ultimately helps oneself (Burton-Chellew and West 2013; Cialdini et al. 1997; Mauss 1954/1967). For example, one might suggest that the "reward" being received is a positive feeling some experience from helping others, also described as warm-glow altruism (Andreoni 1990) and thus that the act was not a generous one. But in many contexts, there is a generosity of giving despite the fact that others, who are not giving, are also benefiting from the reward (e.g., helping the parish church pay the electricity bill). In that regard, the one who gave is, in our view, being generous. We bracket the debate about what altruism is and whether altruism exists or is the same as generosity. We see both terms as pointing toward similar behavior: that of giving of oneself, of helping others without compensation. We find that specific religious beliefs of Catholics and Muslims, and positive feelings about the community one is volunteering in, contribute to the generosity of Catholics and Muslims.

The concept of generosity is closely related to *prosocial behavior,* another term we use frequently. Child psychologists have documented an apparently innate "other oriented" disposition in very young children; we are social beings attuned to each other (Lieberman 2014; Warneken and Tomasello 2006). Prosocial behaviors refer to those behaviors that facilitate living together in groups: acting morally, helpfully, and with self-control (Galen 2012, 876). We use the term in a slightly narrower sense than some might. In our usage, prosocial behavior, or "prosociality," is not just an orientation toward others but behavior directed at helping others in some fashion, through contributions of a person's time and/or other resources.[6]

When we refer to *religion*, we agree with Berger that it is "the human attitude towards a sacred order that includes within it all being – human or otherwise – i.e. belief in a cosmos, the meaning of which both includes and transcends man" (Berger 1974). Yet our definition is more expansive and specifically conceptualizes roles for both beliefs and religious institutions. Scholars ranging from Émile Durkheim to Bruce Lincoln have suggested that religions encompass *beliefs*, "discourse" in Lincoln's terms, that speak of transcendent authority and truth and define a realm of the sacred distinct from the profane. We refer to *religious institutions* as communities that define and organize themselves by reference to particular religious beliefs and practices. These institutions provide continuity for religious communities by interpreting and regulating the beliefs and practices, and claim some authority to do so (Durkheim 1915, 47; Hassner 2009, 21–22; Lincoln 2003, 5–8; Saroglou 2014, 5). This departs somewhat from the thin definitions given by scholars of "religious economics" who state that religion is a credence good with a set of suppliers and buyers (Gill 1998; Iannaccone 1998, 1491). Our definition enables us to address religious communities, their beliefs and practices, and their institutions without prejudicing the analysis toward a strict means–end rationality in religious behavior.

We herein refer to Catholicism and Islam as *mainstream* religions. By mainstream religions we refer to those religious institutions that have a relatively low level of tension with the societies in which they are embedded; in other words, they tend to be part of the ordinary social fabric of a society (Stark and Bainbridge 1985, 23–24). Even if they are a minority in a particular country, they are nevertheless "mainstream" in our usage if they do not require extreme sacrifices as a condition of membership. What constitutes a mainstream religion in any given society may change over time, of course. While both Catholicism and

---

[6] As noted, a number of social psychologists and economists define generosity as behaving cooperatively rather than with self-interested motives (Bendor, Kramer, and Swistak 1996; Cox and Deck 2006; Van Lange, Ouwerkerk, and Tazelaar 2002). Others define it as kindness and altruistic love in which a person acts without "assurance of reciprocity, reputational gains, or any other benefits to the self" (Peterson and Seligman 2004, 326). Space constraints do not permit a discussion of the extensive debate about whether altruism exists, but interested readers might see Batson, Lishner, and Stocks (2015); Cialdini et al. (1997); Fowler and Kam (2007).

Islam have extremist sects, our focus is on the ordinary religions as practiced by the vast majority of adherents.

We next need to consider what we mean by *public goods*. The term typically refers to goods that are both nonrivalrous and nonexcludable. Nonrivalrous goods are those goods and services that can be consumed by one individual without diminishing the ability of others to consume them. If we watch a World Cup match on television, for example, we have not diminished the capacity of anyone else to watch the game, and many additional individuals around the world can join us without detracting from our ability to enjoy it. Nonexcludable goods, on the other hand, are those goods that cannot be limited to others. Once these services have been provided, it is difficult, if not impossible, to exclude individuals from their benefits (Cornes and Sandler 1996, 8–9).[7]

To capture the fact that much generosity by religious adherents is directed at their own religious organization, we use the concept of *club goods*. Strictly speaking, these are goods that are nonrivalrous but excludable. They are produced by individuals in institutions (clubs) and typically restricted to benefit those members who actively contribute in some way to their production. Religious institutions can be thought of as providing a variety of excludable club benefits such as spiritual services, social gatherings, and so on. The extent to which adherents benefit from these services may depend on whether and to what extent adherents contribute to their respective religious club (McBride 2007). We loosen the club goods concept in this book, because most mainstream religious organizations do not require members or guests (nonaffiliated consumers) to contribute to the production of the club good to benefit from it. Anyone can walk into a Catholic church and benefit from the liturgy reading done by volunteer

---

[7] Public goods seldom meet those standards, particularly when considering goods that depend on donations of finite individual resources. We thus acknowledge that the prosocial, generous, and helping behavior of religious adherents is what economists call *impure* public goods. For example, charity is an impure public good. It is not perfectly nonrivalrous or nonexcludable. We can imagine it would be possible for charities to exclude particular individuals from benefits. In practice, however, the major charitable activities typically engaged in by mainstream religions, including the Catholic and Muslim charities we examine here, do not exclude particular individuals or categories of individuals from their charitable aid. Charity is also not perfectly nonrivalrous. Obviously, the giving of charitable resources to one individual diminishes the total stockpile of charitable resources available to an institution to give to others. To the extent that charitable institutions distribute resources indiscriminately and equitably to recipients, we can conceptualize it as an impure public good (Cornes and Sandler 1996, 9–10). For the purposes of readability however, and as a nod to general usage, we use "public goods."

parishioners, for instance, and parents need not volunteer to organize the after-school Islamic education classes to have their child attend them. Indeed, that is part of the inspiration for our study: when benefits are not restricted to contributors, and providers are not compensated, what motivates the contributors to give of their resources? We define *collective goods*, then, as goods provided by multiple individuals, of which club goods and public goods are subsets.

Those with a psychology background might be more familiar with the terms *ingroup* and *outgroup*. For our purposes, they have at their base the notion that individuals' activities, allegiances, and identity are distinguishable between the group of which the individual is a member and the group of which she is not (Deaux 1996). Psychologists expect more generosity toward the ingroup than the outgroup. Defining the boundary of the ingroup can be difficult in practice: members of an Islamic association in Dublin have an immediate ingroup (other association members in Dublin), but is the ingroup also all Muslims? While not technically interchangeable with club and public goods, the ingroup is something of a club: benefits produced by individuals in the group are meant to be consumed only by group members. The outgroup has less in common with a public good, because an outgroup, by definition, does not include members of the ingroup, but a public good could.[8]

Having addressed some definitional issues, what follows is an introduction to how we think about our questions, why we raise these questions, and, in the subsequent section, how we go about answering the questions.

Religious Institutions, Their Communities, and Prosocial Behavior
The distinction between religious institutions and communities often blurs in practice; we maintain it here only to put into relief questions about how the formal institutions of Islam and Catholicism might prompt generosity (Rhodes, Binder, and Rockman 2006). Typically, one would ask what means religious institutions have to monitor the generosity of adherents, and what means they have to sanction those who do not contribute. Can religious officials exclude noncompliant individuals from services or from other benefits? If not religious officials, then do communities informally shun or

---

[8] This literature has also been engaged in an extensive debate about whether the prosociality is just directed toward other members of the religious group or if members help those outside. This raises questions of what constitutes the boundaries of the religious group: is it the local church? Does it extend to a national religious charity of the same religion? And does it count if the donations and volunteer work help nonadherents but the donations and work are given to and/or done by the religious group? (Cf. Galen 2012, 878–880.)

exclude those who do not contribute? Do they have formal rules that allow them to do so, or rules that specify rewards for contributions? Religions often specify that rewards come in an afterlife. Is that the case in Catholicism and Islam, and, if so, is that a motivation for Catholics and Muslims? We should also ask whether the formal structure of a religion encourages or discourages participation: hierarchical organizations, such as the Catholic Church, may limit opportunities to volunteer in the organization. With religious officials and Church structure seemingly distant from adherents, they may reduce adherents' sense of responsibility or goodwill to contribute. Decentralized organizations, such as (Sunni) Islam, may do the opposite (Ahn, Esarey, and Scholz 2009; Hale 2015). Religious institutions also may foster or hinder propensities toward generosity by making it more or less difficult for individuals to know how or what to give (cf. Healy 2000; 2006) and by increasing or decreasing community effects.

A religious community could have an impact on the prosocial behavior of religious adherents because humans, as social beings, are attuned to what their co-equals think of them and adjust their behavior accordingly. Groups affect individual behavior partly through *norms and expectations*. Prosocial behavior becomes something that is required and rewarded by the group. Generosity is simply generalized reciprocity or ingroup cooperation: the donor knows and expects that the "gift" eventually will be repaid by others in the society either tangibly or via benefits to reputation, and that it is given due to group expectations (Mauss 1954/1967; Nowak and Sigmund 2005). As everyone with gaps in their backyard fence knows, if a neighbor is watching, individuals are more likely to conform to the local neighborhood (group) norms.

A variation on this theme emphasizes the importance of a *third-party enforcer* of group norms. Psychologists theorize that having a deity who monitors and sanctions people's behavior makes people more likely to be generous (Norenzayan and Shariff 2008; Shariff and Norenzayan 2007) or that a benevolent God can be an impetus to generosity (Johnson, Okun, and Cohen 2015a; Johnson, Cohen, and Okun 2016). Thus, a religion with such a concept enhances prosocial behavior by providing beliefs about supernatural punishment for those who are selfish and rewards for those who are generous. Generosity of Muslims and Catholics could be caused by beliefs that their behavior is being monitored by a deity or that God provides a benevolent role model (Johnson et al. 2013a).[9]

---

[9] A review of the field is in Tsang, Rowatt, and Shariff (2015).

Taking this one step further, social psychology and evolutionary anthropology suggest that any generous behavior motivated by the need or desire to meet group expectations should be directed toward the ingroup but not to religious outgroups (Norenzayan and Shariff 2008). That is because helping nonmembers would make generous behavior costly to the success of one's ingroup or "club." In other words, group members will be more likely to provide club goods than public goods. Research on minorities indicates that this behavior varies by context: where the group is in the minority, efforts to help will be more focused on the ingroup.

A somewhat different way in which community could affect prosocial behavior is by eliciting positive attitudes, or *positive affect*, of individuals toward engagement in the community itself (Tyler 2011). This view agrees that humans are oriented toward groups, but emphasizes the positive side of that rather than the more negative requirement of meeting group expectations. Humans are relational, and value those relations. Their prosociality may be predicated on emotions such as liking and valuing interaction with other group members, and the sense of solidarity they have with the group (Peifer 2010).

We must also consider that generosity might come from how the community associated with a religion might heighten a sense of *similarity to others*, making individuals empathetic. We would expect that a heightened sense of similarity between oneself and another would result in more generosity. Catholicism and Islam both emphasize the universality of the human condition. We can check if a religiously inspired sense of similarity between oneself and others is a reason that Catholics and Muslims help others, even those not in their specific religious group or religion.

And to state what might be obvious to the casual reader but not to numerous scholars, rituals and discourse about giving, about helping, are likely to matter. How is generosity conceptualized in relation to God and to institutional obligations in the religion? Thus we move to consider the second main area, that of religious beliefs, including the practices that speak to and express them. Here we focus on deservedness, duty to God, rituals, and divine inspiration as key elements of causal mechanisms of generosity in Catholicism and Islam.

Religious Beliefs and Prosociality

Religious beliefs, or discourse, may emphasize other-regarding attitudes and behaviors such as *deservedness*. Members of different religions vary in their view of whether a target of generosity is deserving, and the more they view the target as deserving, the more generous they are (Will and Cochran 1995).

Both Catholicism and Islam hold that the poor and needy are deserving of help regardless of the circumstances or character of the needy individual. There are some distinctions within Islam of who gets helped from zakat funds, while the overall orientation is that the needy deserve help.

Another aspect of beliefs that might affect generosity and collective goods provision is a belief in a *duty to God*. Indeed, Islam emphasizes obedience and a duty to obey God's will and commandments; Catholicism somewhat similarly requires adherence to God's commandments. We term the concept of obedience to God's will as "duty to God." Both religions emphasize helping others, though there may be differences in whether the helping is perceived as a duty. Islam requires, through zakat and *fitr*, giving resources to others.[10] While Catholicism speaks of tithing, tithing is described neither as a formal ritual nor as an obligation. These differences in what the concept entails may lead to differences in responses from Catholics and Muslims to a sense of duty to God.

Helping others could also be affected by the divine inspiration to live a life filled with love from and for God. A spirit of generosity may then come from a sense of *God's grace*, with faith in God working "through, with, and in" the faithful (Benedict XVI 2009; Himes 2006, 18, 19). Pope Benedict XVI made the connection explicit, writing that "charity is love received and given. It is 'grace' (*cháris*)." Serving God opens the door for his love and mercy (Qur'an, Sura 2:177). While they vary in emphases and interpretations, both religions have an understanding of God's grace, that it is through his grace and mercy that one enters heaven and that one loves others. God's grace may be a mechanism for prompting prosocial behavior.

Religious beliefs are intimately connected to the practice of *rituals* of giving: in services, how is giving, charity, or generosity portrayed? While an understudied topic, a few works on wealth and religion and on religious generosity indicate that in religions, the inclination to give generously of time and money is intimately tied to the religious experience and the configuration of religious convictions. Ritual and belief are significant. Miller (1999) found that rituals about giving "reflect the theological differences between denominations" affecting people's perceptions and decisions of why and how much they give (14). Rituals structure how people understand their giving. For instance, they structure whether people

---

[10] *Fitr* is an act of charity that every Muslim with sufficient wealth should do for the poor and needy during the month of Ramadan. Islam also emphasizes nonobligatory giving, or *sadaqa* (Al-Ghazzali 1966; Queen 1996, 49–50).

understand giving as directed toward God or as a membership obligation. They frame how the religion asks its adherents to give; we know that the way in which people are asked to do something has a powerful effect on their response (Andreoni and Rao 2011). Rituals also enhance a sense of community, heightening the impact of community dynamics (Chwe 2001; Ginges, Hansen, and Norenzayan 2009; McNamara 2009, 212–228).

Catholicism and Islam have different rituals of giving. Catholicism does not have a formal institution of giving that is considered essential to the practice and observance of the faith; Islam has several. How do the specific rituals of Islam facilitate the generosity of Muslims? What are the rituals of giving in Catholicism and how do they affect generosity? We need to go beyond theological dictates to understand the arrangements Catholics and Muslims have, and how those affect giving. Generosity may be affected by whether or not there are specific programs established by the parish's diocese or at the mosque or cultural center, and whether there is an organizational effort to increase giving.

The Limits of Religion and Public Goods Provision

Asking questions about how religions prompt and channel prosociality helps us understand the potential of religions to provide social services when the state reduces the scope of its own services. Some argue that a considerable amount of public goods provision is possible without a coercive state (Gill 2013; Leeson 2014; Ostrom 1990; Scott 2009), and it certainly has been demonstrated that under particular circumstances, groups can organize themselves to provide services for themselves (Muchlinski 2014; Tsai 2007). To substitute for the state, social services need to be provided universally, yet mainstream religions cannot compel contributions through taxation in the same way states can. We need to consider what capacity religions have to prompt social service provision by their members. Another consideration is that religious groups, while often thought of as distributing goods to their members, serve nonadherents as well (Cammett and Issar 2010; Cherry and Ebaugh 2014). Why is it that these institutions provide social services to anyone in need; not just to members?

We have disaggregated possible factors within religions, and with reference to Catholicism and Islam, that might lead to generous behavior. This is somewhat artificial, as human motivations and actions are complex and seldom, if ever, singular. There may be multiple factors affecting motivation and behavior. Ours is an effort to better understand the possible impact of specific beliefs and institutions, in isolation and in conjunction with one another.

Research Strategy

In order to answer these questions, we went to Paris, Milan, Dublin, and Istanbul. We studied a Catholic parish and Muslim organization in each city and conducted experiments with adult Catholics and Muslims as well as university students in Dublin and Istanbul, respectively (Catholics in Dublin, Muslims in Istanbul). France, Ireland, and Italy have been and remain crucial to the history and life of the Catholic Church and Catholicism; Turkey plays a similarly significant role in Islam. These four cities enable us to study generosity dynamics of Catholicism and Islam when in majority and minority status. The Western European countries are democracies in which religion can be practiced relatively freely; Turkey at the time of research was a democracy even though there were some limits on religious freedoms (Kılınç 2014; Sarkissian 2015, 90, 117–125). We do not claim to have studied "typical" Catholics or Muslims; there are no such sets of individuals. Organized religions have been affected across time and space by myriad factors that give rise to particular beliefs and practices. However, because basic beliefs and other aspects of religion tend to be shared within a faith, our study contributes to developing a knowledge base about the generosity of Catholics and Muslims. Islam has a wider variety of practices and orientations, some of which vary by ethnicity or nationality, than does Catholicism. We hold national origin and religious orientation constant in Islam by focusing upon the cultural centers established by the Turkish Gülen movement in our four countries (Flynn 2006, 232; Lacey 2009, 301; Pirotta 2008). It is not possible to identify an Islamic movement that all Muslims and scholars would agree is representative and typical of Islam. However, Islam's basic message of charity is constant across the religion, and the Gülen movement has several advantages for our study: it is a relatively mainstream transnational organization within Islam, it is relatively transparent and open about its activities, it is present in our four countries, and it has been especially prominent in Turkey (Kılınç 2013; Kuru 2003; Kuru 2005; Yavuz 2013).

Due to its alleged involvement in political controversies and events in Turkey from 2013 to 2016, the Gülen movement has become of interest to many scholars, policy analysts, and the media. At the time of our research, the Gülen associations were not regarded as controversial and were not implicated in Turkish politics. Indeed, between 2002 and 2013, the movement, at most, was a social ally of Erdogan's then moderate Islamist AKP (El-Kazaz 2015). The movement supported the AKP-led government during election cycles and supported its political and social goals (Hendrick 2009). However, since 2013, the two groups have become antagonistic towards each other. The AKP accused the Gülen movement of having a parallel state structure intending to overthrow the AKP government, while the Gülen movement accused the AKP of eliminating all opposition groups in its path toward authoritarianism (Muedini 2015). The AKP government blamed the Gülen movement for the failed military coup of July 2016. After that event, the movement was criminalized in Turkey. As noted, we did the fieldwork in Turkey and on the Turkish Muslims in the other three cities during 2010. The Gülen community members we interviewed were not in any of the institutions that President Erdogan's government had been purging at the time of writing (i.e., the military, judiciary, police, universities, media). As will become clear in Chapters 4 and 5, the understandings of Islam held by Gülen community members and by Turkish Muslim university students, who were drawn from the general university population at Boğaziçi (not a Gülen-based university), are quite similar. At the time of writing, the Gülen associations in Western Europe are active.

Our case studies included four Catholic parishes and four Muslim associations in Milan, Paris, Dublin, and Istanbul. We accessed these parishes and associations mostly through referrals. We had explained in our contact letters what kind of parish we hoped to conduct the study in: not exceptional, not in an extremely wealthy or poor neighborhood, and not in a tourist zone. With only two Latin rite parishes, there was little choice in Istanbul; we conducted research in the parish of the Basilique Cathédrale du Saint-Esprit, whose head priest was willing to grant access.[11]

Methodology

As part of our broader methodological approach, we combine the advantages of experiments with case studies. Experiments randomly manipulate treatments across subjects and therefore control the environment in which

---

[11] Access to Santa Maria alla Fontana was by direct referral from a scholar of Catholicism in Italy; access to the Church of Our Mother of Divine Grace, in Ballygall, was by referral from the Moderator of the Curia of the Dublin diocese after we had been granted permission by the Dublin Archbishop to conduct the research in the diocese; access to Saint-Pierre de Montrouge was by direct appeal to the head priest; access to Basilique Cathédrale du Saint-Esprit was by direct appeal to the head priest. The President of Intercultural Dialogue Foundation in Brussels put us in contact with the Gülen associations in Paris, Milan, and Dublin. We chose the Yunus Emre Cultural Association in Paris because it was the largest among the six Gülen community centers in Paris. For Milan and Dublin we had only one association available in each city. The cultural centers in Milan and Paris are both located at city centers. The Journalists and Writers Foundation, a leading Gülen-affiliated civil society organization, put us in contact with Ihsander in Istanbul.

the treatments are manipulated. They further allow for quantitatively measurable outcomes across treatment groups (Bowers 2011; Henrich, Heine, and Norenzayan 2010). Case studies and in-depth interviews enable us to probe understandings of concepts and motives, observe behaviors, compare across groups, and learn directly about organizational structures (Gerring 2007; Gillespie and Michelson 2011; Wuthnow 2011). This combination of methods mitigates the disadvantages of either approach separately: experiments often lack external validity and can be hampered by design problems that are hard to anticipate. Case studies and interviews are often challenged because variables (treatments) are not directly manipulated, and interviews only tell us what people think motivated them (Chaves 2010). The use of data from both methods potentially generates more confidence in our conclusions and enables us to refine methods and research questions.

To examine the impact of the theoretical propositions introduced earlier in this chapter, such as the impacts of duty to God or community expectations on prosocial behavior, we use priming experiments on Muslims and Catholics. By doing so, we can test the specific concepts or processes that we think are causally connected (Bargh and Chartrand 2000). Because we prime participants by asking them to write essays (e.g., about their religious community's expectations), the essays themselves become additional data that we can use for understanding effects. The experiments were conducted with more than 800 university students and community adults in Dublin and in Istanbul.

Our case studies complement the experiments and enable us to observe whether the expectations predicted by theory hold; that is, if religious adherents think and act about generosity in the ways expected. In addition, several factors are explored that the experiments do not: ritual, community solidarity, and the impact of minority status. Our case studies are centered on both a Catholic parish and Islamic cultural center in each of Dublin, Istanbul, Milan, and Paris.[12] We pay attention to the sociopolitical context of each city and country in which the parishes and Muslim associations are located. The case study research included more than 200 interviews with Catholic parishioners, Muslim association members, and religious officials, and other data collected through participant observation. The interviews and case studies were conducted with populations separate from those that

---

[12] Carolyn Warner conducted the case studies on the Catholic parishes in Milan, Dublin, and Paris; Ramazan Kılınç conducted the case studies on the Catholic parish in Istanbul and the Islamic associations in all four cities. Adam Cohen conducted the experiments with an American assistant in Dublin and with a Turkish assistant in Istanbul.

were in the recruitment pools for the experiments; the research was approximately at the same time, and done by different researchers, so that findings from one method did not contaminate those of the other.

Our interviews were structured to identify individuals' motivations for particular behaviors. We recognize that what our interviewees tell us may not be what is actually motivating them when they engage in a behavior, or causing them to engage in a behavior (but see Wuthnow 2011). Nevertheless, the interviews are critical for knowing how Muslims and Catholics understand their religions and what they think is going on when they engage in the behaviors we are interested in. If we observe systematic differences between Muslims and Catholics in what they say about their beliefs and behaviors, and that these are relatively consistent within each religious group, we think that the religions have channeled the behavior of their faithful in particular ways. The interviews with parishioners are also critical for getting data on community expectations, community, and religious structure. Interviewees provide many observations about how their religious organization operates. The interviews are not our sole source of data on the Catholic parish and Muslim association case studies. They are supplemented with information-gathering interviews with religious leaders and with documentation on the religions and their charitable organizations.

Because mosques are used only for prayer and are state-supported in some Muslim-dominant countries, our study of Turkey focuses on a Gülen organization rather than on a mosque. We use "Gülen association" to refer to the local organization. When we mean the entire organization at the local, national, and international levels, we use "Gülen movement." This is in keeping with how we use "parish" and "church" for the local-level study of Catholics, and "Catholic Church" or "Church" for the entire organization of the Catholic Church.

Because a book cannot cover all aspects of a topic, we note here what this one will not cover. It does not assess whether Muslims are more generous than Catholics or vice versa. While any such study of that question is beset by methodological and conceptual problems (Galen 2012, 878–880), we set this question aside to avoid getting distracted from our focus on understanding what, within each religion, might prompt adherents to be generous. This is also not a study of the historical forces and broad sociopolitical and economic factors that may affect the overall level of philanthropy of a country, nor trends in generosity within Catholicism or Islam. We are focused instead on finding out what mechanisms in Catholicism and Islam lead adherents to be generous.

Plan of the Book

The book explores the theoretical and empirical implications of the concepts we have introduced in this chapter.

Chapter 2 examines how the structures of the Catholic Church and of Sunni Islam are ill-equipped to monitor and sanction adherents' contributions to collective goods. We provide evidence for this assertion from the four city case studies, the interviews, and the essays that experiment participants wrote. In doing so, we assess systematically the religious rituals that Catholicism and Islam have established about generosity and giving. The Islamic associations have a monitoring structure that encourages giving, in a mild way; Catholics do not. Neither religion has a sanctioning structure that punishes failure to contribute to club or public goods. In finding that the institutional structures and rituals of each religion are insufficient to generate production of club and public goods, the chapter sets up the inquiry into the impact of beliefs.

Chapter 3 unpacks the psychology of religiously motivated generosity. It assesses the experimental evidence we collected from more than 800 university students and community members in Dublin and Istanbul. The results demonstrate that religious primes emphasizing God's grace, duty to God, and deservedness impact the propensities of Irish Catholics to give. The results are less conclusive for Turkish Muslims, and we discuss possible reasons why that is the case. Chapters 4 and 5 take advantage of the rich material in the experiment essays to explore the largely uncharted territory of the meaning of religious terms and beliefs to Catholics and Muslims. These analyses are crucial in uncovering differences and similarities between Muslims and Catholics in how they understand key religious concepts that we think are related to prosociality.

Chapter 6 uses case studies and the interviews to disentangle the potential impact of beliefs and community structures on generosity. It expressly examines the role of beliefs, looking at how Muslims and Catholics understand their generosity and what they think motivates them. It also examines their thoughts about their religious communities, and how that affects their propensities to contribute resources of time and funds. The analyses find systematic differences between Catholics and Muslims in their professed motivational beliefs, with Catholics emphasizing a love for the other stemming from Jesus' love, and Muslims emphasizing a duty to God. We find some similarities in the community influences, with both Muslims and Catholics noting positive social interactions.

Chapter 7 goes one step further in the analysis of community effects. Here we take advantage of our four minority cases – the Gülen association in Dublin, Milan, and Paris, and the Catholic parish of Basilique Cathédrale du Saint-Esprit in Istanbul – to do an in-depth examination of the dynamics of minority communities and generosity. We find that being in a minority status does not change the influence of religious beliefs and institutions on generosity of the faithful. However, we also find that religious minorities give more to their ingroups because, as most observers would expect, the minority groups are concerned about the survival, development, and welfare of their communities in the face of a dominant religious (and secular) outgroup.

Chapter 8 examines the limits and potential of religion and public goods provision in Europe. The chapter uses quantitative and qualitative data to examine the impact of welfare state spending and taxation on prosocial tendencies. The quantitative analyses by and large show that religiosity tempers the substitution effects of a large welfare state on individual-level generosity and contribution to public goods, including for Muslims and Catholics. Using information from our interviews and other field research, we look at some of the larger Islamic and Catholic charitable organizations in the context of the countries they are in; we also examine interviewee responses to our questions about what they think the state and their own religion's responsibility is to help the needy. The chapter shows that the generosity of Muslims and Catholics is relatively indifferent to the status of the welfare state in their country. This chapter also documents how the volunteer organizations in our four Catholic parishes and our four Muslim associations recruit staff and work with state and local agencies, and reveals the limited potential for religious organizations to provide club and public goods on their own.

Finally, the Conclusion highlights the main findings of the book and discusses some of the implications of our methodologies. This leads to a discussion of avenues for future research, as well as some of the limitations of our study. We broach the practical and normative implications of policy proposals to rely on religious (and secular) organizations for public goods provision. We conclude with reflections on the psychology, political economy, and theology of the generosity of mainstream Catholics and Muslims in contemporary Europe.

During our field research, a Parisian Muslim woman in her fifties said that "[g]iving is a duty to God and making people give more is very valuable; because this makes them become closer to God." A Catholic parishioner from Dublin explained her giving this way: "I receive a great sense of community, a great sense of togetherness, of acceptance, of love from people. You couldn't buy that and if you went looking for it you couldn't get it; it comes from the interaction."[13] Neither coercion (through monitoring and sanctioning by the religious institution or community) nor the Golden Rule (through an exhortation to "do unto others as they would do to you") explains our interviewees' motivations. Our interviewees' remarks open the door to a more comprehensive view of the sources of generosity in religions, which we begin to examine in the next chapter.

[13] PM11, DC20.

2

The Charitable Consequences of Institutions and Rituals in Catholicism and Islam

Religious organizations require resources both to accomplish their missions and to sustain themselves as institutions, and they often have as part of their missions the goal of helping others.[1] In short, they need to elicit helping behavior from their adherents. As a Catholic parishioner in Dublin stated, "everyone should play a little part, not just one guy doing five jobs" (DC2). How the institutional structures of Catholicism and Islam get everyone to "play a little part" is the focus of this chapter. As we document below, Catholicism and Islam lack strict monitoring and sanctioning mechanisms that punish failure to contribute, leaving the question of how they generate generosity. In this chapter, we elaborate on some largely noncoercive institutional features of the two religions. To the extent that the institutional structures foster generosity, it is mainly by being conduits for the prosocial orientations of members. Two other important aspects, religious beliefs and positive community affect, also have a notable role to play in eliciting contributions to the collective good, and we address these additional factors in subsequent chapters.

How religious institutional structure affects helping behavior has been studied from several perspectives. Economists and rational choice

---

[1] By institutions, we mean the "rules and procedures that structure social interaction by constraining and enabling actors' behavior" (Helmke and Levitsky 2004, 727). This definition dovetails with classic and contemporary works on religion that note that religion is an institution "that regulates religious discourse, practices, and community," through "formal or semiformal structures" that "vary tremendously" in their attributes (Lincoln 2003, 7). There is an extensive discussion within the field of religious studies on the definition of religion, and some argue that the inclusion of institutions is too "Western" of a perspective. Our point about institutions is that they are structures that produce and reproduce regular patterns of behavior that create capacities for certain kinds of actions and limits on others.

approaches look for institutions with monitoring and sanctioning capacities to enforce group norms and rules, including those about contributing to the group. They have tended to find that the most successful institutions are small sects that can compel compliance through seemingly bizarre dress, behavioral, and sacrificial requirements. Such measures weed out less committed free riders while ensuring the members that remain are willing to bear high costs to sustain the organization and its activities (Berman 2009; Iannaccone 1992; McBride 2007). Sects may also expel members who deviate from group rules. Because sects strongly differentiate themselves from surrounding society, the costs to an individual of being expelled are quite high. Since mainstream religions have relatively easy membership requirements, one would expect them to under-produce collective goods, or not produce any at all.

Another perspective looks beyond monitoring and sanctioning and examines how some institutional arrangements may hinder individual participation. Even if people are somewhat well disposed to help others, and inspired by their religious beliefs to do so, do religious institutions facilitate the expression of this disposition or hinder it?[2] When people have other opportunities, other things they need or want to do with their time and funds, how do religions persuade them to direct some of their resources to their religion?

Certain kinds of structural arrangements seem to be associated with certain kinds of participatory activity, with participatory activity being a prelude to contributions to collective goods. Putnam (1993, 107–109) argues that hierarchical organizations, such as the Catholic Church, inhibit the development of civil society groups and "social capital" that foster the provision of public goods. In hierarchical organizations, members are not required to interact in order to maintain the organization; they are not given the opportunity to do so. They do not develop the trust, camaraderie, or skills necessary to run the organization (Eastis 1998; Hale 2015; Hoffman, McCabe, and Smith 1996; Smith 2006). Because decentralized organizations have more avenues for participation and rely on the inputs of members to sustain themselves, decentralized organizations lead to more cooperative networks between members (Ahn, Esarey, and Scholz 2009). Some of this scholarship assumes people are generally well disposed to help and does not see a collective action problem of the sort that rational

---

[2] Some may be "wary cooperators," cautious about being taken advantage of, others less so (Smith 2006). As we discuss later in the book, religious beliefs and community influences may obviate that caution.

choice people do. We can apply this perspective to Catholicism and Islam. The hierarchical structure within which each Catholic parish church is embedded may create disengagement between the parishioners and the leadership as well as between the parishioners and their sense of responsibility for and identification with the life of the community (cf. Eastis 1998; Hale 2015). Although each Islamic organization or mosque may have some formal internal structures, the structures place more responsibility on individuals for sustaining the life of the mosque/organization. The engagement fostered by this responsibility might, in part, encourage Muslims to be generous. Thus, one would expect that the hierarchical organization of the Church would also inhibit the prosocial orientations of Catholics, all other things being equal. Conversely, one would expect that the nonhierarchical organization of Islam would lead to more engagement of the believers with their community and facilitate cooperative efforts. Yet hierarchical arrangements may have an advantage in that the strongly articulated structures of the Catholic Church may enable it to mobilize parishioners for charitable giving in a way that less centralized movements in Islam cannot.

Relatedly, Catholicism and Islam, as well as other organized religions, have other features that can affect the generosity of their adherents, one of which is their rituals. We treat rituals as a subset of institutions, because they are repeated interactions with a set of roles, rules, and norms about behavior. They are typically part of the "practices" of a religion (Lincoln 2003, 6). We can think about how rituals would affect generosity from two perspectives. From the religious economics perspective, religious rituals can require costly sacrifices of adherents. As scholars of strict sects, gangs, and tribal groups note, participating in costly rituals both demonstrates an individual's commitment to the group and distances them from the broader society (Bulbulia 2004; Decker and Van Winkle 1996; Iannaccone 1988). Even mainstream religions' rituals reinforce group identity and belonging through a group demonstration of what they as a particular religious people do, about what sets them apart. Then, because people are assumed to be more likely to give to their group or, through the rituals, be compelled to sacrifice for it, the rituals that enhance a sense of belonging and that demonstrate commitment to the group lead to club goods donations.

Another perspective on rituals focuses on the impact of the rituals of giving themselves. While an understudied topic, a few works on religious-based generosity substantiate what is likely obvious to the casual observer: that in religions, the inclination to give generously of time and money is intimately tied to the religious experience of rituals of giving. Rituals are part of the religious experience that puts believers in touch with the sacred; often rituals are derived from or seen to fulfill part of the religion's theology. In the context of religious services, they can affect individuals' emotional states, possibly leading to generous responses to calls to contribute funds or time (Corcoran 2015; Wellman, Corcoran, and Stockly-Meyerdirk 2014). Rituals could enhance a sense of community, heightening the propensity to contribute to the group, both through the emotions created and through the fact that in participating in a ritual, individuals are signaling to each other that they are cooperators (Alcorta and Sosis 2013, 577–578; Bulbulia and Sosis 2011, 367–370; Chwe 2001; Collins 2004, 42–44).

Focusing on rituals of giving, Miller (1999, 14) finds that rituals "reflect the theological differences between denominations" and affect people's perceptions and decisions of why and how much they give (cf. Keister 2003; 2007; 2008). Miller explains that how people understand their giving, such as whether it is directed toward God or just a membership obligation, affects giving and that understanding is, in turn, affected by how the rituals of giving are constructed. If giving is directly linked to rituals such as prayer, dedication, or song, there may be more of a sense that giving during services is part of one's spiritual life than that just a perfunctory duty that one fulfills. Smith and Emerson note the significant difference in results between congregations with a "live the vision" approach to rituals of giving and those with a "pay the bills" approach (2008, 128–138).

Though New Testament texts "suggest strongly the centrality of giving and service to the religious life," as do other Church teachings (Catechism of the Catholic Church 1999, 461; Queen 1996, 27), Catholicism has no formal call to give as a sacrament of the faith. There are rituals of giving nevertheless, the most obvious of which is that in services, a collection plate or basket is usually passed around. The Church has developed additional calls to give of funds and time (Conway 1995). In contrast, Islam has several explicitly described institutions and rituals of giving; the most well known is the obligatory zakat (giving of one's wealth to the poor), one of the five pillars of Islam (Hassan 2002).[3] In addition,

---

[3] Catholicism certainly has extensive theological writings on giving and on helping others (e.g., Catechism of the Catholic Church 1999, 2401–2406, 2439–2440a; 2441–2445, 2447–2448, 2459, 2544–2547) which are largely based on biblical sources. The connection with sacred rituals is weak, however. The most that is said in that regard is in the 1992 Catechism, which in 1351 states, "From the very beginning Christians have brought, along with the bread and wine for the Eucharist, gifts to share with those in need" (in Smith and Emerson 2008, 205).

nontheologically imposed collections are also typical in many places of worships after weekly Friday prayers. But to understand what the effect is on Catholics and Muslims of these rituals of giving, we need to note how they are framed.

Mainstream Catholicism and Islam each have a set of theologically prescribed rituals that must be carried out in order to belong to the religion in question. Compared with some religions, these are relatively low cost. Religious economics would not expect rituals of belonging in these mainline religious organizations to require substantial sacrifice by individual adherents for the group, but instead merely be a low-level common denominator that delineates the group. The rituals may have some effect: it is worth asking how the sense of belonging might influence individuals' generosity, and we do so in a later chapter. Here we ask how the rituals of giving express themselves in the lives of parishioners. How do they affect the ability of each religion to elicit generosity and public goods from their adherents? Do the institutions of Catholicism and Islam provide the kinds of monitoring and sanctioning structures that scholars have argued are needed in order to prompt individual contributions to collective goods?

To start answering these questions, we focus on the institutional structures and rituals of Catholicism and Islam as lived and expressed in the Catholic parishes and Islamic associations that we studied in Dublin, Istanbul, Milan and Paris. To preview our results, we find that the institutional structures and rituals of each religion, in and of themselves, are insufficient to generate production of club and public goods. This leads to our inquiry, in Chapter 3, into the impact of beliefs. Before moving to our analyses, we briefly introduce the locations of our case study research.

The Parishes and Associations

We did case studies in four parishes and four Islamic associations.[4] Each parish and association had to raise funds to cover the vast majority of their operating expenses, in addition to fundraising for charitable activities.[5] As we will see, all relied heavily on volunteers to reduce the need for paid staff.

---

[4] See Chapter 1 for an explanation of the choice of cases.
[5] Due to church–state arrangements in France and Italy, some basic restoration work on historic church buildings is covered by the state. Running expenses and newer facilities have to be covered by the parishes/dioceses.

Figure 2.1 Chiesa di Santa Maria alla Fontana, Milan.

In Milan, for the Catholic study, we conducted field work at the parish of Santa Maria alla Fontana (see Figure 2.1). The neighborhood, hemmed in by the Zara, Isola, and Corso Como areas outside the tourist zones of Milan, is modest, with a vibrant mix of Italians and immigrants. The parish had 14,000 parishioners, of which about 2,000 attend mass weekly. It has four priests, including one who had retired but helped with functions. The volunteer groups include the *Società San Vincenzo de Paoli* (Society of St. Vincent de Paul), *l'Oasi* (retired peoples' group), the *Oratorio* (youth center), the Pastoral Council, and the catechism school. Others volunteer (and there is overlap between groups) in the parish office, with the liturgy, and with various celebrations that take place at the church (annual saint day, Christmas sale, etc.). In the parish, but not run by it, is a food bank, staffed by many volunteers who attend the church.

For our interviews with Muslims in Milan, we did fieldwork with the Alba Intercultural Association, the only Gülen community association in the city. The Turkish community in Italy is very small (not more than 15,000), with about 4,000 Turks living in Milan. There are about 200 people affiliated with the association. The association offers weekly religious education lectures, Friday prayer services, weekend school for the Turkish immigrant schoolchildren, and intercultural/interfaith activities.

The Catholic parish in which we conducted our field work in Paris was Saint-Pierre de Montrouge. It is located in the 14th Arrondissement, outside the main tourist sites of the city. It had about 12 paid staff and between 500 and 600 volunteers who run the church office and its main organizations. There were about 50,000 people in the parish's geographic boundaries, of which about 4,000 attend mass weekly (with about 2,100 coming on weekends, excluding the major holidays). The parish is largely middle-class to upper middle-class, with an immigrant community as well, and has six priests and one deacon. There are many active volunteer groups. As in Santa Maria alla Fontana, many parishioners volunteer with other Catholic charities in the parish that are not run by the parish, such as *Secours Catholique*, the *Société Saint Vincent-de-Paul* (SVdP), and the *Comité catholique contre la faim et pour le développement-Terre Solidaire* (CCFD). They are given some support by the parish, depending on the preferences of the head priest and advice of the parish Economic Council. Some 80 percent of its expenses have to be met by tithing and other collections.

In Paris, we conducted fieldwork at the Muslim association of Yunus Emre Cultural Association, which is located in northwest Paris. The Turkish population in France is about 600,000. Almost three-quarters of them live in Paris. The Gülen community has six associations in Paris. The Yunus Emre Cultural Association offers religious and cultural services to its members. It serves about 500–600 people. Some of the activities that the association organizes are weekly religious education courses and weekend school for the Turkish children in which they are taught about Islam and Turkish culture. The association also organizes charitable activities to contribute to the movement's charity work around the world. The organization is also affiliated with a private Turkish school in Paris. Finally, it organizes interfaith and intercultural activities to inform the French people about Islam and the Turkish community.

In Dublin, we conducted our research at the Catholic Ballygall parish of the Church of Our Mother of Divine Grace (see Figure 2.5). Ballygall is outside the city center, in a hilly middle-class Dublin neighborhood. It has about 6,200 parishioners (90 percent Catholic); about 25 percent (1,300) of the Catholics attend mass weekly. In contrast to those in Milan, Paris, and Istanbul, Dublin parishes are known by the name of the parish, not by the name of the local parish church. Ballygall at the time of research had two priests, a sister, and one sacristan, parish secretary (paid), and numerous volunteers in a variety of organizations. The laity was quite involved in religious services, such as facilitating the liturgy and the children's mass, and in baptism and funeral teams. Some in the laity were beginning to get trained to do healing services in response to the paucity of priests. As are all parishes in the Dublin diocese, Ballygall was due to be clustered with others, with the aim of sharing resources.

In Dublin, we conducted our Muslim study at the Turkish-Irish Educational and Cultural Society. The Turkish immigrant community in Ireland is the smallest among all the four cities. At the time of research, there were an estimated 5,000 Turks living in Ireland, most of whom lived in Dublin. The Gülen community has only one association in Dublin, the Turkish-Irish Educational and Cultural Society. The association is the smallest of the associations we included on our study, with about 100–125 members. The association offers weekend religion classes for Turkish schoolchildren. As in Italy, the association's major concentration is interfaith/intercultural dialogue.

Our work with Catholics in Istanbul was in the parish of the Basilique Cathédrale du Saint-Esprit, which has about 200–250 regular congregants out of about 2,000 Latin Rite Catholics living in Istanbul and about 15,500 in Turkey. At the time of research, the parish had three priests; a fourth had just retired before we arrived. The Head Vicar also resides in this parish, as it is the center of the vicariate. Church attendees are largely from three different groups: Levantines (descendants of French and Italian immigrants from the Ottoman Empire), immigrants from the Philippines, and immigrants from Africa, especially from the Democratic Republic of the Congo. The church also receives many Catholic tourists because of its historical importance.

In Istanbul, we conducted our interviews with Muslim members of the Ihsander Association. Ihsander, located in the northwestern suburbs of Istanbul, was an association formed by mostly businessmen affiliated with the Gülen movement. Because organizing around religion is illegal in Turkey, Ihsander could not have official status as a religious association or organization. However, it offered religious education classes and study sessions, and ran several charitable activities. The association had about 350 active members during the time of the study.

Church Institutions and Their Effects in the Catholic Parishes

The difficulties associated with connecting Catholicism to public goods provision can be framed in the following ways: how does a hierarchical organization with low barriers to entry for members and few material incentives and sanctions create club or public goods? To answer these questions, we need to first examine its monitoring and sanctioning structures, and how church structures might provide opportunities for giving and volunteering.

Monitoring and Sanctioning Structures

As is well known, the Catholic Church is a hierarchical organization with a vertical chain of command. That structure was not altered by Vatican II.[6] The Code of Canon Law stipulates that the structure of the Church shall have "no separation of powers" (O'Reilly and Stuart 2014, 208). The bishop holds executive, legislative, and judicial power in his diocese, subject only to the Pope and the Code of Canon Law.[7] At the parish level, Catholic theology privileges the clergy over the laity (ibid., 152, 219–220). Priests, when ordained, take on a different ontological status. They are now the sacramental ministers of God, and even if laicized for violations of Canon Law, still are viewed by the Church as sanctified (Keenan 2012, 42–43; Parkinson 2013, 21). They typically are "incardinated" into a specific diocese or religious order. The religious functions provided at the parish level are run by a priest or set of priests who serve at the will of the bishop of the diocese. This bishop, in turn, serves at will of the Pope.[8] At the discretion of the diocesan bishop, priests can be and, in the countries we studied, are routinely placed in a different parish within their bishop's diocese every six to nine years. Priests answer to their bishops, not to their parishioners. Despite some popular understandings of Vatican II as having empowered the laity, it did not. As one Irish priest noted, "The sense of Church that was promoted over the years, to pay up, pray up and shut up, is still a good description of how the Church operates" (in Weafer 2014, 197). Another noted, "We are still a hierarchical Church and structures haven't changed" (ibid.).

Despite the hierarchical structure of the Church, the Church hierarchy has less control over clergy than meets the eye, particularly when it comes to directing charitable activity or altering doctrine to give it a particular

---

[6] The Second Vatican Council (Vatican II) was a meeting at the Vatican within Rome of Catholic bishops and officials across the world from 1962 to 1965. The emphasis was on adapting the Catholic Church to modernity, and making the Church more responsive to the needs of its adherents.

[7] An archdiocese is a very large diocese that has also been granted the role of "metropolitan see" of an "ecclesiastical province." This grants the archbishop minor supervisory powers over the dioceses within that province. Some parishes are run by religious orders; religious orders typically do not answer to the bishop of the diocese. Religious orders are under the jurisdiction of their order and then of the Pope. Some parishes have been transferred to religious orders; most are within regular diocesan structures, including the parishes in our case studies.

[8] Catechism of the Catholic Church 1999, Part One, Section Two, Ch. 3, Article 9, paragraph 877, 880–886, 894–896 (www.vatican.va/archive/ccc_css/archive/catechism/p123a9p4.htm).

emphasis. Priests have leeway in their own parishes whether or not to initiate projects that the Bishop or Archbishop might advocate. The head priest in a parish has the authority to decide policy, within the bounds of Church policies and the policies of his bishop, within his parish. As the head of the Economic Council of Saint-Pierre de Montrouge in Paris noted, the head priest of the parish picks the causes that are featured during Easter giving campaigns (PC10).[9] The Dublin Moderator of the Curia stated that he had more freedom as a priest in a parish to do what he wanted than he does working directly for the Archbishop of the archdiocese (DC25). In keeping with the reforms of Vatican II, parishes have Pastoral Councils of parishioners usually elected by parishioners or appointed by the priest to three- to five-year terms. Many parishes also have Economic Councils. Both such councils are advisory to the head priest. They have no authority over policy (Coriden and Fisher 2016). These arrangements give priests considerable authority over the operations of their church and parish.

What these arrangements do not do is give priests or the hierarchy the authority to sanction Catholics for not giving financially or for not volunteering. Furthermore, giving is private: pledges and the keeping of pledges for donations are not made public. At best, one might see a small memorial plaque on a pew, for instance, donated by a loved one, but the name of the donor and amount donated is not evident. Those who know how much someone has donated are those who fulfill the bookkeeping offices of the parish church; in small parishes that might be a volunteer. That structure does not give rise to peer pressure or social exclusion if one does not follow through on a pledge or gives less than what might be thought appropriate. Much of the offering comes in the form of cash in the weekly services, so is not traceable to individuals. In addition, priests cannot bar a Catholic residing in one parish from attending the services of another. Indeed, they have no incentive to: it would just create resentment. Although the so-called church shopping that American Protestants engage in is not a common practice among Catholics, some parishioners become regulars at other parishes, usually due to a preference for a particular priest and the programs he has implemented. The consequence of these features is that monitoring depends on the conscience of the individual Catholic.

---

[9] We assigned each interviewee a code to preserve the anonymity of our interviewees. In coding the interviews, we used the initial of the city, religious affiliation of the interviewee, and a number. For example, the first Catholic interviewee in Milan is coded as MC1, the third Muslim interviewee in Dublin is coded as DM3.

As is typical of the so-called mainline religions, the institutional structure of Catholicism provides no serious penalties for not giving. Not giving is not a mortal sin and does not lead to ex-communication. Over the centuries, the Catholic Church has established numerous mechanisms to elicit contributions from the faithful; the institution of purgatory and the pursuit of indulgences to get out of it come to mind. In the parishes we studied, receiving the host, participating in consecrated host during mass was not contingent upon having contributed to the offering or to Catholic charities, nor was it contingent on having volunteered time in the church or in charities.[10] Though the Church states, in the Catechism, that "[t]he faithful also have the duty of providing for the material needs of the Church, each according to his ability,"[11] few Catholics regard this as meaning that it is a sin not to give to the Church.[12] In addition, the amounts and frequency are not specified, and donations "in kind" (of time and other resources) also count. The consequences of not giving depend simply on the conscience of the Catholic, who would have to regard not giving as a sin, confess it, and be given an exculpatory activity by the priest. As to incentives priests can deploy to increase giving, priests can only give a reward by personally thanking giving and volunteering if they know about it.

Those who benefit from the sacraments of the Church are not required to donate funds or give of their time in exchange.[13] For instance, though the priest collects fees for officiating at a marriage ceremony, he does not expect additional donations that, if not forthcoming, invalidate the marriage. Catholics are not excluded from sacraments if they do not donate funds or give time or otherwise provide benefits to the church community.

---

[10] In contrast to not giving, not attending mass weekly is a grave sin in Canon Law, but the failure to attend can be forgiven in confession, and priests do not prevent those who have not been coming to mass regularly from showing up once in a while. They do not follow up with punishment (say, exclusion from partaking in the Eucharist or public shaming).

[11] #2043, www.vatican.va/archive/ENG0015/4/VI.HTM. It is listed at the end of the list of the five precepts of the Church, though it is not introduced as a "precept" (a "positive law" of an "obligatory character"). The Code of Canon Law, governing the functioning and activities of the Church and the faithful, similarly states, "The Christian faithful are obliged to assist with the needs of the Church so that the Church has what is necessary for divine worship for apostolic works and works of charity end for the decent sustenance of ministers" (#222; www.vatican.va/archive/ENG1104/_PU.HTM). Most Catholics are not versed in the Code or the Catechism; the latter was formally issued only in 1992 as a compendium of Catholic theology and doctrine.

[12] Fr. William Saunders, "Tithing," www.catholiceducation.org/en/culture/catholic-contributions/tithing.html.

[13] These sacraments include baptism, first Eucharist (first communion), confirmation, marriage, confession, anointing of the sick, and funeral mass.

Entry to the church or any of its most holy sites is not contingent upon being a provider of club goods. Irish interviewees instead noted that the drawback to the first communion is the expense of the clothes, the gifts to and from relatives, and the large family gathering party that the family of the child is expected to host.

The one evident exclusionary practice, such as it is, is that users of the volunteer services of the Society of St. Vincent de Paul (SVdP), at the parish level, are referred to the parish in which they reside, rather than the parish from which they may have initially sought help. SVdP screens aggressively on that, to discourage abuse or duplication of assistance and to avoid enabling the requester from failing to address the sources of his or her problem by merely going to a new parish center after having exhausted the resources and goodwill of a previous one. SVdP is, however, not run by the parishes. Priests and the Catholic Church have no control over how it organizes its activities.

The Church and the local churches are nonexclusionary. Users of charity services, such as the help centers that are staffed by SVdP volunteers, are not required to be Catholic.[14] They are not asked what their faith is; as noted above, in the case of SVdP, they are asked only if they live in the parish where they are seeking assistance. The head priest in Istanbul also emphasized the nonexcludability of the receivers of charity: "Although most of those who come for help are Christians, especially immigrant Christians, we do not discriminate against Muslims" (IC2).[15]

Given these institutional structures and practices, how does the parish structure of church affect generosity? Parishes have geographic boundaries defined by the Church. Parishioners cannot change them. The point of the parish is to "give birth to new Christians" and sustain the Christian (Catholic) community.[16] Those baptized into the Catholic faith and residing within a parish are considered members of that parish. There is an expectation that they will attend services at the church in that parish. One might think parish structure would discourage generosity, since Catholics are automatically attached to the parish in whose geographic boundaries

---

[14] We use the term "charity" in its sense of being aid to those in need; we understand it sometimes is viewed as a pejorative or condescending term. In response, we refer readers to Benedict XVI's *Caritas in Veritate* (2009).

[15] However, in Istanbul, the parish had to be careful about not being seen to be helping Muslims. If it did help them, it was likely to be criticized by the public and authorities for "doing missionary work by giving food to poor and needy Muslims" (IC 2).

[16] Msg. Lorcan O'Brien, Moderator of the Curia, Dublin Archdiocese, Dublin, Nov. 23, 2010.

they live. This factor is compounded by the fact that parishioners have no choice over who their priest is, in contrast to Muslims, who can hire and fire their own religious officials. On the other hand, because the parish is associated with where they live, the parish structure might enhance Catholics' sense of loyalty and belonging – it belongs to them, they belong to it (Gamm 1999). That could contribute to a willingness to contribute to the parish's activities.

Our evidence on the impact of parish structure is mixed. Based on their residence address, some parishioners we interviewed in Dublin should have been attending a different church, but they preferred the priest and/or activities in a church not in the parish in which they resided (DC2, DC3, DC13, DC16). The vast majority that we interviewed attended the church in their parish of residency, no matter who the priest was at the time or what its activities were. Parishioners mentioned not wanting their funds to go to other parishes or to disappear into the diocesan coffers – even though that is what happens to a percentage of the parish funds. The head of the Saint-Pierre de Montrouge Economic Council said the fact that the diocese taxes the parish, due to its relative wealth, "bothers a lot of parishioners." Many had told him, "I hope what I give doesn't go to the diocese" (PC10). Statements like this potentially indicate that there is a mistrust of the diocesan, or "institutional," Church, given the lack of transparency in what the diocese does with the funds, and a suspicion that the Church's overhead is too high. As an Irish parishioner said of the diocesan administration,

The money they get in from the parishioners, rather than be put into administration, needs to be put back out. I don't know the figures what it costs for the administration but I wonder what part of my pound, my euro, goes back into charity ... I can't actually tell you how much the church gives back into charity. I don't know that. I mean, they [Church officials] do good work, but I think their administrative costs are enormous. (DC9)

Parishes, even the small ones, are large enough that adherents' contributions to the collective good of the parish are difficult to monitor. Our interviewees did not perceive that their giving behavior was being monitored – they never commented on social pressure from others in the parish or in its church. The monitoring capacity of parishes is further diluted by the fact that parishes in modern Europe are not closed societies: most people, if they have jobs, work elsewhere, and their social lives are not necessarily linked to the church. This is another reason why those who attend mass but do not contribute financially or as volunteers are unlikely to be held to account by fellow parishioners. Parishes cannot exclude non-Catholics or lapsed Catholics from living within their boundaries.

While social science theories of collective action expect that being open to all, not just to the ingroup, would reduce incentives for volunteers to donate of their time and energy, the volunteers we interviewed considered helping those in need, regardless of their origin or faith, as a normal part of being human and being Catholic (DC2, DC6, MC14, MC15, PC2, PC6, PC13; cf. Chapter 7).[17] If parishioners were skeptical of where their funds went, they were skeptical of support for the institutional Church, not of support for their parish or their charities. As one Ballygall parishioner commented, once a year there is a special collection "for the Pope; I don't know why, he's got plenty of money" (DC4).

Are there less formal pressures that Church institutions create that might prompt generosity in Catholics? One might be fear. Indeed, it was sometimes mentioned as a motive for obeying, but in the past tense. As one Irish interviewee noted, when she was a child she was afraid to cough in church. "When the priest walked by, you bowed." She added that, "now it is open, it's fantastic that way. I was brought up in fear ... There's not an 'if you don't go to mass God will strike you down' attitude" anymore (DC13). In responding to a question about whether she felt pressure to volunteer, she replied, "no, if I didn't want to help, I wouldn't. I wouldn't feel in any way I'd have to. And I won't let anyone intimidate me" (DC13). A Parisian parishioner stated that "you are free to say 'no'" (PC13). The head priest at Santa Maria alla Fontana said he tries to inculcate a mode of living an exemplary life as Jesus did; this was a thought echoed by other priests in Paris, Dublin, and Istanbul. None mentioned that they had any sort of punitive powers with which to elicit giving behavior. Given their understandings of the sources of generosity as being loved by and love for Christ, sanctions for not giving, even had they been available, would have undermined what giving is meant to be. Put more formally by Pope Benedict XVI, love is charity (*caritas*) and "[c]harity is at the heart of the Church's social doctrine" (2009, 1).

The main pressure from the priest was in the form of creating an obligation by asking someone to help. Although it is rather inefficient, because it requires a lot of effort to affect one or two people, it can work: one parishioner in Paris said that when the new head priest arrived, the parishioner and his wife invited him over for dinner. At the end of the meal, the priest asked them what volunteer activities they did at the church. They sheepishly said "nothing" and immediately volunteered for

---

[17] Given that they had already volunteered, we cannot know if some who did not volunteer was dissuaded by the knowledge they would be helping some non-Catholics.

something (PC14). A parishioner's statements seem to confirm the power of asking: "it's just they put out the appeals, and I got involved, and I suppose the more you get involved the more you get asked to do. One thing goes to another" (DC16). The head priest at Ballygall, in his discussion of the diocese's plan to cluster parishes and share priests across parishes, churches, and services, indicated the importance of personal, direct interaction between the priest and his parishioners in getting them engaged, as well as in helping them in their lives, spiritual and otherwise. He referred the clustering project as "supermarket religion" and said "they've lost the personal touch of the local chaplain ... The whole object of a priest is personal contact" (DC28). Recognizing the Church's institutional limits, he added that "you can never impose on a parish."[18]

How Catholic Institutional Structures Affect Opportunities to Be Generous

We have some evidence that the Church's hierarchical structure may dampen motivation for generosity and reduce avenues of expressing it. For instance, in a diocese, the bishop and the parish head priest pick the main fundraising causes; the parish council only advises. Specific causes may not resonate with all parishioners (e.g., MC14, MC6), and the hierarchical structure disenfranchises them, as does the exclusion of women from positions of authority (the priesthood and permanent diaconate). One adult experiment participant from Dublin wrote, in response to being asked to think about the expectations of their religious community, "I would wish the life of our parish to be more vibrant, more inclusive, more lay engagement. I feel disheartened when the leaders of the church (Priests) retain control of basic issues in parish [*sic*]. Although our parish is not the worst, it could be so much better[,] more vibrant and alive" (EP656).[19] The hierarchical control by the Church of the parish limited the capacity and motivation for volunteerism. As one parishioner commented with regret, she'd like to help out in the parish, but she had not been asked (DC15).

---

[18] To some extent, this effect is time-bound. In Ireland, as elsewhere, the Church used to be a much more powerful institution, much more dominant in Catholics' public and private lives (Garvin 2004). The priest in Ballygall stated, "The Catholic Church here has had such a very powerful influence in government and the state and peoples' lives. Thank God that's gone. We're now down to the real power: the power of the gospel, that's the only thing we have the right to believe in" (DC28).

[19] To retain anonymity, experiment participants were assigned unique identification numbers; each individual is referred to by their identification number. "EP" stands for Experiment Participant.

We also have evidence that because of the paucity of priests, and because of the expansion of activities local churches engage in, the laity may have opportunities to be engaged in the life of the church in the parish, and many become involved. If they didn't, many churches couldn't function. Most would not even be able to deliver the mass on a regular basis. Parishioners, trained to be on a Eucharist team, supplement the priests during mass to deliver the host (wafer) to congregants; others teach Catechism classes to children and to potential adult converts; others conduct hospital and prison visitations; still others volunteer as receptionists or take on other "office staff" duties. In Dublin at the time of our research, the Ballygall parish was holding meetings with parishioners to get input on its future direction. There were indications parishioners felt more inclined to participate due to having been contacted about the parish's fate. The head priest noted that in other parishes he had served, when he encouraged people to get involved, they did so because "they were always seeing it as helping the priest; here they are doing it because it's their parish; they've taken ownership of their parish."[20] Lay activism within the parishes is modest evidence that the exception (decentralization) "proves" the rule: that hierarchical structures discourage the flourishing of generosity.

However, mere institutional opportunity cannot explain the willingness to engage. For that we note, first, the importance of being asked to help. Being presented with the opportunity to give is a critical part of eliciting generous behavior. Many Catholic interviewees said they were asked to volunteer. They had had a predisposition but were drawn in by having been asked, by the priest, by a nun, by a friend. As one Italian woman in her late fifties stated about her extensive volunteering, "I didn't know how to say 'no'; now I'm learning how to say 'no'" (MC5). An Irish man in his thirties noted he was asked to be a communion minister, and asked to volunteer for the parish SVdP group (D32). An Irish woman active in various church service functions noted that "being asked opens the door" (DC1). Being asked was a common theme, to the point where one parishioner regretted the parish wasn't asking her to do more (DC15).

The hierarchical structure, with parishes dependent upon a diocese, would seem to make coordination on charitable activity easier, if the hierarchy of the diocese wishes to encourage that but in fact does not.

---

[20] The priest also cautioned that he was not sure what would happen when the current generation that contributes so much to the parish dies out; he did not know "what kind of people we'll have" in ensuing generations.

The diocese lacks the capacity to compel priests to go along with its orientation. While a bishop can transfer a noncompliant priest to a less appealing post within the diocese, he may find that penalizing priests on specific issues of charity may produce less cooperation in other areas about which he may be more concerned. Monitoring charitable activities in all parishes is often not feasible. The Dublin archdiocese has 199 parishes; Milan, 1,108; Paris, 114; (Latin Catholic) Istanbul, 2.[21] In addition, the Church's parish structure undermines any coordination advantages of hierarchy: with dozens to hundreds of parishes per diocese, and dozens of dioceses per country, typically, there is a lot of duplication of effort, and there is also not much horizontal information sharing. The head priest at Santa Maria alla Fontana observed that "there are 180 parishes in the Milan diocese; each searches for a cure to poverty; but each isn't capable."[22] In recognition of this problem, the Paris archbishop at the time of our research had established a central office for "solidarity," or volunteering and charitable works, and sponsored a set of annual meetings to bring together those in the different volunteer organizations in each parish. The aim was to share information and facilitate useful connections between groups across parishes. Yet this too was not something in which the archbishop could compel his priests to participate: parish engagement was voluntary.

The institutional structure of the Catholic Church appears to offer few earthly rewards to those who contribute. To move up in the hierarchy of the church, one has to be a priest, something that parishioners, by definition, are not. In the three parishes we researched that had parish councils (Dublin, Milan, Paris), to be elected or appointed to the parish council, the main criterion seemed to be willingness to serve.[23] We did not see evidence that council members were in the ranks of the wealthy. Instead, members represented a range of socioeconomic demographics. We were not able to track whether wealthy donors to a parish had been put forward for a private audience with the archbishop or Pope, or whether parish policies, despite the councils, leaned toward that preferred by parishioners who had given substantial sums to the parish. There was no direct evidence that any of these factors obtained, nor was there evidence that parishioners donated

---

[21] Officially, the Istanbul "diocese" is the Vicariate Apostolic of Istanbul. The Milan and Dublin dioceses are geographically extensive.

[22] Don Roberto Viganó, Milan, Oct. 6, 2010. The cited figure referred only to the parishes within the city limits of Milan.

[23] The Basilique Cathédrale du Saint-Esprit d'Istanbul did not have a parish council at the time of research. Nevertheless, parish members did animate a number of internal organizations, such as the Legion of Mary.

in order to obtain influence. Their motivations, as we document in this chapter and in the following chapters, centered on a sense of responsibility and caring toward the parish and toward others.

Astute followers of Catholic theology might note that, starting in 2009, Pope Benedict XVI gave renewed attention to the spiritual utility of indulgences. While it might be an understatement to say that the corruption of indulgences created problems for the Church centuries earlier, what indulgences are, what they do, and how a Catholic gets one is not easy to understand. Because one way to gain a partial indulgence is for Catholics, while "led by the spirit of faith," to "give compassionately of themselves or of their goods to serve their brothers in need," some may interpret this as being able to buy an indulgence (Catholic Church 2006, 28).[24] If one can judge by our interviewees, indulgences do not appear to be a factor motivating Catholics to help the needy. The term was never used by any of the parishioners, old or young, whom we interviewed, nor by the priests, nor did they more generally describe a need to do good works in order to expiate sins and reduce time in Purgatory.

In summary, while its institutions that channel giving should not be discounted, the Church's formal structure is not what leads Catholics to give. As one Irish parishioner cautioned, "Faith is what's important, not the Church. I mean, look, the Church has been corrupt for years. Peter was a lawyer, Paul was a murderer, a couple other guys were thieves, some of the Popes were bastards" (DC10). We turn to examining how the institutional structure of Islam affects Muslims' generosity.

Islamic Institutions and Their Effects in the Muslim Associations

Monitoring and Sanctioning Structures

Islam is a decentralized, nonhierarchical religion with multiple schools of law and social requirements. Islamic religious leaders have no enforcement mechanisms to obtain obedience from their adherents; there are no sacraments in Islam that can be withheld from Muslims by imams or other clerics to obtain compliance with charitable or other cooperative activities. The authority of the religious leaders is established by socially constructed norms and rules, not through theologically imposed religious hierarchies. There are no religious requirements to follow clergy or religious scholars;

---

[24] Plenary indulgences, which could be understood as "full" indulgences, do not appear to be susceptible to that interpretation (Catholic Church 2006, 43–108).

Muslims can follow the teachings of a scholar or leader based on their own judgment. They can change leaders or prefer not to be under the guidance of any religious leader at all. These decisions do not influence the religious status of Muslims.

However, this does not mean that there are no hierarchies in Sunni Islam. Although there are no theologically informed religious hierarchies, there are hierarchies within religious groups that have been shaped by political and sociological factors. Historically, Muslims titled their political leader "caliph," ruling over a caliphate of Muslims, even if they were not in geographically contiguous territories. However, caliph is not a theological title. The caliph had little to no role in shaping how Muslims practiced their religion. After the caliph's abrogation with the fall of the Ottoman Empire, there is no single political leader whom Muslims view as the caliph, even though some fringe groups have declared a caliphate at different times. In many Muslim countries, the state created a bureaucratic hierarchy among those who provide religious services. While imams who lead prayers at the mosques are at the bottom of the hierarchy, there are city representatives within a bureaucratic organization. At the top of the hierarchy is a religious scholar appointed by the government. Most of the time, the state's political considerations strongly shape the composition of this hierarchy.

In other cases, there are religious orders (*tariqah* in Arabic or *tarikat* in Turkish) in which the adherents are organized around a charismatic religious leader. In this case, the authority of the leader is very strong, although there are not many rungs in the hierarchical ladder between the leader and the followers. The personal relationship between the leader and followers is significant in religious orders. Another category of a socially constructed hierarchy is that within religious communities (*jamaat* in Arabic or *cemaat* in Turkish). Our case, the Gülen movement falls into this category. Religious community here refers to "a self-conscious group of Muslims who are coordinated through an informal social network and mobilized to fulfill a mission defined in the idiom of Islam" (Yükleyen 2012, 57). As in religious orders, religious communities also gather around a charismatic leader. However, the authority of the leader is not as absolute as it is in religious orders. There are no strict ritualistic practices in religious communities. Religious communities mostly focus their activities on social issues, not religious rituals. There is a hierarchical ladder between the leader and the followers, and the authority of the leader comes through his or her leadership skills and religious knowledge (Aydın 2004, 308).

In Turkey, the state's Directorate of Religious Affairs (*Diyanet*) oversees religious services. The Diyanet controls all the mosques by appointing their imams and putting the imams on the government payroll. The Diyanet also has a representative in each city and a head representative in each province, and employs imams outside Turkey, particularly in cities where there is a sizable Turkish population. Among our case cities outside Turkey, there are Diyanet-affiliated mosques in Paris, while the Diyanet does not have mosques in Dublin or Milan. The Diyanet also provides other services such as organizing pilgrimage trips and offering religious opinions on certain issues. However, the Diyanet hierarchy does not have any authority over the Muslims who go to mosques. Mosques are used only for daily and weekly prayers and are not the locus of other religious activity. Imams are viewed as prayer leaders and do not have any power over the congregants other than leading the prayers. Imams can also offer religious advice or opinions to the congregants but their post does not give their religious opinions a binding status over the congregants. The Diyanet sometimes organizes charity collections after Friday prayers. The imam informs the congregants about the collection after the Friday sermon, and those congregants who want to contribute can do so when they are leaving the mosque. The institutional structure may facilitate giving but without any sanctioning and monitoring mechanisms attached to the collection. The congregants are free to decide whether to contribute or not to the collections, and their contributions do not influence the service that they get at the mosques.

In Western Europe and in Turkey, Muslims who want to have a broader experience of Islam beyond daily prayers offered in mosques often form and engage in religious associations. Some in Western Europe develop mosques, as well. The Gülen movement has not done so. This may be because they are keeping with their organizational model as developed in Turkey, and because they wanted to have more opportunity to interact with the broader Muslim and non-Muslim populations. While the Gülen associations have not operated mosques, they usually have had a dedicated space that could be used for daily prayers. At the time of our research, the associations did not have imams and did not offer regular prayer services. As we mentioned in Chapter 1, we focused on Muslims in the Gülen movement to be consistent in nationality across the four countries we were studying and because the movement was fairly open and accessible to researchers.[25] The Gülen movement can be considered a loosely

---

[25] For further information on the rationale of choosing the Gülen movement, see the section on Research Strategy in Chapter 1.

hierarchical religious community (or *cemaat*). It adheres to the teachings and practices of Sunni Islam but has its own social organization that offers religious education programs, such as study sessions, and mobilizes its followers to give to various causes.

Religious communities have informal social networks through which they can enhance their mission that is inspired by religious teachings. As is the case in other religious communities, the Gülen movement focuses on social, educational, media, and philanthropic activities in addition to providing religious services such as forming study groups and providing a religious education for the children. There is a loose hierarchy within the movement even though local organizations have strong autonomy in their decision-making. The movement has local associations led by a community leader appointed by the representative organization in the city, whose leader in turn is appointed by the country-level organization. The leader in each association is responsible both to the people in the association and to their superiors. In the larger cities, there is a representative above the local association's leader (in Milan and Dublin, the leader of the association is also the leader of the organization in the city) who reports to the country representatives. The local associations have relatively autonomous decision-making structures. They each have an executive board that identifies potential activities they plan to engage in based on their own resources.

Association members are not sanctioned if they do not give time and money. Association leaders and boards cannot expel someone from Islam for failing to contribute. The services offered by the associations not only are for those who contribute to the association, but are open to all, sometimes even to non-Muslims. The associations in each of the four cities we studied have weekly adult religious study meetings in all cities, and weekend religious classes for children in Dublin, Milan, and Paris, cities where the children otherwise would not learn about Islam in public schools. The associations try to attract as many people as possible to the study sessions and classes, accepting anyone who is interested. For instance, one of our interviewees said she invited her daughter's non-Muslim school friends to the association's weekend school to show them the kind of religious knowledge that Muslims learn (MM29). In Istanbul and Paris, the Gülen movement has private, full-time schools. Access to them is not contingent upon congregants' contributions to the associations. At the time of our research, the school in Paris was underenrolled and administrators were recruiting beyond active association members in an effort to increase enrollment. The Gülen schools in Istanbul were prestigious and one might expect that being an active member would make a difference in getting a space for one's child in the schools. In schools in which admission did not require a central placement test, contributors could have been favored in enrolling their children in the schools. However, in Turkey, most of the prestigious private schools enroll students through a central placement test, so the association's school administrators cannot choose their own students.[26]

In the four cities studied, Muslim associations put a special focus on interfaith dialogue activities. In Istanbul, the association put Muslims in contact with non-Muslim minorities through regular meetings and programs. In Paris, Milan, and Dublin, they reached out to the broader community through dinners, trips, and academic and cultural programs to promote interfaith dialogue. Most of these activities were with those who were not Muslim; clearly, being a contributor to the association is not a requirement for participation. Most of the time, the associations try to reach out to leading members of the community regardless of their religious background. Being in an influential position rather than contributing to the association made the difference in getting a spot in these programs. Further, those who want to attend these types of programs could almost always find a space (PM1, MM6, DM5, IM17).

The Gülen associations also provide help for those in need through charity campaigns organized by their networks and through an organization dedicated to charity, *Kimse Yok Mu* (KYM; Is Anybody Listening?). For the local campaigns organized by the associations, there are two types of charities. One contributes to the general collection initiatives led by the movement, such as aid to Pakistani flood victims. In the second type, the local members of the association organize ad hoc collections based on the local needs. KYM usually identifies the causes and organizes individual campaigns for each cause through its website.

How Islamic Institutional Structures Affect Opportunities to Be Generous

The organization did not operate as a strict top-down hierarchy, so there were numerous opportunities for adherents to participate, donate, and volunteer. Most of the decisions related to the local associations are taken at the local level. Within each association, the adherents meet weekly in

[26] When the tension between the AKP and the Gülen movement surfaced after 2013, there were widespread allegations against the movement that the movement's networks within the state fed exam questions to Gülen sympathizers.

smaller groups of eight to twelve people to discuss day-to-day issues of the association. These weekly meetings are where important decisions about the community are taken. Depending on their availability, each participant in the group takes responsibilities to be completed within the week ahead. The local members in the association play a role in balancing local and central interests and priorities. They take cues on priorities from the movement leadership, while implementation of those priorities at the local level requires a consensus in weekly meetings. For example, one issue that the Dublin association board was discussing during our visit was whether to rent a bigger place for the association in the city center in order to incorporate more interfaith dialogue activities, in addition to the services that the association already provided. Interfaith dialogue was something encouraged by the Gülen movement, but the congregants in Dublin were unwilling to take the steps to rent a bigger space because they thought they were not financially ready for such a move. Since the local members fund local associations and their activities, and money transfers from other cities are rare to nonexistent, most of the local decisions are taken by local initiatives.

The impact of the decentralized structure, and small local associations, seems to have been to foster a sense of responsibility among adherents to contribute in time, funds, and other resources to the association and its causes. Those outside Turkey felt a responsibility to help the Muslim community become established and to improve its image. An interviewee from Paris noted that "we need strong intercultural organizations to change the Muslim image in France" (PM1). Others also noted this issue (e.g., MM5, MM29, DM11) and explained that their contributions were motivated by a desire to elevate the status of the Turkish Muslim community in their respective cities. Another common explanation was based on a desire to provide proper education (which also includes religious education) for their children (e.g., PM6, PM11, PM28). The words of a woman from Paris in her fifties are illustrative: "When I was raising my kids, we did not have these associations in Paris. I tried my best to raise my kids in a Muslim way but I could do it in a very limited way. I was unlucky. I do want my kids to be lucky in raising their kids by having this kind of facility [meaning the cultural association]" (PM11). In Turkey, many expressed a desire to help their local community and to maintain the association. The orientations indicated a stronger sense of prosociality than a sense of contributing only to avoid social retribution or denial of religious resources.

The lack of strong monitoring and sanctioning mechanisms in Islam, including in the Gülen movement, means that, as with Catholicism, mainstream Islamic religious organizations are vulnerable to free-riding and collective action problems. They nevertheless produce club and public goods. Although the institutions of Islam provide some vehicle for giving, they are not sufficient to account for people's commitment to contribute.

A question to ask is whether Muslims revived the historical institution of waqf in mobilizing the congregants to provide charity and public goods. In Islamic law, the institution of waqf, or pious foundations, created the mechanism for wealthy Muslims to establish organizations that helped to provide social services. Waqfs had a religious role in that they were "pious acts" that helped the founder's after-life status, and also discharged "the obligation of giving charity" (Singer 2002, 25). Waqfs also could provide employment to family members and prestige to the founder (ibid.). Waqfs were a significant vehicle for charity in the Muslim world from the eighth until the nineteenth century, when by and large they were appropriated by states (Çizakça 2001; Hennigan 2004; Kuran 2001; 2016; 2011, 97–116). They were "the chief vehicle for formal philanthropy" by Muslims (Singer 2002, 16). Although those who developed the institution of waqf justified their decision based on Islamic sources including the Qur'an and hadith, we do not see any direct references to it in the Qur'an (Kuran 2001, 844). It was developed under classic Islamic law between the seventh and tenth centuries. Accordingly, "a waqf was a foundation that a Muslim individual established by turning privately held real estate into a revenue-producing endowment" (Kuran 2016, 522). Once a private property was endowed as a waqf, it was supposed to serve the public function stated in its deed. The state or ruler did not have the right to take over any waqf property. The founder of the waqf stipulated the function and procedures of the management of the waqf, and the founder appointed the manager. Although a waqf served charitable functions, it also benefited the founding family since its properties were secured from state takeover and family members could be salaried caretakers of it (Kuran 2016, 422–425). The laws about waqfs provided that a waqf was supposed to serve to the function that the founder specified in the deed; its mission and activities could not be changed over time. For these reasons, waqfs were unable to adapt to new conditions; they became stagnant over time. By the early twentieth century, governments in Muslim states confiscated the resources of the waqfs and took over many of the public functions that waqfs had served over centuries (Kuran 2001).

In the late twentieth and early twenty-first centuries, Muslim-dominant countries, including Turkey, developed Western-style nonprofit organization laws to regulate charitable institutions (Kuran 2016, 444–447). In Turkey, foundations (*vakıf*) and Islamic charitable associations (*dernek*) are the two leading institutions through which charitable functions are legally established. While setting up a foundation requires relatively more resources, setting up an association does not require capital. In foundations, most decisions are made by a board of executives, and the board members are not responsible to the beneficiaries. In associations, members or beneficiaries carry relatively more power. They elect the board members and make key decisions (Hatemi and Oğuztürk 2014). In all four countries studied, the Muslim respondents were affiliated with associations. The Gülen movement set up foundations in Turkey mostly to establish universities and sometimes to contribute to other social functions such the Journalists and Writers Foundation. However, most local organizing has been through the vehicle of associations. Our respondents did not have a systematic understanding of what waqfs were and how they could be revived in contemporary world. Only one interviewee explicitly referred to waqfs, when explaining the necessity of giving in the Ottoman Empire: "Our ancestors founded waqfs even for very trivial things such as protecting the birds" (IM12). This contrasts with the extent to which our interviewees spontaneously brought up various examples of generous behavior (e.g., that of Abu Bakr), verses from the Qur'an, and other Islamic practices that encourage giving. If our respondents had a systematic understanding of waqfs, this likely would have been evident in the interviews. The interviewees' focus was on giving to their association or to activities that were sponsored by the foundations, with virtually no attention to the association or foundation's status in Islamic law or tradition.

However, as we will discuss in detail in Chapter 6, Muslim respondents had a strong affiliation with their associations and praised their engagement with their communities. This affiliation, though, seemed to have less to do with the historical institution of waqfs and more to do with community ties.

Rituals of Belonging and Giving

Being repeated in a structured way, rituals may act as institutions in stimulating giving for religious adherents. The rituals of belonging and giving can constitute a framework that leads Catholics and Muslims to give time, effort, and financial resources to their associations and other causes.

Catholicism

Catholic rituals of belonging exact some opportunity costs in time and effort, but are low in comparison to the rituals of strict sects and cults.[27] Potentially, some of the rituals of belonging, such as the prohibition against using birth control, are costly. As is well known, most West European Catholics ignore some prohibitions to which they object. The alert reader may note that where Catholics are in the minority and in a society that persecutes or discriminates against religious minorities (or against Catholics in particular), adhering to Catholic rituals *is* costly. One can say likewise for Islam. Because the effect of minority status is a significant topic, we address it in a separate chapter. Attending mass and going to confession weekly are required by the religion, but in the large urban societies in which we conducted our research, individuals are not ostracized by the religious community nor punished by religious leaders for not observing traditional Catholic practices. In the contemporary period, observing practices in Catholic-dominant or even mixed Christian societies does not isolate adherents from the broader society. The religion, as practiced, is "low tension" (Stark and Finke 2000, 143).

Catholic rituals of giving do not enable Catholics to signal to each other their commitment to the group. Giving is private: in our four parishes, the object into which one puts one's donation at mass was a deep, dark bag. What one dropped in would not be visible to those sitting nearby nor to those facilitating the passing of the bags between pews. Annual pledges could be mailed in or electronically deducted from one's bank account; the only church official in the know would be the bookkeeper (Figure 2.2).

In addition, in the French, Italian, Irish, and Turkish Catholic religious services (mass), monetary giving was downplayed. While the passing of the collection basket is a ritual, it is not a sacred one and is not treated as such in services. Even the term "collection" indicates it is not thought of in spiritual terms. It is not an "offering" (to God or even to the Church). In our parishes, there were collections at each service, but they were not incorporated into the other parts of the service; the priest did not link giving or the collection with any spiritual or other sacred themes or symbols. At most, the priest stated that the collection or collections were

---

[27] There are formal rituals of entry, routinely summarized, for children, as baptism, first communion, and confirmation. Children and adults must take classes to be "confirmed" as Catholics. The opportunity costs for children appear to be similar to children whose parents raise them in evangelical or other Protestant churches (Gwin et al. 2009, 28–29; Smith 2003).

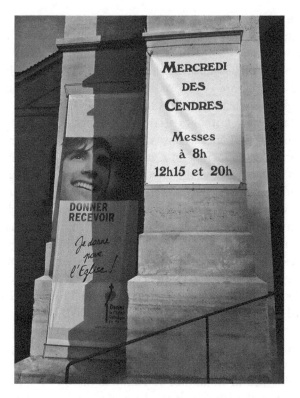

Figure 2.2 Poster at Saint-Pierre de Montrouge for annual diocesan pledge drive ("denier de l'Église") and Ash Wednesday, Paris.

for one or another item.[28] The collection followed the liturgy reading and the short homily (sermon). The liturgy readings follow the Church's theological calendar, so do not necessarily focus attention on the upcoming collection. A priest at Santa Maria alla Fontana commented that in the fifteen minutes he has for his homily, it is difficult to develop themes connected to the liturgy readings, particularly if he tries to make them relevant to parishioners' lives. He added that "you Protestants are better at that" (MC22). The readings and sermons are not followed by congregational or other singing linked to the collection. For instance, at Ballygall, just after the sermon at the children's mass (attended by quite a few

---

[28] In Istanbul, all the collections after the services go toward the expenses of the priests and the church. Since the church has a small number of congregants, it needs more help for its own functioning as compared with other cities. We were told that the internal financing was enough for operating costs of the church.

parents and grandparents), the priest announces how much was collected the last week, and what the different colored collection bags are for that will be passed around. Then a lay person reads the profession of faith (the Nicene creed), then there is another prayer reading from the liturgy, then the passing of one bag, then another (numerous services observed, November 2010 and May 2011).[29] There is a slightly different order at adult masses (the prayer reading comes after the passing of the collection bags). Afterward, the bags disappear into the back of the church, and the priest starts to get set up for the Eucharist. The prayer of blessing for gifts is for the bread and the wine that become consecrated during the Eucharist, not for the collection that just took place. In neither version of the mass service is the collection explicitly linked to individuals' religious life; it more tends to interrupt the flow of the service. Processes were similar in Milan and Paris. While many of our interviewees noted that the Eucharist is the most emotional and community-reinforcing part of the mass, the collection takes place prior to it, or well after it, such that any potential connection between the Eucharist and the collection is lost. Indeed, most interviewees could not remember a particular sermon in the past three to six months that had mentioned giving or helping others, and with no linkage of the collection to a call to give, the collection ritual did not have a strong role in explicitly calling forth generosity (e.g., DC9, DC13, DC14, DC16, MC14, MC18, PC4, PC7, PC8). Instead, some pointed out that it was the overall service that inspired them (MC14, PC8).

In Istanbul, the collection was even less linked to the religious purpose and spirit of the service: it came at the very end of the service. Two children from the parish collected money for the church after each service. The head priest stated that in addition to weekly collections, the church organizes four major fundraising events throughout the year: one of them, for the church, is in April; one for Vatican is in December; one for missionaries is in October; and one for Caritas during the Lent period, in which congregants are given a donation envelope to return with their contributions (Figure 2.3).

Given this framing of the collection process during services, we would not expect Catholics to make connections between sacred religious duties or experiences and giving. Rather, giving might take on a more perfunctory, "secular" character: it pays the bills. Indeed, that is what parishioners

---

[29] The text of the Nicene creed can be found at www.vatican.va/archive/ccc_css/archive/catechism/credo.htm. It dates from 325 CE, with revisions in 381 CE. The readings prior to the Eucharist are the "liturgy of the Word," in contrast to the "liturgy of the Eucharist."

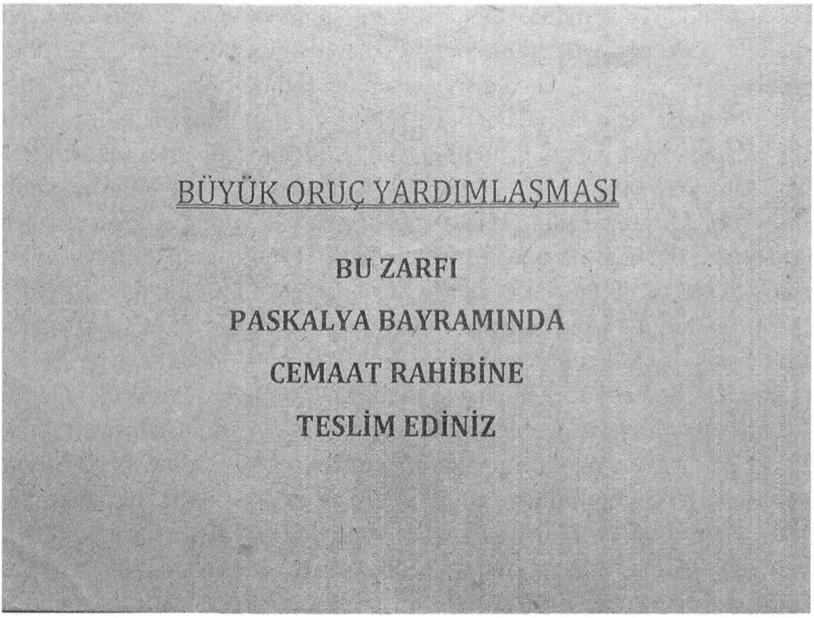

Figure 2.3 Envelope for the Lent collection, Basilique Cathédrale du Saint-Esprit, Istanbul. English translation: "Lent support. Hand in this envelope to your priest at the end of the Lent."

in all four cities told us. Giving during the services was not interpreted as a spiritual or religious act; it was more often seen as helping to pay for the utilities, for the priests' salaries and retirement funds, and, rather resentfully, for diocesan expenses (PC10, DC9). As one parishioner noted, she gives to the parish because she is in it; because she "benefits from it" (PC13). Another commented that it is not "an offering in the sense of sacrificing; it is not an expression of sins; it is a 'thank you' for all the happiness and joy I have received" (PC11). This parishioner stated a common view: "the principle duty of Catholics is to aid the parish because it lives on donations." Further, the parish constitutes the spiritual community that is an essential part of her faith. To sustain that, she feels a responsibility to contribute.

As has been found in American parishes (Smith 2008), European priests were reluctant to be vocal about asking for funds. They were discrete. For instance, at Saint-Pierre de Montrouge in Paris, one finds a small brochure on a table near the main door, with the bulletins, that is labeled "The collection: why? for whom? how much?" After answering the first two questions, it suggests what might be an appropriate contribution during the mass. That suggestion is on the back of the brochure – it is the last

Figure 2.4 Saint-Pierre de Montrouge collection brochure.

thing one reads, so, again, it is discrete. The head of the parish Economic Council said that they developed this in response to confusion from the currency conversion from the French franc to the euro – people were no longer sure what was a reasonable amount to put in the collection basket at mass. The brochure suggests two euros for the head of the family, and to add another euro for each additional member of the family who participates at mass (Figure 2.4). It concludes by saying that "your participation is a sign of your confidence in the life of the body of Christ" – it does not even repeat the word "donation" or "gift" – it instead steers the notion of funds toward "participation." The head of the Economic Council noted that in the year since they produced that brochure, contributions went up, despite the recession, from an average of 1.5 euros per person to 1.84 euros per person (PC10).[30]

One Irish mother who always took her young children to mass explained that giving during the collection is a lesson for her kids: "with the collection

---

[30] At the time of our research, one euro equaled about US$1.40. The positive impact of a suggested amount, which amounts to a focal point, on giving behavior has also been noted in debates about tipping at restaurants and in other service sectors.

baskets going around I always give ... Money would always be put into the two bags – it wouldn't matter if it were for a snail farm or the homeless. Have kids put it in." The important thing is the giving: "kids see that someone needs help. [They] have to know it's needed and goes to somebody." Her children seemed to have picked up on the idea, applying it in unexpected contexts: one evening one of her young sons wanted to sleep in his chair instead of in his bed. She told him, "Sleep in the bed, there are poor children who don't have a bed." His brother said, "Mom, why don't you let him sleep in the chair and give his bed to the poor children?" (DC13).

The parishes rely on that ritual of giving being ingrained in their parishioners. The head priest at Santa Maria alla Fontana quipped that there is a saying in Milan that "the works of the Church are done on the advice of the rich and the money of the poor." He noted the one or two euros per week of parishioners attending mass added up to a substantial, and reliable, amount of funds.[31] The lengthier statement of an Irish Catholic summarizes many of the thoughts interviewees expressed when asked about religious services and giving: "It's voluntary, you don't have to give. I feel very obliged to support my church in that envelope ... And the first collection (at mass) is for the priests (and even some of that goes into the archbishop's house which people don't know and I think they should). I have a little bit of difficulty with the two [collection] baskets, especially the second one, which is for 'share.' It's for building churches in Dublin. There's no churches that have been built. So I don't know where the money goes. I really don't know where the money goes. It goes into the Archbishop's House but I don't know what they do with it." As to how much she gives, she said, "I work it out proportionately of my income. The more money I have the more money they get." When asked if she gives to the Church because of its religious teachings, she responds that she doesn't, and explains: "Everything has to be funded no matter what it is, whether you feel you have to or you want to give it. Practically, the priests have to live, the church has to be funded. It's a practicality to me. I want to give it. I can see the money that we give is put back into the [local parish] church. I can see it. It's not as if the church's gotten all dilapidated ... The money's there and you can see. It's a beautiful church and it's well maintained" (DC9). She noted that the parish church did get a new roof. Giving of financial resources is largely a practical matter, not

---

[31] Don Roberto Viganò, Milan, Oct. 6, 2010.

Figure 2.5 Ballygall parish Church of Our Mother of Divine Grace, after a Sunday mass, Dublin.

one that has direct spiritual meaning, and not one that is viewed as an obligatory sacrament.[32]

In Dublin, Paris, Milan, and Istanbul, the need for volunteers is sometimes mentioned at the end of the service. As noted above, recruitment tended to happen by word of mouth and by the priest or other official asking individuals if they would consider taking on a role. In other words, volunteering is not regarded or conceptualized in the religious services as something that serves a spiritual or religious sacrament. Volunteers are free to (or "left to") impute their own meaning to their contributions.

For most, if not all, interviewees, there was nothing specific about the mass or a priest's sermons that they could recall prompting or inspiring them to be generous or other-regarding (e.g., DC21, DC22). As one noted, "all is linked" in the religious service (MC14; cf. PC4, PC7, PC17, PC18). An Irish interviewee (DC2) said of giving that "it's not drilled into you," and he could not recall sermons that specifically talked about giving. Another, an elderly parishioner, said, "It's not the pitch" (DC3). For many,

---

[32] This corresponds to findings in the United States that "Catholics tend to view money and material possessions as having little or nothing to do with religious or spiritual issues" (Starks and Smith 2013, 4). Miller (1999) observed in her study of a US parish that "although the Roman mass clearly offers a rich symbolic universe for participants, in this congregation … it seems to be disconnected from the financial or material realm of people's everyday lives" (68).

attending mass has no effect on giving; rather, it "keeps you in touch ... Life is funny. There's people that never come to church that may be more charitable. Coming to church is just something you like to do" (DC11). To the extent the interviewees reflected on the teachings of their faith, most noted, in the words of one, that everything in the faith propels one toward "consideration of others" (MC14). An Irish parishioner observed that "certainly there are sermons that talk about Gospel stories which have examples of giving" (DC1). Irish parishioners noted that "they never really ask [for money]; they never say 'we want your money'" (DC2); it's more that parishioners hear "if you could, please give." This is a fine point, but to the parishioners' minds, it makes a difference. One added that "it's a great parish for giving, whoever has it, gives. No one is banging on your door" asking for money (DC2).

The passing of the collection basket at mass does generate a response from most attendees; while the parishes do not rely solely on that for their income, it is one part of it. Many interviewees said they give as they can, and don't discriminate between causes or programs and beneficiaries (e.g., DC2, MC18). In the Ballygall parish, a retired man noted, laughing, that "they're always lookin' for money for something, they're a basic source of charity in Ireland ... they've always looked after the poor" and "there are always boxes rattlin' in front of you." He indicated that requests were not made explicit during services, adding that the priest might mention that there is a collection for one or another charitable organization going on outside the church after mass but that the priest doesn't push it (DC11; cf. MC6). Another Ballygall parishioner stated that the priest "never does ask for funds, he never ever does" (DC1).

Interviewees noted they tend to give at services, though quite a few also mentioned giving financially via automatic payments, or larger amounts on special occasions, such as Easter, when the diocese and parish priest might have chosen several causes to support that season. Respondents varied considerably on whether particular causes led them to give more, for instance, to help Christians in the Middle East or missionaries in Africa, or whether they gave to the causes picked by the priest (e.g., DC2, DC21, DC22, MC4, MC5, MC18, PC3, PC19).

There are other ritualized acts that raise funds for church functions: purchasing candles to light and place at an altar as a prayer for someone (PC10) or making a donation to a religious order that then prays for the donor (DC9). Commenting on an order of nuns she sends donations to, an Irish parishioner explained, "We have nuns down there who are praying for us. You can write to them and give them your requests, they're coming from good women." She added, laughing lightly, "Hopefully He's listening" (DC9).

Given the unmonitored rituals of giving in the Church, its officials might, in turn, say of Catholics, "Hopefully, they'll respond." We turn now to the possible impact of rituals in Islam.

Islam

There are not strictly monitored rituals of belonging to the community among Muslims. Some potential practices might include attending weekly programs conducted by the associations in our four research sites, attendance at annual pledge meetings that the associations organize, or attending some community events. Other than these practices, there are no visible dress codes or other rituals of belonging. That many women in the organization wore a headscarf could be a potential ritual but there were several women among our interviewees who did not follow the practice. Furthermore, Muslims are distinguishable for their dietary restrictions (such as not eating pork and avoiding alcohol), but these did not seem to play a role in the giving, monitoring, or sanctioning of the members. These practices can distinguish Muslims in the non-Muslim majority settings and they might have faced some bias in Paris, Milan, and Dublin, with the presumption that adherents would have to be more committed to sustain that practice in those cities.

Doctrinally, the most significant religious practice of giving in Islam is zakat, which is compulsory for all Muslims who have sufficient material resources. As one interviewee in Paris pointed out, zakat is mentioned in the Qur'an several times, right after daily prayers are mentioned. Its importance is due to the positioning: the daily prayers are considered the most significant Islamic ritual (PM24).[33] The ritual thus is given an important place in Islamic theology, by being one of the five pillars of religion. Depending on the type of property and wealth that a person has, different percentages should be given to others in need. In general 2.5 percent of a person's wealth should be given away annually. Each Muslim who gives zakat calculates the amount and personally gives it to those in need, or an individual can give it to certain associations that play an intermediary role between givers and recipients. In its practice today, there is not a specific ritual about the way zakat is given; people are responsible for doing it themselves. Historically, some Islamic states monitored

[33] Some references in the Qur'an include 2/43, 2/83, 2/177, 4/77, 5/55, 9/71, 21/73, 22/78, 98/5.

people's wealth and their corresponding zakat obligation. Relevant for our query about which structures within Islam may provide monitoring and sanctioning mechanisms that prompt giving, even when political authorities have monitored the zakat, religious institutions have not had the authority or capacity to monitor the zakat contributions of Muslims. Monitoring is self-imposed by individuals. The Islamic associations do not have any power to impose the requirements on their congregants, nor sanction any congregant's failure to practice zakat. Congregants are free to give their zakat to whomever they want or whatever cause they choose. The associations can only remind them of the duty.

Although this is the practice among many Muslims whom we interviewed and observed, zakat historically has been interpreted and implemented in a variety of ways. In the Qur'an, zakat is treated "as a purifier of property" (Kuran 2003, 276) and seen as fulfilling an obligation to God to help the needy. It has been viewed as a good deed that brings rewards in the afterlife (Singer 2002, 22). The Qur'an mentions categories of people to whom zakat may be given: "the poor, the needy, zakat administrators, potential converts and Muslims who might yet renounce Islam, manumitted slaves, debtors, people fighting for God, and wayfarers" (Kuran 2003, 278). In the early years of Islam, zakat was seen as a charitable gift. After the Prophet Muhammad founded a state in 622 in Medina, zakat became the basis of the new polity's tax system. Over time there was variation in the bases on which zakat was assessed. States used zakat revenue for military purposes, operational expenses, and to help the poor (Kuran 2003, 277–280). In the era of imperial Muslim states, non-Islamic taxes replaced zakat, such that gradually zakat gained a narrower meaning, that of charity (Singer 2002, 24–25). Although there are exceptions, most contemporary Muslim-dominant states leave decisions regarding zakat transfers to individuals. The Turkish state does not have a zakat collection system. The decision to pay zakat is left to the individual Muslim's conscience. Our respondents seemed to be aware of this responsibility and paid special attention to it. They mostly regarded zakat as charity, not a state tax.

Another ritual, that of fitr, also known as *zakat al-fitr*, is a charitable contribution given to the poor in the month of Ramadan, the month during which Muslims practice ritual fasting. Fitr is obligatory for all Muslims, whether male or female, minor or adult, so long as they have the means to donate (Ali 2014, 18). Someone from the household pays the required amount for the family members before the prayer of the Eid el-Fitr, the festival that Muslims celebrate after the month of Ramadan.

For each family member, an amount that can feed one person for one day is required. The Islamic associations can play an intermediary role in collecting and distributing these charitable gifts. However, their intermediary role is not prescribed by Islamic teachings, but a matter of convenience: those who do not have time to search for the poor to give to can give their contributions to their associations. As with zakat, the associations do not have any mechanisms to compel donations. Even though the ritual is time-specific, it is not tied to specific religious ceremonies, so Muslims can give their fitr contributions anytime within the month of Ramadan. If a Muslim decides not to give fitr, there is no human mechanism for sanctioning the decision.

In addition to these theologically based compulsory donations, there are other religious rituals of giving. An optional ritual of giving is *sadaqa*. It can be given anytime, in any amount. Sadaqa is any giving beyond zakat and fitr. In Islamic teachings, voluntary work and good deeds are considered sadaqa. The legitimate receivers of sadaqa are the same kind of people who are eligible to receive zakat, with the addition of close family members (Singer 2006, 315). When zakat was imposed in early Islamic states, sadaqa, as a praiseworthy yet voluntary practice, became a major means to help the poor (Kuran 2003, 278). Although it is encouraged by the theology, there are no means through which it can be monitored. Muslims can give to anyone in need or to any charitable organization, such as to neighbors, their relatives, to student funds, or simply to collections after weekly Friday prayers. Religious institutions have little to no role in controlling Muslims' giving by way of sadaqa. In Islamic theology, there is a shared understanding that sadaqa can expiate sins and improve one's standing before God. Sadaqa can also protect the givers from disasters and life troubles. Those who have legitimate reasons not to fast in the month of Ramadan, such as pregnant women, can give sadaqa to fulfill their requirements (Singer 2006, 315). In comparison to the history of zakat, it is more difficult to trace the historical evolution of sadaqa, as it is a voluntary act (Singer 2006, 316).

How did these rituals affect the generosity of our interviewees? First, it was clear that the effects of these institutions of giving on Muslims varies somewhat, depending on their degree of engagement with the associations. For those who are less engaged with the associations, the religious rituals, particularly zakat, encourage them to give more. As a Muslim in Dublin stated, "The best criteria of giving is [sic] determined by Islam through the zakat. It's my aim to give my zakat annually. If I reach that goal, I feel very happy" (DM30). However, many interviewees, especially those who were more active in the associations, did not even mention zakat or fitr in their interviews. When asked why they did not refer to these religious rituals of giving, they responded that those were required for everyone and giving in the amount of zakat was just a duty. To them, real giving is giving beyond the required amount of zakat. It seems that most interviewees internalized the requirements of zakat and fitr and did not consider them part of their generosity. As one Gülen member in Istanbul stated, "After we got to know '*hizmet*,' we stopped calculating our zakat amount. What we give to the association is much higher than what we are required to give as a zakat requirement" (IM11).[34] Zakat and fitr seem to establish the minimum levels of giving for more religiously active Muslims, and set a target for less active but still religiously observant Muslims.

In the associations, giving and charity were not addressed directly in religious sermons. In Milan, the association provided Friday prayer services but there was no ritual of giving at those services. This is in line with the practices in regular state-run mosques in Turkey. However, a donation box is available at the associations, and those who would like to contribute put money to this box. Especially in Istanbul, Paris, and Milan, encouraging giving was a priority of the associations and often mentioned by interviewees. At the time of research in Istanbul, the members were trying to raise funds for a dormitory project for university students. In the four cities studied, the associations were also soliciting donations for Pakistani flood victims.

Although giving is not part of the sermons and religious experiences, and associations do not have control over how congregants perform the religious rituals of giving, each association has annual events to collect charitable contributions from its members. These are not theologically imposed rituals; that said, some of our respondents gave a religious justification for these practices. For example, a businessman from Istanbul referred to the early Muslims' practice of gathering contributions at the time of emergencies and stated that "the closest friends of the Prophet, Ebu Bekir and Ömer, are known for their competing to give" (IM18). This point is clear in the annual fundraising pledge that Gülen associations organized, usually during the month of Ramadan. In these meetings, members pledge donations in two categories: (1) the amount that they pledge to give throughout the upcoming year and (2) the amount that they pledge to raise from others (mostly sympathizers but not active members).

---

[34] *Hizmet* is the Turkish shorthand for the movement among its followers. It means "service."

We were told that sometimes there may be two separate events for each category (IM18). In the pledge meeting, people announce their pledges in front of all the attendees in the room. The meeting is not open to the public; only those invited can attend to the meeting. The money coming from the annual fundraising event is used to sustain the associations and to fund their educational, social, and religious activities. Most of the time, contributors include most or all of their zakat obligations in their pledges (e.g., IM16, PM24, MM1, DM25). In justifying these events, some members voiced their belief that these types of collections were conducted at the time of the Prophet Muhammad (e.g., IM18, MM13, PM7). Though, as with other *hadiths* (sayings of Muhammad), the historical veracity of that example may be debated, it nevertheless serves as an important reference for those who quote it (Hallaq 1999).

Certainly, the public nature of the pledging would lead to pressure to pledge, and to pledge at the highest level one could sustain. To that extent, the associations have a structural feature that may motivate giving. This gives Islam, or at least the Gülen movement, a peer pressure sanctioning (and/or incentivizing) mechanism – one has an incentive to gain community approval by giving, and one is concerned about the sanction of community disapproval if one does not give. A middle-aged man from Istanbul, when talking about his giving during the pledges, mentioned that he compares his giving with others. He approaches the publicity of his giving in positive terms, as this encourages him to give more because he compares his giving with those whose circumstances are similar to his (IM14). When talking about the pledges, the respondents referred to them as "incentives" (IM18) and referred the practice's origins in Islamic history (PM7). Some interviewees mentioned another hadith, that the Prophet Muhammad encouraged his companions to "compete for the good" (IM17). However, the associations do not have a well-developed capacity to monitor the actual donations nor means of sanctioning those who miss their pledged targets (PM24, MM21, DM25, IM25).

There are other ad hoc collections in the community. If the association notices a critical need, for either the association's local activities or a disaster in some part of the world, it organizes special fundraising events. For example, the associations in Dublin, Istanbul, Milan, and Paris had organized events for victims of the earthquake in Haiti and the floods in Pakistan. Another community-based nonritualistic way of giving, called *kermes* in Turkish, is organized by women who do not work outside the home. The term applied to their collaborating to make hand-crafted articles that they would sell at a busy public place or during special occasions. Related to this, the women also come together to cook and sell food to raise money for particular projects of the association (e.g., PM8, MM2).

In short, the compulsory religious rituals of zakat and fitr and voluntary ritual of sadaqa are important for the Muslims, as they set the expectations that God has for the faithful. Muslim organizations do not have any control over how the congregants perform their obligations. They can offer mechanisms through which congregants perform these religious practices, but they do not have the means to monitor their members' compliance nor sanction noncompliance. The rituals are personal, with several ways that the individuals can perform them. The associations themselves come up with other events through which they can facilitate the giving of their congregants. The annual pledges, the annual collections before Eid al-Adha, and specific collections are among these. However, these practices are not stipulated by Islamic teachings, so the congregants are not "theologically" responsible to contribute to these. Muslims contribute nevertheless, leading us to explore in subsequent chapters the role of religious beliefs and community engagement in their charitable activity.

Conclusion

As we have demonstrated, the Church and Islamic associations do not have institutions that, through their monitoring and sanctioning structures, can compel "generosity" or giving and volunteering. At best, both organized religions remind adherents of the religious values of giving and provide outlets for them to do so.

For Catholics, the religion relies heavily on prosocial dispositions encouraged by its doctrines that advocate being helpful to others. The Church's institutional sanctions are nonexistent and Catholicism's spiritual sanctions are weak. The religious rites and rituals do not exclude on the basis of whether or not one has contributed. For Muslims, the main structural feature that encourages giving is the Gülen associations' annual fundraising meetings, in which invited members publicly declared what their donation to their association would be. Follow-through was not strictly monitored nor sanctioned.

The institutional structures that were found to contribute to the provision of public goods for both Catholics and Muslims were generally decentralized, where laity were asked and encouraged to take on leadership roles within their particular religious community. Accordingly, institutional exhortations to encourage giving were generally downplayed, and instead people were encouraged by more informal channels, such as word of mouth, a church official making a request directly of an individual, and associational activity, to produce public goods. Formal institutional sanctions and incentives were not driving factors.

Both religions have formal mechanisms of giving; Catholicism the collection at mass, Islam the zakat and fitr. We also noted other mechanisms that may be less ritualized, such as the annual fundraising drives of the Church and informal giving in Islam (sadaqa), as well as the more formalized legal structure of the waqf, or Islamic foundation. Interviewees were aware of the fundraising institutions of their religion, with the exception that only one Muslim interviewee seemed cognizant of waqfs and their role in Islamic charity. That is not to say that the others were not; instead, it seemed that interviewees were focused on giving to their associations and related movement, but not concerned about the status of them in Islamic and state law. It is difficult to say whether this is a trend; certainly, there is variation in what Catholics and Muslims understand to be the requirements of their respective religions. It becomes clear that, as studies of altruistic behavior in other contexts have found, organizational structures help elicit and channel the direction of giving and volunteering (Healy 2000).

Neither Catholicism nor Islam has strong sanctioning or monitoring systems; Islam perhaps has a stronger one than Catholicism, but neither religion could be characterized as being a strict sect. Indeed, the main sanction for Muslims is an internalized belief that one has a duty to God that if not fulfilled will result in real losses on earth, as well as real disfavor from God. The main monitoring mechanism is also an internalized belief that God is watching one's behavior. A secondary mechanism is in the form of the public declaration of giving, with a relatively weak follow-up mechanism (no public chastisement if one does not follow through, for instance). Catholicism lacks both those sanctioning and monitoring mechanisms. Clearly, the institutional structure can provide opportunities for Catholics or Muslims to be generous; whether they will respond, however, is not a function of the institutional structure – that cannot compel them to do anything. Instead, the institutions must rely on the prosocial orientations, the beliefs of their adherents, and the positive affect they feel for their religious community.

One might object that we have downplayed the possible role of reciprocity fostered by institutional structures: for the small parishes, and for the Gülen associations, the fact that adherents would see each other repeatedly might encourage helping behavior. Even if there is some sense of reciprocity leading to cooperation (perhaps more so in the Gülen associations than in the Catholic parishes, because of size and because of the public pledging ceremony), our two religions do not have the means, except via beliefs, to punish noncooperators. An expansive view of beliefs could include, as we explore in later chapters, community expectations – but even those are mild, and hardly enforced, when it comes to financial giving and volunteering. Our results point to a factor that tends to be overlooked in the debates about "rational cooperators": the extent to which prosociality and internalized religious beliefs may facilitate generosity and public goods provision. What becomes apparent in our case studies and experiments, as the next chapters show, is the extent to which the religious beliefs and community engagement activate and channel prosocial tendencies in individuals.

3

Generosity, Public Goods Provision, and Religious Beliefs in Catholicism and Islam

An Experiment

Organized religions devote considerable resources to setting out their beliefs and trying to ingrain them in potential converts and adherents. Having seen in the previous chapter that the institutional structures of Catholicism and Islam have a very limited capacity to prompt prosocial behavior in the faithful, we now investigate what impact different beliefs have on generosity. It is something that Catholic and Muslim religious officials in Dublin, Milan, Paris, and Istanbul told us they would like to know, too. Religious beliefs and their effect on helping behavior are something of a black box to social scientists, and even to those with the responsibility for perpetuating them. Our research into this "black box" is centered around the idea that different religious beliefs and community practices might influence people to be more, or perhaps less, prosocial, and that this could be expressed in how much they contribute to creating and maintaining club or public goods.

In this chapter, we describe a variety of pathways through which both religious communities and beliefs might affect the prosocial behavior of religious adherents. From these pathways, we develop hypotheses that we then test via psychological experiments. In short, we asked people to think about various aspects of religion, through what experimental psychologists call a priming procedure (Bargh and Chartrand 2000), and then we measured people's propensities for making monetary donations both to their own religious institutions and to more general public goods. The chapter proceeds by laying out the rationales for the propositions we test about specific beliefs, then by describing the experimental procedure, presenting the analyses, and discussing our findings. To preview the results, two experimental conditions, God's grace (where participants were asked to reflect generally on the grace of God) and deservedness (where participants were asked to reflect on the deservedness of the recipients of aid), affected giving in the Irish Catholic participants; none did in the Turkish Muslim participants. We probe our data further and look into why we did not obtain results in the Turkish Muslim case.[1]

Hypotheses about Religious Beliefs and Generosity

We focus on propositions derived from the theologies of Catholicism and Islam and from findings in social psychology and other fields. The first of these propositions looks into the possible impact of community expectations on prosocial behavior. Many different academic fields, including psychology, consider humans to be very social creatures, attuned to what other people think of them, and thus inclined to behave in ways that try to manage other people's views (Richerson and Boyd 1998). When groups have norms and expectations about how people should behave, including whether they should be generous, we expect that people will be influenced to act accordingly. One defining feature of religious groups or communities is that they have ideas about what is moral behavior (Durkheim 1915, 44; Graham and Haidt 2010). Thus, when a Catholic or Muslim group has ideas and norms that encourage generosity, we expect that adherents will contribute to public and club goods because of those group ideas, norms, and expectations. They may perhaps fear being excluded or sanctioned by the group if they do not contribute generously.

People tend to be more generous when they perceive an expectation that other people in their group want them to live up to group norms about cooperating (Kurzban 2001; Satow 1975; van Rompay, Vonk, and Fransen 2009). Religions are often structured to encourage a sense that one is part of a group, with the result that adherents feel connected to members of their religious group (Lincoln 2003). Adherents tend to want to avoid being ostracized or punished for failing to be a good member of the group. Thinking about the expectations of one's religious community may primarily make people donate to causes that are related to the group, and not to people outside the group. This draws on the idea that people powerfully identify with their own group, or "ingroup," and prefer it to other groups, or "outgroups." If this is the case here, when it comes to generosity, thinking about one's religious community's expectations should encourage Catholics and Muslims to prioritize helping their ingroups, and would be expected to make them oriented toward club,

---

[1] As we describe below, participants were drawn from both public universities and religious communities (parishes in Dublin, Gülen associations in Istanbul).

rather than public, goods (Cialdini et al. 1997). Islam and Catholicism consider integration into and cooperation with a community to be a way of serving God. Because both Catholicism and Islam promote serving God by serving others within their community, group members' beliefs about the normative expectations of the religion should lead to prosocial, cooperative behavior (Abrams et al. 1990, 97–119; Kniss and Numrich 2007, 56–57). We formulate our first proposition as follows:

Hypothesis 1: *Thinking about the normative expectations of one's religious community leads Catholics and Muslims to donate to club goods.*

Another possibility, though, is that both Catholicism and Islam are religions that emphasize a universality of humanity and the value of compassion. If so, then making people think about their religion might bring to mind values like universal compassion, potentially prompting generosity in a more global way, evident in donation to public goods. Because both religions recognize and teach a universality of humankind and the value of compassion, Catholics and Muslims may not always prioritize their own group (Luke 10:25–37; Matthew 25:31–40; Qur'an, 2:177). Instead, they may be empathetic with others, regardless of group affiliation. A sense of similarity to other people should accentuate this feeling, because it would encourage a participant to see herself or himself in a needy person's shoes. Such thinking should extend beyond group boundaries of ingroup. We thus expect Catholics and Muslims to be more generous when prompted to think about religious teaching about how all people are similar to each other, and that this generosity would even be evident in public goods – not restricted to one's own religious group.

Hypothesis 2: *The sense of being similar to all other humans fostered by their religion makes Catholics and Muslims more likely to contribute to the production of public goods. The effect on the production of club goods will be less pronounced.*

Religious writings and group norms in many religions, including Catholicism and Islam, stress the idea that other people deserve help. Religious discourse may emphasize additional other-regarding attitudes and behaviors such as deservedness of someone in need. Previous research has found that adherents of different religions vary in their view of whether a needy person is deserving; the more they view the target as deserving, the more helpful they are (Will and Cochran 1995). Key tenets of both Catholicism and Islam hold that the poor and needy are deserving of help regardless of the circumstances or character of the needy individual

(Queen 1996, 26–28, 47–48). Catholics and Muslims should exhibit more helping behavior when their thinking about someone in need is couched in terms of deservingness, and that helping would not be subject to a bias toward their own group members.

Hypothesis 3: *Thinking about the concept of deservedness promoted by their religions should lead Catholics and Muslims to be more generous toward others, no matter the others' religion.*

Our fourth hypothesis starts to bring us to some potential differences in the effects of our experimental prompts on Catholics and Muslims. Religious discourses and community understandings of the notions of duty and obedience to obey God's will and commandments may operate differently in the two religions. While both Catholicism and Islam value and expect people to help others, there may be important differences in whether this norm is seen as more of a duty or as more of a voluntary activity. Through Islamic concepts and behaviors like *zakat* and *fitr*, giving resources to others, many Muslims see such giving as being commanded by God, whom Muslims have a duty to obey (Al-Ghazzali 1996; Queen 1996, 49–50). Catholics often do not perceive giving as a duty to God. Tithing is not described in Catholicism as a formal ritual or as a duty, even if it is a common and valued practice. Rather, Catholicism can better be described as emphasizing voluntary choice about whether to practice such generosity, and to model oneself after Jesus' generosity, but not in an obligatory way. For these reasons, we expect that when our experiment asks people to think about their duty to God, the belief would resonate more with Muslims than with Catholics, and be evident in their subsequent generosity to club and public goods.

Hypothesis 4: *Thinking about the concept of duty to God makes Muslims more generous toward others, and makes them more likely to contribute generously to both club and public goods. This concept should have less effect on Catholics.*

While this concept should have a greater effect on Muslims' generosity, we now turn to a concept that may affect Catholics more so than Muslims. While feeling a duty to God to help others could result in generosity, as we have just discussed, generosity could also be promoted by a divinely felt inspiration to feel God's love and to radiate that love to other people. A Catholic might say, then, that a spirit or practice of generosity could come from feeling a sense of grace and a faith that God is working "through, with, and in us" (Benedict XVI 2009, 1; Himes 2006, 18, 19; Kozlowski 1998, 282; Queen 1996, 27, 50). Catholicism specifically teaches that "faith, hope, and charity" are an expression of God dwelling within the generous person (McBrien 1980, 991), and as Pope Benedict XVI explained, "Charity is love received and given. It is 'grace' (*cháris*)" (Benedict XVI 2009, 3).

Islam has some similar ideas as well, holding that one is generous "for the love of God," and thereby gives generously to others. When Muslims serve God in this way, they open the door to God's love and mercy (Qur'an 2:177). In a sense, then, the terminology and emphasis and interpretations may differ slightly between the two religions. However, both Catholicism and Islam have an understanding of this concept that we are referring to here as being generous as an expression of God's grace, by which one can love and be generous to others, and ultimately enter Heaven. So, we hypothesize that making participants reflect on God's grace would make people more generous to those within and without one's religious group (club and public goods). We also anticipate that this effect could be more evident in Catholics because of the explicit way that God's grace is discussed in Catholicism, relative to Islam.

Hypothesis 5: *The inspiration of God's grace that is fostered by their religion makes Catholics and Muslims more likely to contribute to the production of both club and public goods. The effect should be stronger on Catholics.*

Our final hypothesis, and experimental prime, concerns religion in general. One of the main motivations for our research project was that conventional wisdom, and some empirical support, holds that "religion" (as a general concept) may promote generosity. We wanted to know what more specific beliefs and norms could be responsible for generosity and prosocial behavior. Religion is a multifaceted concept, including factors as diverse as community expectations, God's commandments, and God's grace. Thus, it is not obvious which aspect of religion, if any, would make people more generous in everyday life or when people are interviewed about religion or when religion is primed (Galen 2012, 885; Ritter and Preston 2013). However, acknowledging the body of research that tests whether religion prompts generosity, we test this expectation. We do so in keeping with some studies of prejudice and religion that suggest religion heightens within group identification, thus encouraging adherents to favor club goods over public goods (Pichon, Boccato, and Saroglu 2007; Shariff and Norenzayan 2007).

Hypothesis 6: *The general concept of religion will prompt both Catholics and Muslims to contribute to collective goods. Catholics and Muslims both are more likely to contribute to club than to public goods.*

Methods and Data

As we have mentioned, our experiments were designed with the idea that getting participants to think about specific religious aspects, like religious community or duty to God, might affect their generosity, evident in a charitable donation to a group related to their religious in-group (we considered this a club goods donation), or to a group that has a general, largely secular, identity (we considered this a public goods donation). Our experiments rely on the strong likelihood that Irish Catholics, through religious education and attendance at services, would have been exposed, at some point in their lives, to standard teachings of Catholicism, and that Turkish Muslims, likewise, would have been exposed to standard teachings of Islam.[2]

The experiments were designed to assess the ways in which our hypothesized mechanisms impact the likelihood of participants to make a charitable donation either to their religious ingroup (conceptualized as a club goods donation), or to a secular group charity (conceptualized as a public goods donation). The anonymous experiments used primes of the focal constructs. Priming experiments make a certain concept or psychological process salient (Bargh and Chartrand 2000).[3] Some experimentally validated ways of priming religion are already in the psychology literature. Some prior experiments, for example, have made religion temporarily psychologically salient to people by asking them to unscramble sentences that did or did not have religious words, like divine or spirit, in them. In one famous experiment, this subtle religious prompt made people more generous in an economic game ostensibly played with an anonymous partner (Shariff and Norenzayan 2007; also Ahmed and Hammarstedt 2011, but see Gomes and McCullough 2015). But we do not know from that experiment what it is about religion that made people more generous. We therefore sought in our experiments to prime specific aspects of religion, including duty to God, community expectations, religious notions of similarity to others, religious notions of deservedness, and God's grace. As noted, we also included a prompt that just asked people to think about their religion, in a more general way. Finally, we included a neutral control prompt. We measure club and public goods provision in a behavioral way,

---

[2] There may be some variation in knowledge due to variation in instruction, frequency of exposure, and self-selection into study groups. However, participants were randomly assigned to the experiment prompts, so there should be no systematic bias in knowledge levels affecting outcomes.

[3] We use "prime" and "prompt" interchangeably when referring to the focal constructs.

by gauging actual donations to charities (club or public). By doing this, our priming experiments test whether specific concepts are causally connected to the outcomes of interest. The experiments are not structured to see how chronically salient ideas of duty to God, or community expectations, etc., relate to collective goods provision, but whether temporarily making one of these constructs more salient resulted in prosocial behavior.

After such prompts, we asked our participants if they wanted to donate any of their experimental payment to charities, ones related to either club or public goods. Our hope was that through this experimental design we could assess whether specific aspects of religion, temporarily made more psychologically salient through a specific prime, could have a causal impact on people's generosity.

We conducted a set of experiments in Catholic-dominant Ireland and in Muslim-dominant Turkey in the fall of 2010 and the summer of 2011. In Ireland, we solicited student participants from University College Dublin and community participants from Catholic parishes in Dublin. In Turkey, students came from Boğaziçi University in Istanbul, and community participants were adult Muslim Gülen association members in Istanbul.[4] As explained in Chapter 1, our research was conducted well prior to the Gülen movement being targeted by Prime Minister and then President Recep Erdoğan as an enemy. For participation, Irish students were offered 10 euro, Turkish students were offered 10 Turkish lira, Irish community members were offered 25 euro, and Turkish community members were offered 25 Turkish lira.[5] Experiments were conducted in university classrooms for the students or at churches and community centers for the community participants.

We studied both students and community members because each of these kinds of samples has advantages. Students are less variable in demographic characteristics like age and education level, so their participation should provide more confidence in the effects of our experimental primes. Community members are more representative of the society at large, and vary in demographics like age and education level, so we could potentially

---

[4] The Dublin adult community experiments were conducted in Inchicore Parish; St. Brigid's Parish of Cabinteely; Knocklyon Parish; St. Josephine at River Valley in Swords; Parish of the Annunciation, Rathfarnham; and in St. Fergal's Church, Ballywaltrim. The adult community experiments were conducted in Istanbul with the Ihsander community associations.

[5] Both universities are public. For a discussion of the status of the Gülen association at the time of our research, see Chapter 1. See the Online Appendix for explanation of amounts chosen (Explanation of Participant Payments).

see if variables like these are important in understanding the links between religion and generosity (Henrich, Heine, and Norenzayan 2010; McDermott 2013, 608; Rozin 2003). The parishes and Islamic associations from which we recruited the community members for the experiments were not the same as those from which we recruited interviewee participants. The university students were also independent of the interviewee pools.

Our anonymous experiment essentially consisted of a questionnaire in which participants were randomly assigned to write an essay about one of the aspects of religion we have discussed or about the desk and chair they were sitting at. The latter was a neutral control condition that had nothing to do with religion or generosity.[6] Writing an essay in response to a prompt was the experiment prime. Comparing people's generosity in any of the religion conditions with people's generosity in this control condition would tell us if religion affects generosity.

After doing these essays, participants were asked to mark on a form how they wanted to be paid for the experiment – did they want to keep any or all of the money for themselves, donate any part of it to a charity associated with their religion (a club good: a Catholic or Muslim children's charity), or donate any or all of it to a secular public good (the United Nations Children's Fund, UNICEF). We instructed the participants that they could divide their payment any way they wished and that the total across the three categories should total the amount of their experiment payment. These choices were made as anonymous as possible, as participants turned in their forms and were paid individually in a room separate from the main experiment room, and not by those who were affiliated with the institution that recruited them to participate (their religious institution in the case of adult community members, their university in the case of university students).

At the end of that procedure, participants were told they actually would be given their whole payment, and they could do with it what they wished; they were thanked and debriefed. For our dependent variable in this experiment, that is, people's generosity, we assessed whether people donated any funds to the club good (the ingroup charity) and/or whether they donated any funds to the public good (the secular charity, or UNICEF).[7]

---

[6] See the Online Appendix for experiment protocol (Study Codebook).

[7] While most participants gave either all or no proportion of their payment, several participants gave only a portion. If we conceptualize our dependent variable as the proportion of payment given, the resultant nonnormal distribution of our dependent variable violates the assumption of normality and is not amenable to parametric analysis as a continuous variable. For this reason, we collapse it into a dichotomous variable indicating whether an individual gave any proportion or not of their payment. We have

Results

Our main goal was to deduce whether any of the specific religious beliefs meant to be triggered by the essay task affected the likelihood of Catholics and Muslims making a donation to their religiously affiliated group (the "club" or ingroup), or to a secular charity not affiliated with their religion (the public good). We used logit regression analyses to see if donation probability varied across the essay conditions. We ran these analyses separately for Turkish Muslim and Irish Catholic groups in order to see which belief constructs tend to be more important for the generosity of Muslims and Catholics, respectively.[8]

Impact of the Experimental Primes

Within the first set of models, we examine the impact of each prompt on the predicted probability of giving, in relation to the control group. We present our results as the probability, predicted by the model, that individuals receiving particular primes made a club donation or a donation solely to the public good (UNICEF).[9] The experimental results in Figures 3.1 and 3.2 are shown as discrete marginal effects. We might think of this as the difference in the probability, predicted by the model and based on the data, that individuals made a donation when compared with the control group. Figure 3.1 presents marginal effects for whether Irish Catholics made club and public goods donations, while Figure 3.2 presents marginal effects for whether Turkish Muslims made club and public goods donations. The *y*-axis depicts the difference, compared with the control group, of the predicted probability of making a donation. The *x*-axis depicts each prime, and the accompanying point represents the marginal effect of each prime compared with the control group. The lines emerging from those points

also conducted OLS analyses on the proportion of the payment given and as ordinal logistic regression analyses while coding the donations variables with categories of no donations, partial donations, or full donations. Neither departs systematically from the results presented here, and all regression results are available in Online Appendix Tables OA.1a and OA.1b.

[8] For the experiments, "Catholic" refers only to Irish Catholics, and "Muslim" only to Turkish Muslims. See Tables A.6 and A.7 in the Appendix for experiment participant demographics.

[9] We present our results in Figures 3.1 through 3.4 visually as marginal effects. Because the marginal effects calculated from logistic regression depend to some degree on values assumed to be taken on by other variables in the model, we present full regression tables in the Appendix, Tables A.3 through A.5, with raw coefficients. The marginal effects presented here were calculated at the average of the predictions (Buis 2007; Long and Freese 2006, 113–116; StataCorp 2013, 10–11).

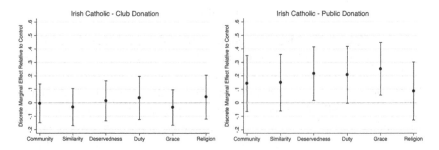

Figure 3.1 Change in predicted probability of making a donation to club and public goods, Irish Catholics.

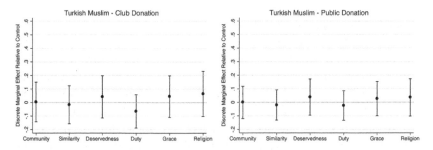

Figure 3.2 Change in predicted probability of making a donation to club and public goods, Turkish Muslims.

represent the 95 percent confidence interval. To the extent that those confidence intervals do not intersect 0, we can speak of that prime as having a statistically differentiated effect from the control condition.

Interestingly, as Figures 3.1 and 3.2 demonstrate, we find that none of the essay primes affected donation probability for either Catholics or Muslims to the club good.[10] This runs counter to our first hypothesis, which predicted that when Muslims and Catholics think about the expectations of their religious communities, they would be inclined to donate to their community. For public good donations, on the other hand, Catholics showed several differences across essay conditions. Those in the

---

[10] We find differing and statistically significant results between Irish Catholics on whether our student or community samples were more or less likely to have made a donation. The student experiment groups in our Irish Catholic sample had a 15 percent lower predicted probability of making a club goods contribution than individuals in the community sample, while students in the Turkish Muslim sample had a 13 percent higher predicted probability of making a club goods donation than individuals in the community sample. We see similar relationships for both groups with public goods donations (Appendix Table A.3).

deservedness group had a 22 percent higher predicted probability of making a donation than those in the control group, and those in the God's grace condition had a 25 percent higher predicted probability of making a public goods donation. For the Muslims, again, the essay condition did not affect the probability of donating.[11]

To summarize the results of our experimental analysis, the various religious primes had differential effects across the Catholic and Muslim samples. While Irish Catholics tended to respond to the God's grace and deservedness primes, priming these belief constructs did not have any effect on Turkish Muslims' giving. We found no significant impact of any of our five specific religious primes, nor of the general religion prime, on Muslims' donation behavior. There are several possible explanations for why the primes did not elicit results among the Turkish Muslim population that invite further investigation, and we assess those reasons in the discussion of experimental results.

Demographic Characteristics and Religiosity

Within the second set of models, while maintaining our interest in the impact of the primes, we wanted to see how robust those findings were when we also included the demographic characteristics of the participants. Accordingly, we asked our participants demographic questions pertaining to their religiosity, sex, education, age, marital status, and self-described socioeconomic status. Using this information, we constructed logit statistical models, like those presented in Figures 3.1 and 3.2, but this time we added the demographic information to see its influence on our results.

Since our subjects were randomly assigned to the experimental primes, we can be relatively confident that any differences across conditions are due to the primes. By the same token, our research subjects were not randomly recruited, so the effects of our demographic variables such as age or religiosity may not generalize to a larger population. At the same time, the exercise provides a useful means to further test the robustness of the impact of the primes, and it gives us some cautious insight as to the impact of demographic characteristics in our own experimental sample.

We collapsed our socioeconomic data into three mutually exclusive categories: low, medium, and high (we omitted the medium status variable

---

[11] We note that duty to God also comes very close to achieving the conventional 95 percent confidence threshold for statistical significance in the public goods donation model for Irish Catholics, with a 21 percent higher predicted probability of making a donation when compared with those in the control group.

from the model and use that as a reference category to describe the effect of the low and high socioeconomic status). We also used a simple indicator for whether an individual was married. We collapse individuals' educational attainment into three categories: those who had finished high school or lower, those who had started but not (yet) finished university, and those who had at least finished university or had gone on to attain an advanced degree (with those who had started, but not completed college used as the omitted reference category). Due to a distinctly different distribution of ages, we categorize the Irish Catholic and Turkish Muslim respondents into different age categories.[12] In both groups, the age group of 18–24 is used as the reference category. We also included gender. Finally, our scale for religiosity is based on a mean response value to a battery of eight Likert scale questions pertaining to each respondent's religiosity (Online Appendix, Study Codebook; Cohen et al. 2017).[13]

Like the previous analyses, we ran logistic regression models. The results, available in Appendix Tables A.4 and A.5, show that most of the demographic characteristics are not important determinants of generosity, and the results of the primes are quite similar to those obtained without the demographic variables.[14] The one demographic factor that does have an impact is religiosity. In both the Irish Catholic and Turkish Muslim samples, religiosity is positively associated with club goods donations. Figures 3.3 and 3.4 present predicted probabilities illustrating the relationship between increasing religiosity levels and donation results.

The relationship is remarkably similar in both the Irish Catholic and Turkish Muslim samples. Our religiosity variable ranged from one with individuals with very low levels of religiosity to seven for individuals with high levels of religiosity. For the Irish Catholic populations, individuals

---

[12] The Irish Catholics are sorted into five age groups: 18–24, 25–36, 37–55, 56–70, and 71+. The Turkish Muslims are sorted into three age groups: 18–24, 25–36, and 37+.

[13] We removed the marriage variable from the Turkish Muslim analysis due to its very high degree of covariance with several variables in the model, specifically the sample and age variables. Its inclusion does not change the substantive model results, and it does not itself have a statistically significant impact.

[14] In none of the models was socioeconomic context, marital status, level of education, or gender a statistically significant factor. Like our previous analyses, the primes have no statistically significant effect in the Turkish Muslim models (Appendix Table A.5) or in the club goods model for Irish Catholics (Appendix Table A.4). However, God's grace continues to have a statistically significant and positive impact for the Irish Catholic public goods model (Appendix Table A.4). Deservedness comes close to achieving statistical significance at the conventional 95 percent confidence interval in that same model.

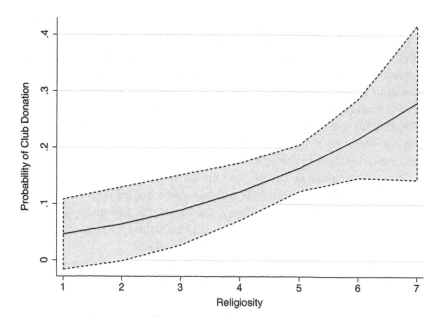

Figure 3.3 Irish Catholic religiosity and predicted probability of club donations.

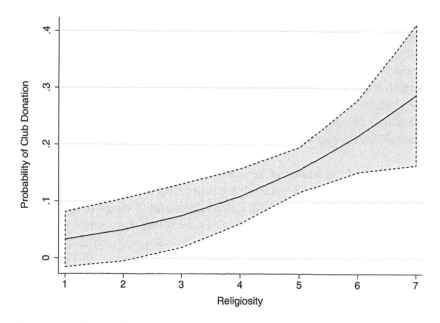

Figure 3.4 Turkish Muslim religiosity and predicted probability of club donations.

with the lowest levels of religiosity, at a value of one, have only about a 5 percent predicted probability of making a donation to the religious club (Catholic children's fund). However, the most religious individuals, with a value of seven, have a 28 percent predicted probability of making a donation to the religious club. Similarly, Turkish Muslims with the lowest levels of religiosity have only a 3 percent predicted probability of making a donation to the religious club fund, while Turkish Muslims with the highest levels of religiosity have a 29 percent predicted probability of making a donation to the religious club fund (Islamic children's fund).

With the important caveat that the participants were not randomly selected, the experiment results provide some suggestive evidence that the higher an individual's religiosity, the higher the probability that individual would make a donation to the religious ingroup. Religiosity had no effect on individuals' donations to the public good.

We checked the average religiosity of our community and student samples, and found that in Ireland, community members had a score of about 5.4 on our scale of 1–7 (7 being highest), whereas students scored an average of about 3.5, and that difference is statistically significant. Community members were substantially more religious than students in Ireland. In Turkey, community members scored an average of about 5.9, whereas students scored an average of about 4.5; the difference is also statistically significant. This makes sense and reassures us that our samples were not an aberration. We would expect people recruited to the experiments from within parishes and branches of an Islamic association to be more religiously observant, on average, than those who were recruited out of university settings. It also makes sense that, if they were going to donate at all, those more religious participants who had been recruited from their parishes and Islamic association would have been predisposed to think of the religious group first.

Discussion of Experimental Results

To sum up, we found some evidence supporting our hypotheses about the impact of religious beliefs about deservedness and God's grace (hypotheses three and five) for Irish Catholics. These beliefs apparently prompted Catholics to donate to the public good, in our case, UNICEF. We had expected, due to the religion's emphasis on considering all humans as equals, that thinking about their religion's teachings on the deservedness of the needy, Catholics would be prompted to help, regardless of whether the target was of the same religion or not and hence not discriminate between the club and public good. To some extent this was borne out, in that Catholics overlooked the religious charity, perhaps more so than we expected. Similarly, for God's grace, our interpretation of Catholic beliefs suggested that Catholics would donate without consideration of whether the target was Catholic or not. This was the case: Catholics tended to target the nonreligious public good. Indeed, none of the beliefs had a consistent effect on the donation to the Catholic charity.

For Muslims, none of the beliefs we tested had any significant impact on their donation behavior, whether donating to the religious charity or to the secular, public good. Controlling for the primes and demographic features, religiosity had a significant effect on donations to the religious charity for Catholics and for Muslims. Demographic characteristics had no effect on donation behavior for either Catholics or Muslims.

With these results in hand, some anticipated and some not, we can now turn to trying to explain what worked and what did not, and what we can learn about research on religion and generosity as a result. Why did some but not all of the results come out as predicted, and why, especially for our Turkish Muslim participants, did our primes seem to not have any effects on generosity? One factor may be due to the process of priming. Priming tries to make a concept more salient to a participant, to see if that changes their behavior. If the concept is not there at all, there is nothing to activate. On the other hand, if a concept is already highly salient, it may not be possible for the prime to further activate that concept. If duty to God, for example, is a highly important concept for Muslims, priming it would not have an effect on their generosity if they were already going about their day thinking about duty to God regularly (Bargh and Chartrand 2000). Our interviews, discussed elsewhere in this volume, lend some credence to this interpretation, insofar as Muslims did point to duty to God and expectations of their community as factors in their generosity.

Another interpretation of our results is more methodological and relates to some choices we made in designing our experiments. In order to facilitate comparisons and equality of treatments, we needed to keep the donation options as similar as possible between the two religions. To accomplish this, we constrained the list of charity organizations in the experiments. In addition, our ingroup charities ("Catholic Children's Fund" and "Muslim Children's Fund") were specific to people's religions but not to their local community or parish. While many of our Muslim participants wrote in a preference for their own association, many of our Catholics may have preferred the public good charity (UNICEF), given the salience of the church's clergy child sex abuse scandal at the time of the experiments. If Catholics tended to avoid donating to the Catholic

Children's Fund because of the clergy child sex abuse scandal in Ireland, we might expect to see mentions of the scandal and perhaps critical comments about the Church in the essays that responded to the primes that might more be associated with the Church as an institution, such as "religion" and "community expectations." In addition, we might expect the topic to be brought up in our interviews and in some of the essays, as indeed it was (see Chapters 4–6).

All in all, the charities to which we constrained choices may not have been some people's preferred charities, and, indeed, some participants wrote notes on their donation forms expressing a preference to donate to something else. If we include individuals who wrote that they would prefer that their donation go to a different organization or that they would keep the money and donate it later themselves, we find that there are substantially more Muslim donations and that Muslim community members were more likely to have made a donation than students, though the individual primes still have no statistically significant effect. However, coding our donation measure in this manner would be problematic. Much like telephone surveys where respondents who did not vote in a previous election, to save face, might report they had, there are certainly reasons to believe participants might report they would donate later while ultimately keeping the money.[15] For this reason, we examine the most conservative measure of giving – those individuals who noted their money would go directly to one of our pre-chosen charities and who never had an expectation of receiving the money themselves. Choices we made about which charities to offer to our participants and how to code their donations are important to keep in mind when interpreting results.[16]

A simple analysis of donation behavior can help us see if that might be what happened. Table 3.1 indicates the total number of donations made across the experimental population to the charity options.[17] Overall, participants were slightly more likely to have given to the public good than to the club good: about 17 percent of respondents gave to the charity of their religion, while over 20 percent of respondents gave to the secular charity.[18]

---

[15] We report results in the Online Appendix, Table OA.3C.

[16] There is some evidence that due to the clergy child sex abuse scandals, American Catholics redirected their donations to secular organizations and those of other religions (Bottan and Perez-Truglia 2015; Hungerman 2013).

[17] For ease of reading the text, figures are rounded to first decimal point. In tables they are presented to second.

[18] Included in each of those percentages are the 8 percent of participants who split their payment between both the religious and the secular charities.

Table 3.1 *Proportion of participants making a donation*

Donation Type	Total Subjects	# Making a Donation	% Making a Donation
Club donation	689	115	16.69
Public donation	689	144	20.90

Table 3.2 *Proportion of participants making a donation, by religion*

	Catholic Sample			Muslim Sample		
Donation Type	Total Subjects	% Making a Donation	% Including Donation Later	Total Subjects	% Making a Donation	% Including Donation Later
Club donation	337	16.62	17.21	352	16.76	56.25
Public donation	337	31.45	34.72	352	10.8	12.78

Table 3.2 points out some interesting differences between the Catholic and Muslim samples. Catholics were less likely to have made a donation to the club good (16.6 percent) and more likely to have made a donation to the public good (31.5 percent). This may indeed have been an effect of the clergy child sex abuse scandal that was highly salient in Ireland at the time of our experiments. Muslims were more likely to have made a donation to the club good (16.8 percent) than to the public good (10.8 percent),[19] which is what one generally might expect: people prefer their in-group. In addition, as Table 3.2 shows, a relatively large number of Muslims indicated that they would donate to a preferred charity later. Fewer Catholics did so. This may be due to an institutional difference between Islam and Catholicism affecting the community members. Because the Turkish state controls the mosques in Turkey, where our Muslim experiment participants were, the nonstate Turkish Islamic associations have members more attached to the associations they elected to join. In contrast, Catholics typically are members of parishes by default of

[19] The differences are statistically significant at the 95 percent confidence interval.

where they live. While many of our Catholic participants may have been repulsed by the Catholic Church's child sex abuse scandal and so avoided donating to the club good, they shifted their donations to a credible secular alternative, UNICEF.

Another possible explanation for why the primes had no systematic effect on Muslims' donation behavior, but two primes (God's grace and deservedness of those in need) did on Catholics, is that there may be country-specific differences between Ireland and Turkey and thus differences in behavioral responses to religious beliefs. However, there are several reasons we do not think such differences explain the results. The experiments focused on religious beliefs that should be relevant in any country, not country-specific moral norms. We tested religious constructs that were not unique to particular national versions of a religion (e.g., we did not test the capacity of "Saint Patrick" to elicit prosocial responses in Irish Catholics). As we discuss later, interviews with Muslims and Catholics in Paris, Milan, Istanbul, and Dublin indicated that respondents were consistent within their faith traditions regarding their reasons for engaging in prosocial behaviors. In addition, some scholars find Turkey and Ireland to be comparable in the role of religion in civil society and not so far apart in some aspects of their development (Arslan 2001; Garvin 2004; Schneider, Krieger, and Bayraktar 2011). Thus, we are not inclined to interpret our results in terms of Turkish-Irish differences.

We also considered whether the Islamic practice of zakat would have an impact on people's generosity in our experiments. One might reason that if a participant engages in zakat, they would feel no need to be generous in our experiments. However, most Turkish Muslims pay zakat once a year, usually during Ramadan, which was not when our experiments were conducted. It is not likely that zakat contributions undermine the donations that Turkish Muslims make at other times. We thus do not think that the practice of zakat would have interfered with our experiment.

Qualitative Essay Analysis

One more way that we can assess whether our primes had an effect on generosity is to see what people said in the essays they wrote in response to the prompt. While a weaker test of the impact of the primes on generosity, we could see, for example, if people primed with God's grace were more likely to mention charity and generosity in their essays than people who were in the control condition. We had research assistants code whether

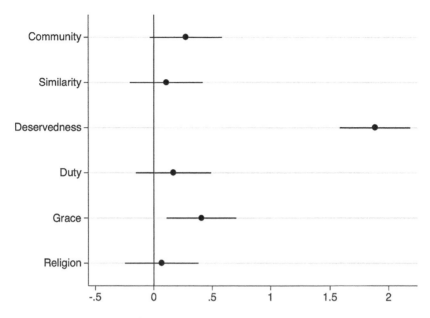

Figure 3.5 Essay prompts and Irish Catholic mentions of charity. Note: Confidence intervals intersecting zero indicate that a relationship is not statistically significant.

sentences in the essays mentioned volunteering, giving of money or offering, or other charitable behaviors.[20] We then used OLS regression analyses on the content-coded essays. Figures 3.5 and 3.6 visually present the results of our analysis, with the x-axis depicting raw regression coefficients and the y-axis depicting our primes.[21]

While we do not want to give these results too much weight because they are about mentions of charity rather than actual charitable behaviors, we did find that Catholics who were in the God's grace and deservedness conditions were more likely to mention concepts related to charity than those in the control condition, and it was those two prompts that led to the behavioral outcome of donations.[22] The other prompts had no noticeable,

---

[20] See the Online Appendix for the Code Sheet for Experiment Essay Content Coding. Individuals who did not leave a written essay response were coded as having made no mentions of charity. Some 108 Irish and Turkish essays were randomly selected and recoded for checks of inter-coder reliability. These checks resulted in a Krippendorf's alpha ratio value of 0.853.

[21] We count the number of times in an essay that a participant mentions a concept related to charity or generosity.

[22] We present our regression results as Appendix Table A.8. We note here that deservedness had a noticeably large impact on charitable mentions in both our Irish Catholic and

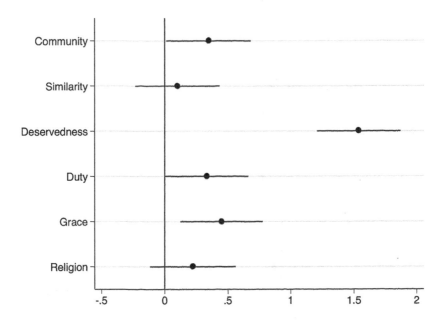

Figure 3.6 Essay prompts and Turkish Muslim mentions of charity. Note: Confidence intervals intersecting zero indicate that a relationship is not statistically significant.

systematic effect on Catholics' mentions of concepts related to charity. For Muslims, four prompts resulted in more frequent mentions of charity in their essays: community expectations, deservedness, duty to God, and God's grace, our first, third, fourth, and fifth hypotheses. Given that these beliefs made our Muslim participants more likely to be thinking about generosity, while their writing the essays did not affect their actual donations in our experiment, we can only wonder if the donation options we gave were not well suited to tapping into the Muslim participants' generous tendencies.

Conclusion

The experiments found that Catholics were more likely to be generous when prompted with the concept of God's grace or with the concept of

Turkish Muslim qualitative models. This is likely at least partially because the prime asked about religious teachings on the degree to which individuals deserved help, and mentions of help was one of the content categories our coders used to identify mentions of charity.

their religion's teachings about the deservedness of those in need. They also showed that for Catholics, those constructs led to more frequent mentions in the essays of concepts related to charity. The experiments found no impact of the six religious concepts we tested on Muslims, though they did show that the concepts of religious community expectations, their religion's teachings about deservedness of those in need, their duty to God, and God's grace led to more frequent mention in their essays about concepts related to charity.

We caution that our studies are not a comprehensive test of the impact on generosity behavior of every conceivable religious belief in Catholicism or Islam. Nor do the studies engage the debate about whether the religious, however defined, make "better neighbors" (Ahmed 2009; Blouin, Robinson, and Starks 2013; Putnam and Campbell 2010, 443–492; Stegmueller 2013). We have advanced the study of causal mechanisms underlying the provision of public goods by members of two world religions. We focused on specific religious beliefs, not generalized moral norms that might be diffused in a country or culture. Furthermore, the beliefs we analyzed are not unique to any given national culture or national "version" of Catholicism or Islam (Johnson and Cohen 2014). Nevertheless, we are cautious not to overgeneralize from our samples. Further research in other contexts is necessary to assess the consistency of the mechanisms across locations and cultures. For instance, collective goods provision could be affected by differing institutional arrangements. Institutions may foster or hinder propensities toward generosity by making it more or less difficult for individuals to know how or what to give and by increasing or decreasing the above-discussed community effects. Further, our studies were conducted in democratic countries. How religious beliefs and community expectations affect club and public goods provision in other political contexts is a question for further research (Alexander and Christia 2011; Healy 2006). We might expect, for instance, that where a religion is under threat from a regime, ingroup dynamics would heighten the impact of religious community expectations in order to help the group survive (Sarkissian 2015; cf. this volume, Chapter 7). What the impact would be on individual-level beliefs, such as duty to God or God's grace, is less clear. Additional cross-national comparative research is necessary to explore these questions.

With our donation measure and our analyses of the participant essays, we note that there were some interesting results as well as some puzzles to solve, which makes us think more deeply about religious concepts and the choices researchers make in designing their experiments and coding schemes. One question is just what the different belief constructs, our prompts, meant to our Muslim and Catholic experiment participants. Chapters 4 and 5 investigate.

4

The Meaning of Religion to Catholics and Muslims

What do the terms associated with religious beliefs prompt adherents to think about and to feel? One of the questions social scientists who study religion often face is knowing what religion means to their participants. Policymakers and politicians face similar questions. If they are going to promote or oppose "faith-based initiatives," for instance, it might be useful to have more information about what "faith" and its related concepts mean to the faithful, and whether these are the same or different across particular religions. For instance, how do members of different faith communities understand "religion"? What kinds of thoughts and emotions does the word elicit? Our research enables us to provide some initial answers, recognizing that beliefs, thoughts, and feelings are affected by contexts and social practices.

We can examine what some other concepts derived from religion, such as God's grace and duty to God, mean to adherents of different faiths. Do Muslims have fairly uniform or varied understandings of those terms? Do Catholics? Our experiments used an essay prime format that asked respondents to write about what a randomly assigned topic made them think about and how it made them feel. The task had the potential to elicit a variety of emotions and thoughts: participants were not constrained by instructions to write a coherent essay justifying an argument, nor were they required to think strategically. We used the essays as primes for the generosity experiment; we also can use them to investigate what thoughts and feelings our participants have about various topics. While many experimental psychologists use essays to prime certain concepts (e.g., a terror management researcher might ask a participant what they think dying will be like; Greenberg, Solomon, and Pyszczynski 1997), when used for priming purposes, researchers do not often report on what people actually say. They simply lump together people who got one essay prompt into one group (e.g., the mortality salience group) and people who got another prompt into another group (e.g., the control group). In this and the next chapter, we unpack the content of the essays, to see what people think and feel when prompted by specific religious concepts.

This chapter, which discusses the religion, God's grace, and duty to God responses, is closely linked to the next, which discusses the essays about deservedness, community expectations, and similarity to others. It proceeds as follows. We first discuss the nature of essay primes and what, in general, we might learn from them. We then review and assess the meaning of "religion" to our experiment participants. We next explore what Muslim and Catholic participants thought and felt when they were prompted with the concepts of duty to God and God's grace. What becomes apparent is that each concept elicited a range of thoughts and feelings, some more focused on the concept, others going in perhaps unexpected directions. Note that rather than correcting the grammar, punctuation, and spelling of the essays, or rather than putting in [*sic*] after every error, we have quoted verbatim from the essays. We have verified the accuracy of our transcriptions.

Validity of Essay Primes

Recall that we conducted the experiments among students at Boğaziçi University in Istanbul and University College Dublin (UCD) in Dublin, and among adult community members of the Gülen association in Istanbul and of Catholic parishes in Dublin.[1] In the experiments, we asked the participants to write an essay on the thoughts and feelings that a particular religious topic elicited in them. Each participant was asked to write only one essay, in response to only one "prime," to which they had been randomly assigned. Then, we assessed their generosity, measured as their willingness to make a donation, to either a religious (club good) or secular (public good) charity. This measurement was taken after respondents wrote the essays in response to particular experimental prompts. The participants did not know that the essay question would be followed by a donation question. Our hope was that through this experimental design we could assess whether specific aspects of religion, temporarily made more psychologically salient through a specific prime, could have a causal impact on people's generosity.

---

[1] For details, see Chapter 3.

Here we briefly comment on whether our procedure of priming religious thoughts and feelings via essays is a valid thing to do. Issues of validity in experimental research are nuanced, and there are several different kinds of validity to consider, such as internal and external validity. Internal validity refers to how valid it is to have confidence in the cause and effect relationships. Here, we might ask whether it is valid to think that differences in what people say in their essays, or in their donation behavior, can be validly attributed to the different essay conditions. In the case of people getting different topics about which to write (different essay prompts) and then writing different essays or donating differently, we are confident with regard to the internal validity. People were randomly assigned to receive different essay prompts, so any preexisting differences between conditions (say, in people's propensities to donate) should be equally balanced between experimental conditions.

While considering whether these essays are valid indicators of anything, we could consider the idea of manipulation checks – seeing if the essay primes indeed brought up the thoughts and feelings we assumed they would. Indeed, it is reassuring that Catholics who received the community expectations and religion prompts were more likely to mention norms. Similarly, Muslims who received the community expectations prompt were more likely to write about norms. While not necessarily theoretically noteworthy, we did see that Catholics who received the prompt about their religion's teachings on their similarity to others were more likely to discuss how they were like or unlike others, and the same for Muslims. Similarly, Catholics who received the deservedness prompt were more likely to talk about deservedness, as were Muslims. Such tendencies validate that the essays, at least sometimes, got people to think about what we asked them to think about. Strikingly, as mentioned at the end of Chapter 3, for Catholics it was when the prompts they responded to led them to write about charity that they were more likely to donate to the public charity. Those conditions were God's grace and deservedness of the needy. As also mentioned, while we had no behavior results for Muslims in the experiments, four of the prompts (community expectations, deservedness, duty to God, and God's grace) led to more frequent mentions of charity. We can only wonder if the donation targets had been different, whether the behavioral results would have corresponded to the essay mentions of charity.

We also often saw that, while individuals may not have directly addressed the specific issue raised in the prompt, they still talked about similar concepts that those prompts brought to mind. This is theoretically sensible and seems to provide evidence for the validity of the essays. One example of this is that Catholics who received the duty to God prompt and those who received the God's grace prompt were more likely to talk about divinity. The prompts are concepts that, in Catholicism, have to do with divinity. Similar findings emerged for Muslims. Muslims who received the community expectations or duty to God prompts were more likely to talk about a third-party enforcer. Many of the concepts referred to in the essays were directly related to the essay conditions.[2] Yet as we will note below, there was also a range of topics, thoughts, and feelings elicited by some of the prompts. When, for instance, Muslims were prompted with deservedness, they were more likely to write about concepts related to deservedness, but they also were more likely to write about the state and about religious doctrine. As our subsequent analyses of the essays indicate, this seems to have been because Muslims thought about the role of the state in helping the needy, and thought about what their religion instructed on helping those in need.

In addition to providing assurance that our essay prompts tapped relevant concepts, there might also be instances when respondents brought up further thoughts and concepts not anticipated by current social psychology research on religion. Pointing out these instances can help further refine how we assess attitudes and beliefs while also aiding in the development of new future hypotheses. An example of this, as we discuss below, involves the use of the concept of "religion" to explain religion's impact on various phenomena. As our discussion illustrates, the reason "religion" has prompted contradictory impacts across previous studies is because it likely does not prime individuals in a consistent manner.

Other differences between conditions were not randomly assigned. We did not randomly assign people to be community members or students, to be Irish or Turkish, or to be Catholic or Muslim. As a result, we can probably be less confident that any Irish Catholic/Turkish Muslim differences can be validly attributed just to religion, in no small part because any number of things could be confounded with being Irish Catholic versus Turkish Muslim, such as language or economic conditions. Indeed, being Irish and being Catholic are completely confounded in the experiments, as are being Turkish and being Muslim. That said, because our focus was on religious variables, it is plausible that our results had more to do with being Muslim or Catholic than with being, respectively, Turkish or Irish.

As a source of data about what these religious concepts make people think and feel, the essays are surely useful. A concern might be that

---

[2] For details, see Appendix Tables A.9 and A.10.

participants do not accurately report on their thoughts and feelings. People might censor themselves if they have unpalatable thoughts and feelings. But we do not think this is a problem in our study because people did say negative things (e.g., many Irish Catholics talked about the clergy child sex abuse scandal within the Church) and because, more importantly, the essays were anonymous.

Another validity issue we want to briefly mention here concerns a different kind of validity, external validity. This refers to how generalizable our findings are beyond the particular participants or contexts that we studied. We did not draw a random sample from all Irish Catholics or all Turkish Muslims. These were people from particular cities, particular educational institutions, or particular religious institutions, and they were furthermore people who volunteered (one could say generously) to participate in our experiments. For instance, we hardly think Irish Catholic university students at UCD who volunteered to be in our experiments are representative of all Irish Catholic university students, let alone all Irish Catholics. Be that as it may, it is easy to say the issue of generalizability requires more research (which all undergraduates say in their undergraduate theses), and we agree, but we also think that one should not rush to condemn the external validity of our project without thinking through the ways in which it matters. Is there some particular reason to be concerned about a particular way that UCD is not representative of Irish universities more broadly, or that the churches from which we solicited participants are unique in some way that would have an impact on people's religious thoughts and feelings in responding to our essay primes or in their donation behaviors?

At the same time, we are cautious not to overstate the relevance of implications stemming from claims that cannot be attributed to differences systematically derived from the random assignment of essay prompts. The value of the exercise is to further assess the internal validity of our essay prompts, to advance tentatively possible rationales explaining differences in the impacts of these essay prompts, and to present some interesting unanticipated responses from the essays that might help refine measurement of these concepts and potentially provide fodder to interested researchers to develop new deductive hypotheses.

Religion

Scholars who use experiments to try to assess the role of religion in prosocial behavior have to make assumptions about what religion means to people. Some have argued that the reason religion prompts cooperative, other-oriented helping behavior in people is that it prompts a perception that a fearsome God "is watching you" (Norenzayan 2013); others argue it prompts a perception that "God is loving you" (Johnson et al. 2013a). In the former, one helps only because God will punish noncooperators; in the latter, one helps because one feels loved, so one generously gives help as an expression of love.

In measuring religion's effects on prosocial behavior, psychologists have often conflated possibly distinct concepts, leading to ambiguous results, including to a difficulty of determining, for instance, which kind of God or what other aspect of religion the participant had in mind (Preston, Ritter, and Hernandez 2010). Further, political scientists and sociologists have tended to treat religion as a dummy or ordinal variable measured most often through frequency of prayer or religious service attendance. The multiple meanings of religion to adherents, which may well affect how "religion" influences behaviors of interest, are underexplored.

The essays written by our respondents provide valuable insight into these debates. We see from our own study within and across Catholicism and Islam that "religion" prompted a range of emotions, associations, and thoughts. The experiment participants who had been randomly assigned to the "religion" prompt received the following instruction:

Think about your religion or the religion you grew up in. Describe your religion or the religion you grew up in. What does that make you think about? How does that make you feel?

We find that "religion" elicits a mix of negative and positive feelings from Catholics and Muslims. The quantitative analyses of the content-coded essays found that Catholics were more likely to mention norms, rituals, doctrine, and disillusionment, and Muslims more likely to mention rituals, doctrine, divinity, and disillusionment (Appendix Tables A.9 and A.10). The essay condition did not increase the likelihood of either Catholic or Muslim participants to make more mentions of charity-related concepts than did the control condition. Some Catholics criticized the Church hierarchy, particularly for its rigid structure based on control and sexual abuse stories. While many were positive about Catholicism generally, they were critical of the Church as an institution. Catholics, we hasten to add, also commonly voiced very positive feelings about religion, particularly referencing concepts such as love, charity, spirituality, and prayers. A number referred to the Church as a source of positive influences.

Similarly, many Muslims were critical of the stricter versions of Islam. They described how religion controlled people's lives rather than allowing people to control themselves through their own will and choices. They also made references to how people commit evil acts in the name of religion. As noted above, quantitatively, Muslims were more likely to express disillusionment. However, many Muslims also wrote about their positive feelings towards Islam. In doing so, they mentioned the morality, love, respect, inner peace, and happiness that their religion brings, as well as concepts such as giving and prayers.

Irish Catholics

Among the Catholic students and community members, the religion prompt elicited quite a few responses focusing on Catholicism as an institution.[3] Illustrating starkly negative attitudes with regard to the institution itself, one student wrote that she "feels sick to be a part of this religion due to the sexual abuse stories" (EP438).[4] One said that, "with the current scandal within the church, I have no 'faith' in the Church" (EP472); still another that "the Catholic church is very corrupt. I usually have negative thoughts about religion because it is so corrupt and full of crime" (EP561). This participant went on to distinguish between "belief" and the Catholic Church, concluding her essay with, "I think belief is wonderful but the Church is too oppressive and hypocritical to be thought of well" (EP561). Another student expressed the somewhat critical view that the Catholic Church, like "any other church or faith," is an "institution that wants people to believe it has answers and control people" (EP493). "Control" was echoed by other Irish Catholic student respondents (EP527, EP565), with one perhaps seeing this as a good thing: "this is one of the best ways to keep societies civilized" (EP565).

While quite a few students commented without criticism that they "grew up in a Roman Catholic household" (EP534, EP577), others indicated religion was "forsed upon us" in school (EP472, EP454), at home (EP493), or generally: "I think many people attend [mass] not out of desire or want, but rather out of fear, insecurity, or just being forced to go" (EP574, EP536). The prompt led one to comment that while she was "against the Catholic Church and don't practise I wouldn't want to be any other religion, for the fact that it's the most laid back" (EP472). The

---

[3] At the time of our research, Ireland was roiled by a Catholic Church clergy child sex abuse scandal, revealing that the Church hierarchy had been actively complicit in protecting priests and other religious officials who had or were sexually abusing children.

[4] Each experiment participant essay was assigned a code; EP stands for "experiment participant" and the number is their code number.

essay concluded on a negative note about getting "annoyed about their 'teachings' etc." (EP472). The view that Catholicism was the "most laid back" contrasts with a view that "it is a very traditional or conservative religion" (EP415). Some essays had mixed thoughts: "Religion is a good and bad thing. I prefer to keep an open mind and hope for the best" (EP548).

In addition, reflecting perhaps religion's diminished role as a credible moral compass in society, many voiced the view that, as one participant put it, "for me it has no value. If humans had as much faith in themselves as they do in a God then maybe we could sort out our own problems instead of waiting for God to do so" (EP415). Another concluded, "My religion doesn't make me think about much but I do pray if I am in need of help or if someone is sick" (EP441). The minimal space religion takes up in their lives was echoed by other essays: "Don't really think much about religion; ... feel rather indifferent at most times" (EP448). That essay also mentioned how the participant was "made to feel 'guilty' about not practising my religion," and it ended on a negative note of referring to the clergy child sex abuse scandals.

Irish Catholic community members, too, often expressed dissatisfaction with the Church as an institution. There were a number for whom "religion" generated negative thoughts, such as disillusionment "with the way my Church is run. I have no problems with the basic message of Christianity – my problem is with those leaders of my Church who have failed to lead" (EP300). Another Catholic wrote of a number of Church policies with which she disagreed and then stated, "I also took a strong dislike to the church after the controversy arose about abuse in state run institutions, they [were] run by Catholic priests and nuns and they ruined many a child's life and scarred them both physically and mentally. Catholic religion is old fashioned and outdated and after all the bad things happening in the world I am struggling to even believe in God" (EP345; also EP636).

For some of these community members, disillusionment or anger at the Church was the main focus of the essay; for others, "religion" triggered a mix of thoughts, such as of "history, tradition, ritual, the power of prayer" as well as "the loss and pain and harm and destruction that has been done in the name of the Catholic religion and other religions so the sorrow and shame of that" (EP317). This participant also said she felt "sad at the role of women in the Catholic church," and then ended on a positive note: "I love being part of my religion because of the message of Jesus Christ but also because of my family and my grandparents and the sense of belonging, continuity and tradition" (EP317). "Religion" generated another mixed response in the participant who wrote, "in essence I am a Roman Catholic but identify more with Protestantism, e.g., freedom of clergy to marry and women to be ordained but I have never entertained the thought of leaving my religion" (EP352). Another participant (EP586) also had mixed feelings including both guilt and comfort (EP448, EP515) or a mix of helping in times of difficulty along with worrying about the end of life: "I worry a lot and wonder what will happen at the end of my life" (EP577).

Throughout, for Catholic community members, a frequent refrain prompted by the religion prompt was that of disagreement with the teachings of the Church: "A lot of rules are man made. They are not the teachings of Christ" (EP676, EP658, EP641, EP613). Others did not express disagreement with Church teachings but made a point of distinguishing between the Church and the faith (EP592, EP607, EP636, EP300, EP317, EP345, EP352).

Several essays indicated that the prompt made them think about religion as a general topic, sometimes in a negative light, sometimes in a positive light. As one student wrote, "I also feel religion is extremely contradictory as not everyone believes in one God. It creates too much division within society and creates a prejudice among people. Religion, in my opinion, has caused more trouble than it has solved problems" (EP460). On the other hand, there were those who expressed more positive emotions and thoughts in response to the prompt about religion. One who indicated she was a devout practicing Catholic wrote, "My religion gives me hope when I am feeling low or lost ... Religion makes me think about doing good and being a bit more charitable" (EP536). The essay concluded with a sentence about praying "to guide me in the right direction or to help me with difficult exams or problems I may have" (EP536). Another indicated that Catholicism "gives people a start on knowing right from wrong" and that he thinks of it "more of the spiritual side" and is rather reflective about it (EP571). His last sentence was about thinking about "how God can help me accomplish [my goals] if I am worthy" (EP571). One noted that the institutional religion was less important than "forming a personal relationship with God and being moral, faithful and respectful" (EP574). Another said religion gives her "hope" (EP431) and another referred to religion as her "Rock" (EP630).

As with the students, religion prompted some positive thoughts among community members as well, such as the participant who said she has "always felt extremely comfortable with my religion and derive both satisfaction and consolation from same" (EP285). Another noted,

"As I have got older I tend to turn to religion in times of trouble" but that "Day to Day tend to forget about religion" and that "it should be more important for me" (EP293). One woman stated that "it makes me feel that I've someone that I can turn to pray to" and mentioned that "in being at the Church there was a great feeling" (EP333). For another participant, "It makes me feel secure to know my religion and believe in it" (EP606). For some, the positive thoughts were about the sacraments, e.g., "I feel a sense of fulfilment after attendance at mass," though even this participant, in reflecting on the strength of his faith, mentioned the clergy child sex abuse scandals, saying he has "never felt unsure or put off by scandals in the church" (EP365, EP592).

Positive thoughts spanned multiple beliefs and belief constructs within the religion. One Catholic wrote, "It has given me an explanation of what life is about ... the belief in God who created me, sustains me and wants me to live a full live and after that to enjoy his presence forever. It gives me a sense of worth – I am precious to God – amazingly!! – and a sense of belonging to the community of Christians. It also gives me a sense of solidarity with all humanity ... and that having been blessed ... I should share what I can with those less fortunate." Yet here too, the thoughts turn somber, as she continued, "Unfortunately, being made up of frail humans, the Church has had many problems with fulfilling Christ's mission— – but this does not detract from the mission itself" (EP607). Another wrote, "I pray every night, and always chat to God. I thank him for my day, and if I have something that I am worried about I will ask for his help ... I feel that I always have someone to talk to because of this and am never really alone" (EP526). Another participant described the religion she grew up in as "one of love your neighbor, self respect and respect of others and we were also taught to offer a helping hand when you saw someone in need" (EP613). She too mentioned the comfort of having "God to call on when things get a little too much," then concluded by expressing some dissatisfaction with "the way the hierarchy in the church expects adulation," criticizing the hierarchy's policies on women and celibacy for priests (EP 613). Other participants brought up the "sense of community" and how "Religious services i.e. baptisms, marriages, and funerals are valuable rituals that add to the richness of my life" (EP663, EP365).

The religion prompt apparently did not tend to prompt Catholics to think their behavior was being watched even though it often prompted them to "think about God. Eternity and my relationship with God. Although I am full of doubt it encourages me to do good" (EP366). Another wrote that it "makes me think about and feel strong sense of right and wrong and moral issues although I try to be tolerant of the convictions of others (not always successfully)" (EP373). One wrote about "fear instilled in us if we did not behave" (EP587). Even this remembrance of fear was washed out by the final statement that "I am glad to say that my faith has developed into a mature relationship with the Lord" (EP587). One who wrote of the joy that has resulted from her trying "to live out the moral teachings of the Bible and Gospel's within" also wrote, "I've found it a wonderful challenge and also struggled to live up to it many times. For me it's a win win situation following this way of life" (EP630). Another mentioned thinking about "the gospel message and how I suceed or fail to live it in my daily life" (EP636). Another wondered if in her disagreeing "with some aspects of this religion ... means that I am not respecting this religion" but did not convey a sense of her actions being scrutinized by a watchful God (EP641). Rather than see a watchful God, many indicated, as did this participant, that "my God is a very loving, forgiving and merciful one." She went on, however, to express sadness and concern about the actions of the Catholic hierarchy in the clergy child sex abuse cases and on other issues (EP658).

Some had little to say: "I think been brought up in the Roman Catholic Religion is fine but other religions are ok also" (EP382). For another, "My faith means a lot to me. It brings me closer to God ... Without God and my faith I would not have coped" (EP676). Several noted how Catholicism was part of their childhood because "there was no other religion to compare it with at the time I was growing up; one always attended mass and confession because that was what was done" (EP592, EP608).

Turkish Muslims

For Muslim students and community members, thinking about religion elicited a variety of emotions and thoughts. Religion was often seen as manipulated or created by people to control others and as something creating obligations to be fulfilled. A sense of God watching and waiting to punish infractions was largely absent; potential divine punishment was seen to come more from religious institutions or the community. For those who had more positive emotions and thoughts, they did not directly describe a benevolent God. Religion was just associated with peace and good feelings.

Many Muslim student responses conveyed a sense that religion was imposed, that it removed free will and choice (EP1, EP8). While one thought it was socially "imposed," mentioning her hometown, she differentiated the social context from the perhaps more theological, writing that

"Islam as a religion is open to questioning" (EP76). Just as some Catholic students saw control as a feature of their religion, some Muslim students noted a controlling aspect to religion. One, having stated that "religion and rituals of religion are not divine aspects but created by human beings," concluded her essay saying, "Religion is one of the most ideal ways of managing people" (EP8; also EP29, EP76, EP87, EP90, EP106). Another wrote it was "invented by people to ensure order," and labeled it "offensive" (EP15; also EP141 and EP29). Still another associated Islam with directing "individuals to good and right" and added, "The requirements of religion are intended to create order" (EP87). One noted it helps to ensure morality and "ensure solidarity and cooperation within societies" (EP136).

The theme of oppression of women came up in some essays: one participant associated Islam with an "oppressive attitude of men towards women," saying "it never evaluates men and women as equal" (EP106).[5] Some thought that religion was "misinterpreted from time to time and this increasingly makes our community conservative and imposes certain restrictions on people" (EP87) and that it prevented "free thinking" (EP106). Others noted a lack of choice, that the religion (Islam) "was already chosen for me" (EP90), with its "practices imposed" (EP76). "I was told you are Muslim because your parents are Muslim" (EP90).

One participant saw Islam as "fictional" (EP15), another said that the "unchangeable rules" are "threatening" (EP136). Some associated religion with evil: not that religion itself was evil, but "most of the evil, or in other words bad, behaviors are performed in the name of religion and I think it is the best way to exploit people" (EP15). One thought Islam particularly stands out as an oppressive religion: "Especially in Islam we clearly see the oppression imposed on people by means of threatening people with hellish tortures" (EP106).

Another theme among Muslim students was religion's contribution to morality, to teaching people to be good. Their view of this was sometimes positive, sometimes negative. "I think religion is only a set of principles that determine our morals and behaviors" (EP50). These thoughts led the student to conclude, "When I think of my religion, I feel I am on the right way. But I also feel alone." Another also associated his religion with morality and peacefulness, and found joy in fulfilling its requirements (EP112).

---

[5] Exploring whether there were systematic gender differences in essay responses merits further analysis but is beyond the scope of this work. As we show in results presented in Chapter 3, gender was not a factor in donation responses to the primes.

Others described Islam's belief system and required practices (EP67). Some started their essays in a neutral tone, "As my family is Muslim, I was also brought up as a Muslim," went on to discuss whether they fulfilled the requirements of the religion, then noted some negative aspects, such as teaching children "'You should do that; otherwise you will burn in hell,'" but concluded, "I am pleased to be a Muslim" (EP128). One expressed some distress at how "My religion makes me think that many obligations of mine are difficult to fulfil, although I know that they are not. I do not feel good regarding this issue" (EP22).

And just as with Catholic students, religion elicited some positive thoughts: one student associated it with "tolerance, love and respect" (EP22); another said that it provides confidence and help (EP36); still another that it makes them "feel good" and brings "inner peace" (EP100). One noted how religion helps them "live well and morally" and that with the "beauties of my religion" they "feel much better" (EP121). The essay makes clear the mixed thoughts and emotions: even as the participant expressed positive thoughts about Islam, the second to last sentence of the essay brought up a fear of falling short: "I am faithful but don't feel comfortable as I don't fulfill all the requirements of my religion" (EP121). Another described the confidence it gives her: "No matter what kind of a barrier I meet, I have my omnipotent Creator from whom I can seek help at any time. This always gives me a feeling of confidence and helps me meet my fears and overcome them" (EP36). Another saw it as quite helpful in "hard times but also at times when I was very happy" (EP43). This positive view was tempered by the concluding admonition that "no matter what happens, religion is not a reality one should slavishly commit to" (EP43).

Similarly, a number of Muslim community members expressed thoughts of thankfulness about being Muslim (EP191, EP232, EP244, EP171, EP757). For many, the religion brought to mind peace, with some writing that it "gives inner peace" (EP171, EP186) or "As we live in peace and happiness in Islam, I wish that all Muslim people would live in peace and happiness and that Islam makes them choose the right path" (EP250; also EP696, EP723, EP778). For one participant, the religion prime led him to write "Islam: To live for peace, solitude, endless divine light and the love of God" (EP778). The multiple associations that "religion," here Islam, had for participants is evident in one woman's statement: "Islam is one of the most beautiful religions in the world. We love all the creatures as they were created by God. Islam suggests beauty, goodness, solidarity, forgiving, loving and respect. Thank God for being a Muslim" (EP270).

Some community members associated the requirements of the religion with good outcomes: "The orders and prohibitions imposed by Islam are the unique concepts that make man a real man ... [Islam] is the religion of gaining, heralding, rejoicing, assuring, and securing" (EP191). Another put it this way: "All of the rules and commands are for finding happiness in this world, and in particular after death" (EP769). In a slightly different vein, some noted what Islam brings in this and the afterlife: "My religion offers well-being both in the world and hereafter" (EP214; also EP782). For another, it touched on a sense of grace or God's love: "My religion involves being filled with God's goodness, and firstly loving people and remembering that they are very valuable, because they are God's people" (EP749). One participant noted, "Islam is a religion of tolerance and sharing" (EP221).

While the religion prompt did not mention a duty to God, for some community members, it elicited comments revealing a sense that participants needed to do things for God: "What can I do for God today?" (EP191, EP186, EP257). In a slightly different vein, another saw the religion as creating something to belong to so he would "not live aimlessly" (EP723). For one participant, "religion" brought to mind thoughts of mortality even as it brought to mind generosity: "The Islamic religion promotes giving as its foundation. In our religion, which has the belief in the Day of Judgment and life after death, there is resurrection after death and being accountable to God for our deeds" (EP764). One understood religion to be a means to an end: "Religion is the way of becoming a servant of supreme God and expression of appreciation" (EP267).

Some participants described what the religion commands: "Our religion commands us to be generous and honest. It tells us to live not only for ourselves but for others as well" (EP199, EP713). Another participant stated, "My religion commands me to live out human values to the maximum. Due to my religion's commands I learned to look at all of the creatures in mercy. I learned to value humans" (EP713). Another man stated, "God commands us to 'help.' Helping means giving the blessing of God. The poor are also benefitting from these blessings. So they should also give. Our community wants to live this and wants to keep this alive" (EP732). One participant emphasized what he must do: "I must please God and gain his approval because the Almighty God created me when I was nothing" (EP755).

What was apparently absent in the adult Muslim community member essays, in contrast to both Catholic student and adult community member essays, was a sense of disillusionment or anger at "the religion," with religion being interpreted as the institutions or hierarchy. There were no critical comments about how the religion is interpreted by religious authorities or society (in contrast to the Muslim students, who did have critical comments). In addition, what was strikingly absent in the adult Muslim community responses were any comments about how the message of Islam has been distorted, twisted, or changed by religious authorities or adherents. There was no sense that the religion was imposed or constraining. As one stated, "Religion is freedom of conscience" (EP240). Participants did not state that they disagreed with the teachings of Islam as interpreted by religious authorities over time.

This may stem from several factors. First, Sunni Islam is a decentralized, nonhierarchical religion, and religious authorities are chosen by the community members. This gives adult Muslims the option to choose the community in which they feel most comfortable; they can leave and join another if they become frustrated with their community. Those who remain would have a more positive view of their association and religion. The student participants probably did not belong to a specific religious community. They may have associated "religion" with the religious community and teachings in which they were brought up instead of a community they deliberately chose. A final point of interest is that although in Turkey the state runs the mosques and pays the imams' salaries, none of the adult community participants associated "religion" with that. Because Sunni Islam does not theologically impose institutions, Muslims might not associate particular institutions with their general understanding of religion.

We turn now to more specific aspects of religious belief, including God's grace and one's duty to God.

God's Grace

There has been very little discussion in social science about what impact the belief of God's grace might have on the generosity of religious adherents of any faith, let alone the understandings of God's grace within specific faiths, such as Catholicism or Islam. We hypothesized that it would be a concept that would resonate with Catholics and that if filled with a sense of God's grace, they might be generous. Indeed, as we discussed in the previous chapter detailing donations made in our experiments, this is one of the primes that led to a higher likelihood of Catholics donating their participant payments to a charity.

While Islam may not be as explicit about the grace of God, it does convey that when Muslims are filled with love for God, they are generous toward others and, conversely, that when they are generous toward others, they will be filled with God's love and mercy, the latter being a concept closely associated with "God's grace." Participants who had randomly been assigned to this prompt were given the following instruction:

Think about God's Grace. In what ways does your religion say it means to be filled with God's grace? Describe what things you can do to be filled with God's grace. What does that make you think about? How does that make you feel?

Interestingly, as the quantitative analysis of the content coding showed, God's grace also was a concept that led both Catholics and Muslims to write about concepts related to charity. In addition, this prime led to a higher likelihood that both would mention concepts relating to rituals, doctrine, and divinity (Appendix Tables A.9 and A.10). Finally, this was an essay condition that led to a higher likelihood than the control condition that Catholics would donate some or all of their participant payment to a charity.

Although Catholics mentioned different feelings and thoughts about God's grace, they all mentioned positive things that included compassion, caring, love, and giving to others. To some, it elicited feelings of connectedness to God and other people, while others wrote of being joyful with God's love and thankful to God. Few Catholics stated some criticism of the church because of its strict rules and scandals and put God's grace into a different category. As opposed to our initial assumptions, we did not see much difference from Catholics in the way Muslims interpreted God's grace. The prompt elicited similar feelings and thoughts for Muslims as for Catholics. Some Muslims equated God's grace with wholeheartedly believing in God, while others saw it as avoiding evil. For some Muslims, the prompt elicited feelings of forgiveness, sharing, happiness, tranquility, and generosity.

Irish Catholics and God's Grace

The university students had mixed reactions to God's grace. One student stated that God's grace means being "full of the goodness of God" and "full of compassion and love for others" (EP408; EP462, EP522). She added that it makes her "think of all the goodness there is in the world" (EP408). One noted it means feeling "closer to god ... and to feel safe when I participate in mass or confession as it allows me to acknowledge any of my wrong doing" (EP563). Another noted that "it is as simple as just loving another human being" (EP423). Others noted it means having "a positive attitude towards life" (EP433), acting "spiritually towards others around you"

(EP492), or being "accepting of others" (EP557). For one, the concept had no bearing on his life: "God's grace is an abstract idea for me, one that is not relevant in my daily life. I honestly don't even know what it is" (EP513).

Many community members also took the prompt in a positive direction. The community members tended to write about God's grace as a gift, as something that let them feel peaceful, connected. One parishioner's words provide a clue to how God's grace could be linked to generous behavior in Catholics: "God's grace is the gift of faith – a generous gift," and it means "to be a good Christian and by doing so, filled with a sense of goodness to my fellow man/woman" (EP650). To some, God's grace meant "to feel comfortable with God" and to think "how I could be a better person" (EP287) or "live in harmony with God" (EP289). A woman wrote that "to be filled with God's grace is to fulfill our inheritance as God's children and be united with Him." She concluded her essay with the thought that "grace means the Lord is with us" (EP394). Another commented on "the birth of a child. The grace of god is in that child forever" (EP601).

For Catholics, the God that came to mind with this prime tends to be benevolent and caring. "God's grace" led some to think of "praising and thanking God for everything" (EP289, EP350). Some mentioned feeling thankful (EP326, EP601), "lucky" (EP336), or "safe" (EP332). One concluded that it "makes me think about prayer, peace of mind and happiness it makes me feel good" (EP309). Several others also noted God's grace "make me feel complete, whole, connected, full of joy, courage to face difficulties" (EP394, EP651). For some the connections were complex: when filled with God's grace, "we are more active Christians and we can appreciate the special gifts the Lord has bestowed on us. It is one of the greatest gifts a person can receive," and that in turn made her want to share it, "hoping that people will see the goodness of God's grace" (EP353). One stressed "God's grace is free" (EP360).

God's grace seemed to make parishioners feel comforted: "I feel God is with me in all things that I do. And places I go. He is there for me at all times" (EP372, EP595, EP612, EP657); another noted feeling "at peace" (EP400, 589), and another "happy and at peace" (EP664). One noted it made him think about "the goodness and forgiveness and love of God" and that it made him feel "After Communion and Confession a feeling of love and warmth, a feeling of never again offending God" (EP380, EP336).

Thoughts of helping others were common (EP295, EP359, EP664, EP681, EP339, EP350, EP595, EP601). As EP295 summarized, it meant having "compassion, patience and caring towards people" (EP295), and that "I get a great feeling of peace when I give my time and love to others" (EP295). One explained, "To be filled with God's grace I can be kind and good to those who need it" (EP339, EP350, EP595, EP601). Another noted it made him think about "becoming a better disciple of the Lord" (EP303); yet another that it made her "think of all the needy people in the world who are starving" (EP599).

For another student, God's grace meant acceptance of oneself "by God as a good person" (EP450). Others seemed to understand that one could have God's grace even if one didn't "live such a strict Christian life" but seemed unsure (EP505). This may be because, according to one participant, God's grace is not "referred to very often at Mass or other religious ceremonies" (EP506). The concept seemed to enhance some Catholics' sense of connectedness to other Catholics: "you feel a connection to god and more part of his followers" (EP443).

For others it brought to mind a struggle to believe, and they voiced their skepticism about their religion, particularly in light of the recent clergy child sex abuse scandals in the Church (EP413) or personal losses (EP447). For one, it led her to reflect on the time she did not spend practicing her faith or thinking about and "talking to God" (EP479). Others questioned the "logic" of their religion: "it makes me think of how hypocritical religion can be, if humans are created by God but imperfectly so, then isn't he/it making it incredibly hard for anyone to be 'filled with God's grace'?" (EP533). One student felt "angry" because of "the rules the Church demand you must follow" (EP453); another commented that "it is not easy to follow these rules and the 10 commandments. On some level it seems almost pointless in trying" (EP473). Other negative thoughts included that of "dying people or people who are ill, who must have to think about this a great deal" (EP450), or feeling "sad that I feel I am no longer filled with God's grace" (EP506).

As with the students, some adult Catholics mentioned needing to keep "God's and the Church's commandments," including going to "Mass and the Sacraments" (EP303, EP394). For another it was less about the rules and more about remembering that "God's grace is with us all, all the time we need to remember it's there and behave in a manner befitting of his grace" (EP625). One parishioner, who wrote extensively on what God's grace meant to him, and after having mentioned that it made him "think about what one can do to make the little bit of the world one affects a better place and be open to the needs of others," ended his essay with the comment, "Often I feel that my response has been inadequate, especially on a close, personal level, and also that a peaceful life of gardening would be very pleasant" (EP611). While an expressed preference for a life of gardening was unique, his essay was indicative of how the Catholics in the community participant group (adult parishioners) responded to "God's grace": with thoughts and feelings of peace, of caring for others, of spiritual comfort, and tranquility. These thoughts, rather than norms, obligations, or similarity to others, were also associated with the behavioral outcome of generosity in the experiment.

For some, it made them "think about my attitudes to others especially those who might be different to me" (EP339); for another, "it makes me think of humanity as a whole," as well as being "satisfied and happy" (EP359). One parishioner associated God's grace with "His intervention in my life" and concluded with the thought that "Allowing God in makes me feel good not only about myself but those around me" (EP386).

Of the community participants, only one of the "God's grace" essays had any comments about the recent clergy child sex abuse scandals (EP650). Overall, thoughts were much more about joy, peace, and helping others than about the institutional church or rules or hypocrisies of it, in contrast to what was often evoked in the religion and community expectation primes.

Turkish Muslims and God's Grace

The prompt of God's grace led some to query the logic of their religion's theology: "In order to be filled with the blessing of God, we are to accept the requirements stated in the Qur'an and fulfill them. What this situation makes me wonder is if God is a holy being that gives without expecting a return, why did He lay down conditions?" (EP28). For another, God's grace "is only towards humans who believe in Him wholeheartedly" (EP138). Some community members likewise stressed faith and how fundamental it is to life and the afterlife (EP172, EP254), or, as one said, "Nothing can happen in the world without the blessing of God" (EP239). This participant mentioned, as did others, how "we must work as much as we can to deserve the blessings provided for us by God" (EP239). For several, thinking about God's grace led to analyses of theological require-ments and beliefs: "I need the blessing of God in order to feel his grace" (EP115, EP126).

It led some to feel "peaceful ... happier and I am more grateful" (EP35). As one man put it, God's grace "makes me feel happy" (EP99). Another participant noted feeling peaceful and more confident: "there is no positive behavior I cannot perform" (EP56). For one, it meant "being able to keep away from evil as much as possible" (EP42).

As with Catholics, God's grace meant, for some, thinking of others and helping them (EP14, EP49, EP93, EP115, EP164). It is God's grace that enables them to "Become more loving towards human beings" (EP138). Many focused on the rituals that need to be done and rules that need to be followed (EP59, EP71, EP75, EP99, EP126). For one, God's grace led to the conclusion that "Gaining the love of God and fulfilling our prayers may not make us happy in this world but it is an indication that our life after death will be good" (EP66).

The prompt led several community participants, similarly, to think of helping others (EP771, EP779). It led some to think of sharing their wealth with others and sharing "the goodness God has granted us" (EP183, EP218, EP722, EP725). Some cited, as participants had in response to other primes, the words of the Prophet Muhammad: "A person is not really a Muslim if he goes to be satiated while his neighbor goes hungry" (EP198). This participant concluded by writing that "Even a smile on the faces of the people we help is worth everything" (EP198). Some mentioned helping others "for the sake of God," not for the sake of the recipient (EP254, cf. EP249, EP269), and that this "makes me happy" (EP272). God's grace prompted another to think of how "We gave up the wealth of the earth to be accepted to God's eternal Heaven. This is why Muslims are generous" (EP688). For another, everything is done "for God's sake," including writing the experiment essay itself (EP721, EP752). Another explained, "If we do everything for God's sake, his grace will pour down on us" (EP725). A number of the essays included the thought that since everything the believer has is given by God, it is inevitable that one uses those gifts to "gain his grace" (EP725).

One community member said, "I feel tranquil and safe" (EP192). One woman said she feels tranquil "when I help people" (EP218). One elaborated that, "As Muslims, owing to our faith in destiny, we understand that we are always filled with the benevolence of God. We know that God is always with us, protects us, takes care of us and also helps us" (EP205). Another member noted how God is always with him, and that that helps him persevere during stressful times and gives him "indescribable pleasure" during "happy times" (EP233). God's grace made him think more broadly about what God has taught him: "I have learned how to be well-intentioned, keep my patience and love people" (EP233). Similarly, the prompt led some to say, "I feel very happy and pleased" (EP269, EP740). God's grace made them reflect on how "Our life is continued through the kindness of God" (EP740).

The essay condition did not elicit uniformly positive reactions. For some, thoughts were about how, in life, "God may make mankind suffer various distresses" (EP110, EP21, EP66). One mentioned falling short and needing to ask for God's forgiveness (EP7).

Rather strikingly, despite our expectations that the concept would not be as familiar to Muslims than to Catholics, none of the Muslim participants challenged or corrected our use of the term. While it did not lead to statistically significant donation behaviors in the experiment, it was one of the primes that, for Muslims, led to noticeable (statistically significant) mentions of charity-related concepts in their essays, more so than in the control condition. As seen above in the community sample, many of the essays clearly indicate an orientation toward helping others.

Duty to God

Because we had hypothesized that a religiously inspired belief in having a duty to God to be generous, to help others, would prompt prosocial actions, we included as one of the experiment primes that of "duty to God." Participants received the following instruction:

Think about your duty to God. What does your religion say is your Duty to God? Describe your duty to God. What does that make you think about? How does that make you feel?

We can see in the spontaneous responses to essay primes in the experiments some differences between Catholic and Muslim understandings of "duty to God." Catholics tended to reject the idea that they had a duty or obligation to God, whereas Muslims tended to accept that they did and then described the duties. Catholics tended to turn the discussion to one of to whom or to what they have a duty, or what kinds of rules they should follow.

While some Catholics simply understood duty to God as performing tasks such as going to church, many did not feel that they had a duty to God. Rather, they stated that they had a duty to themselves and others. In some Catholics, the prompt elicited the love of others, while in some it elicited obeying the Ten Commandments. Others suggested that God's unconditional love does not impose any duty on believers. Some defined duty as being "a good Catholic." This prompt did not lead Catholics to have a greater likelihood of mentioning charity-related concepts, but it did for Muslims. Muslims expressed a strong feeling of duty to God in their essays. Many referred to pillars of Islam as duties, while others mentioned simple tasks like being thankful to God. Some, particularly among the adult community members, mentioned giving, charity, and helping others as a duty to God. It was clear that Muslims saw their good deeds toward others as part of their duty to God. In our quantitative analyses of the content coded essays, while both Catholics and Muslims tended to mention concepts related to rituals, doctrine, and divinity, Catholics also mentioned disillusionment, whereas Muslims referred more often to a third-party enforcer (Appendix Tables A.9 and A.10).

Irish Catholics and Duty to God

Views of duty to God in the Irish Catholic student population tended to subject the religion to critical analysis. One student started her essay with the statement, "I often question religion" (EP407), and then wrote, "My 'duties' to God make me think about other religions that might make more sense." Another wrote, "I don't believe I have a 'duty' to any higher form of being" (EP487). She does "believe the 10 Commandments are something to stand by" (also EP496, EP509). Several mentioned obeying the Ten Commandments or obeying God's commandments, or, in a similar vein, being "a good Catholic" (EP284, EP299, EP364, EP399, EP623), interpreting the Ten Commandments to mean to love or help one's neighbor.[6]

Others interpreted the prompt as what their religion tells them they should do: "My religion says I should do the following: To obey God and respect him ..." (EP457, EP518, EP526). Some interpreted it narrowly as a duty to God to "go to church, normally every Sunday" (EP553). The interpretation of what they should do is rather looser than what the Catholic Church might want. As one Catholic student wrote, "In relation to my duty to God, I see my duty as fulfilling my goals and aims in life" (EP508, EP535). There were a number who expressed beliefs along these lines: "my duty to God is first and foremost to love others as you yourself would like to be loved" (EP461, EP467, EP471, EP481). Similarly, a number of Irish Catholic community members responded that they had a duty to love their neighbor or love others as they love themselves (EP284,

---

[6] The Church's formal teachings on the Ten Commandments do not include "love thy neighbor" as a commandment; that association appears to stem from two other sources, Leviticus 19:18 and Matthew 22:37. In the latter, Jesus' response to a question about "which is the greatest commandment in the law" includes, as the second greatest command, "You shall love your neighbor as yourself."

EP292, EP335, EP351, EP364, EP367, EP402, EP644, EP678, EP684, EP685). One noted the duty to God "is to love, love with all my heart" and then went on to discuss the importance of loving God (EP584).

For some community members, the prompt made them think of how similar they are to others. One participant responded, "My religion guides me to be as one with my fellow human beings" (EP319); another, "We are all children of God and we should be there for each other ... My neighbour is the same as me" (EP319).

Community members sometimes questioned the idea of having a duty to God, adding, "I feel I have a duty to myself and others that I try and live a Christlike life" (EP299). One summarized a view expressed by many that "I don't feel I have a duty to God because I believe God gave me life as a free gift without me asking for it" (EP588, EP660, EP594, EP652, EP660, EP675). One commented, "I don't know whether I have a *duty to* God. I feel I have a duty to myself and to others that I try and live a Christian life" (EP299, EP588). The prompt elicited surprise in some, who responded, as did one man, "Duty to God is something I have never thought about. I can only relate it to duty to family and friends, even at that I cannot grasp the concept of duty to God" (EP671).[7] Another wrote that the duty to God "is to carry ourselves in an honourable manner" and concluded the essay by saying the duty is "to live in a way as much as possible that portrays the word of God but not necessarily the church" (EP594).

Some avoided the idea of a duty to God, and instead wrote about a duty, leaving off the idea of a duty to God or to anyone. As one man wrote, "I believe I am on this earth for a specific purpose. My duty, as I see it, is to seek to define that purpose and then do it." A little further in the essay he mentioned a "duty to live in accordance with gospel values" and, to conclude, said that "my duty is, as outlined by Jesus (and by my religion), is to love my fellow humans by being respectful and helpful and doing no harm" (EP634).

The prompt elicited some negative comments about the Catholic Church, as well, for some student participants: "I believe in God but not in the role of the Church" (EP553), and "I feel it is important to note religion and religious differences have been the cause of countless wars and conflicts ... religion has killed too many people" (EP508). And, most

---

[7] The respondent concluded by noting it was something they would investigate later: "I cannot comprehend our duty to God. As a result of this, duty to God is something I will try and go into detail at some future stage."

succinctly, "Religion says that our duty to God is important. This makes me feel pressured" (EP580). Sometimes the negative feelings were about God. One participant wrote, "Sometimes in life when bad things happened I ask myself if there is a God up there" (EP346) but nevertheless concluded that their duty to God "is to try and do good things in life and threat [NB, likely "treat"] people the way I like to be treated."

Also perhaps reflecting the absence of a sense of a duty to God, many did not seem to respond directly to the prompt, instead starting their essays by noting, "Well, without God in my daily life, my life would be very empty" (EP614); "I love my Roman Catholic faith and feel well informed when I read about it" (EP307); or "True God I love. I think he gives me the grace to be a good Christian" (EP337). This latter participant added that he had a duty "To respect others as they respect me, to be kind to all people as they are to me" (EP337). Another wrote, "I like to involve God in my everyday life" (EP381).

Turkish Muslims and Duty to God

For Turkish Muslim students, the primary response to the duty to God prompt was that there is a duty to "take refuge in Him and say prayers asking for forgiveness" (EP10). Many indicated the duty is to believe in God and perform ritual prayers. Many expanded on their duty, saying it requires them to keep the five pillars of Islam (EP4, EP17, EP3, EP38, EP45, EP65, EP70, EP95, EP98, EP127, EP146). Thinking about those requirements led to a number of participants reflecting that they "do not fulfill any of these" (EP24) or that "I believe that I should do much more" (EP38), leading some to "feel guilty" (EP70). Some thought about the impact that duties to God have, noting they are "effective in shaping our thoughts and acts in life" (EP65, EP38, EP81, EP104).

Community members also indicated that a duty to God exists. Some respondents wrote of duty to God, "The first one is to believe in God," and then noted that other duties are "written in the Qur'an or defined by our Prophet" (EP706, EP780, EP174). Many listed their duties, with most of them focused on the five pillars of Islam (EP238, EP261, EP275, EP282, EP738, EP745, EP753, EP767, EP780). One listed practicing the pillars of Islam as a duty and added that the more pious among Muslims also give more to charity than the required amount (EP780). The variation came in how they described the duties. Some cast "duty to God" as "My religion tells me," rather than as a duty to God (EP212, EP217, EP745), while noting an obligation to help people (EP217, EP745). One expressed the same duties in different words: "my religion orders me to pray with my body, spirit and wealth" (EP212). Another pointed to the Qur'an, hadiths, and the work of the leading scholars to identify the real duties to God without specifying what those might be (EP174).[8]

Some separated a duty to God from duties prescribed by the religion. For the former, one noted, "I think my duty is to become a good person"; for the latter, the same student said she was required to "perform the *salat*, fast, pilgrimage to Mecca and zakat" (EP104, EP116, EP155). Some indicated that while the religion (not God) requires "several duties," "I think that none of these is necessary" (EP24). Others responded that the main duties were "to be honest, hard-working and to be fair" (EP81, EP153), even though they were aware of the theologically prescribed duties. Some community members also thought the duty was essentially to help others (EP756). As one put it, "If I am trying to be a rose, I should also try to make my surrounding a rose garden ... My religion recommends giving, not being selfish" (EP212). God "orders" Muslims to "be loving people" (EP212). One participant included "helping the poor and orphans" as a religious duty (EP745). Others did not address the theme of duty to God, but stated, "To gain God's love we should be helpful to people" (EP785, EP208, EP217). The quoted person also cited a hadith, "The best of people are those that bring most benefit to the rest of mankind" (EP785).

Another recurring theme among Muslim community members was the duty to teach others about God and Islam (EP651, EP194, EP261, EP201, EP212, EP767, EP208, EP774, EP733). After giving information about the five pillars of Islam, one community member added that "we have another important duty, which is to tell others what we know [about Islam] to make them also enjoy our pleasures" (EP767). One woman specified that her duty to God is to teach people that Islam is about love (EP212). Another participant wrote that the duty is "making God known and telling the beauties of Islam" (EP261). Another wrote that the duty to God was to remind others about their duties as servants of God (EP201). Some mentioned the duty to teach children and relatives about God, because knowing God would make them better human beings (EP208, EP774, EP774).

Several participants indicated complex thoughts about having a duty to God. One female student observed, "I don't think that I comply with these requirements and that there are people who strictly comply with

---

[8] Recall that hadiths do not have the same theological status as verses from the Qur'an; however, they appear to serve as a guide and reference point for a number of the experiment participants.

these requirements. I do not think that is possible ... is there anyone matching these definitions? Of course ... our Prophet is a person meeting these requirements." She indicated her "interrogation" of religious issues "scares me" (EP17). One wrote that "there is a huge gap between the things I saw in Islam and what was taught to me [in elementary school]." She noted a "paradox between symbols, beliefs, restrictions" (EP98).

The prompt led some respondents to feel thankful to God for their lives (EP95, EP24, EP116). One saw thanking God as her "greatest duty" (EP153). Many community members also were succinct, writing concisely, "Promoting virtue, preventing vice" (EP194, EP255). Some cited the Prophet Muhammad for being an example of promoting virtue and preventing vice (EP255). For one woman, thinking about duty prompted her to write, "My sole target in life is to gain the approval of God" (EP174). Another wrote, "I think our greatest duty is conduct all of our affairs around the idea of making God pleased" (EP720). One stated duty as living in harmony with the environment, animals, and nature (EP255). Another simply said worshipping, refraining from evil deeds, and giving charity to those in need were the main duties to God (EP738). Another had a similar list but included a duty to God not to harm to others (EP217). Another simply identified duty as being thankful to God for being healthy and for the worldly beauties that he gave (EP201). Another included "to love all God created" as a duty (EP275).

The Muslim participants seem to have had a more homogenous sense of duty to God than did Catholics; that is, both the object of the duty (to God) and what the duties were rather consistent, with many citing the five pillars of Islam, and then some elaborating on what that meant in their lives. This makes sense in that "duty to God" is a clear concept in Islam, with children routinely being taught the "five duties" or pillars. While this prime did not lead to statistically significant behavioral outcomes in donations, as our content coding analyses showed, it did prompt Muslims to have a higher likelihood of mentioning charity than did the control condition (Appendix Tables A.9 and A.10).

Conclusion

In this chapter, we have examined the content of the randomly assigned essays that individuals wrote, which were intended to prime a particular dimension of religious belief. We noted that the exercise is valuable in assessing the validity of our essay prompts, in assessing why various essay prompts either did or did not prompt generous behavior from participants, and in examining responses that may have been unanticipated by previous literature to help us refine our measures and to provide a base of information that might help drive deductively formed future hypotheses.

This review of the experiment essays indicates that concepts associated with religious beliefs can elicit multiple meanings for Catholics and Muslims. For instance, what comes across in the survey of the religion prompt is that, as we had expected, it elicits a myriad of thoughts and emotions, with participants expressing a wide range of belief constructs in their religion. There was no singular interpretation of what religion meant in either faith, something that should be a cautionary note to researchers who want to study the impact of "religion" on behavior. The Catholic essays showed little support for the idea that "religion" prompts people to be prosocial because it prompts people to be cognizant of a watchful or punitive God. Catholics did not indicate they were concerned about a watchful God when thinking about "religion." The most consistent thought seemed to be about the corruption of the Catholic Church (hypocrisy of the leadership and clergy child sex abuse). In contrast, the Muslim essays in response to "religion" revealed a belief that God was watching how they lived and that in order to please God, the participants needed to live their lives in a certain way.

Duty to God, among the Irish Catholic sample, prompted varying responses, with many suggesting they had more of a duty to themselves and others. Muslims, on the other hand, typically identified strongly with the idea of having a duty to God. We also found in our survey of the grace prompt that responses tended to be much more positive, focusing on concepts of joy, peace, and providing help to others. It was much less centered on the institutional church, its rules, or perceived hypocrisies embedded within the Church among Irish community members. Somewhat surprisingly, we found that Turkish Muslims did not correct our use of the term "grace" or claim the concept was alien to them, but that it tended to elicit generally, albeit not universally, positive responses.

Having focused on three beliefs that involved divinity, we now turn to a set of beliefs that may be more focused on relations with others. What thoughts and feelings do these prompt in Catholics and Muslims, and what are the similarities and differences across the two religions in their writings about those concepts?

5

Religious Communities, Prosociality, and Connections to Others

In this chapter, we examine how religious teachings on three concepts about individuals' connections to others are reflected in the thinking and behaviors of Catholics and Muslims at the individual level. We do so through a study of the experiment essays about the deservedness of the needy, one's similarity to others, and the expectations of the religious community. These concepts touch directly on the religious beliefs and understandings of Catholics and Muslims about their connections with others. Religious teachings on deservedness, similarity, and community expectations typically are assumed to influence individuals' prosocial behavior. Though the participants produced a wide array of reactions within each prompt, we can nonetheless see some generalities within each for both Catholics and Muslims.

As we elaborated in greater detail in the previous chapter, our analyses of the experiment essays are helpful in elucidating the primes that had statistically significant impacts on either making a donation or mentioning charity as a concept. They enable us to learn about what thoughts and feelings the priming concepts elicit in Catholics and Muslims. In so doing, the essays provide depth on the mechanisms linking the concepts to giving to and helping others, and may also show us why some of the primes do not elicit statistically significant impacts.

Recall that the experiments were carried out among students at Boğaziçi University in Istanbul and University College Dublin and among adult community members of the Islamic Gülen association in Istanbul and among adult community members of Catholic parishes in Dublin.[1] We asked the participants to write about how a particular religious topic

---

[1] For details, see Chapter 3.

made them think and feel. The question that enabled us to measure their experiment-prompted generosity, asking whether they wanted to donate to religious or secular charities, came after the essays; participants were not yet aware of that donation question when writing their responses to religious concepts. Rather than correcting the grammar, punctuation, and spelling of the essays, we have quoted verbatim from them. We have verified the accuracy of our transcriptions.

Deservedness

We first consider what Catholics and Muslims think and feel when prompted with the concept of what their religion teaches about people in need who deserve help. Much previous research has concluded that members of different religions vary in their view of whether a target of generosity is deserving, and the more they view the target as deserving, the more generous they are (Bean 2014; Bekkers and Wiepking 2011; Will and Cochran 1995). This perspective does not fully allow for the possibility that in some religions, deservedness may simply be defined as being in need. Both Catholicism and Islam emphasize helping those in need, without reference to circumstances; think of the Christian parable of the prodigal son. Here, with the essay prompts on religious teachings about "people in need who deserve help," we can see to what extent our Catholic and Muslim experiment participants reflect this view. The prompt was:

Think about people in need who deserve help. What does your religion say about people in need who deserve help? Describe their circumstances. What does that make you think about? How does that make you feel?

The prompt seems to have led to a fairly consistent focus on helping the needy, in contrast to other primes that led to responses going beyond the concept being activated, an observation confirmed by the content-coded analyses (Appendix Tables A.9 and A.10). As we discussed in Chapter 3 in detailing donations made in our experiments, this prime was associated with a significantly increased likelihood of Catholics donating their participant payment, and it was also associated with a higher likelihood that both Muslims and Catholics wrote in their essays about concepts associated with charity. We first review the Catholic, then the Muslim, participant essays.

Irish Catholics and Deservedness
Some Catholic students described the ways in which organizations affiliated with the Church, or the local parish church itself, help people in need

(EP405, EP464, EP434, EP455) or, in reference to rising poverty, said that "something needs to be done about it" (EP420). Many, even those who had "lost a lot of faith in the catholic church following recent events" (EP455), noted that Catholicism teaches them "to treat your neighbor as you would like them to treat you" (EP455) or to help those in need (EP405, EP420, EP426, EP449, EP499, EP511, EP530, EP539, EP569). The Good Samaritan was mentioned a number of times (e.g., EP539, EP544). One parishioner commented that thinking about what her religion taught about the needy deserving help reminded her that she needs "to remember how blessed and fortunate I am and that 'helping' is a requirement, a necessary part of who I am, not an 'optional extra.'" She ended her essay reflecting that "I need to do more giving, more reaching out" (EP291). Some commented on "how lucky I am" (EP306, EP622); one used the term "blessed" (EP618). Thinking about those in need deserving help led others to be "grateful for the life I have" (EP357).

Several parishioners also mentioned recent, more societal-level events. Lack of trust in Church institutions came up, "as it seems they can't be trusted any more than political institutions" (EP666). Another said, "What upsets me the most is the blindness with reference to incest and abuse in our society" (EP680), then linked it to the "economic mess," and she concluded, "We all individually hold a key to mutually helping each other in Ireland" out of those problems (EP680). For many students, being asked to think about "people in need who deserve help" immediately brought to mind those suffering from Ireland's recession (EP355, EP363). As part of the socioeconomic concerns, one parishioner noted that "it is very difficult to know who is hungary anymore" and then referred to local aid efforts in her parish (EP377).

Thinking of religious teachings about people in need deserving help led one parishioner to comment that the recession in Ireland "has turned us back to God who gave us all we had in the first place" (EP618). Some parishioners also brought up socioeconomic issues (EP622, EP673). One participant stated, "my religion says there will always be people in need who deserve help, there will always be people who have more than others" (EP320). He then commented that that makes him feel "how unjust our world can be and how lucky I am to be in the position to help those who are less well off than I am" (EP320, EP673). The prompt led people to think about how "There are so many people who need help" (EP646). One Catholic parishioner wrote, "Social justice is very important and there should be help for people in need. The resources of the world should be shared by everyone" (EP593). One, while noting that his religion teaches that "Christians should follow the example of Christ and the early Christians," wrote that "current society is failing to meet the needs of all sectors; there appears to be an increasing divide between those who are well educated and those who are not; increasing lack of ethics and responsibility on the part of elected representatives" (EP322). Many echoed the sense that helping is an obligation or expectation (EP329, EP363, EP311, EP642, EP680). One said the situation of people in need deserving help makes her think that "I should help people in need as best I can" (EP306). Some referred to the Ten Commandments, stating "to love God and love your neighbour" (EP378, EP646). Another wrote, "We may not always be able to help people with donating money – my religion has taught me that – it is to give yourself" (EP640, 642). Others put it slightly differently, saying that Catholicism "tries to encourage you to help those in need" (EP298, EP306, EP357, EP673) or that their religious belief is that "if I can help anyone by any donation I am pleased to do it" (EP370).

The prompt also made them think of being in another's shoes: "If it was us in that situation we would be very grateful of some assistance" (EP405). Nevertheless, afterward, when given the opportunity to donate part of her participant payment to a charity, she declined. Another, in a related vein, thought of how those in need "have as much a right to comfort and safety as myself or anyone else" (EP420). Another Catholic student thought about "the extenuating circumstances that have lead people to be in these situations" and that she could just as well wind up there if unfortunate (EP464, EP491; also EP370).

Others reframed it as "I believe people in need should be helped" (EP412), without indicating that they should participate in helping. Some said they "feel sorry for people in need" and "feel that I should help them" (EP455). Another student said he felt "sympathetic towards people in need and despite the fact I don't often donate I feel I should" (EP499). For some, the concept made them "feel sad and sorry for them [those in need]" and a bit helpless: "I feel like I want to help them as much as I can but its very hard to know what to do" (EP434, EP490). One added, "Contributing money is not the way I want to help" (EP490). Others hinted at or mentioned feeling guilty: it "makes me feel like I should be doing more to help people in need" (EP449, EP569, EP469, EP530, EP539). Another said that "it makes me feel sad thinking about people who are in need of help" (EP555). And she concluded, "Tossing some spare change has always seemed futile and ineffective to me" (EP469). For others, the thought of those in need deserving help made them feel thankful for "my privileged life" (EP464; also EP482, EP555).

Parishioners also varied in whether the feelings associated with helping were good or bad. The prompt led many to comment that the act of helping others makes them feel good. As one Catholic community member offered, "When I help people in need it makes me feel good, and like I am spending my time in a good way" (EP311, EP328, EP646). Others said that "it makes me feel interested in better understanding of peoples circumstances and assisting where I can" (EP369). The prompt also sometimes led to feelings of "sadness," helplessness (EP329, EP377, EP503, EP633), anger (EP363), or confusion (EP666). As with the students, some voiced a sense of being "inadequate ... I would like to be able to do more" (EP377). Such thoughts sometimes led people to feel a bit guilty; as one Catholic woman wrote, "I feel like Im being selfish because I've got it good, and I should be greatful to have a house, food and clean water" (EP622).

One parishioner saw it as a difficult challenge to "be the face of Christ to our fellow human beings" in responding to people in need (EP590). For some, it appears that when they feel that needs are overwhelming, the perceived magnitude of needs stymies their generosity. For yet others, that perception pulls at their heartstrings and they donate. Examples of the latter include the parishioner who concluded his essay writing, "may God please help all the families who are suffering from starvation" (EP503). Another admitted he feels "pretty helpless at times" (EP673). The prompt led some to think about personal experiences of being in need such as having lost a job (EP597), others about specific events in the Irish Church, namely, the clergy child sex abuse scandal (EP609).

Some students discussed the moral and sociopolitical dimensions of people in need. One stated there is a need to "divide wealth more evenly" (EP412). One mentioned that Church teachings are that "people in need who deserve help should get it" and noted this does not necessarily happen, because the state more often helps those in need (EP426). Another pointed to the institutional failings of the Church, saying that "the Catholic Church puts forward a very 'help the needy' attitude, but tends to ignore this at the highest levels" (EP498). One said that "religion does not play a major part in helping people." She described some of their problems, such as being homeless, poor, or depressed, and said that "they are not dealt with through religion" (EP555). It seems to be a view that religion is in a realm separate from these kinds of issues. Another said that "people shouldn't have to *deserve* help, if someone isn't in a fit state of mind they still need help and we should give it → even if they don't deserve it" (EP449). She used another example to challenge the very concept of deservedness as a basis for helping the needy, pointing to some homeless who "may not be trying to help themselves, they may have done this to themselves but we should still help people" (EP449). This was stressed by another Catholic student, who said, "I think the word 'deserving' is unnecessary. If a person has a need they need you're help. There should be no real consideration of their addiction etc." (EP569; this participant did "draw the line at helping a paedophile"). This tends to be in keeping with expectations about Catholics' attitudes toward helping those in need (and was voiced by some of the interviewees). That said, some thought "too many people ask for state aid without trying things" (EP511); another commented, "To me 'deserve' means 'entitled to' and that feeling that you deserve something just because of a particular situation in your life doesn't sit well with me" (EP575).

Parishioner participants, likewise, mostly reasoned that people should be helped no matter what led them to be in need of aid; whether one "deserved" help was not in question. As one said, "My religion says that all people in need deserve help regardless of what lead to their circumstances" (EP403). Another said, "For my religious beliefs I have always believed that a person in need of help is the same as a person who has what he needs. He is a son of God, too, just like me" (EP597). This participant, as well as others, noted similarity with others: "we are all human and all in need somehow" (EP403, EP590, EP593, EP640). Another put it as: "All people are created in the image and likeness of God and to be loved and cared for accordingly" (EP665). One even challenged our wording of the prompt, responding, "I feel no matter what someone has done in their lives – everyone deserves help – who are we to judge who 'deserves help'!" (EP640).

Some differentiated between those who deserved help and those who didn't, with the latter having gotten themselves into a bad situation perhaps through using drugs (EP298). One parishioner discussed at some length that while he believed that "But for the grace of God, there go I," he also finds "it most difficult to help those who are afflicted with addiction." Yet his reason was not that these individuals had created their own problems, but that "I know and accept that I cannot cure them, control them or change them." This made him "feel very limited as to what I can do" (EP665). A number of participants reflected on the diversity of material needs (EP370, EP391) and on how needs are not merely material (EP369, EP378, EP391, EP618, EP666, EP673).

In summary, common thoughts and feelings among the Irish Catholics were that Catholicism teaches that the needy deserve help; that there is guilt in relation to the needy; that there is a sense of perhaps not doing enough to help; that there was a bit of division between some who thought that the needy deserve help no matter how they got into their situation, and others who thought "deserve" represented "entitlement"; and that religion did not help the needy, either as an institution or as a belief system that would help people deal with their needs.

Turkish Muslims and Deservedness

In asking Muslim students to think about people in need deserving help, we elicited a range of comments, many of which indicated that the participants' religion tells them, or suggests to them, that they help those in need (e.g., EP12, EP5, EP77, EP40, EP54, EP64, EP92, EP96, EP108, EP132, EP158). We see in the responses of most of our Muslim participants that being needy is what makes one deserving of help and that one did not have to do something or be something, other than needy, to be "deserving" of help. As one participant put it, "everyone is tested in a different way in life ... God orders us to help needy people" (EP77, EP132). A few pointed out that "According to my religion ... helping such people is a good deed" (EP47). Several quoted from the hadith, and commented that helping the needy is both a religious duty and "a humanitarian duty" (EP92, EP158). As one stated of people in material or spiritual need, "Our religion also obliges people to help these people" (EP158), and they quoted the hadith, "A person is not really a Muslim if he goes to bed satiated while his neighbor goes hungry" (EP158).

One student thought religion was not central to helping those in need: "I noticed that when I saw needy people, I could fight for them and help them instead of praying to God for them. Therefore, my feelings were never based on religion" (EP26). Another's thoughts demonstrate the complexity of religion's possible role in helping the needy. While she first stated that "I think helping is one of the essentials of being Muslim," this participant went on to voice concern about the sincerity behind helping the need: "if you help people just because it is a requirement of religion, that is not right" (EP137).

Community members also discussed whether Islam requires helping the needy. Many Muslim community members quoted the same hadith mentioned by some students, "A person is not really a Muslim if he goes to bed satiated while his neighbor goes hungry," indicating that to be a Muslim is to help those in need (EP167, EP175, EP188, EP227, EP242, EP258, EP784). One said, "It is this hadith that shapes my thoughts, lifestyle, and decisions" (EP784). One wrote that "the neighbor" in the hadith should be extended to include places in Asia and Africa (EP167). Another participant quoted the hadith, "There are two tempers that God loves: good manners and generosity; and there are two traits that God disparages: bad manners and meanness" (EP209). One seemed to see it as a way of ensuring God would help them, should they wind up in a difficult situation: "I know that if I help them [the needy] now, God will help me when I end up in difficult conditions" (EP195).

Some community members saw helping others as an explicit directive: "Islam stipulates helping every person who is in a difficult position" (EP247, EP264, EP735, EP748, EP750, EP759). The quoted participant said Islam does not care about the needy person's background (not "religion, language or race") (EP247). As an example, he mentioned the humanitarian support that Turkey gave to the victims of floods in Pakistan and the earthquake in Haiti (EP247). Another mentioned the satisfaction of helping the needy – "Giving a hand to a person in need gives human being happiness in this world" – and added that "regardless of what we get in return, we help because this is an order from God" (EP748, EP264). Some defined need not only in material but also in spiritual terms (EP735, EP750, EP258, EP219). One suggested praying as a way to help the needy: "we help them financially as much as we can, but through prayers we also don't leave them alone and give moral support" (EP258).

Many mentioned complying with the "principle suggesting 'work not for yourself but for your Muslim brother'" (EP168). Others saw it as "A Muslim is a brother of a Muslim. Therefore, we must help our brother" (EP181, EP219). For one participant, thinking about the needy deserving help elicited thoughts of empathy: "We could be in difficult circumstances just like them" (EP181, EP195, EP258, EP219, EP175, EP209, EP762). Another said that even if a person does not have resources, they should help the needy by encouraging others to help (EP209). Islam's teachings on the needy deserving help seem to inspire thoughts of empathy and identification with others' circumstances.

A number of participants indicated that they were conscious of God assessing their actions in response to those in need. Many described God's favoring those who "spend their wealth in God's way" (EP209), with one going on to explain that "God approves of morality and generosity whereas He dislikes immorality and meanness" (EP209). As with the students, some noted that "need" could be moral or material (EP219, EP258, EP735, EP750). One community member wrote that God's statements on the necessity of taking care of the poor, orphans, and the needy made him feel responsible and mentioned the Prophet Muhammad's example as a source of inspiration to help the needy (EP748). Another mentioned that she would not feel comfortable when she met with God (in the hereafter) if she had kept money for herself even when she knew that someone needed it (EP175). Also as with the students, some noted that "God tests every Muslim" in how they use their wealth and how they live their life, "accordingly, the rich have responsibilities to the poor" (EP237; also EP759), and "This is called Zakat" (EP237). One participant saw helping as an opportunity to invest in the afterlife (EP784). Along the same line, another wrote that giving charity protects one from life troubles (EP762).

One student observed, "Helping the needy is above religion, language and race ... My religion directs people to help people in need without making any differentiation. Human is human" (EP154). Some brought up socioeconomic inequalities and injustices (EP5, EP12, EP26, EP79). Quite a few discussed the circumstances and feelings of those in need (EP33, EP40, EP158). Some voiced mixed feelings about the needy: "Sometimes, beggars influence me negatively" (EP152). As with the Irish respondents, some Muslim participants commented that needs are both spiritual and material (EP77, EP108, EP158).

Some who had discussed the unfairness of circumstances that leave some people in need ended their essay with a disclosure: "Although I consider myself a good person, I also realize that I don't think about these social matters very much" (EP96). Another commented, "If I didn't write these [comments about the needy] down, I would forget about them" (EP152). For others, the prompt elicited an essay criticizing their society, stating that "neither the religion nor morals are given importance and people ignore the needy and continue to self-indulge" (EP154).

The prompt also brought up feelings of sadness (EP26, EP33, EP40, EP163) and thoughts of being "very lucky" (EP26, EP96, EP137). While none of the participants said they felt hopeless in the face of those in need deserving help, they noted they struggled sometimes to provide enough help. As a student wrote, "If there is nothing I can do, I say prayers for them" (EP163). The prompt led some participants to feel "sad" because "there is no equal income distribution in our world" (EP219). This community member said Muslims should share their wealth with others, citing the hadith, "None of you truly believes until he wishes for his brother what he wishes for himself" (EP219). The participant mentioned a trip to Africa the previous year, noted the poverty there in comparison to the relative wealth in Turkey, and raised the necessity of helping those living in miserable conditions.

For others, thinking about the topic created a happier thought, in that, "to help someone and make someone happy, gives me happiness" (EP715;

also EP784, EP168). One saw it not so much as helping but as a requirement to "be useful to all mankind" (EP712); another flatly stated, "We cannot be selfish" (EP762). For some, the prompt led them to think about the good in their religion because "it protects the poor and those in need" (EP 750; also EP219).

A number of participants brought up zakat as a means of helping the needy (EP54, EP40, EP77, EP64). One student commented that in Islam, the material needs of the poor "are met by methods such as zakat" (EP108). For another student, fasting during Ramadan is something that "really makes people think of hungry people" (EP152). Another discussed the explicit teachings of Islam about helping the needy, and their meaning, seeing zakat as a means of enabling those with sufficient wealth to "fulfill their religious obligations." For this student, zakat "underlines the importance of cooperation," with cooperation being the participation of the giver and recipient in the exchange (EP157). Another explained that "Islam suggests that everything a person owns was originally granted by God and that all such possessions are temporary" (EP163).

To summarize Catholic and Muslim responses to deservedness, there was little discussion of what makes one "deserving" of help – if one needs help, one deserves help, regardless of how one came to be in that situation. Most Catholics focused on people's needs and saw those as justifying help. One deserves help merely by being a fellow human being in need of help. Some admitted to conflicting feelings about certain kinds of needs, say, of drug addicts or pedophiles, and others noted a wariness of being taken advantage of. Of interest, none mentioned Catholic rituals of giving, such as offerings at mass or annual pledges. Generally, Muslims saw being in need as the reason one is deserving of help, and that Islam instructs them to help others. Some took pains to point out that religion is not necessary to generate a response to those in need deserving help. Being human is sufficient. Further, there is no distinguishing between people when it comes to being deserving of help. And participants noted that Islam's institutional features, such as zakat, are mechanisms through which Muslims help the needy.

Community Expectations

Studies of prosocial behavior have found that group norms of reciprocity may enhance generosity. We hypothesized that Catholicism and Islam would channel that effect, in that both religions create groups that have a set of norms and expectations about religiously inspired acceptable and desirable behavior. We gave our experiment participants the following instruction:

Think about the expectations of your religious community or the religious community you grew up in. Describe what your religious community expects of you. What does that make you think about? How does that make you feel?

The prompt elicited a range of responses from Catholics and Muslims, with Catholics tending to mention things associated with norms, rituals, doctrine, and disillusionment, and Muslims mentioning norms, a third-party enforcer, rituals, doctrine, and concepts related to divinity (Appendix Tables A.9 and A.10). As we discussed in Chapter 3 in detailing donations made in our experiments, this prime was not associated with an increased likelihood of Catholics or Muslims donating their participant payment (Figures 3.1 and 3.2). It was not associated with a higher likelihood that Catholics wrote in their essays about concepts associated with charity, but it was associated with a higher likelihood of Muslims doing so.

Irish Catholics and Community Expectations

The Catholic students by and large did not voice a sense that their religious community had strong or strict expectations of them, even though as Irish children they had had Catholic religious education in school (EP437, EP459, EP484, EP486, EP507, EP558, EP570). One noted "no judgement" (EP546). This may reflect the loosening of the Church's grip on Irish society, as well as norms post–Vatican II. Some mentioned expectations of doing good, avoiding wrong-doing, passing on the faith to their children (EP411), adhering to a "moral code" (EP436, EP484, EP521), and being expected to "treat others as we wish to be treated" (EP579). These listings were devoid of descriptions of feeling pressure. As one wrote, "each to their own is how I feel" (EP417). This participant noted, "I did not grow up in a particularily oppressive or forceful religious community" (EP417); another stated, "I don't feel pressured" (EP437). Some mentioned the rituals one is expected to observe (mass, confession), then said, "but I don't" (EP459). Another mentioned following "whatever the majority are practicing" (EP514).

On the other hand, there were those who said that their religion "wants me to conform fully to the religion. Some of these things can make me feel angry or annoyed" (EP430). Another mentioned that the community "expects all within my community to act the same ... All must comply with certain regulations and rules" (EP488, EP551). Hypocrisy of the Church was mentioned a number of times. As one noted, "I feel that a lot of authoritative figures in the religion do not conform themselves, and are hypocrites" (EP430). One noted, "Although I agree with the Christian opinions and expectations, some make me feel claustrophobic and isolated from others" (EP468). She added, "I don't believe in some of the rubbish that is attached to the Church," pointing to the expectation to attend "services at Easter and Christmas" (EP468). Another discussed how society has changed "while religion is remaining the same," and that could lead one to feel "restricted." The participant then commented how she felt "discriminated and isolated from my religious community" because "teenagers are left out" (EP488).

The consequence of thinking about expectations was, for some, that it "makes me feel like part of a community even though I'm not an extremely religious person" (EP436). For another, the thoughts led to questioning "whether God is real or not" (EP484). For yet another, thoughts led to the conclusion that, "As there are numerous different religious communities, I find it hard to believe which one is right" (EP486). Thoughts often became negative: "the Catholic church is very elitist and blind to modern peoples' needs" (EP507). For another Catholic student, thoughts turned to a conflict with a parent about religious hypocrisy (EP573).

Another mentioned the expectation "to be involved in following the guides/rules of the people who teach about my religion." This led to thoughts about being involved, because "having a sense of community is important," but she indicated that did not affect her: "if I choose to be more involved in my religious community, I would prefer to do so 100% out of my own individual choice, rather than feel obligated/over-influenced to do so" (EP497). Community expectations led some to think about not just expectations but what the meaning of the community was, what the point of faith was, and whether God exists (EP573).

Irish community members also discussed whether there were community expectations to be generous. The community expectations prompt generated a range of thoughts and emotions in the adult parishioners. One participant started by saying the first expectation is "that we feel part of the community" (EP390); another commented that their religious community had wanted "more and more" people to attend mass "to keep the faith strong." Seeing this kind of commitment "makes me feel strong and know that people are willing to give up there time to do this" (EP379).

Many listed the basic rituals such as attending mass (EP655). Many also listed helping with volunteer work (EP390, EP302, EP316, EP371, EP638, EP653, EP655, EP662), observing the Ten Commandments (EP296), and honoring and worshipping God (EP596). One said the expectation is that of "being reverent and respectful" (EP596); others noted being a good person (EP316, EP318, EP341, EP348, EP358, EP602, EP624, EP653, EP656, EP662, EP669). Some commented that it was the community that helped them do these things (e.g., EP348).

Many community members commented on the change in expectations over time, noting that the Church they grew up in was much more strict and demanding than the Church or parish community they are in now, where "nothing is expected of you" (EP669, EP677). One noted how expectations of participation in rituals have "changed greatly," where the emphasis now is on reconciliation, "confession" (EP323). Another participant stated that expectations, overall, have changed, getting looser (EP354, EP631). The latter participant then commented on how one has to be an active participant now, and that the days of "duty" to an institutional church are gone: "The church is the people. People are the church" (EP354, EP617, EP624). Still others commented on a relaxation of rigid expectations to attend mass and go to confession, with some pointing to the Church's loss of authority "due to abuse by the Church on children" (EP368). Another commented on how "Pre-Vatican II" the "fear of punishment was all-pervasive" (EP393), and that while things are, as others have commented, far less rigid now, the community is "divided": there is that which has a "loving God" and that which is being "tested" by "the [clergy child sex] abuse which has been prevalent in Ireland and world wide" (EP393). These thoughts led her to reflect on changes in the Church, its being male-dominated, and aspects of living as a "baptised Christian." She concluded by wondering what would happen to the Church (EP393).

Others, like most of the students, said that "the religious community does not expect alot from you. It is entirely up to you to spend the amount of time you spend involved in religious activities" (EP315). This participant made no mention of normative expectations nor the lack thereof; she thought it was more about the time commitment. This was echoed by others (EP602, EP603, EP624, EP627), including one who said, "I tend to think more about my own wishes, choice, search, faith, journey etc. rather than about the communities expectations" (EP638, EP655). Some reflected on the consequences of this, wondering if it comes at the cost of a "close community." That in turn led to feelings of disappointment (EP627). One stated, "I am keen to engage and bring about a more caring and faith filled society. The apparent lack of expectation frustrates me" (EP656, EP669). Indeed, for one participant, commenting about the Church's *lack* of expectations led him to "think maybe that the church needs to be a bit more visible outside the actual building itself, maybe a bit more active in society, etc." (EP603).

Thinking about community expectations did often lead to thoughts about the community, which one participant declared "is a joy to be part of" (EP315, EP596). As another commented, "people know and care about you" (EP316); another associated it with living "very contented as a family" (EP358). In other words, more of the essay was devoted to reflecting on positive aspects of the community than on its expectations (EP368, EP631). The thought of community expectations left some feeling "good about myself knowing that I am giving back to my community and living my beliefs" (EP296), and others said that "none of my siblings are practicing Catholics ... I think I will say a few prayers for them" (EP304). Another mentioned feeling close to her deceased relatives when she prayed, and how that was "a great feeling" (EP596).

Some clearly associated the term "religious community" with the institutional Church. As one wrote acerbically, "I think my religious community expects people to live by rules that are 1) outdated, 2) not followed by a lot of religious leaders." She expressed anger, noting the hypocrisy of "pregnant women not allowed to marry on main alter in church and early morning or late night while behind the scenes the clergy were abusing children" (EP327). Her essay ended with "I love to go to some services where I can feel an emotional bond to God ... but [I] have lost a lot of faith in the clergy" (EP327). Another commented that "the Vatican now wants to control my thoughts and actions. They seem to be in a different world to me," with the expectation that one "obey[s] their rules without any thought" (EP643). He distinguished that "community" from "the community I am in daily," about which he had much more positive things to say; at the end of the essay, he explicitly contrasted it with the Vatican (EP643).

There were a few who thought much was expected of them in terms of volunteer time. As one woman put it, "I think that there is quite a lot expected of so few" (EP371). She expressed a sense of being "disheartened" with "the Church, State, and pillars of society" (EP371).

Clearly, writing about the expectations of their religious community led many to think broadly about what they thought the community was and what had happened to it. The focus was not just on its expectations but on varying views on the meaning of community. This variation in what the respondents meant by community was even more widespread among the Muslim respondents, as we discuss next.

Turkish Muslims and Community Expectations

As the content-coded results confirm (Appendix Tables A.9 and A.10), the prompt elicited a range of responses about community expectations. One participant wrote that the religious community "does not put much pressure on me," noting nevertheless that "Muslim" is on his national identity card (EP11). Another said, "The community where I live has certain restrictions and expects me to live within these restrictions. However, I don't regard this as pressure" (EP39). Still another indicated that there are expectations, even if not expressed verbally: "you feel that you will not be welcome if you don't fulfill them" (EP46). One stated flatly, "Different ways of thinking and discussion are not allowed" (EP69); another stated that one has to conform and hold the "right" beliefs (EP82, EP103, EP120).

What participants considered to be "the community" ranged from family (EP83) to the entire country (EP62).[2] One student rejected the idea that the community mattered at all: "The point is not what a member of the community wants from you; the point is what your religion requires from you" (EP142). This thought led the participant to discuss the contradictions that sometimes are evident between the community and "what God wants from me" (EP142, also EP149). One participant noted the difficulty of determining what the relevant community is: because "we live in a complicated community I do not know according to whom and what I should act." She went on to note a sense of pressure to follow "the requirements of my religion" (EP25). Another said there are expectations to follow basic rules to "not misbehave" and went on to stress that "I do not have to account to anyone but God regarding my religion" (EP89). Another also thought of her "religious responsibilities," rather than about the community's expectations (EP123). Another thought the idea that the community would have expectations of her as "ridiculous ... Religion is an internal phenomenon" (EP162).

Some differentiated between religion and its expectations, and the community and its expectations, saying that the former is "more important" and that the religion expects "me to help all human beings without discriminating" (EP177, also EP234). Another also started with "the things that

---

[2] This may be due to how mosques are organized in Turkey. Since mosques are used only for prayer purposes and controlled by the state, what the religious community is may be less clear to the Turkish students than it is for Catholics. This is probably not the case for the Muslim community member participants, since they had joined a particular religious community. For Catholics, doctrine and practice locate the community in the parish and in the Church. See also our discussion of cemaat in Chapter 2.

God wants from me as a Muslim" and then wrote that the "religious community expects us to pray, respect, love, help, promote solidarity and support one another" (EP775, also EP777). One stated that the religious community she grew up in "has no direct expectations of me" (EP279). Another did not mention community expectations at all and instead focused on the religion, which requires that he be "an ethical person following my religion's commands and prohibitions" (EP716, EP776). Likewise, a man commented that respecting his parents "is a must" and "helping poor people is a necessity in our religion" (EP736, also EP764). The focus was less on the community's expectations and more on what they perceived to be the religion's expectations (EP769). For others, the main thought was "we should do everything for God ... If you are in a financially good status you should help the poor" (EP280). For another, community expectations prompted him to respond, "Our religion tells us to create goodness and to help those in need" (EP763).

Some student participants mentioned that their religious community expects them to follow rules (EP18) or rituals (EP120), to be "morally good, fair and honest" (EP62, EP88, EP89, EP123), helpful (EP113), or live up the community's ideal of a "good person" (EP119). Some saw this as a good thing (EP88): "I have no doubt the community in question is thinking of my well-being." Others saw it as more constraining: "The community in which I grew up expects me to do what it has done until now" (EP149). Many community member Muslims also noted the community, and the religion, did have expectations of them: they "expect us to love all human beings" (EP173; also EP235, EP761). Some felt that the community expects one to "become a good servant of God and become beneficial for the community we live in and mankind" (EP253, EP761), to "respect each other's beliefs" (EP276), to help one's "relatives and neighbors" (EP714), and to "live my life according to the Islamic rules, and then to orient myself, as an individual, to the community" (EP751). Some stated that they had an "obligation" to help others, to be "useful to other people" (EP761), though they did not state that this was directly due to the community's expectations. One said the community expected him to explain religious obligations "to other people" (EP777).

Some community members similarly seemed to interpret the question as asking what the function of the community was (EP781): one participant commented on how "we learn good behaviors and habits" in communities (EP184). Another said, "It teaches me to live my religion in a more accurate way" (EP193); yet another said, "People need a good friend or a community not to go astray from the truth and give in to their bad instincts" (EP197). She added that her religious community "teaches us not to live based on only this world but also to desire good things in the other world" (EP197). Similarly, another stated that the community "teaches us to serve as a community" (EP204). Others saw their community as having the purpose of affecting "the moral behaviors of society" (EP226). For one, it was that "My God has chosen this community for me" (EP763), and for another, that "God introduces us as equals" (EP766).

For some students, the prompt led them to think more broadly about Islam and other religions, describing how they "realized that there is a very thin line between members of Islam and the people that were introduced to us as impious" (EP119), that is, opining that there may be few differences between Muslims and non-Muslims. One had critical observations of community-based restrictions that some Islamic communities put on their followers in Turkey, such as the banning of listening to music (EP62).

As the above essay analyses show, some Catholics noted the basic requirements of the religion (attending mass, for instance). Some thought of the institutional church, with which they had a negative image; most noted that the Catholic community had very low expectations of them, especially at the parish. A few regretted the low expectations, seeing it as reducing the community feeling. A number had warm thoughts about the local community. For our investigation into sources of generosity, what is significant in the Catholic essays is what is absent: Catholics tended not to write about helping their community or adhering to the particular rules it had. The norm of reciprocity was not vocalized. Muslims perhaps reflected a stronger sense that their religious community had expectations of them, but many nevertheless pointed out that what really mattered was God's expectations of them, and that the community functioned to help them meet those expectations. The community also helped them help others to meet God's expectations.

Similarity to Others

There is a considerable literature in social psychology on the role of empathy and perceived similarity in prosocial behavior. Empathy promotes prosocial behavior, and people help others whom they perceive as similar to themselves (Batson 2014; Cialdini et al. 1997). We surmised that if Catholicism and/or Islam taught people about how they are similar to others, the prime would elicit generous behavior. Instead, as discussed in Chapter 3, the prime had no statistically significant effect on the behavioral outcome in the experiment, and the experiment essays reveal that asking

Catholics and Muslims about how they are similar to others and what their religion says about that leads to a range of responses, including rejection of the idea that people are similar to each other. This prompt gave participants the following instruction:

Think about how you are similar to other people. In what ways do the teachings of your religion say that you are similar to other people? Describe how the teachings of your religion suggest that you are similar to others. What does that make you think about? How does that make you feel?

As evidenced by the essays, it seems that even for those who see their religion as teaching them that they are similar to others, the concept does not necessarily lead them to think of helping others. This essay task led Catholics and Muslims both to mention, unsurprisingly, concepts related to self/other identification, but also rituals and doctrine (Tables 4.1 and 4.2). The prime did not lead to a greater likelihood of Catholics or Muslims donating their payments (Figures 3.1 and 3.2) or more often mentioning charity-related concepts.

Irish Catholics and Similarity to Others

As with other prompts, this one elicited a range of responses and associated thoughts. Several voiced the belief that we are "all created equal in God's own image" (EP410, also EP416, EP483, EP543); "we are all sinners but will be forgiven on the last day" (EP410, EP510, EP529); and we are "all God's children" (EP429, EP440, EP543). One commented about "god as the higher authoritative power" (EP416), and went on to think about "the many religions around the world" (EP416). One woman thought about how "the catholic tradition make all its followers at the same level as creatures of God," which she saw as a good thing, in that one could see fellow Catholics "in a 'real' way," but on the other hand, it led her to think about "the 'hypocrisy' of religious thought where disequality manifests itself in a very clear way" (EP419). One noted a similarity to others because "I am caring" and that her religion "has thought [sic, probably "taught"] me to be caring ... to be giving and to share" (EP520). This led her to "feel like we are all part of one group" (EP520). Another noted, "As a roman Catholic we are taught to love all humans as equals" (EP572). He thought that was a "good guideline," the idea of which "makes me feel happy" (EP572).

One noted that while the teachings of the religion do not "say that I'm similar to others," they do teach that "we are all 'equal'" (EP424). This respondent commented that he supported the "belief that all people are equal but if my religion began to imply that all people are similar I would have serious problems with that" (EP424). Some community members similarly commented about having "similar needs and wants as most" (EP294, EP288). For one participant, this led her to "think about others who are suffering and need help and support" (EP294). One man stated, "My religion teaches charity and equality for all ... It makes me feel part of a family community and therefore give assistance to whoever needs it" (EP632, EP674).

One observed that the way people are similar to each other is in being "out for themselves" (EP439). She mentioned that her religion teaches that "everybody is the same in our feelings ... [and] in the way we think and feel about God." But she added, "I don't really agree with this belief at all" (EP439). This brought up feeling "disconnected" from her religion and "other people from the church" (EP439). Another had a different take on a similar theme: that Catholicism points out that people are similar in that "they are quick to judge and condemn others" (EP510). She said this led her to "think about my own morality" and "reminds me that I am only human" (EP510).

The essay condition of religious teachings about similarity led several to focus on the Catholic community: "we all share the same beliefs; we gather at mass to express these beliefs and pray to God" (EP435, EP458, EP465, EP495). The prompt also brought up feelings of being "part of a community ... sometimes it gives me hope," and it made her think "about how I live my life" (EP435). One commented, "Your similar in a way that you are told to obey, certain rules" (EP470, EP483). For one woman, "this makes me feel a part of something and accepted" (EP483). As with a few others, one man commented that the Bible "cannot say we are similar to others. We are only similar because we were born Catholic." For him, similarity came from "the clothes we wear, the place we live," and so forth (EP470).

As with the students, some community participants focused on "other people who share my religion," noting they are similar because they "Frequent the sacraments together" (EP286, EP376, EP645), or because "we are 1 body and 1 with the Lord" (EP621). The prompt led some to think of the religious community and how they felt a part of it (EP286). One woman commented, "It makes me feel good and comfortable to sit at mass and feel the same as others" (EP376). As with the students, a number of participants explained their similarity to others in terms of a common religion: "we all believe in the one God" (EP349, EP395). One participant concluded that she is similar to others in "living our daily lives as

Christians ... and in the universal hope that we will all be reunited in the life hereafter" (EP395). Another responded, "We are taught to treat people the way we would like to be treated" and that she tries to "see the good in people. It is not always easy" (EP598). One woman said that the religious teaching made her think about how "In some ways I feel unequal" because of people living in poverty. "This makes me feel the need to be generous with the world's goods" (EP362). One saw the religion as creating differences between her and those who are not religious (EP667); another thought of how "other religious beliefs are different from mine," with none the exclusive "path to find salvation" (EP670).

After noting commonalities with "fellow Catholics," one participant said that the "commands of the church are to love God and our neighbours as ourselves," and it was in this way that she understood the Church to have teachings on similarity with others (EP645). Some emphasized that "we are born in the image and likeness of God" (EP288, EP384, EP626, EP639, EP679), or that "in god's eyes we were all created equal" (EP340, EP362, EP582, EP583, EP628). As one continued, "We have all got a deep need of God, whether we realize it or not – in that way we are similar" (EP582). One woman reasoned that "we have all been created by God and therefore we all are similar" (EP384); others, that "we share a common human nature" (EP312) or a common fate, saying we are "All heading to ultimate death and we can't bring anything with us" (EP661). Expanding on that, she noted, "I am similar to other people, according to my religion, because we are taught to love others as I love myself" (EP312). One man responded, "My religion teaches me that we were all born with original sin and Christ came on earth to redeem and save us. Being human we are all prone to human weaknesses and failings. My religion gives me comfort and a feeling of security and companionship with other people" (EP401, 674, EP583, EP632). As another said of how all people have worries and problems, "there is a whole community there to help if we would only ask" (EP621). Thinking about the religion's teachings on how one might be similar to others led him to comment on how his faith creates a comfortable, reassuring sense of community.

For some students, the prompt led them to wonder how everyone could be treated equally if they behaved so differently, with some people being, for example, charitable, and others not (EP410). This participant also saw a contradiction in priests preaching that Catholics are all equal "despite a church hierarchy being in Rome" (EP410) or that "women are still discriminated against by the Catholic Church. This makes me feel angry and slightly sad" (EP458). One who commented that "religion makes us feel similar because we all worship the same beliefs" said that "it makes me question religion and what is so great about it" (EP465). One woman concluded with the negative thought that "it also makes me feel like I don't like being generalised with all people of my religion all the time" (EP495). Not surprisingly, some students stated they disagreed with Catholic teachings that they are all similar, as they thought this impeded their individuality: "I am a strong believer in individuality. I believe each person is different and unique" (EP543).

Some community members also were skeptical that everyone can be equal. A community member noted that because "all people have obvious similarities likewise each individual unique"; this is "Not a fruitful topic" (EP398, EP647). She nevertheless continued with a discussion of the Church's teachings about individual choices determining "our lasting fate: ie sin → hellfire, virtue → heaven" (EP398), and how she did not see generalizations about people as applying to her. Another woman saw the Church teaching that "God makes us all unique and unlike one another ... [it] teaches us that we are similar in ways based on human values, love and kindness" (EP647). One community member noted being struck by how different people can seem to be ("When I meet people from other continents") and that she then remembers "that all of the Biblical characters were from the Middle East – and they inspired our own values and customs" (EP583). One woman said her religious teachings instruct her to treat "all people as equals" and "ignore certain dissimilarities eg. colour, race, status, etc. We are all equal before God" (EP674). Another saw the similarity through Catholicism's teachings that "This power of God to heal is for all God's children everywhere on earth and He has no favorites" (EP626). One participant concluded that she felt she needed to ask God "To comfort those who suffer through the actions of others" (EP679).

For another, writing the essay about similarity to others led her to think about how people fall short if they are not "giving their complete devotion" to "the faith" (EP440). One said she was taught in her religion (Catholicism) that "everyone is different" and that it was her own thinking that led her to see that people "can be similar" (EP485). She did note that "religion tells us to do to others as we would want them to do to us" and that "in this way we are all similar" (EP485).

There were few comments to the effect of "but for the grace of God, there go I"; on the whole, similarity was a complex topic that elicited a variety of thoughts and feelings. It seldom prompted thoughts or feelings of empathy with others, something that has been hypothesized to affect generosity or prosocial behavior. Interestingly, this topic seemed to prompt as many thoughts of community and of helping others as did the community expectations prompt, and the tenor tended to be positive. At the same time, many commented on how God makes people unique.

The prompt did not always elicit essays that seemed directly responsive. One participant simply said, "I like my religion. I like going to mass and saying my prayers" (EP308). In another response, the participant commented that the Ten Commandments apply to "everyone," which made her think about needing to be "conscious of the people around me," which meant "I'll have to work a lot harder" (EP628).

Turkish Muslims and Similarity to Others
Some saw the similarity in having "the same religion," "the requirements of religion, pillars of religion," which led to the comment that "I don't feel good … If we help someone just to avoid being punished after death, we might as well not help" (EP6). Another saw Islam as the reason "We resemble each other and constitute a whole" (EP159).

Some community participants also focused on commonalities with other Muslims, such as having a common faith in God and "faith in the Prophet" (EP196, EP252, EP281, EP729). One invoked the hadith, "A Muslim is a mirror of another Muslim" (EP730). One man stated, "I believe that religion has one source and thus its doctrines bring people closer and they resemble each other" (EP248). It is not so much that the religion teaches that people are similar to each other as that the religion's beliefs and rules make people similar (EP248). Another participant voiced that view as well: "In fact human beings don't resemble one another. People resemble each other because they perform their prayers" (EP268). One man emphasized that Islam teaches that "Muslims are equal" (EP765). He then noted, "A trouble affecting my equal is also my trouble" (EP765), indicating a sense of empathy brought about by a sense of others being equal.

Other comments were more universalistic. One participant did see Islam as stipulating that "we are all the same no matter what our race, religion and color is" (EP63) or that "everyone has a desire and a common joy" (EP118). For some, thoughts of similarity brought on thoughts of equality: "Our religion suggests that everyone is equal in the eyes of God" (EP41). This led to thoughts of being with "people who understand me, love me and feel happy around me" (EP41). Some saw the religion as erasing status distinctions between people (EP78). For another, "it may mean that 'you're all sisters and brothers,'" yet "this has nothing to do with similarities among people" (EP13). A male student wrote that Islam suggests that "every human being is different from another," even though it also "says that we all descend from Adam and that we are equal," which "makes me feel relieved" that others are like him (EP109).

Some community participants stated that "all human beings were created equal by God" (EP166, EP236, also 274). The fact that "I have some needs like eating, drinking" led one to think he was similar to "other people" (EP787). Religious teachings affected this participant's view that "I should think of others" (EP787). Some noted there can be differences, such as in "our religions or languages," but "we resemble each other no matter what the religion or language is" (EP236, EP717). The religion teaches nondiscrimination. One woman noted that all human beings "share the same world, sun and moon" (EP281). Another stressed that "We regard it as a duty to live together with people without discriminating against people because our Prophet recommended this" (EP274). It also "orders us to help each other" (EP274). As one commented, "Our religion also advises us to live for others because all of us have common characteristics" (EP176). One participant stated that Islam teaches that "all human beings are valuable as they are servants of the Creator" (EP166).

Other essays talked about people being different, with one student commenting, "It makes me think that I'm different from others" (EP118). Another similar comment from another student: "I do not look like the people who comply fully with the religion" (EP20). One stated that although people were basically the same physically, "in terms of spirituality, almost no human beings resemble one another" (EP94). She viewed Islam as suggesting that everyone "was created in the same way but differs from one another" (EP94). A community member also focused on difference: "My religion makes me feel different. The target is not being the same but being different, yet living my religion always makes me feel different" (EP170). A student said that "we are all reflections of God" and that God evaluates people "equally" but that the things people do during their lives "make them different from one another" (EP122).

Some did not think Islam instructed the faithful on the topic of being similar to others. "My religion has no unchangeable approaches on the resemblance of people to other people" (EP145), one wrote, commenting that any beliefs about this were created by people. Another student stated, "I do not know what Islam suggests on this subject" (EP122). She did say that "we are all reflections of God" and that God evaluates people "equally" but that the things people do during their lives "make them different from one another" (EP122). In contrast, another who also was not sure what

Islam had to say about being similar to others said she thought of how "similarities in physical appearance and character" and how being raised in the same religious "environment" can lead people to be similar to each other (EP3, EP34). Another noted the same thing, and then said, "I just know that religion tells me I am equal with everyone no matter what their religion is" (EP27). In turn, that led to her wishing that "the prejudice of the believer towards the unbeliever and vice versa would end" (EP27).

Responses seldom led to thoughts of helping others. Instead, there were mentions of whether or how religion created similarities, other aspects of being similar or not, and problems associated with those topics (EP34, EP55). One student observed, "Being good or evil could be an inborn characteristic. Then isn't it God that created this difference from the beginning?" (EP107). One concluded that "being united with a person or a community should not be based on being a member of the same religion" (EP55). Another saw religion as a means of establishing "resemblances between ourselves and many other people" (EP57); it was not the religion that suggested people were similar, but the belonging to it that created similarities.

For some, the prompt brought forth thoughts about following "the way of our elders who taught us the religious and moral rules" (EP203). One, while not commenting on whether or how Islam teaches that he is similar to others, thought about how "Islam is not only about this world but also about the afterlife." He concluded, thus, "So I should love and help other people" (EP760). One woman commented about how "when I read the Qur'an, I feel very comfortable and happy … When I think of God, I feel tranquil" (EP230). Another participant also concluded by saying, "the presence of God, which provides for all our needs, relaxes me" (EP717, EP728).

Our survey of the Catholic and Muslim essays on similarity to others can be summarized as finding that Catholics brought up a wide array of ideas that emphasized both similarities and particularities of individuals. While some equated all human beings as the creatures of God, others saw them as different because God created every human being as unique. To some, religion did not teach that human beings are equal, while to others it encouraged its adherents to love all humanity. Some thought that everyone is similar because of their belief that everybody is born Catholic. The idea of being similar led some participants to not judge or condemn others quickly. For instance, one saw the idea of being similar as hypocritical because she thought that women were discriminated at the church.

Muslims also did not come up with one unified view on similarity to others. While some participants saw all human beings as equal regardless of race or religion, others saw themselves different from the rest. While some acknowledged that religion does not have any fixed viewpoint on the similarity to others, others saw themselves as similar to others because all are the servants of God. To some, human beings are similar, as they are all reflections of God, but for others, they are different because God created them different.

Conclusion

In this survey of results from the experiment essays about the deservedness of the needy, community expectations, and similarity to others, we have seen that concepts associated with religious beliefs are imbued with multiple meanings, some more so than others.

We noted in Chapter 4 that the experiments led to no statistically significant results for Muslims' generosity behavior based on the essay condition to which they had been assigned. That being said, it is clear from the essays that the Muslim participants were highly attuned to the responsibility of helping those in need. This came through strongly in the deservedness essays.

The essays show that we cannot assume that religious terms will be "neutral" or "positive" in the minds of experiment participants (*pace* Pichon et al. 2007). For instance, while both Catholicism and Islam have teachings about how people are all equal, in response to being asked about their religion's teachings on their similarity to others, Catholics and Muslim often discussed whether this was actually the case, and some pointed out that similarity is not the same as being equal. For some Muslims and Catholics, thinking about what their religion said about the deservedness of those needing help led to feelings of helplessness in the face of intense needs. We cannot assume that the concepts mean to the adherents what we think they do.

Another concept that had a meaning that seemed a bit different from what social scientists have tended to give it was "community expectations." When asked what the expectations were of their religious communities, a number of Muslims pointed out that what was more important were the expectations of the religion, of God, as opposed to the community. The latter was a means toward the end, and thus not in itself the primary source of moral behavior. Most Catholics, including the adult community members, indicated the community did not have high expectations. Some pointed to changes in the Church over time as contributing to that. Because the Church does not have a monitoring and sanctioning capacity for financial donations, and because that capacity is weak to nonexistent in Islam, as discussed in Chapter 2, Catholics' and Muslims' perceptions of community expectations may also have been low. Also, what Catholics and Muslims identified as the community varied: it could be the parish, the Islamic association, the society, the Catholic Church as an institution, or the worldwide community of believers in the respective faith. This heterogeneity in delineating what the community was may be due to the relative openness of the two faiths in interacting with multiple groups and layers in their societies, and the fact that their adherents are not hived off in strict sects that structure and monitor the bulk of their lives.

Taking Chapters 4 and 5 into account, the essays on religious concepts about one's relationship with God show that we cannot assume that religious terms mean to the adherent what outside observers and researchers assume. For instance, "God's grace," seemingly a positive term, generated comments in the Catholic essays about the corruption of the Church, about personal losses, religious hypocrisy, and guilt, in addition to the expected, more positive thoughts of peace, tranquility, and caring for others. Similarly, although God's grace might be more familiar as a Christian concept, the essays showed that God's grace also resonated with Muslims.

As opposed to many scholars' tendency to present Islam as a religion in which the idea of a "watchful God" prompts people to behave in certain way, the essays did not necessarily confirm this tendency. However, the essays also showed that Muslims have a strong feeling of duty to God as compared with their Catholic counterparts. While both Catholicism and Islam have teachings about human equality, in response to being asked about their religion's teachings on their similarity to others, Catholics and Muslims often discussed whether this was actually the case, and some pointed out that similarity is not the same as being equal. For some Muslims and Catholics, thinking about what their religion said about the deservedness of those needing help led to bleak feelings of powerlessness in the face of overwhelming needs.

The essays also reflected some sociological realities. In the essays by Catholics, societal issues such as the Irish recession were often mentioned. Some of these essays contained concerns about events in the Catholic Church, particularly the clergy child sex abuse scandal, in which it had become apparent that the Catholic hierarchy had for decades tolerated and protected priests and other religious officials who were sexually abusing children. Perhaps not surprisingly, "disillusionment" was a common theme in the Catholic essays from the community expectations prompts. We also saw a manifestation of some shifts in Catholicism across generations, in that Catholic adults noted that expectations are much less rigorous than when they were children, while some Catholic students commented that they did not feel any pressure. Changes in the Church due to Vatican II, as well as changes in society, likely contributed to those perceptions. Similarly, the less critical stance of the adult Muslim community members may have been due to their having deliberately chosen to join the Gülen movement, one of several Turkish Islamic religious associations they could have joined. In contrast, Muslims generally did not associate community expectations with negative thoughts, emotions, or events.

The recognition that sociological circumstances shape how people respond to primes should be a reminder that context is important (Bargh 2006). We cannot simply ask, "What does religion prime?" without further considering that religion may prime different things for people in different circumstances and contexts. Essay primes are one tool social psychologists use in experiments, but seldom are the contents of the essays analyzed. In this and the preceding chapter, we took the opportunity to do so, in order to better understand what a set of key beliefs means to Catholics and Muslims. In the next chapter, we examine which of those beliefs the adherents themselves see as connected to their generous behavior, and what motivates their contributing to their religious communities.

6

Belief, Belonging, and Giving in Catholic Parishes and Muslim Associations

Immediately after taking office in 2001, US President George W. Bush signed an Executive Order creating the Office of Faith-Based and Community Initiatives, declaring, "Faith-based and other community organizations are indispensable in meeting the needs of poor Americans and distressed neighborhoods" (Bush 2001). In May 2014, Turkey's Prime Minister Recep Tayyip Erdoğan stated that religious charities "contribute to the just distribution of welfare and wealth" (Erdoğan 2014). Bush's and Erdoğan's views are not exceptional. Many countries rely explicitly or tacitly on organized religions to carry out social welfare functions. To engage in these activities, including sustaining the organizations themselves, organized religions require resources from a variety of sources, most especially their adherents. While debates continue about whether state-provided social welfare displaces ("crowds out") religious charities and religious belief, and whether the organized religions are more capable of providing social welfare than is the public sector (Dahlberg 2005; Fridolfsson and Elander 2012; Gill 2013; Hungerman 2005; Traunmüller and Freitag 2011), less attention has focused on what should be a critical question for politics and policy: what motivates religious adherents to contribute to the charitable work of their religions? Clearly, political leaders see religion as an important source of charity and social welfare provision. Do the faithful themselves think their religion is a source of their charitable actions? And if so, what aspects of their religion do they think are influential?

In this chapter, we address these questions by studying what Catholics and Muslims think motivates them to be generous toward others through their giving and volunteering. To recap what we discussed in Chapter 1, both Islam and Catholicism encourage other-regarding, charitable acts, and each uses the examples of their primary religious figure as behavioral

143

standards. Catholicism and Islam also differ in important ways. Though New Testament texts "suggest strongly the centrality of giving and service to the religious life," Catholicism has no formal call to giving as a sacrament of the faith (Catechism of the Catholic Church 1999, 461; Queen 1996, 27). In contrast, Islam has several explicitly described institutions of charity, the most well-known of which is the zakat, one of the five pillars of Islam (Benthall and Bellion-Jourdan 2003, 7–44; Kozlowski 1998).[1] Catholicism is hierarchically organized; Islam is decentralized. Catholic beliefs stress choice; Islamic beliefs stress obligation. We are interested in whether these differences manifest themselves in how adherents of the two religions view their responsibility to give and help their organizations.

Through our case studies in Chapter 2, we have seen that the institutional structures of Catholicism and Islam do not have effective monitoring and sanctioning mechanisms that might prompt individuals to help others. Through the experiments in Chapter 3, we have seen that Catholics respond with generosity to the concepts of God's grace and what their religion says about the deservedness of the needy. We also found indications that concepts of God's grace, duty to God, community expectations, and deservedness prompt Muslims to think about concepts related to charity. Chapters 4 and 5 showed the range of thoughts and emotions that the full set of religious concepts, hypothesized to prompt people to behave generously, brought forth. We turn back to our case studies to see what it is in those beliefs that leads Catholics and Muslims to be generous, and to learn what it is in the religious communities that elicits volunteering and donations of funds. The in-depth interviews within our case studies enable us to probe concepts and motives and find out how generosity is lived in the parishes and associations.

As major world religions with a growing share of the world population, Catholicism and Islam are significant potential generators of charitable giving and volunteering. Understanding whether and, if so, how, Catholics' and Muslims' beliefs create motivations to give is an essential step in increasing our knowledge of how religions contribute to public welfare. While it is commonly stated that all religions have a "golden rule" of helping others, it does not automatically follow that all religions use the

---

[1] Although there are not mechanisms to monitor whether Muslims practice zakat, or obligatory charitable giving, and there are many Muslims who do not, and although how it is practiced has changed over time (see discussion in Chapter 2), zakat is typically thought to be one of the key requirements of Islamic practice. We discuss below what our interviewees thought of it.

same theological beliefs to ground that rule or that the adherents understand them in the same way (Prothero 2010). The goal of this chapter is to contribute to an understanding of what role the adherents think their beliefs are playing in their motivations to give to their religious organizations, including volunteering their time and effort.

The literature that specifically focuses on religion and generosity tends to give weight to two factors that affect generosity at the individual level. Some argue that the key factor prompting helping behavior is the intrinsic beliefs, others that it is the community aspect of the faith (Graham and Haidt 2010; Putnam and Campbell 2010). Those who stress the role of beliefs debate what aspects of religious faiths create differences in the generosity of their adherents (Miller 1999; Smith and Emerson 2008; Tropman 2002). They examine the content of the beliefs, with some arguing that what matters is a perception of a punitive deity, and others that what matters is a perception of a benevolent deity or sensations of spirituality (Hadnes and Schumacher 2012; Johnson et al. 2013; Lee, Paloma, and Post 2012; Shariff and Norenzayan 2007; Stanczak 2006). Those who look at the role of community focus on religion and social engagement (e.g., Bartkowski and Regis 2003; Candland 2000; Djupe and Neiheisel 2012; Miller and Yamamori 2007; Unruh and Sider 2005; Wuthnow 2009; Wuthnow and Evans 2002). The community is seen to affect other-oriented behavior through its norms and expectations. This dovetails with the emphasis of the economics of religion school on the monitoring and sanctioning capacities of the religions (Berman and Laitin 2008; Cnaan 2002, 296; McBride 2007). What remains to be explored is whether there are systematic differences between how community expectations in Catholicism and Islam are perceived by community members, and how this affects Catholics' and Muslims' contributions to the collective goods of the group.

In addition, an overlooked variable in the study of cooperative interaction is the "positive affect," that is, positive emotions that members might have toward a group (Tyler 2011). The positive affect individuals have toward their group can be an integral part of helping and engaging with others (Collins 2004). It thus is something that may have a role in generating generous actions by Catholics and Muslims (Corcoran 2015; Fowler and Kam 2007; Smith 2006). While a rational choice approach would see this as a mere quid pro quo – individuals give and volunteer because they get a commensurate emotional satisfaction out of doing so, a "warm glow," to quote economists (Andreoni 1990; Hungerman 2009) – this feature of a religious community's role in public goods provision needs more attention from political scientists. An intriguing hint comes from a study of "what terrorists really want." It finds what is key is affective ties to others: friendship and community (Abrahms 2008). Positive affect highlights the importance of a prosocial orientation in generating collective goods. The implication is that individuals are not just strictly rational, selfish noncooperators who can be induced to help each other only with monitoring and sanctioning mechanisms.

Building on these literatures on individual-level attitudes on faith and belonging, we assess whether the faithful themselves are aware of the influence of belief and community on their generosity, and see whether there are differences between Catholics and Muslims in how they think about their prosocial, generous behavior that leads to provision of club or public goods. Learning the ways people describe their actions provides a window on how, if at all, their religious beliefs and communities have affected their understanding of generosity. In this chapter, we are interested in the religious motivations of the faithful in their giving to others, including volunteering in activities intended to help others.

The chapter is based on 218 semi-structured interviews with approximately 25–30 individuals in a Catholic parish and in a Muslim association in each city. Parishes and associations were chosen on the basis of referrals, and the process of gaining access varied by city. We recruited both those who attend regularly and those who are on the membership rolls but do not attend regularly. We also recruited from a range of socioeconomic strata.[2] All interviews were conducted at locations of the interviewees' choosing. This was typically a room in a building owned by the parish or association, in their home, a café, or restaurant; some interviews were held at the interviewee's place of business. The field research was conducted in various months from May 2010 to May 2011, taking pains to avoid major religious holidays that might have over-primed generosity. For each city, we spent approximately four weeks with a religious group.

The interviews lasted between thirty minutes and two hours. They included questions about what interviewees think their faith's teachings are on generosity and helping others, what their obligations and responsibilities are to help others, and why they think they engage in helping, giving actions. We asked what their interaction is with their religious community, and whether, how, and why they volunteer in it or give funds to it or other organizations. We invited them to comment on anything we should have asked them about but did not. With the exception of some

---

[2] See Chapter 1 and Tables A.1 and A.2 in the Appendix for information about locations, access, and interviewee demographics.

Catholics in Istanbul, each interview was conducted in the mother tongue of the interviewee.[3]

We systematically assessed the interviewees' responses to our questions by reviewing the recorded interviews and noting emergent themes. We compared these across groups in different cities, and between religions, in order to see whether themes were unique to locations or whether they were common across groups in the same religion, and to see whether interviews needed to be assessed again for nuances regarding themes. This technique enables us to see themes that a more quantitative approach, with the content coding of word or counting word frequency, may miss. It also forces us to note themes that may not accord with prior expectations (Leech 2002; Lofland et al. 2005; Schaffer 2006; Thomas 2006). We are not constructing ideal types that are meant to represent or apply to all Catholics and Muslims; we have the more modest goal of drawing on Catholics' and Muslims' discussions of their generosity to examine how, if at all, they find their religious beliefs and communities influence their giving.

Our interviews show that Catholics and Muslims articulate different faith-based motivations in their contributions to their religious communities. Generally, Catholics do not feel or believe that they have a duty to God to help others and to be generous to their organizations. Instead, they think of their giving as helpful for the needy and an expression of God's grace and love. In contrast to Catholics, Muslims often link their giving to fulfillment of a duty to God. To Muslims, the act of giving for the sake of God is more important than its beneficial consequences for the recipient. The religious community plays a significant role in both Catholics' and Muslims' giving. Catholics and Muslims indicated that they derived emotional satisfaction from helping the community. While much research has tended to stress the role of communities in monitoring and sanctioning individuals as a means of compelling "generosity," Catholics' understandings of their religious community does not conform to that model and Muslims' only slightly.

Belief and Charitable Giving

Our Catholic interviewees were emphatic that their generosity is not a duty and that they are not facing a punitive God. To the extent that our Catholic

---

[3] Some Catholics in the Istanbul parish were immigrants from countries of which the interviewer did not speak the home country language. In those cases, the interviews were conducted in Turkish or English, depending on the preference of the interviewee.

parishioners understand their generosity as coinciding with the teaching of the faith, they understand it as stemming from love for one another, from following Jesus' example of loving one's neighbor. In line with the Islamic emphasis on obedience to God's will, our Muslim interviews demonstrated that Muslims see their giving to their religious institutions as fulfillment of a duty to God. For Muslims, love for God cannot be separated from the idea of duty to God.

Only two of 94 Catholic interviewees answered "yes" to the question: "do you have a duty to God to help others and to give?," and each immediately qualified it as a "requirement," not a "duty" (PC17), saying, "God requires you to help others" (DC22).[4] As an Italian interviewee in his thirties stated, "Jesus didn't say 'you have to do this.' Jesus said 'this is the path, you choose'" (MC6). An Irish parishioner echoes this view: "God gives me a choice. God prompts me and he allows me to say yes or no and I know if I say yes he's going to be there with me all the time." (DC9). The common theme was interpreting their generosity as coming "from love" (DC20, PC5). It seemed linked to a sense of God's grace. Many interviewees see this love as a source of charity and voluntarism toward others, but they do not see this as the point or goal of such love (DC1, DC11). Many cited the Gospel of Matthew's famous saying, "Inasmuch as ye have done it unto one of the least of these my brethren, ye have done it unto me" (Lindsell 1965, 1482, 25:40). An Italian Catholic parishioner in his forties interpreted the verse as Jesus saying, "[G]o encounter others, including the poor; don't abandon them" (MC13). Jesus is telling him what to do, but he does it because of God's love, not because of a duty to God (or Jesus). An Irish parishioner stressed that helping and giving is "not a duty, there have been opportunities. I was drifting a bit, the door opened" (DC1). Another responded that "you're not morally bound, I suppose, to give … It's part of Catholic teaching to be charitable, part of your religion and belief that you must help the deprived." He used the phrase "must help," but he rejected the idea that helping others was a duty or obligation to God (DC11). It was a general "you should" and not one mandated by God (DC2). Our Catholic interviewees understood that they should help others, but did not see that as a duty to God; they linked it instead to the importance of everyone contributing to the community: "charity is part of Christian life" (PC7).

---

[4] We assign each interviewee a code to preserve the anonymity of our interviewees. In coding the interviews, we used the initial of the city, religious affiliation of the interviewee, and a number. For example, the first Catholic interviewee in Milan is coded as MC1, the third Muslim interviewee in Dublin is coded as DM3.

Another responded, rejecting the idea of a duty to God, that "nothing is obligatory" (PC2). Some explained their helping others with reference to empathy: "it could be me in that situation" (PC4).

A striking difference with Catholicism is that none of our 124 Muslim interviewees answered "no" to the question: "do you have a duty to God to help others and to give?" Islam emphasizes obedience to God's will. If God's will is that the individual be generous, then religiosity affects generosity by raising Muslims' sense of an obligation to God. It is "for the love of God" that one gives to others (Qur'an 2/177). This belief is a significant factor in our Muslim interviewees' understanding of their generosity. The vast majority understands their giving as a duty to God. Most Muslim respondents think that when they give, they give from resources that belong to God (e.g., IM2, IM20, PM7). They see their money and belongings "as God's deposit" on them. A male interviewee in his thirties from Istanbul illustrates this point: "We do not see money and our belongings as our own property. We see them as God's deposit on us. We can fulfill our responsibility if we use that deposit properly. Giving for the sake of God is one way of fulfilling that responsibility" (IM7). A number of respondents (PM5, MM1, MM6, IM24, DM9, DM16) mentioned the following verse from the Qur'an to emphasize that what they had was not for only their consumption: "Behold, God has bought of the believers their lives and their possessions, promising them paradise in return" (Qur'an 9/111). In explaining their motivations to give to others, the interviewees also referred to Muslims from the time of the Prophet Muhammad and their giving as a model. It was clear from their answers that the interviewees established a direct link between religiosity and giving, as giving is considered a significant religious duty. To show the centrality of giving in religious teachings and history, one Muslim from Istanbul noted, "Abu Bakr [the first caliph and the closest friend of the Prophet Muhammad] used all of his wealth for the sake of God and to help others" (IM18).[5]

While our interview questions did not ask directly if interviewees thought "God is watching you," very few Catholic interviewees (PC17, PC14) thought that God or Jesus would judge them based on whether or not they were helping others. Those few who mentioned being judged explained that the duty to help is toward others, not God. We owe our

---

[5] Many respondents mentioned Abu Bakr as an example of generosity and giving. The veracity of the belief that the caliph Abu Bakr actually used all his wealth to help others is difficult to establish. However, we should note that many of our respondents thought of him as an exceptional example of being generous.

neighbors our assistance; God will judge later what one has done with one's life (PC17, DC16). A French interviewee mentioned being "Pascalian," referencing Pascal's wager and also pointing to the verses of Matthew 25:41–46 in which Jesus condemns to hell those who did not aid him by aiding others (PC14). Not only is it good to help others, but not doing so could have unpleasant ramifications in the afterlife. This interviewee pointed out that generosity is from the heart, not merely "what is due" to another person. Even for those who perceived a judgmental God, generosity is not a duty to God; it is a manifestation of God's love in them.

In contrast to Catholics, many Muslims stated that God has been and will be judging them for their generosity or for the lack of it. Many Muslim interviewees argued that if they do not give funds, God causes them to lose money anyway because they have not fulfilled their duty to God. For example, one of the interviewees said that whenever he skips helping his association, he is caught by a traffic cop and has to pay as a fine the money he otherwise should have given to his association (PM3). An interviewee from Istanbul echoed the point: "If you do not give to the places that you are required to give, that [amount] will be taken from you eventually. You will experience a problem and lose it anyway" (IM13). These respondents see these incidents as reflections of God's compassion: God is warning them, with what they perceive to be gentle nudges, about their misbehavior (e.g., PM3).

To Catholics, because Jesus' and God's love does not have to be earned, earning it through giving to others (or to God via donations to the church) is irrelevant. A parishioner from Istanbul said, "God loves those who follow what Jesus did [meaning helping those in need]," but she did not view this as something one had to do to gain God's approval (IC13). An Italian Catholic said he understood the teachings to be saying "resemble Jesus more" (MC14). An Irish parishioner explained that "it's voluntary, you don't have to give. I feel very obliged to support my church" (DC9). She mentioned that "[i]f you're asked to do something or somebody suggests something, or you have a thought, you have a responsibility. I don't know whether you call it faith or spirituality or responsibility" (DC9). Parishioners who linked their giving with specific scriptures often noted, as one concisely stated, that "there are only two commandments that matter: love God and love your neighbor" (DC10).

To Muslims, though, God's love needs to be earned through pleasing God. Pleasing God requires fulfillment of duties, charitable giving being one of those. To some Muslims, the duty is paying the zakat, and pleasing God through good work. Many interviewees, especially those who are more engaged in the associations, did not even mention the obligation of zakat. When asked why they did not refer to zakat, they responded that zakat sets the minimum amount of giving. To them, real giving is giving beyond zakat. When asked if zakat motivates him to give more, a Parisian male respondent in his fifties replied: "Zakat and fitr are of course important. They are part of our religion and we have to respect them. And we fulfill our responsibilities of zakat and fitr. But how can we do all the activities that we need to do by only relying on zakat?" (PM18). While duty to God was prevalent among the Muslim interviewees, it was not only a feeling obligation, but also an effort to please God through fulfilling duties.

The main message our Catholic interviewees conveyed is that they do not feel or believe they have a duty to God to help others, to be generous. As one French Catholic put it, the idea of an obligation to God "has no sense" (PC4). A Dublin parishioner said, "God gives me a choice" (DC9); another said the duty was a "duty to find out what you should believe" (DC10). Some Catholic interviewees noted, instead, a sense of obligation to the priest or nun: when they were asked if they would be willing to take on a task, they accepted because they were being asked by a religious official they viewed with respect and/or whom they admired (DC6, MC2, MC15, IC3, IC7). Similarly, as we mentioned in Chapter 2, a French parishioner said that when the new head priest (*curé*) arrived in the parish, the priest asked him and his wife what they did in the church? The interviewee said he and his wife immediately signed up to be volunteers (PC14). A parishioner from Istanbul said that "when Father Giorgis asks our group to do something, we do our best to please him" (IC3). Another parishioner, an immigrant from Thailand in the same church, concurs: "we are a small community and the priests here cannot do everything in the church. We should make things easier for them" (IC7). Some noted they gave it some thought, particularly when the volunteer activity required a significant commitment of time and energy (MC14, PC13, PC16). In keeping with this, some interviewees spoke of "intelligent volunteering," not just "blindly giving" of time and money (MC14). Many said they were asked to help out with a specific activity or group and did so from a desire to help and a sense of responsibility. The interviewees indicated that, on the whole, they did not volunteer out of a sense of duty to God.

Instead of duty to God, many Catholics mentioned family upbringing or schooling as main reason why they are generous and engaged in helping behaviors. An older Irishman stated that "it's something in you, [it] all stems from parents," adding that when he was young, "everybody was poor at that time in Ireland. You shared anything you had and you contributed that way in life" (DC11, DC12). A Parisian parishioner said it was "natural" because she had been raised by people for whom it was, and that the "fact that it was natural for them is also linked to the faith, also linked to the fact that they are believers" (PC19). A devout French Catholic raised in the Church and who frequently attends mass and leads volunteer groups in the parish credited his participation in Boy Scouts as giving him his sense of wanting to help others (PC10). Others understood their generosity as being part of the "Catholic culture," which is something they became aware of as adults (MC13), or having a "social Catholic" upbringing and having a "1968 generation" background (MC5). One parishioner, who mostly saw her generosity as influenced by her upbringing, pointed to a culture of giving as well: "Irish people are very generous, anyways, because we had nothing. And our history tells us we had nothing. So we are generous when we have it" (DC9). Still others cited an experience with a religious order or group (DC11, MC14, MC17, PC13). One summarized the source of the helping orientation as "being brought up within the Catholic Church to help. It was part of your religion; it's engrained in all of us. We're all what we were born into" (DC11). A Milanese parishioner saw his Catholic upbringing and the Gospels as having taught him to "go encounter others, including the poor, do not abandon others" (MC13, MC16). Another said the faith leads one toward "a consideration of others" (MC14). Catholic interviewees linked their helping others to a belief that that is what Jesus would want, not out of a sense of duty to God. A middle-aged Parisian Catholic summed it up as "charity is a part of Christian life" (PC7).

Finally, a common refrain was that of actualizing one's faith (PC11). As an Irish parishioner said, "I kind of feel from my own personal faith, to make it real, I need to be doing something" (DC14). For some, generosity is both in Church teachings and automatic. As one active (retired) Ballygall parish volunteer put it, it is "very much so" in church teachings. But, he added, "I never really think about; it's part of life, you just help people out. Basically, if I was in same situation it's nice to know people are there for you to help you out; that's it; it's part of the teaching, alright, of Catholicism" (DC12). Another Ballygall parishioner said, "I would say it's a basic Christian principle that in some way you share; if you can do it, maybe a few coins, and then the church does provide a vehicle for that … ; I'd see it as being a fairly basic tenet" (DC14).

The Muslim interviewees strongly indicated that since giving is a duty to God, the act itself is more valuable than its consequences that produce collective benefits. An anecdote that a Parisian woman (PM11) told clearly shows this outlook. When one of her neighbors declined her request to help her religious association, she considered finding a job in order to be able to contribute more to the association, instead of asking others to give funds to it. Although she could have contributed more money to the association by working than she would have been able to collect from others, she changed her mind because, in her view, this option would have prevented her from helping others to fulfill their responsibility to God. She thought that all Muslims have the responsibility to give and that by prodding them to donate funds, she was helping them fulfill that responsibility. She saw this as in itself very valuable (PM11). Along these lines, the interviewees often talked about how the stories of the generosity of the companions of the Prophet Muhammad influenced their own giving. Those role models were linked to a duty to God to give to others. One Muslim from Istanbul noted: "Why did God give us our resources? It is for us to use those resources wisely and responsibly ... Abu Bakr used all of his wealth in the path of God and to help others. He is a good model for us to follow" (IM18).

As a motivation for their giving, Muslims emphasized fulfilling their responsibility to God rather than solving the actual problem that the help targeted. An Istanbul interviewee stated that God tests a wealthy person to see if they would give or not, while God tests a poor person to see whether or not they would be patient. To the interviewee, both of their responsibilities (to give and to be patient) are to God, not to one another (IM14). Another respondent concurred that he had a responsibility to help the poor and needy "to gain God's approval" (IM21). Another Muslim from Istanbul echoes: "When we give to others, we actually invest in ourselves. At first sight, it looks like we did something for someone else. But in reality, we discharge a big responsibility in transferring God's property to those in need" (IM18). A man from Milan concurs with these points: "If I help someone, I do not expect any gratitude from that person in return ... I help that person because God asks me to help those in need" (MM6).

In keeping with this view, our Muslim interviewees conceptualize their giving to their religious associations in terms of their duty to God. A Parisian Muslim, for example, explained her support of the religious association as fulfilling her responsibility to God since the association reaches out to "those who are in material or spiritual need" (PM5). It was less a matter of helping a community of coreligionists than of fulfilling an obligation to God (MM3, MM11, PM11, DM12, IM5). In contrast to the Catholic Church, there is no equivalent idea of a community of faithful as the *body* of a holy figure, but members want to support the community because they believe that by doing so they fulfill a duty to God.

Given the obvious difference between Catholics and Muslims in their understanding of the relationship between duty to God and giving, one might argue that the differences they identified are a function of using secular and religious language to explain motivations for personal and community actions. The implication is that the reference to duty to God among Muslims is a derivation of the fact that Catholics are more secularized than Muslims. This argument is less persuasive for our cases. Although different people in different religions could understand duty to God in different ways, we think that duty to God is by definition a religious concept. Both Catholic and Islamic teachings have always emphasized helping those in need and being other-oriented. Furthermore, our Catholic interviewees spoke about helping others in religious terms, with frequent reference to the Gospels and to the example of Jesus; they just did not view contributing to the collective good as a *duty* to God. As one said, it is "truly a disposition of the heart" (PC3).

Belonging and Charitable Giving

As the previous section indicated, Catholics and Muslims often referenced their religious communities when speaking of their generosity, their giving, and their volunteering. Almost all the Catholic interviewees mentioned the importance of their immediate communities and their parishes for their giving. They explained their helping behaviors in terms that indicated a positive orientation, or "positive affect," for group interaction. Catholics who gave of their time often said that they liked to be with people and to be collaborating in a helpful undertaking. To them, the engagement enhanced their religious life. The community also fostered a sense of trust, which may have facilitated giving and volunteering. Muslims similarly emphasized the role of community in their giving. Although duty to God is the major motivation to support their organizations, attachment to their communities also motivates Muslims to give. Muslims often mentioned the satisfaction that they receive from being engaged with their communities. While much research has tended to stress the role of communities in monitoring and sanctioning individuals as a means of compelling "generosity," Catholics' understandings of their religious community do not conform to that model and Muslims' only slightly. Instead, positive affect for the community is a dominant theme.

Catholic parishes formed the context for the religious community most of our interviewees spoke about. Interviewees also spoke of the organizations they volunteered in and the religious orders where they attended seminars. Parishes are, for Catholics, the place where "new Christians are born and raised" (DC25). Our interviewees varied in their involvement and attachment to their parish; they all explained their helping behaviors in terms that indicate a positive affect for group interaction. Individuals who gave of their time often voiced that they liked to be with people, to be focused on something, to be collaborating. It was clear from observing the activities of the Society of St. Vincent de Paul at Santa Maria alla Fontana in Milan, and the *Pain Partagé* group at Saint-Pierre de Montrouge in Paris, that the charitable work was as much a magnet and outlet for warm socializing as it was for the activity itself. Catholics see their generosity as inhering in the community. One Ballygall parishioner stated that "it's a basic part of your Christianity, it kind of flows from a kind of basic Christian community. The basic Christian community should not be an inward community it should be an outward community; so I think that's the basis of it; and then the Catholic Church takes that up in its various ways" (DC14). Another noted that Catholic teachings stress the sense of community, the obligation to the community. He said, "Teachings of faith: all community isn't it? Love your neighbor I suppose is the basic tenet and how that manifests itself in practice ... fundamentally the teaching is, ... you're helping your neighbor as the lord told us to help our neighbor" (DC16). A Parisian Catholic woman in her late thirties commented on how refreshing it was to be engaged in a group that worked for no pay, in which no one was trying to "move up in rank," no one was trying to "earn something for themselves," and in which everyone was focused on something that would benefit others (PC19). For many, the engagement with their religious community in a volunteer project was a key element of living their faith.

There were hints that the religious communities, that is, the parishes, fostered trust, which in turn gave adherents more confidence in giving to them. Our interviews show that Catholics are more comfortable in contributing to their own local churches (MC13, PC10). Some Ballygall parishioners, as well as the head priest (DC28), expressed concern over the impending merging of parish operations ("clustering"), thinking the community spirit of the parish would be diminished. Father Brendan Quinlan noted it seemed the Church had "lost the personal touch of the local chaplain" (DC28). Some parishioners were concerned that people might not be as willing to volunteer or give if their efforts went to a bigger entity less known to them. A Catholic parishioner in Dublin indicated the power of familiarity and trust within the community for eliciting generosity. In speaking of the planned "clustering," he said, "I probably wouldn't volunteer if somebody came from another parish and said 'do you want to do this?' I'd be very suspect ... I'm fine if the priest I know signs the checkbook but not if I don't know the priest" (DC10). Familiarity within the context of their religious associations may have facilitated some giving by Muslims, as well. Several noted that knowing the specifics of the works to which they donated time and funds gave them confidence to give more. A businessman in his fifties stated, "What motivates me is to see what is being done. That opens my eyes. That gives me new ideals and dreams. When you are in the movement and see what is being done, you understand the need and your worldview is shaped accordingly" (IM21, PM1).

Catholic interviewees expressed a strong sense of being connected to others, of having a responsibility to others: "Something just in me says you must pay back, you must give something back to society; God obviously is working in me, my faith is there, otherwise I wouldn't do it" (DC9). Interviewees expressed a sense of reciprocity: it is a matter of "treating others as you'd like to be treated yourself" (DC3). Another Dublin parishioner said, "Basically, if I was in same situation it's nice to know people are there for you to help you out" (DC12). A Santa Maria alla Fontana Catholic noted that she tries to give of herself to others as much as possible. She sees her giving "as a bit of circle in life: you give then as you get older you may need others to assist you" (MC1). Another stated that she had, for a long time, "a sense that I was blessed in my life, fortunate in my life, I know there are a lot of people for whom life is a lot harder; if I could help people, I'd like to" (DC1; cf., PC3). A Parisian Catholic observed that the fact that the parish community was the "place of confession" was a reason she gave to it (PC11).

Many Catholic interviewees are fond of the parishes they belong to, and they like working in the groups they are in or have volunteered with before. Parishioners expressed satisfaction with their experiences of working with other parishioners in the various organizations they volunteered in, and feelings of affection toward the priest, sister (nun), or friend who invited them to get involved (e.g., MC2). This was evident among the congregants of the St. Esprit Church in Istanbul (and was also voiced by a number of the experiment participants in their essays, e.g., EP368, EP596, EP655). The community provides a sense of belonging. While the older volunteers mostly referred their loyalty to the church (IC5, IC6, IC20), the younger and immigrant members mostly addressed the friendship within the church (IC3, IC10, IC23, IC24). The participants of a church-based volunteer group, the Legion of Mary in Istanbul, indicated how they deepen their friendship while doing "good things" for others (IC3, IC10, IC25). In the words of a Filipino woman who migrated to Turkey in 1990s: "when I first came to Turkey, a friend brought me to this church. I felt at home and since then I contribute to the church either financially or by volunteering" (IC3). For most of the immigrants, the church is seen as a place where their problems are addressed within small friendship groups. No one voiced a concern about peer pressure or being socially sanctioned for not contributing or volunteering. An Irish parishioner, in explaining why he volunteered at the parish, said he couldn't quite put his finger on it – "I can't really point to any Damascus moment here or a homily or see it on the walls, it's just they put out the appeals, and I got involved." He added that "it's also enjoyable, it's one of the main things" (DC16).

In all four parishes we studied, Catholics spoke of the powerful effect volunteering has on their experience of their faith. A Milan parishioner stated that "sharing unites a bit of the heart" (MC15, PC13). To many, helping within the parish or with a Catholic charity is seen as furthering the work of Jesus or of the Church in the world. Those Catholics who volunteered in activities that sustained the religious life of the parish, such as the children's ministry, reading the liturgy, or being on the baptism or funeral team, often noted that doing so enabled them to attain a greater understanding of their faith and noted that that was important and rewarding to them (e.g., DC1, DC2, PC3, PC19, DC13, IC16, MC5, MC14).

Many Muslim respondents also mentioned that the close friendship among the members of the community was an important factor in creating a giving-friendly environment. They noted that because they see other members of the association at least once weekly, they develop social bonds. A furniture storeowner from Istanbul described the relationship between friendship and giving in the following way: "Being involved in this movement made giving part of our personality. It is because you become part of a new social environment. Here, we compete to do good things ... I cannot stop working in the face of the needs of so many people" (IM17).

One of the key factors both Catholic and Muslim interviewees mentioned when asked why they give or volunteer was that they received so much more than they gave, thanks mostly to their engagement with their communities. The interviewees voiced surprise at the extent of the positive impact their helping others had on themselves. In Milan, several parishioners commented on the friendships they have developed through their volunteer activities, and that that inspires them to keep volunteering (MC1, MC2). Several others, who volunteered with *Caritas Ambrosiano* in Milan, said the "spirit of the group" was a key part of what kept them engaged (MC25, MC26). For some, including the *Caritas* volunteers just mentioned, this spirit had something of a transcendent quality that was life-giving: "it's oxygen" (PC19). Many interviewees who were volunteers said they got back more than they gave, that they thought it was more rewarding for them than for the people they helped, and that they learned from those they helped. As an Italian Catholic stated, "I get repaid abundantly" (MC4, MC2, MC3), echoing the feelings of an Irish Catholic parishioner who stated, "I get as much pleasure out of doing it as benefit to the parish" (DC6). A French volunteer stated that "one receives a thousand times more than one gives" (PC13; also PC19, PC5). One noted that "our success is the joy and smile of those who participate" (PC2). A number of interviewees voiced that by helping they are "giving thanks for what you got" and that because of this they want to "help the people who aren't" healthy or otherwise "ok" (DC2). A retired Frenchwoman said she feels she's been "spoiled by life" and got involved because she wanted to "give back" some of what she had received (PC3). A retired woman in Istanbul also mentioned her satisfaction when she saw that "the needs of the poor immigrants are met" within their volunteer group (IC16). The complex role of community for Catholics was summarized by one parishioner: "I receive a great sense of community, a great sense of togetherness, of acceptance, of love from people. You couldn't buy that and if you went looking for it you couldn't get it; it comes from the interaction" (DC20).

In addition, many Italian and French Catholic interviewees mentioned that the interaction between "giver" and "recipient" itself was critical; for them, it was a fundamental point of generosity – not just to give but to interact with the recipient. A number of interviewees strove to alter the term "recipient" so that it would not have the connotation of an impersonal exchange or unidirectional act. The recipient was a person whom Jesus wanted them to love, and that meant to help, to be next to, to acknowledge their presence and needs. Notably, many of the Catholic charitable organizations are also trying to refashion notions of charity and "recipient" (MC20, PC2, PC9, PC22, PC24). A volunteer group that provides meals for the homeless and destitute in the parish of Saint-Pierre de Montrouge, Paris, not only prepares and serves the meals but also dines with those they are serving. The experience for all concerned is personal, and the volunteers value that. They tended to speak of it as a manifestation of their faith, noting how Jesus interacted, sat, and dined with the people he was helping.

Muslims also stated how much they receive by giving to others. However, Muslims did not, in contrast to Catholics, phrase things in terms of wanting to "give back" to their community or of receiving so much more than they gave to the community. When they said giving actually increased what they originally had, they mostly talked about how God increased their own spirituality, well-being, and happiness. Association members often noted how they felt satisfied with helping the global initiatives of the Gülen movement. Many interviewees thought their relationship with the movement was special. The most often cited endeavors of the movement were the establishment of schools in poorer regions of the world, especially in Africa, the intercultural activities of the organization, and the sacrifices of the young recruits of the movement, especially graduates of prestigious universities in Turkey, who go to very poor countries as teachers (e.g., IM21, PM7). Donations to the movement in support of the international projects were more common in Istanbul and Paris, where the local associations were relatively better established and on less precarious financial terms than in Milan and Dublin. Many of our respondents in Istanbul and Paris, where the movement was large and had relatively wealthier followers, stated that they took foreign trips to see the activities of the movement abroad. Interviewees commented that the trips informed them about what is done with their donations and increased their inclinations to volunteer in and give to their associations (e.g., IM21, IM29, PM1, PM5, PM7). A respondent from Paris mentioned how his trip to Pakistan to help the victims of Pakistani flood deepened his relationship with the movement and led him to give more time and money (PM7).

Members of both religions also evinced a practical approach to their generosity with their community. For Catholics, the view was very much that someone has to take responsibility to make sure the priest has money to live on, that the electricity bill gets paid, that the leaky roof gets replaced (DC9, MC13, PC11). The duty was toward their community, not toward God. As one Parisian said, "the principle duty of Catholics is to aid the parish because it lives on donations. The state can repair the building up to [that which was built prior to] 1905 ... but all salaries etc. are the parish's to pay ... I benefit. I'm grateful. I make the Church for me. There's a community. One has a desire to donate in one's turn." In noting that she donates 10 percent of her savings, she said she sees it "as a duty to the parish, to the community, to the place of confession, not to God" (PC11).

Several Muslim female respondents emphasized the necessity of having local organizations and schools to provide a high-quality Islamic education for their children (e.g., PM6, PM11, PM28, MM3). The words of a woman from Paris in her fifties are illustrative: "When I was raising my kids, we did not have these associations in Paris. I tried my best to raise my kids in a Muslim way but I could do it to a very limited extent. I was unlucky. I do want my kids to be lucky in raising their kids by having these facilities [i.e., the cultural association]" (PM11). A woman in her early thirties in Milan concurs: "The weekend school helps our kids learn more about our own values in Italy. It is a big challenge for us to raise our kids here. The cultural center is our biggest help with that. Without that, we may lose our future generations. We should do our best to keep the cultural center open" (MM3). Interviewees sometimes voiced a concern that if they do not donate funds, their children, in the words of one, "will not have proper facilities and will be in danger of losing their identity" (PM28). One theme that most Muslim respondents noted was the image of Muslims in Western Europe. They saw their contributions as being a way to help elevate the status of the Muslim community in their respective cities (e.g., PM1, MM5, MM29, DM11). Certainly, Muslim and Catholic religious organizations are open to "free-riders," adherents who do not contribute. However, our interviews indicate that there is a core in the communities who, along with seeing generosity as having a divine basis, along with finding engagement rewarding, are prompted to act out of a sense of responsibility to the community: the bills must be paid.

One question that arises about the role of community in giving is whether or not the community sanctions members who do not give. Among Catholics, there was no mention of social retribution or pressure if they did not give financially or volunteer. Partly, this is built into the structure of financial giving in the church: it is private. Pledges and the fulfilling of annual pledges for donations are not made public. At most, those who know how much someone has donated are those who do the bookkeeping for the parish church; in small parishes that might be a volunteer. That structure does not give rise to peer pressure or social exclusion if one does not follow through on a pledge or gives less than what might be thought appropriate. There is no monitoring, and no sanctioning, of giving behavior during mass because giving is anonymous. With regard to volunteering, some Catholics feel they have a responsibility toward the community, but they do not perceive any social pressure from that community. They reason that the community needs the aid of each to run: "everyone should play a part, not just one guy doing five jobs"

(DC2, DC14). Asked why she volunteered, a Frenchwoman stated, as if it were obvious, "there was a need; I responded" (PC6). Yet even those who voiced this view rejected the idea that they might owe the parish or other Catholics something: as one said, "no, if I didn't want to help I wouldn't. I wouldn't feel in any way I'd have to" (DC13). Another parishioner, in Paris, summarizes what was often indicated: "you are free to say no" (PC13). The parish does not banish parishioners who do not give, who do not volunteer. They are free to take part in services, to send their children to First Communion preparation classes (staffed by volunteers), for instance, and to partake of charity services if need be. As an Irish parishioner who volunteers for the local branch of St. Vincent de Paul put it, "we never ask if you're going go to church, what religion you are, none of our business. We help anybody, whether they're black, Muslim, there's never any question about it." He then added, "the way I look at it, it's hard enough for me to try to save me own soul, never mind somebody else's" (DC12).

Like Catholics, Muslims' social engagement in their communities constitutes an incentive rather than a sanction in their giving. While Muslims do face some peer pressure to pledge to give, they do not face any retribution from the community if they do not give funds or volunteer. One issue that was raised in the interviews was the format of annual pledges of the members to the religious association. As mentioned in Chapter 2, the annual pledges are relatively public. While contributions are entirely voluntary, the pledges of the contributors are publicly announced in the room in which the fundraising event is organized. This creates a peer pressure mechanism among the participants. An Istanbul respondent emphasized the social dimension of giving (IM17). He used a Turkish proverb when explaining the impact of peers on giving: "*Üzüm üzüme baka baka kararır*": "Grapes darken by looking at each other." In other words, people mature (or develop habits) by learning from their peers. Some interviewees mentioned a hadith: to "compete to do good" (MM6). The statements of a respondent from Istanbul shows that "duty to God" comes into play in fulfilling the pledges as well: "When we pledge an amount, we feel that we promise God to give that amount. When we make the payment, we feel we are fulfilling our promise to God" (IM22). In the words of a respondent from Istanbul, "Organized programs by the movement of course influence our giving. If we were alone, we would not give this much. We should remind [each other of] the religious duties of each of us. This is what the movement does in a systematic way" (IM18).

Members of the Islamic associations had developed close-knit ties between each other in each city. Many respondents mentioned that the close friendships among the members of the community were important in creation of a giving-friendly environment. They noted that because they see other members of the association weekly, working together on various projects together, they develop social bonds. A furniture store owner from Istanbul mentioned friendship and giving equally: "Being involved in this movement made giving part of our personality. It is because you become part of a new social environment ... The place that I like the most is my village. I love to live there. Sometimes, I think about going back to my village and living there. However, when I go to my village just to visit, I miss my friends in two weeks" (IM17).

The faiths do affect *how* their adherents give and volunteer. Despite differences in some aspects of theology, both Catholicism and Islam emphasize community-building projects (Kniss and Numrich 2007, 9). The Catholics and Muslims we studied aimed their giving at efforts that helped to maintain their own community (such as their religious services and infrastructure), and that helped the broader community (such as antipoverty and joblessness projects and building and running schools and health clinics locally and overseas). Many Catholics manifested their belief in loving one's neighbor by volunteering for programs that helped the community in general by way of helping specific individuals. For instance, in Paris, volunteers with the Saint-Pierre de Montrouge *Pain Partagé* (shared bread) project collected food donations, then prepared and hosted a lunch each week for low income and homeless people in the neighborhood, and dined with them at the lunch. This created a sense of connection and social recognition for individuals who otherwise had few or no social interactions, and created a community within the larger area in which the parish is located. Volunteers took care to note which regulars were absent any given week, and followed up to check on them. A group of women in the church in Istanbul had frequent meetings for worship and for planning of community projects. The members of the group emphasized how the small group meetings deepened their friendship and encouraged them to help the community (IC3, IC10, IC25).

Attributing the motivation to their sense of a duty to God to help the needy, Muslim volunteers in Istanbul collected monetary and in-kind donations for the people living in a poor neighborhood who were the victims of a small-scale flood. To interact with the victims in person, the volunteers made a group trip to the neighborhood that was closest to the location of their association. Some of the group members hosted some of the victims at their own homes until conditions improved. When helping those in need, they did not expect gratitude from the victims, as they saw their volunteerism as an outgrowth of a feeling of duty to God to help others, not a duty to those in need. This again highlights a contrast between Catholicism and Islam. For Muslims, the religious inspiration for helping was a sense of duty to God; for Catholics, God's love and loving one's neighbor.

Conclusion

The interviews add a dimension to our understanding of the role of beliefs and institutions in the generosity and public goods provision of Catholics and Muslims. While the experiments focused on a necessarily limited set of religious-based constructs, including expectations of one's religious community, the interviews, being somewhat open in structure, enabled us to learn of additional factors that influence Catholics and Muslims and deepen our understanding of how Muslims and Catholics understand some of the concepts we did test for. We saw that many Catholics attributed their giving to their upbringing as much as to any specific religious belief, and that many responded when asked out of a sense of wanting to help the community or others and out of a sense of responsibility. Muslims also evinced a concern for their community and a desire to help. The extent to which such orientations are due to religious-based socialization is something we cannot probe with our data, but warrants exploration in the future. The findings are sensible and perhaps not surprising, reinforcing research showing that prosociality and generosity is not a one-dimensional phenomenon.

The interviews reveal important differences in the ways Catholics and Muslims consciously think about their generosity to their organizations and its connection to their faith. Catholics do not understand generosity, or helping others or giving financially, as a specific duty to God. Instead, if they give it a religious frame at all, they frame it as inhering in love for and love from Jesus. To them it is a choice. Many also tied it to a sense of responsibility to their religious community. This is similar to findings from studies of Catholics in the United States (Keister 2007; Miller 1999; Smith and Emerson 2008). Volunteering was described both as a desire to help and as a joy at the spiritual and emotional experience of helping and being involved with other people. Some also tied their giving and helping, their orientation, to their upbringing and the examples of their parents or the education they got in a youth group such as Scouts. We saw hints of this in the experiment results: duty to God had no effect on Catholics, and in their essays, many declared they did not have a duty to God; if anything, they had a duty to others.

In contrast to Catholics, Muslims often link their giving to fulfillment of a duty to God and pleasing of God. The emphasis on duty to and pleasing of God is a dominant factor in Muslims' accounts of why they give to their associations and to those in need. In the mind of many Muslims, the act itself is what is of primary importance since it is regarded as fulfillment of a duty to God; the beneficial consequences for the recipient are secondary. Similar to Catholics, attachment to their communities also encourages Muslims to give more. Engagement with the religious community is intrinsically rewarding. While the experiments did not corroborate empirically that Muslims respond to duty to God, analyses of their essays indicated that that concept, as well as deservedness, God's grace, and community expectations, did consistently prompt thoughts of charity.

What our experiments were not set up to test was the positive affect of community engagement. As much of the work on prosociality reasons that humans are prosocially helpful to each other only when compelled to be, such as by group norms or group-based monitoring and sanctioning mechanisms, we focused on community expectations. The interviews allowed us to find out what the lived experience of Muslims and Catholics is in their volunteering for and giving to their communities. Through these case studies, we learned that for Catholics and Muslims, engagement in volunteering, in helping activities with their religious communities, leads to positive feelings toward the community, which prompts continuing engagement and contributions. Catholics' comments about being asked to help indicate that positive feelings toward the one who asked them make a difference in their response. They do not, however, see helping as an obligation to God and they do not fear social or religious sanctions if they say "no." Because of its relatively smaller size in our research settings and because of the way the Gülen movement is organized, our Muslim interviewees were in more tightly knit groups than were our Catholic interviewees. Some Muslims mentioned competing with each other "to do good," indicating some sense of community-based pressure to contribute. Overall, we find, contrary to expectations of the literature that emphasizes monitoring and sanctioning within groups to obtain cooperation, that Catholics and Muslims see their generosity as motivated by the positive emotions they feel toward their respective religious communities. As one Catholic said, "God loves those who give while smiling" (PC14). In the next chapter, we will examine the extent to which these motivations and feelings are affected when a group is in religious minority status.

7

Religious Minorities and Generosity

During the fieldwork for this study, a Catholic Filipino woman in her forties working for a professional babysitting company in Istanbul enthusiastically talked about her involvement in her church, particularly her helping immigrants coming from the Philippines (IC18). Yet she added that she would have been involved in her church even if she had been in her home country. The message was that it was not being in a small minority group that motivated her to help others, but her faith. A Muslim community leader in his thirties who oversaw a weekend school for children in Dublin pointed out its importance for boys and girls for learning more about their religion but indicated that "opening of the institutions of education is our duty regardless of where we live" (DM25). He implied that being part of a small minority was not the reason he volunteered in his religious organization. Catholic and Muslim congregants in Istanbul and Dublin, respectively, indicated that being part of a small group strengthened their ingroup social ties while heightening a sense of urgency about survival in an alien culture. Other scholars have found that ethnoreligious minorities often engage in volunteer work, helping their own and the broader community in which they find themselves (Cherry 2014; Kniss and Numrich 2007). How does being in a minority religious group influence an adherent's generosity?

There are several streams of thought on how small groups, of which religious minorities are a subset, might foster prosocial behavior. One is based on the idea that small groups facilitate the development of social ties that then inspire the giving of time, effort, and material resources; another is based on the idea that people are "generous" when under surveillance and threatened with sanctions for not helping the group.

Drawing on the first perspective focusing on the development of social ties in small groups, we might reason that being in a small community increases the positive "emotional energy" (Collins 2004; Corcoran 2015; Lawler 2001) that members feel, leading to more generosity. Katie Corcoran reasons that "commitment to religious groups is achieved and maintained through collective religious rituals, which produce 'collective effervescence' – a strong, shared emotional experience that connects participants to the collective" (Corcoran 2015, 688; Collins 2004). Other scholars suggest that being in a small group may increase the intensity of one's religious faith. To the extent faith affects generosity, one would expect those in the small group to be more generous (Clemmons and Hester 1974; Whitehead and Stroop 2015, 661; Wuthnow 1994). Andrew Whitehead and Samuel Stroope (2015) explain that in small-group settings, individual participation in group activities is highly encouraged. The increased participation may result in a deepening of religiosity and faith, without changing the understanding of the giving or the goal of it. Finally, members of small groups may get more training in administrative skills; these skills then transfer to civic engagement and volunteerism within and outside the group. The group, on average, needs more help from each member to run its organization than does a larger group (Dougherty and Whitehead 2011; Whitehead and Stroope 2015). Thus, in small groups, individuals have more opportunities to practice administrative, communication, and leadership skills. Once they have learned these skills, the costs of remaining involved or taking up a new activity are lower (Whitehead and Stroop 2015, 661).

In a somewhat different vein, drawing on the economics of religion, we might focus on whether the small group has incentives and sanctioning mechanisms to elicit the desired behavior of contributing to collective goods (Berman 2009; Hale 2015; Iannaccone 1994). Small groups should be able to encourage their members to be more generous than large groups because individuals typically are better able to monitor each other's behavior (Stark and Finke 2000). There are thus more social pressures to be generous in small groups (Hale 2015; Hoge and Augustyn 1997; Olson 1965). Large groups, with their loose monitoring capabilities, will have more free-riders (Stroope 2012). Also, the stronger in-group dynamics in small groups leads to greater emphasis on each member helping the group survive (Feldman 1984; Van Vugt, Roberts, and Hardy 2007). This effect is reinforced to the extent group members cannot get what they need or want elsewhere, a situation in which religious and ethnic minorities find themselves when wanting to practice and maintain their religious and cultural traditions. Being more dependent on their group, they are more likely to contribute to its survival (Hechter 1987). There is some research on US nonethnic minority congregations that finds that being a religious minority (relatively speaking) does lead to less free-riding and more giving per capita (Brewer, Jozefowicz, and Stonebraker 2006). While the giving is attributed to better monitoring and sanctioning, group survival may be a factor.

To our knowledge, there have been few systematic comparative studies of how or whether the status as a distinct religious minority affects the generosity and prosocial behavior of adherents.[1] Our research on Catholics in Istanbul and Muslims in Dublin enables us to explore some possible effects. To preview our conclusions, we find that minority status does not change the way Catholics and Muslims understand their religious beliefs about helping others, and it does not change the impact of their institutions on their prosocial behavior. What the minority status changes, somewhat, is the target of the generosity. Religious minorities focus more on helping their group, because, as one would expect, they are concerned about the survival and welfare of their community. They also develop a positive affect toward one another.[2] Furthermore, their religious institutions are a base from which they develop programs to maintain their traditions, help newcomers, and support less fortunate members. In short, being in a minority situation does not lead congregants to interpret religious beliefs on generosity differently; however, it has an influence on their giving for social and community-based reasons.

Some might expect that understandings of religious beliefs and the structures of the religious institutions that affect generosity would be changed by the group in order to foster group survival. What we find, instead, is adherence to the same beliefs as coreligionists in majority contexts and replication, to the extent possible, of the institutional features of the religious tradition. Our interviewees indicated that maintaining the religion in its beliefs and institutions was a primary goal.

Minority status does have an impact on the target of adherents' giving. Catholics and Muslims in minority settings were a bit more focused on helping their own local group than on more broadly oriented financial giving and volunteering. Catholics raised concerns about the declining Christian population in Istanbul and Turkey, while Muslims raised concerns about the necessity of having sufficient resources to sustain their religious traditions. We need to note, however, that Catholics and Muslims in majority contexts also thrived in the small volunteer associations they

---

[1] Brewer, Jozefowicz, and Stonebraker (2006) compare US Lutherans in a majority Lutheran city to Lutherans in a majority Southern Baptist city.

[2] We caution that in majority contexts, adherents who joined volunteer groups within their congregations also developed a positive affect toward the community.

participated in. Our study is not able to assess whether being in a minority environment led congregants to give more than those in a majority environment on a per capita basis.

In line with the main theme of the book, the analysis of beliefs and institutions of generosity in Catholicism and Islam, we look into whether minority status influences the ways in which people understand and channel their generosity and how their religious institutions affected that. We do not assess whether the minorities were "more generous" than the majority groups we studied in those same cities. We first give a brief description of the Catholic community in Istanbul and Muslim community in Dublin. Then, we examine the relationship between minority status and understandings of beliefs and institutions on giving and compare our findings with the literature.

The Catholic Community in Istanbul and the Muslim Community in Dublin

Catholics in Istanbul and Muslims in Dublin are not just small groups, they are small groups in a context in which the majority is of a different religion. In addition, many of them are ethnic minorities. As we will see, interviewees voiced concerns about the small size and future of the group. The groups' demographics warranted those concerns. In 2010, there were about 15,500 Catholics in Turkey, with about 2,000 Catholics living in Istanbul, and about 250 regular congregants in the parish in which we conducted our research, Basilique Cathédrale du Saint-Esprit (IC1). Although the Catholics of Saint-Esprit were the members of the same parish, they came from various backgrounds. One set of congregants is descended from French and Italian immigrants (Latin Catholics or "Levantines"), a population present in Istanbul since sixteenth century. Largely due to Ottoman Empire and Turkish state policies, most Levantines have retained their Italian or French citizenship; they have not become Turkish citizens.[3] Another, and a bit larger group, is Catholic immigrants from the Philippines, most of whom migrated to Turkey for jobs. A third group is that of Catholic immigrants primarily from African countries, who left behind difficult conditions in their home countries. The parish also has a small

---

[3] During the Ottoman period, they kept their Italian and French citizenship because it was more advantageous for them. Ottoman Sultans gave them special privileges ("capitulations"). After the establishment of the Republic, they were allowed to stay in Turkey but were not allowed to become citizens unless they married a Turkish citizen.

number of Turkish converts. In addition to these groups, the church, which is itself historical and in the middle of a historical neighborhood, serves many Catholic tourists who come as visitors and worshippers.

Muslims in Ireland are a religious minority, with a population of about 30,000. Of them, about 5,000 are Turkish, with most of them living in Dublin (Flynn 2006, 223).[4] At the time of research, the Gülen community had only one association in Dublin, the Turkish-Irish Educational and Cultural Society (TIECS), with between 100 and 125 members. The members are mostly first-generation Turkish immigrants, with a few non-Turkish members. They have varied socioeconomic backgrounds and include software engineers, education professionals, small business owners in the textile or food industry, and graduate students. TIECS provides them both religious and cultural services. In contrast to the Catholic minority in Istanbul, the Turkish Muslim minority in Ireland is more homogenous in ethnic background.

One point that needs to be addressed is the extent to which Catholics and Muslims feel free to practice their religion and feel unthreatened in Istanbul and Dublin, respectively. Both Turkey and Ireland guarantee freedom of religion for the minorities in their constitutions and legal documents. However, there are concerns about social exclusion and marginalization of both Catholics and Muslims. Turkey long has had more exclusionary policies toward institutionalization of religious minorities. Although the state removed several discriminatory policies between 2000 and 2011, there are social biases and stereotypes against Christians. Furthermore, several Christian groups face difficulties in opening places of worship, and they lack legal religious status, which makes it difficult for them to engage in legal transactions as a corporate body (Kılınç 2014; Sarkissian 2015, 90, 117–125). Muslims in Ireland are free to practice their religion and establish organizations to represent themselves. However, Ireland is not free from the rising Islamophobia that has spread in Europe (Flynn 2006). Our interviewees were concerned about the stereotypes against them and were taking initiatives to decrease the biases.

Minority Dynamics and Generosity

To preview results, minority status for Catholics and Muslims did not change how the congregants understood generosity. We did find that the

---

[4] Interview with Sinan İlhan, Vice-Consul at Turkish Embassy at Dublin, Nov. 20, 2010.

small group environment created a positive affect among the members of both faiths, or, as Corcoran would put it, "emotional energy" (Corcoran 2015). It is not clear if this is necessarily the outcome of being in a minority environment, because we found a similar positive affect among the congregants in majority contexts who participated in small groups within their own organizations. Second, the religious minorities were concerned about group survival: it was frequently mentioned by interviewees as a key reason they gave financially and in time and effort to their organizations. Minority status influenced the target of giving and led Catholics and Muslims to support their own organizations. The arguments that minority environment increases the intensity of faith, civic skills, and monitoring and sanctioning did not seem to be important for our cases. There did not seem to be overt retribution for enjoying the benefits of the group without contributing. However, it is likely that the small group sizes made it easier for members to notice who contributed to group efforts and who did not, and it is possible our interviewees had internalized the social norms, such that there was no sense of being monitored or sanctioned by the group. We should also note that because we used the same set of interview questions for Catholics and Muslims in majority and in minority contexts, we can have some confidence that the minority context interviewees were not prompted by us to think of their minority status when answering questions.

Positive Affect and the Community

Both Catholics and Muslims mentioned the importance of their respective communities and talked about how they enjoyed being part of their small groups. In general, both groups appreciated the existence of like-minded people within a country in which they had a minority status. Where congregants in majority and minority status often mentioned the religious and social importance of their engagement with their religious community, congregants in minority status also noted that the feeling of togetherness helped them face the difficulties of being a religious and ethnic minority and that they were motivated to help because of the assistance they had received earlier from the community.

We see the community affect in comments of the Latin Catholics in Istanbul. Of various groups among the Catholics in Istanbul, their connection to the Church is a long-standing one, compared with the relationship of the newer immigrants to the city. For the Latin Catholics, the churches and schools have been a locus of community building and socialization. Just as we often heard those in majority status in our four cities say, an

Istanbul Catholic congregant stated that "the church is important to me for keeping and practicing my religion" (IC19). Yet indicating that the parish had a special role due to minority status, interviewees talked about how the parish played a role in maintaining social ties with community members. To many, it was nice to develop friendships with other Catholics through the religious and community-based activities at the church (IC19). Echoing this, another interviewee stated that "the church is a place for Catholics to socialize among themselves in their own ways in a Muslim country" (IC20).

One can easily notice a strong engagement and positive affect among the immigrant Catholics in Istanbul. Many volunteered and financially supported the parish's initiatives. A group of Filipino women in the church in Istanbul illustrates how being a minority group creates a small group interaction and facilitates giving. These women combined giving, community activism, and worship as a way to keep their group identity, to help one another, and to contribute to other initiatives of the church. They formed a local branch of the Legion of Mary that brought them together for weekly prayers and organizing meetings afterward. To a woman in her late forties, who led the Legion of Mary meetings, these meetings allowed the group to deepen the ties among them, to create collaboration opportunities among the members, to help the new immigrants mostly from Philippines, and to contribute to the church (IC3). This woman started the group to "provide the kind of support that I got when I first came to Istanbul fifteen years ago" (IC3). She mentioned that they found jobs for the newcomers through using their networks. To her, they "became the first contact point for many new Filipinos coming to Turkey" (IC3). Another Filipino woman concurred: "It is important to have the church and our group in Istanbul. It helps us keep up with our religion. It creates an opportunity to help one another" (IC10). On the weekends, the participants of the Legion of Mary organized bake sales to raise funds for new immigrants, as well as social gatherings to create a forum for their families to come together. That almost all the women in the group mentioned the help they received from the church when they first arrived in Turkey indicates that the minority context fostered a sense of empathy and wanting to give back. The members also mentioned how being involved in the group deepened their intimacy and friendship (IC3, IC10, IC18, IC25). The religious institutions are the same, but the intention is focused more on specific minority needs.

One woman parishioner illustrated how it is not easy to see whether being a minority or being part of a religious community is the motivation behind the prosocial behaviors. She said the church inspired her community engagement. She was thankful that Catholics had a church in Istanbul that made their collaboration and community work possible: "I am grateful for my friends here. We help the new people to settle in. We organize programs for the immigrant women. We also help with other functions at the church" (IC18). She added, "I was raised as a Catholic and I have been involved in the church in Philippines as well" (IC18). Her comparison of generosity in her home country and in Istanbul suggests that she would have been generous whether in a Catholic-majority or Catholic-minority country.

Many of the African immigrants, most of whom were from the Democratic Republic of the Congo, worked as street vendors in Istanbul and said they were inspired to help due to the help they had received when they arrived. A man in his forties explained the difficulties he experienced when he first came to Istanbul in the early 2000s and how people at the church helped him: "I came to Istanbul because a friend was already here. I had several problems, financial problems, finding a job, finding a place to live. Several issues. But my friends and congregants from the church helped me at that time" (IC14). He then became involved in several volunteer activities at the church. In his own words, "I became a helper for the newcomers. This is a way to pay back to those who helped me in the past" (IC14). Another Congolese immigrant in his thirties had a similar experience. He considered the church an important forum to get connected with other friends, who were "faithful and committed to helping others" (IC24). To him, "it is the close friendship that I like the most here. It is like a refuge in an alien land" (IC24). The Congolese immigrants, who often had little or no disposable income, volunteered more than they made monetary donations to the church. They had all received some help from the church when they first arrived at Istanbul. An indigenous Catholic confirmed this point by indicating that the church had always been concerned with the newly arriving immigrants and tried to make life easier for them in Istanbul as they settled in (IC9).

Muslims also mentioned small group interactions and a positive affect toward their communities within a minority context. Muslims in Dublin spoke of TIECS as an important institution that provided a forum to connect Turkish Muslims and help them keep and deepen their religious and cultural traditions (DM3, DM13, DM17, DM23, DM29, DM30). Being a venue for the Turkish immigrant community might have increased the positive affect, or "emotional energy," among the Turkish congregants in Dublin. To a salesman in his twenties, the center helps building friendships and deepening spirituality: "When I am here with friends, I can enjoy strong friendships and experience our own religious traditions. The cultural center provides a level of friendship and spirituality that we cannot find elsewhere" (DM3). Another interviewee concurred with the Catholic interviewee whom we quoted above (IC24): "the cultural center is like a refuge for me where I can feel the warmth of friendship among fellow Muslims" (DM21).

Since most of TIECS members were Turkish immigrants, some interviewees emphasized ethnic-based community links more than religious motivations when asked about their involvement. A male interviewee in his thirties explained his support of the cultural center with reference to what the center provides for the Turkish people (DM13). To him, the center facilitates "strong collaboration among the Turkish people," organizes aid for the needy within the community, and "helps the newcomers in their first years" (DM13). An engineer in his thirties said, "I am not a very religious person but I like being part of this community because this is probably the only association in Dublin that takes community involvement projects for the Turks seriously" (DM23). To another interviewee, "the projects for the Turkish immigrants" that TIECS organized appealed her. She liked "to experience Turkish culture with friends in the association" (DM17). Another woman, who works at a restaurant, echoed the point: "TIECS offers a strong venue for socializing for Turkish people in Ireland" (DM29). Another woman in her late thirties addressed the support that TIECS provided for the new Turkish immigrants to Ireland: "it is a great opportunity for the newcomers to know that there is a place that they can go and get help" (DM30).

Interviewees also addressed the importance of the cultural association for forming community ties among Muslims, especially during the religious holidays. The respondents found these gatherings particularly important: social ties become more meaningful at emotionally charged times of the holidays. A café owner in his late thirties found these gatherings significant for keeping in touch with other community members, as well as celebrating the holidays together in a non-Muslim country. Although he was not a regular contributor to the functions of the cultural center, he said he contributed to the events that aimed to bring the Turkish community together, particularly during the religious holidays: "I want to play my role in the representation of our culture here in Dublin. I usually provide room and food for the events at my place when the events contribute to the experience of our cultural richness" (DM28). In a similar vein, another interviewee mentioned that he liked the religious-based social function of the cultural center. To him, "the weekly meetings make it possible for community members to socialize with one another. In these meetings, we find an opportunity to talk about spirituality and religion" (DM6). He found this an important addition to Muslims' social life, as these opportunities were rare for the Muslim minority in Dublin (DM6).

Being in a small community seems to play a positive role in both Catholics' and Muslims' involvement in and giving to their communities. Both sets of congregants referred to friendships and community ties in their respective religious organizations. They raised the importance of keeping up with their values, helping one another out – particularly newcomers in immigrant communities – and connecting with people during important festivals and religious programs. However, the statements of our interviewees on religion, community, and giving are not much different from the statements of those congregants who live in majority contexts. As we described in Chapter 6, Catholics in Paris (e.g., PC6, PC10), Milan (e.g., MC13, MC14), and Dublin (e.g., DC2, DC10, DC12, DC13) and Muslims in Istanbul (e.g., IM14, IM17, IM18, IM22, IM24) mentioned their satisfaction with working with the community and the social ties and friendships that they develop within their congregations. What stood out in the minority context was the motivation of reciprocity many interviewees mentioned, and the importance of the community for providing a welcoming context in which to socialize. Being engaged in the community reaffirmed people's religious and ethnic identities and practices.

The argument that the minority environment would increase the intensity of faith and the civic skills of the congregants seemed to influence little to none of the giving of the Catholics and Muslims. During our interviews, congregants referenced several religious concepts in explaining their giving (i.e., IC15, IC20, DM16, DM25); however, based on the interviews, it is difficult to say if being in a small group increased the intensity of their faith and led to more giving. The congregants mostly referenced the deepening of social ties and friendships (IC10, IC18, DM10, DM15). Similarly, it is also difficult to say that being in a small group increased the congregants' administrative and civic engagement skills. In contrast, the interviewees raised the concern that the lack of sufficient human resources prevented them from having better-organized events (e.g., IC 7, IC24, DM5, DM25). It seems that the perception of and satisfaction from being in a small community may have encouraged some to give more time and resources to their institutions (IC7, DM16); however, this does not necessarily mean that they administrative and civic engagement skills than those active in groups in the majority contexts.

Group Survival

Catholics in Istanbul and Muslims in Dublin were cognizant of their religious minority status, and that was a factor in their contributing time, funds, and effort to their communities. For the bishop, priests, and congregants in Basilique Cathédrale du Saint-Esprit, the survival of the church in Istanbul was definitely a significant priority. The religious community in the church was very small. Most of its members did not have Turkish citizenship and some were newly arrived immigrants. The bishop and priests clearly underlined that the Church did not get any external support for its operational costs (IC1, IC2, IC8, IC27, IC28). Although the congregants in the church contributed to other collections such as Vatican-administered campaigns and Caritas-administered charities, most of the contributions from the congregants were used for the functioning of the church (IC8). According to one of the priests, "we are completely supported by our congregants without any international help even though the recent laws allow us to receive external support" (IC8). This is a conscious decision to make sure that the church has the capacity to sustain itself (IC8). A number of interviewees saw their contributions as crucial for the survival of the church. They thought the church was essential for both spiritual (IC6, IC16, IC25) and social functions (IC14), which in turn they viewed as central to their own lives in Istanbul.

To many interviewees, the church was a place that helped congregants sustain their cultural and religious traditions. The Latin Catholics saw the church not only as a place of worship but as a place of cultural regeneration. A retired man in his late sixties described the role of the church in his upbringing. That person, who also attended the Catholic school affiliated with the church, discussed the cultural festivities that he had in the church during his childhood. To him, "the church is everything about my own life" (IC6). Raised as a minority child, the interviewee had limited cultural exposure to the Catholic traditions in the city, but the church provided that. In turn, he wanted to transmit that to future generations: "The existence of the church means transferring not only our religion but also our culture to the Levantine sons and daughters" (IC6). Another person in his sixties also shared this thought by saying that "seeing like-minded people on the weekends [in the church] helped maintain our identities as Latin Christians" (IC22). In the words of a jewelry store owner in his late fifties, "We were always different. I went to a French school affiliated to our church. We used to get together in community picnics and church settings. Our church and school allowed us to maintain our identity in an increasingly conservative Muslim country. As our parents did in the past, we take every effort to continue these institutions" (IC22).

A male teacher in his thirties saw the Catholic school as an important transmitter of Catholic culture and values (IC13). To him, it was only through the school that their children could retain their Catholic identities, and only this could guarantee a thriving future for Turkish Catholics (IC13). By providing a Catholic environment, the school "allows the children to be raised as Catholics and be proud of their religious identity" (IC13). Interviewees who mentioned having attended the Catholic school agreed (IC6, IC16): "the school helped me and my children keep up our own values" (IC16). They voiced concern that the school did not have as many students and resources as it did during their childhood. This, to them, was alarming for the future of the Catholic community in Turkey (IC6, IC16). As one said, "the children [who go to public schools] may not feel the level of confidence that we had about our Catholic values" (IC6).

Since the Catholic community in Istanbul is a mixture of groups, there was a minority dynamic at different levels among the congregants. Some Latin Catholics indicated that their numbers, as compared with new immigrants, are decreasing every year (IC6, IC22). To them, it became very difficult to sustain the church, which they, in turn, consider to be the repository of the Christian traditions (IC6, IC22). An elder congregant lamented that "the youth is leaving from Turkey to Europe and America. Without the new immigrants, the church will lose its members quickly and face the threat of extinction" (IC22). An older congregant who is also a historian of the Catholic minority in Turkey said that "the number of Levantines has been steadily decreasing in the church for several decades" (IC20). A retired congregant in her sixties was also concerned that the decreasing Levantine Christian population in Istanbul may make it hard to sustain the church (IC16). She noted that "our population is shrinking. This is a serious issue for the church and the school" (IC16).

For other Latin Catholics, their dwindling number caused them to become a minority group within the congregation. The changing demographics of the church made it less a place of cultural regeneration for Latin Catholics, although it still is a religious and spiritual center. An interviewee said that "the immigrants from the Philippines and Congo help the church expand its members. This is great for its survival. However, the church is not a cultural forum for Latin Catholics like myself any more. It is becoming a multi-national religious house of worship. This is totally different than past, but may be not necessarily a bad thing" (IC6). To some, the new immigrants provide new life to the church. A Latin Catholic stated that it was "good to receive new immigrants because they help maintain the church" (IC5). However, he was also concerned that the Latin Catholics would "become a minority in the church and have less influence on its future" (IC5). Not everybody sees this as a negative development. To one retired woman, the church could survive thanks to the support of the new immigrants, but the same thing could not be said for the school, which requires high tuition to meet its expenses (IC16). She saw the effort to help the new immigrants settle in the city as an effort to maintain the Catholic institutions in Istanbul (IC16): "we may like it or not but the future of the church is changing. We help the new Catholics who will maintain the church" (IC16). A woman in her early thirties concurred: "immigrants are new blood to the church to remedy the problem of the shrinking Catholic population in Istanbul" (IC21). Similarly, she believed that helping the new immigrants was an investment in the future of the Catholic church in Istanbul (IC21).

The immigrants also considered the church a forum in which they could maintain their religious traditions and pass them on to their children. As a Filipino woman stated, "having a church in Istanbul is important for practicing our religious traditions here" (IC10). A woman in her forties said that "the church is important for my daughter to learn more about Christianity. She goes to a public school and learns nothing about Christianity there. It feels good that she at least learns something at the church on the weekends" (IC25). While the church was becoming a more cosmopolitan Catholic entity, both Latin Catholics and immigrants saw the church as an indispensable part of their life in Turkey.

Consistent with concerns about the shrinking Christian population, and with suspicions about Christians using charity to proselytize among Muslims, the Saint-Esprit Church directs most of its charity toward the Catholic minority groups in Turkey. The regular beneficiaries of the church's charity programs are Christian refugees in big cities and poorer Christians in Eastern Turkey. One of the priests in the church indicated that Christians from Iraq who fled after the US invasion of 2003 constituted a significant group that the church supported (IC2).[5] In addition, the church organized donations to Christians in rural areas of the Eastern provinces, particularly in Van (IC2, IC20). The funds helped by "providing vocational courses, establishing small carpet making machines in their neighborhoods, and making funds available for small business ideas" (IC20).

---

[5] We conducted our fieldwork research in the summer of 2010, before the Syrian refugee crisis emerged.

Two priests from the church mentioned the importance of Turkey for the Christian history and the necessity of having a Christian existence in a historically significant country (IC8, IC27). One, in his mid-seventies, made this point clear: "The numbers of Christians, in this country which houses several treasures from Christian history, is shrinking. I think it should be one of our priorities to sustain the Catholic Church in Turkey. That is our responsibility to our history and traditions" (IC27). While the priests spoke of the church's historical legacy, parishioners were more focused on immediate social and religious needs.

We caution that we cannot conclude that the church's emphasis on helping Christians is because of their minority status per se. On the one hand, several church leaders raised the concern that the existence of Christianity in Turkey was under threat (IC1, IC2). This concern might have led them to collect donations for other Christian groups in Turkey, as noted. On the other hand, the resources of the church in Istanbul are very limited, and this might have led the church members to be selective in whom they helped. Furthermore, one priest said that the broader Turkish community was very suspicious of them having missionary activities toward Muslims, and this led them to limit their help to Christians (IC2). In his words: "we also want to provide help for the Muslim poor but this gets misunderstood easily. We are accused of trying to convert them with small material incentives" (IC2).

Finally, although group survival was a great concern to many congregants, to some members, particularly the younger Latin Catholics, it was not a significant factor in their involvement in the church nor in their generosity. A man in his early thirties explained his involvement in the church in more cultural, less religious terms and was not concerned about being a religious minority in a Muslim-majority context. He was involved in the activities of the international charity organization of the Roman Catholic Church, Caritas, particularly in its activities for children, and saw his involvement as having more of a humanitarian mission: "regardless of our religious affiliations, we need to help those in need. This becomes an even more urgent matter when those in need are innocent children" (IC11). Although he seemed more cosmopolitan and humanitarian in explaining his volunteering, he was selective in deciding which organization through which to channel his charity. He trusted Caritas because of its connection to the Catholic Church (IC11). Similarly, a woman congregant working for Caritas identified her mission as "helping the needy without any regard for who that person is" (IC21). She did not mention minority status.

Similar to their Catholic counterparts, many Muslim interviewees raised concerns about establishing strong institutions that would enable their ethnoreligious community to survive and flourish in Ireland. Similar to how many Catholics viewed the church in Istanbul, the Muslim interviewees saw community gatherings at their cultural center as crucial to holding the Turkish Muslims together in a Christian-majority country (DM11, DM18, DM25, DM26). As one congregant stated, "the cultural center helps us to keep our values; without it, it is difficult to live as Muslims in Ireland. Even if we can keep our values, our future generations may not" (DM26). A community leader in Dublin said, "[W]e're a minority group in Dublin. We use each and every opportunity to utilize our members here. Any contribution coming from our members is welcome. This can sometimes be monetary contributions, at other times, just inviting their friends to our programs. Each effort, even a very small one, is valuable to us" (DM25). Another concurred: "we all need to help the association as much as we can. This is the only way to keep it working. We are only a handful of people in Dublin" (DM11).

Another factor that might have led to a concern to have viable institutions in Ireland was the increase in anti-Muslim sentiments throughout Europe. In the words of a Muslim doctoral student, "we need institutions to represent us better in Western Europe. Our future is hijacked by extremist groups elsewhere who do not even live in this country. We should represent ourselves as real Muslims and not let others to represent us without our consent" (DM18). Another interviewee agreed: "it is important to keep our religious values here in Dublin but it is also important to let others know about our values so that they do not fear from Muslims" (DM19). A woman interviewee brought up the stereotypes against Muslim women in Europe and suggested that the Muslim institutions were needed to empower women and help defeat those stereotypes (DM24). She continued: "we need more women's programs to connect with other women. Only in this way, can we melt the bias against us" (DM24). Another Muslim shifted the discussion to being a Muslim in a European setting: "we need to create institutions that teach us how to be both Muslim and European, and others about our own values. They should also know that we are Muslims but not alien to their values. We embrace European values as much as we embrace our religious traditions" (DM11).

Muslims in Dublin considered weekend school as a tool for their children's socializing with other Muslims. Many also looked at the weekend school from a group survival point of view. They considered it a place of learning through which the children keep their Muslim identity (DM4,

DM19). To a woman in her early thirties, the weekend school was "the only place where kids learn about Islam and Turkish culture." Maintaining the school was important for the future of Muslims in the country (DM12). A textile company owner in his mid-forties was interested in supporting the cultural center particularly because of its work with the children (DM19). To him, "developing these educational activities is crucial for the future of Muslims in Ireland." Another interviewee indicated that "the limited number of educational institutions for Muslims in Dublin makes the weekend school an urgent priority" (DM25).

Muslims also commented that their children needed a social environment in which they could learn about religion and culture, and make Muslim friends. To many, TIECS created opportunities for the children to socialize in the context of common religious and cultural values. To a congregant, the center helped "the kids make friends who share similar values and backgrounds. This is important as they feel very different at school. Getting more Muslim friends at the weekend school makes them feel self-confident about their values" (DM10). That Muslims are a minority in Ireland increased the need for a place in which both the community and the children could sustain their religious values and traditions. However, it is not clear if this was an outcome of a religious awareness or being in a minority status. For example, although a community leader in Dublin stated that "the kids improve their knowledge of Islam in the weekend school," he did not raise concerns about being a minority in a non-Muslim majority country (DM25). The fact that many Muslim interviewees in Turkey also raised the necessity of conveying the religious message to children makes it difficult to isolate the impact of minority status on this reasoning.

In addition to developing the children's knowledge of Islam, a couple of parents talked about the academic support that their kids got from the cultural center's weekend school. One mentioned how important it was for the "kids to get extra support from the center for their success at [public] school" (DM9). This interviewee went on to relate the children's academic success in public schools to acceptance of them as Muslims. She said that "when we help our kids succeed at school, they will become self-confident and be more proud with their Muslim identities. This will help their integration without assimilation" (DM9). Another parent made a similar point: "It is important that the kids learn more about religious values and still be very successful at [public] school. The weekend school plays an important role in making both happen" (DM15).

As with their Catholics counterparts in Istanbul, Muslims in Dublin used most of their giving to sustain their local institutions. Those who contributed to global causes directed their funding to the charity organization affiliated with their religious community, Kimse Yok Mu (KYM). Many Gülen followers mentioned that they gave their contributions for global humanitarian campaigns to KYM because they trusted it to help people in real need. Muslims had a feeling of ownership of KYM and saw it as part of their community. The views of an engineer were typical of other Muslims: "I have trust in KYM that they will direct the aid to the needy. I don't have any suspicion on how the collected money will be used" (DM5). But it is difficult to say that this feeling was an outcome of living as a minority in Dublin; Muslims in Istanbul also had a similar feeling toward the KYM even though they were in a Muslim-majority country.

Some interviewees considered TIECS's interfaith dialogue initiatives as an extension of the necessity to reach out to non-Muslims in an effort to create a safe zone for Muslims in Ireland. To a graduate student, "interfaith dialogue increases our acceptance by the Irish people. The more they interact with us, the more they see us as normal people, their fears disappear as we become normal in their eyes" (DM1). He continued, "[W]orld opinion about Islam puts on us a duty to challenge the stereotypes against Muslims" (DM1). One interviewee explained that she supported the association because "interfaith dialogue creates a more comfortable environment for future generations of Muslims in Ireland" (DM27). Another congregant concurred: "I try my best to volunteer for all the interfaith initiatives. We will keep facing more stereotypes in the future. It is our duty to prevent the spread of groundless stereotypes against us. We should stop complaining and do something about it. Reaching out to non-Muslims and letting them know more about Muslims, to me, is the best way to counter these stereotypes" (DM5). One interviewee, a teacher, voiced a similar view, explaining the necessity of dialogue with non-Muslims in Ireland: "if we want to leave a safer place for our children in Europe, we need to reach out and establish bridges of understanding with the broader community here" (DM9). In addition to countering stereotypes, some congregants saw TIECS as a means to connect to the broader Irish society through religious dialogue. A software engineer in his early forties stated that the cultural center enabled Muslims to establish meaningful relations with non-Muslims. Though they already interacted with non-Muslims before the cultural center was founded, the center changed the nature of those relationships by making cultural exchange the framework of their social relations. He said that "the cultural center forces us to think the ways in which we reach out to others as confident 'Muslims' ready to collaborate with non-Muslims for the resolution of social issues and community matters" (DM20).

Muslims did not speak about whether or not being a minority played a role in their support of these programs. Nevertheless, it seems that when negative sentiments about Islam were on the rise in Europe, Muslims perceived a greater threat to the group's existence. The interviewees indicated more urgency about developing links with non-Muslims when their existence was less established in a given country. This was apparent in Muslims' attitudes toward interfaith dialogue in other cities of the study. Muslims in Dublin and Milan more often spoke of the necessity of dialogue than Muslims in Paris. This issue became even less relevant in Istanbul where Muslims are part of the majority population.

The findings on being a religious minority and on giving among Muslims in Ireland easily translate to understanding the minority dynamics in France and Italy. There are many similarities between Dublin and Milan Muslims in terms of the role of group survival in their giving. In both cities, Muslims constitute a small minority, and in both, Gülen-affiliated Muslims have only one cultural center. In both cities, the associations emphasize community ties. They work to develop the resources of their religious communities and sustain their religious and cultural traditions. Since the Muslim communities in each city are small, most of the efforts and contributions of the congregants go to the domestic institutions. In both Dublin and Milan, Turkish Muslims also worked on interfaith and intercultural activities to develop positive connections with the broader society.

Muslims in Paris shared several of the characteristics of their counterparts in Dublin and Milan; however, they had a more established position in Paris than Muslims in the other two cities. There were several cultural centers in Paris and relatively more Muslims affiliated with the Gülen movement. Although protecting their traditions was still a significant priority for Muslims in Paris, they channeled their giving beyond sustaining their institutions. In addition to giving to KYM, like their counterparts in Dublin and Milan, they contributed to institution-building outside France and took responsibility to meet the needs of new schools or institutes in developing countries. In this regard, they were more similar to their Istanbul counterparts, who were in a religious majority context. This seems to indicate that as minority communities become established and stable, the target of their giving becomes similar to the giving of those who live in Muslim-majority countries.

We found little evidence of strict monitoring and membership requirements playing any role in the giving by Catholics and Muslims in religious minority status. The institutional structure of the parish in Istanbul and the

Gülen association in Dublin were similar to their respective counterpart structures in the majority contexts. As we explored in Chapter 2, those structures were typical of mainstream, "low tension" religions. Even though the Catholic congregants, particularly the immigrants, met within small groups on a weekly basis, they did not mention any social pressure to join those meetings, and membership requirements were loose: one had to sacrifice little to be a member. Additionally, congregants in majority status were able to form small groups within their larger community. What seems more to have been a factor is that to the extent congregants valued their religious traditions and socializing with others in their traditions, and if they could not find substitutes elsewhere, they were motivated to contribute to their minority group. Where there was "high tension" was in the groups' being religiously distinct and, in some instances, ethnically distinct, from the larger society they were in. But it would be a stretch to say that the small group environment of the minority religions generated stricter social monitoring or membership requirements.

The major drivers of generosity among Catholics and Muslims were faith and community, as demonstrated in the earlier chapters. The interviews indicated that being a religious minority played little role in both Catholics' and Muslims' giving and no role in the ways that Catholics and Muslims understood the relationship between religion and generosity. However, as the religious communities became smaller, the concern of group survival, in terms of religious and cultural traditions, seemed to increase. Congregants in majority contexts were more likely to give to different causes and organizations beyond their own. In the smaller communities, giving was more focused on the needs of the local organizations. For example, Muslims in Paris, who were the most populous of the three groups, voiced fewer concerns about the future of their existence in France as compared with Muslims in Ireland and Italy.

The interviews with the religious minorities demonstrated that their understandings about religious teachings on generosity, on beliefs about helping others, were no different from those in majority groups. As demonstrated in greater detail in Chapter 6, Catholics put more emphasis on duty to the community and upbringing, while Muslims put more emphasis on duty to God. We have not observed differences in the understandings of the congregants in minority and majority contexts. For example, Catholics in Istanbul considered their giving as something that pleased God even though they do not see it as a duty (e.g., IC13); this was no different from the beliefs of Catholics in Milan and Dublin (e.g., DC9, DC10). Similarly, being asked by a priest rather than having a duty to

God was a motivation for volunteering for Catholics in Istanbul (e.g., IC3, IC7), as well as Catholics in Milan (e.g., MC2, MC15), Paris (e.g., PC14), and Dublin (DC6, DC9). Likewise, Muslims in Dublin (e.g., DM9, DM16), Milan (e.g., MM1, MM6), Paris (e.g., PM5), and Istanbul (e.g., IM7, IM18) had similar views on considering giving a duty to God. Along the same lines, Muslims in minority contexts (PM5, MM3, MM11, PM11, DM12) shared the same view as Muslims in majority contexts (IM14, IM21, IM5) that fulfilling their responsibility to God was more important than solving the actual problem of the recipient of the help.

Conclusion

The Catholic parishioner in Istanbul and the Muslim community leader in Dublin that we mentioned in the beginning of this chapter were both right that being in a minority status does not change the way that Catholics and Muslims interpret their religious teachings and institutions on generosity. However, our analysis has also shown that the close social ties and the fear of survival among minority groups led them to give to their ingroup more in comparison to their counterparts in majority settings. In the minority settings, groups developed intimate social ties and were concerned with the survival of their communities. For this reason, they were supportive of the mechanisms to help newcomers, maintain their traditions, and protect the welfare of the less fortunate members. In short, minority status may influence the type of giving for community-based social reasons. As other scholars have found in regard to ethnoreligious immigrants in the United States, minority status does not seem to change the way the faithful interpret religion (Cherry 2014; Kniss and Numrich 2007).

Catholics and Muslims noted the joy of being together in a context dominated by a different religious majority. Both groups mentioned positive affect toward their fellow community members. There seems to be an "emotional energy" stemming from being in a small minority status. This emotional energy led the members to give to their communities more. The members in both communities expressed that they helped one another in facing the difficulties of living in a different setting in which they are a minority. The Catholics in Istanbul experienced minority dynamics at different levels as they are composed of both indigenous (Latin Catholics) and immigrant (Filipino and Congolese) Catholics. The Latin Catholics prioritized the protection and enjoyment of their cultural traditions, while immigrants were concerned about helping newcomers and forming mechanisms through which they could support one another. Turkish Muslims shared a similar type of minority feeling as they were mostly first-generation immigrants and had similar problems stemming from having a minority status.

In keeping with the sociological argument on emotional energy, the small group environment created an "emotional energy" among the congregants and motivated them to contribute to their institutions. Both Catholics and Muslims mentioned the importance of their communities and talked about how they enjoyed being part of their small groups. In general, both groups appreciated the existence of like-minded people within a country in which they had a minority status. Our evidence does not allow us to discern whether this is an outcome of being a minority religion or of developing a positive affect toward their communities regardless of their minority status. As noted in earlier chapters, we found that Muslims and Catholics in majority contexts spoke of strong, positive community attachments to and feelings for their religious organizations. This similarity makes it difficult to measure the isolated impact of minority status on giving behaviors.

The parish in Istanbul was small but not through a deliberate attempt to sustain the close connections that small size fosters. Rather, in Catholicism, for nearly all parishes including all those we studied, parish size is determined by geographic boundaries, which, in turn are determined by the Church hierarchy (Code of Canon Law, n.d., Code 515). Catholic congregations have no control over the geographic size of their parish, nor over the minimum or maximum number of parishioners in that parish. They cannot split of their own accord if they think the parish has too many Catholics in it, nor merge with another if they think they have become too small. The one trend we observed was that in Dublin, parishes were being "clustered," with priests and other staff pooled to serve multiple parishes, not just one. The Archdiocese was doing this in order to mitigate the consequences of a dearth of priests. In Islam, there is much more opportunity for groups to split and control their own size. That said, the Turkish Muslims in Dublin and Milan were of such small numbers that splitting was out of the question. In Paris, where there was a relatively larger Turkish population, there were six communities organized around six associations established in different geographical locations of the city. In Istanbul, the association we studied was one of several and served the northwestern suburbs of Istanbul. There were many small groups within that association. Generally, the Gülen movement regulated the formation, merger, and splitting of groups, in cooperation with the local associations.

Threats to their survival also seem to influence the giving of Catholics and Muslims. Catholics and Muslims addressed the issue of survival from similar and different perspectives. Both groups raised the issue that they needed to have institutions to keep their unique cultural and religious traditions and transmit those traditions to the younger generations. Among the Catholics in Istanbul, the Latin Catholics were especially concerned about the disappearance of their cultural heritage. This was indicated in their concern not only about the church, but also about the school affiliated with the church, as they saw it as a carrier of cultural traditions. Recent immigrants were more concerned about the welfare of the newcomers and maintenance of the church to keep up their religious values. A few Catholics mentioned that Christians should have a strong presence in the lands where Christianity first emerged. For Muslims, the main issue was establishing strong institutions to meet the needs of the new generation of Muslims and to keep their own cultural and religious traditions in a non-Muslim majority context. Muslims were also concerned about their relationship with the broader society, as they felt threatened by an increasing anti-Muslim sentiment in Europe. Yet rather than look inward in a defensive reaction, this concern inspired them to develop interfaith and intercultural dialogue initiatives with the broader society.

This chapter investigated, largely through interviews, whether being in a minority status influences Catholics' and Muslims' religiously motivated generosity. We found that the religious motives congregants attribute to their generosity does not change in minority contexts even though the target of giving may be somewhat different. In the next chapter we explore another contextual factor that may affect religious-based generosity and ask: does the welfare state undermine the generosity of Catholics and Muslims?

8

The Welfare State, Religion, and Generosity

In October 2010, as Italy was recovering from the recession, there was a controversy about housing for some of the Roma in Milan. The Cardinal Archbishop of Milan, Dionigi Tettamanzi, had criticized the mayor's decision to limit public housing options, stating, "We hope the state takes up its responsibilities." The vice mayor fired back, "Housing for gypsies? The Curia should open up its real estate holdings" (Foschini 2010). The exchange captures two views of the welfare state: one, expressed by the Church, is that the state has responsibilities to social welfare that it must adhere to; the other, voiced by the Milan mayor's office, is that the Church has not only the responsibility but also the resources to provide social welfare.

With the collapse of many states and the retrenchment of social services, recent research has asked what fosters the provision of welfare and social assistance services outside of the state or government (Cammett and MacClean 2014). There has been interest in the United States and Europe in whether faith-based organizations, including organized religions, can deliver state-funded welfare services as well as or better than secular organizations (Bielefeld and Cleveland 2013; Ferguson et al. 2007; Fischer 2008). Some have suggested that as the welfare state retrenches, faith-based organizations will pick up the slack. Research on both perspectives has largely ignored how faith and religious organizations might enable a religious group to provide public goods, and what the role of faith and religious organization structure is in the existence and success of the activity. This chapter addresses these gaps by providing systematic information on whether religious adherents are more likely to give than the less religious, on what motivates Catholics and Muslims to volunteer in or give to faith-based "welfare" activities, and on the institutional structures within those religions designed to deliver welfare services.[1]

Standard expectations are that greater welfare state spending generally makes individuals less likely to provide public goods voluntarily. In this view, people are less likely to help others through volunteer work or to make material contributions to charities. The reasons are twofold. First, as the state takes care of social welfare, people feel less responsible and feel less need to help out. We can think of that as a shift in responsibility. Second, people have less discretionary income to give, due to paying taxes to support the welfare state. We can think of that as a tax on generosity. One would expect that these effects could obtain, but be muted, in religious individuals.[2]

Some scholars expect that these dynamics also affect religiously motivated generosity. Research has shown that there is a "crowding out" effect on religiously motivated generosity from state-supplied social welfare, with the logic being that if the state provides the social net, there is no need for individuals or religious organizations to do so (Andreoni and Payne 2003; Hungerman 2005). Other studies have found its effects to be complementary or inconclusive (Dahlberg 2005; Fridolfsson and Elander 2012; Scheepers and Te Grotenhuis 2005, 461). Still others argue that people who have a more elastic preference for religion reduce their religiosity in more expansive welfare states. In other words, fewer people are religious, but those who have a strong preference for religion would be less likely to reduce their religiosity and thus less likely to reduce their religiously inspired charitable activity (Gill and Lundsgaarde 2004). The effects in Catholicism and Islam have not been studied. Applying this reasoning to the impact of state subsidies to religion, if the state subsidizes an organized religion, the religion's upkeep costs may be reduced, relieving followers of the "need" to give for that purpose, and therefore reducing their "generosity."

In light of economic crises and the retraction of welfare states in Europe and elsewhere, knowing how nongovernmental entities elicit public goods provision is important. Some scholars suggest that when governments reduce the supply of public goods, the private sector fills in (Ferris and

---

[1] That said, we need to be clear that we are not trying to test the effectiveness of faith-based initiatives, nor the perspective that as the welfare state retrenches, faith-based organizations can fill in and do the job.

[2] What has been studied are the views within different denominations about individual responsibility versus societal responsibility for welfare. This has been done without attention to the extensiveness of the welfare state (Davis and Robinson 1999).

West 2003; Gill 2013; but see van Oorschot and Arts 2005). On the other hand, research indicates there may be limits on the effectiveness of private supply of social welfare (Davis and Robinson 2012). Religious groups have constraints in providing social services at the level the state does because of their need to create club goods for their adherents: they need to sustain their own organization and minister to their followers. They also lack the coercive taxation powers of the state (Warner 2013). Prosocial behavior prompted by religion is unlikely to generate the same level of funding.

We take advantage of public surveys in Europe, including in Turkey, to subject a series of hypotheses about the relationship to quantitative analyses. We then present interview data we collected in our four primary countries of interest (France, Ireland, Italy, and Turkey) to analyze how the welfare state interacts with both Catholicism and Islam. The interviews include those with leaders of major religious charities in each of our four countries, as well as with parishioners and local religious officials. We also test state subsidies to the organized religions and the impact of that factor on public good provision by religions. Generally, the logic is that if the state helps to pay for a religious organization's operating costs, individual adherents will feel less responsible for donating to help the organization maintain itself and run its programs.

Overall, we find some intriguing indications that the crowding-out hypothesis is indeed muted by the religiosity of adherents: they contribute anyway. Why Catholics and Muslims may do so has been discussed in other chapters. We expand on that discussion here with an analysis, in four case studies, of adherents' views of the welfare state in their country, of their responsibility to help the needy, and of their religious organization's responsibility to do so. We proceed by first presenting our quantitative analyses and findings. We then briefly describe the historical context of the welfare state and religious charities in each of our four countries, and go on to present our case study results. To preview the commentary, the leaders of the main Catholic and Muslim charities in our four countries had a willingness to work with the state in providing social welfare locally and internationally, viewed their organizations' role as essential but insufficient, and viewed their organizations as providing a means for religious adherents to practice the generosity inherent in their religious beliefs. The case studies show that no matter what the state does in the realm of social welfare, Catholics and Muslims believe they themselves, and their religious organizations, have a responsibility to help those in need. We conclude with a summary of results and a comment on the prospects for faith-based organizations to substitute for reduced state welfare provision.

Hypotheses

To better understand the relationship between religion and the welfare state, we develop six hypotheses. Our survey data, described in further detail below, enable us to assess whether there is a relationship between the extensiveness of the welfare state and people's view of the responsibility that individuals bear for helping others. To the extent there is a relationship, we also examine whether that relationship is affected by the religiosity of individuals.[3] The data do not measure whether people in countries with smaller welfare states and/or lower tax rates actually spend more time doing volunteer work; we are measuring whether crowding out first affects whether people think individual citizens should be directly helping others. Readers who are less interested in the technical details may prefer to skip to the discussion of results.

First, we assess the general relationship between the extent of welfare state expenditure and the degree to which survey respondents feel individuals have a responsibility for actively helping others. We might alternatively conceptualize this as the degree to which respondents support the contention that individuals bear responsibility to provide goods and services that assist their fellow citizens (public goods). Because the welfare state takes on responsibility for providing social protection for society's needy, citizens, whether religious or not, may feel individually absolved from such responsibility. Having theoretically consented to the state taking on these welfare functions, and with many contributing through taxes in funding those functions, individuals may believe they no longer need to help with their own independent contributions. As a result, Hypothesis 1 suggests that welfare state expenditure is negatively related to support for the idea that individual citizens are responsible for public goods provision.

Hypothesis 1: *The higher state welfare expenditures, the less likely individuals are to support citizen responsibility for public goods provision.*

There is reason to believe, on the other hand, that increasing degrees of religiosity are generally associated with greater individual public goods provision. Religious organizations typically emphasize the importance of adherents' contributing to charitable projects. As a result, we would expect

---

[3] Approximately 34 percent of the sample who answered the question identified as Roman Catholic, 12 percent Protestant, 9 percent Eastern Orthodox, 2 percent other Christian denomination, 0.05 percent Jewish, 5 percent Muslim, 0.2 percent Eastern religion, and 0.3 percent other non-Christian religions; about 37 percent stated that the question was not applicable to them.

that higher levels of religiosity are associated with stronger levels of support for individual responsibility for public goods provision.

Hypothesis 2: *The greater the religiosity of individuals, the more likely they are to support citizen responsibility for public goods provision.*

Besides religious individuals being more likely to contribute to public goods provision generally, it is possible that religious individuals have some sort of intervening influence on the negative relationship between welfare state expenditure and support for citizen responsibility for public goods provision. This can express itself in two possible ways. First, it is possible that highly religious individuals intensify the negative relationship between welfare state spending and individual public goods responsibility when compared with their secular counterparts. The welfare state takes on social welfare provisions that have typically been the purview of religious organizations. The highly religious are particularly impacted by the welfare activities of the state and even less likely to support individual responsibility for public goods provision as a result.

The other possibility, however, is that highly religious individuals mute the negative association between welfare state expenditure and citizen responsibility for public goods. This is because, despite the welfare state encroaching on the traditional role of religious organizations, the theological emphases on charitable giving help to mitigate this relationship among the highly religious. In other words, not only would we expect highly religious individuals to support individual public goods provision generally (as assessed by Hypothesis 2), but we would also expect them to do so in a way that lessens the severity of the expected negative relationship between welfare state expenditure and individual public goods provision. We formally test our hypothesis by stating that we expect highly religious individuals will mitigate the negative relationship between welfare state expenditure and individual public goods provision. However, we acknowledge the possibility, unstated in our hypothesis, that highly religious individuals may make the negative association between expenditure and public goods provision more severe.

Hypothesis 3: *High levels of religiosity diminish the negative association between welfare state expenditure and support for citizen responsibility for public goods provision.*

Relatedly, it is possible that higher taxes (used to support the welfare state) are associated with lower levels of discretionary income that can be used to engage in charitable activities. Such taxes may also discourage time spent on such activities. As a result, we expect the following:

Hypothesis 4: *The higher the levels of taxation, the lower the likelihood of individuals supporting citizen responsibility for public goods provision.*

Just as we hypothesize that highly religious individuals might either mitigate or intensify the negative relationship between levels of welfare expenditure and individual public goods provision, we also assess the degree to which highly religious individuals influence the hypothesized negative relationship between levels of taxation and individual public goods provision. Here, higher taxation rates are not necessarily crowding out the ability of religious organizations to provide public goods and services, so we do not expect that highly religious individuals will further intensify the negative relation between taxation and individual support for public goods provision. At the same time, because religious doctrines emphasize the importance of charity, we do expect that highly religious individuals might mitigate the negative association between welfare state expenditure and individual public goods provision.

Hypothesis 5: *Highly religious individuals diminish the negative association between taxation and support for citizen responsibility for public goods provision.*

Finally, we assess the impact of state subsidies to religion. If the state subsidizes the cost of maintaining a religious organization as an institution, it may relieve the burden on individual members of providing time and resources toward maintaining it. As a result, we might expect, among specifically religious individuals, that a higher degree of state support for a particular religious organization is associated with less individual public goods provision. For instance, in Italy and France, the state pays for the major repairs of Catholic churches, that is, the buildings themselves (in France if built before 1905); arrangements for monasteries and nunneries are similar. In Turkey, the state runs the mosques but does not fund religious associations. In Ireland, the state has funneled considerable social welfare and education funds through the Catholic Church. Whether it makes sense to consider these as core functions of the religion (and thus subsidized if the funds come via the state) is a subject of debate in the literature. Presumably, the impact on the generosity of individuals would still be to reduce their donations and volunteerism, since the funds and services are coming from the state (and, thus, their taxes).

Hypothesis 6: *The higher the number of subsidies to religious organizations, the lower the likelihood of religious adherents supporting citizen responsibility for public goods provision.*

Quantitative Analysis

Data for our analyses come from Round 2 of the European Social Survey (ESS) (European Social Survey 2004),[4] the Government Finance Statistics Dataset (International Monetary Fund 2015) from the International Monetary Fund, the Expanded Trade and GDP dataset (Gleditsch 2013), and the Religion and State Project (Fox 2011), resulting in more than 47,000 individual observations across 25 European countries.[5] In order to capture the priority that individuals give to contributing to public goods independently of the state, our central dependent variable of interest utilizes data collected from Round 2 of the European Social Survey.[6] Respondents were asked the degree to which they agreed with the statement that "citizens should spend at least some of their free time helping others." We construct a dichotomous (yes/no) variable from this information coded as 1 for respondents who agree and as 0 for respondents who either disagreed or who were ambivalent[7] to develop a measure illustrating individual support for citizen responsibility for the provision of public goods. Because the survey question asks about contributing free time, rather than funds, we avoid the possibility that an individual would think citizens are responsible for funding the welfare state through taxes.

We assess the size of the welfare state using data from the Government Finance Statistics dataset of the International Monetary Fund (IMF). All data related to national expenditure and taxation were collected for the year 2008 as a percentage of GDP, providing the earliest and most comprehensive data available from the IMF in relation to the totality of our countries of interest (International Monetary Fund 2015). We focus on the expenditures of government most likely to compete with services provided by religious organizations and most pertinent to potential crowding out:

---

[4] The 2004 ESS Round 2 data have the advantage of including all four of our case study countries. Italy was removed from Round 2 due to a sampling problem, and the data presented in the main text exclude Italy as a case. However, while the ESS cautions that its sampling experts have not signed off on the Italian data, they are available for separate download. We integrated it into the main dataset and reran our models including the Italian data, which we present in Online Appendix, Table OA.5. The results including the Italian data do not substantively depart from those presented here.

[5] See the Online Appendix, Table OA.4, for descriptive statistics for all variables.

[6] We provide a greater degree of detail for all of our variable descriptions in the Online Appendix. We also provide code for recreating our dataset and all statistical analyses at: http://cambridge.org/9781107135512.

[7] As a robustness check, we also ran our results against an alternative ranked variable using ordinal logit regressions. These are presented in the Online Appendix, Table OA.6. The results do not deviate systematically from those presented here.

expenditures on social protection reported as a percentage of national GDP. As a check for the influence of national wealth, we include a measure of GDP per capita collected from Kristian Gleditsch's Expanded Trade and GDP Data (Gleditsch 2013). In order to test Hypotheses 4 and 5 regarding taxation rates, we collected data from the IMF's Governance Finance Statistics database. We examine taxes on individual income, profits, and capital gains.

Our measure of religiosity is from a question in Round 2 of the ESS in which participants were asked, "regardless of whether you belong to a particular religion, how religious would you say you are?" and responded by self-classifying on a scale of 0 ("not at all religious") to 10 ("very religious"). For the hypotheses in which we are interested in simply categorizing whether individuals are highly religious or not, we create a dichotomous variable between the highly religious and others. We do not expect a subtle movement in religiosity among individuals who are not particularly religious (from 1 to 2, for example, on a religiosity scale from 0 to 10) to register much of a mitigating impact on the relationship between welfare expenditure and public goods provision. Instead, it makes sense to differentiate the highly religious, who are more likely to be involved with their religious organizations and who have more likely internalized religious messages, from less committed members.[8]

Finally, we assess Hypothesis 6 with data collected by the Religion and State Project (Fox 2011), which provides dichotomous indicators on several dimensions through which the state may subsidize religion. We sum these together to have a count of the number of different types of subsidies provided by government to religious organizations.[9]

We control for a variety of individual-level attributes with data collected from Round 2 of the European Social Survey. These variables include age, gender, number of household members, education, whether individuals were retirees, household income, marital status, an individual's self-identification on a left to right political scale, and religiosity.

---

[8] Thus, while religiosity ranges from a scale of 0 (not religious) to 10 (very religious), for the interaction term, we isolate only the most religious individuals. We did so by only including those individuals at least one standard deviation away from the mean value of the religiosity variable. We code everyone who answered as 8 or higher on the religiosity scale as highly religious and assigned a score of 0 for everyone else.

[9] Due to a lack of cross-national, comparative data, it is not possible to assess the "volume" of subsidies. The number of programs enables us to measure the extensiveness of the degree to which the state is supporting religious organizations. In Online Appendix Table OA.9, we run analyses disaggregating these measures and running each subsidy individually.

Given our dichotomous dependent variable and multilevel data with individuals nested in countries, we ran hierarchical logit regression models.[10] We use the shorthand of "individual public goods provision" to refer to our dependent variable of the extent to which individuals think people "should spend some of their free time helping others" (European Social Survey 2004).

Results

We present here only predicted probabilities for our key statistically significant variables of interest. Readers are invited to examine full tables of regression results located in both the Appendix at the end of this book and the Online Appendix.[11] Figure 8.1 presents the predicted probabilities that individuals support citizen responsibility for public goods provision, given varying levels of state expenditure on social protection. We find support for the contention of Hypothesis 1 that the higher state welfare expenditures, the less likely individuals are to support citizen responsibility for public goods provision. We see that every percentage point increase in expenditures on social protection as a percentage of GDP is associated with a decreased predicted probability of individual public goods provision. We see that very low levels of expenditure on social protection are associated with high predicted probabilities of public goods provision. For example, when expenditure on social protection is on the low end, at 8 percent of GDP, the predicted probability that individuals will support individual responsibility for public goods provision is very high, at a little over 85 percent. However, the greater government expenditure as a percentage of GDP, the lower the predicted probability. By the time government expenditure reaches very high levels of 23 percent of GDP, the predicted probability of support for citizen responsibility for public goods provision decreases to just under 70 percent.

We also find strong support for Hypothesis 2, that higher levels of religiosity will be associated with stronger support for citizen responsibility

---

[10] We rescaled the survey weights as appropriate for hierarchical models (Rabe-Hersketh and Skrondal 2006, 824).

[11] Due to the greater ease with which our statistical software produces predicted probability graphs for logit models rather than multilevel logit models, Figures 8.1–8.4 were run on logit models with clustered standard errors rather than the hierarchical models that serve as the basis of our primary analyses. Full regression tables of these primary models are shown in Appendix Tables A.11 and A.12. As comparison of Appendix Table A.11 and Online Appendix Table OA.8 reveals, the clustered logit models used to produce these figures yield very similar results to the hierarchical models.

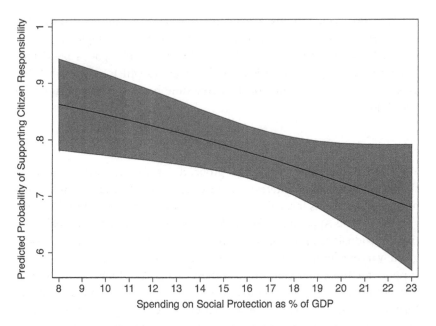

Figure 8.1 Social protection spending and predicted probability of supporting citizen responsibility for public goods provision.

for public goods provision. In each of our statistical models[12] each unit increase in an individual's level of religiosity is associated with an increased likelihood of supporting individual responsibility for public goods provision. This relationship is illustrated visually in Figure 8.2.

Furthermore, we find support for Hypothesis 3, that highly religious individuals diminish the negative association between welfare state expenditure and support for citizen responsibility for public goods provision. We assessed the interaction effect between welfare state expenditure and religiosity and their subsequent impact on support for citizen responsibility for public goods provision. We present a predicted probability plot (Figure 8.3) examining the nature of the interaction between high religiosity and social welfare spending and their relationship to individual support for public goods provision.

Figure 8.3 demonstrates the predicted probabilities for expenditure on social protection in our interaction model for both highly religious and non-highly religious individuals. The figure graphically illustrates the mitigating impact high levels of religiosity have on the negative association

[12] See Appendix Table A.11.

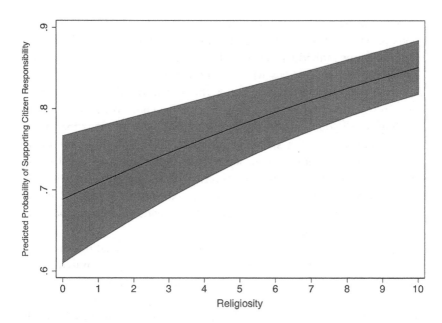

Figure 8.2 Religiosity and predicted probability of supporting citizen responsibility for public goods provision.

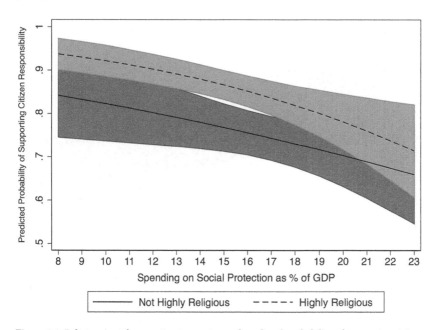

Figure 8.3 Religious/social protection interaction and predicted probability of supporting citizen responsibility for public goods provision.

between government social welfare expenditures and individual public goods provision. The dotted line indicates the predicated probabilities for highly religious individuals, whereas the solid line indicates the predicated probabilities for individuals who do not self-identify as highly religious. There are two notable results. First, highly religious individuals are more likely to support citizen responsibility for public goods provision than are non-highly religious individuals. The second notable result is that, while the relationship between spending on social protection and support for public goods provision is still statistically significant and negative for highly religious individuals, the severity of the negative relationship between public goods provision and welfare expenditure is reduced among the highly religious when compared with individuals who do not self-identify as highly religious.

Hypothesis 4 stipulates that the higher the levels of taxation, the lower the likelihood individuals support citizen responsibility for public goods provision. Figure 8.4 visually represents this relationship. The model assesses the impact of individual taxes on income, profits, and capital gains on support for citizen responsibility for public goods provision. In Figure 8.4, we see that every percentage point increase in these taxes as a

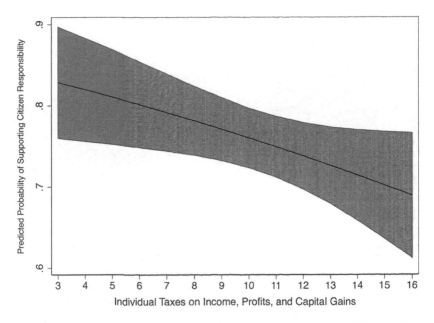

Figure 8.4 Taxation rates and predicted probability of supporting citizen responsibility for public goods provision.

percentage of GDP is associated with a decreased likelihood that an individual supports citizen responsibility for public goods provision.[13]

On the other hand, our models provide little support for Hypothesis 5, suggesting that high levels of religiosity diminish the negative association between taxation and support for citizen responsibility for public goods provision. The coefficient on the interaction term[14] is not statistically significant, suggesting that highly religious individuals have similarly diminished support for individual responsibility for public goods provision as their less religious counterparts at increasing levels of social welfare provision. Our sixth hypothesis states that higher levels of subsidies to religious organizations should result in lower likelihoods of support among religious adherents for citizen responsibility for public goods provision. However, we find that the number of different government subsidies has no statistically significant impact on the views of religious individuals that they should spend time helping others.[15]

While we have no a priori theoretical expectations about denominational effects, we are also interested in variation in the degree to which various religious traditions are associated with individual support of a responsibility for public goods provision. Here we examine the same models we analyzed previously, but we replace religiosity with categorical variables assessing the religious affiliation of survey respondents. The potential categories include Catholics, Muslims, Protestants, Orthodox, and an "other" category.[16] Each of these categories is assessed against individuals who responded that their religious status was "not applicable," and we take this as meaning these individuals are not members of a

---

[13] Our interest here is in creating a broad and generalizable portrait of the relationship between religion and the welfare state pertinent across a broad array of European religious groups (and less religiously observant individuals). In Online Appendix Table OA.10, however, we analyze only those individuals who identify specifically as Muslims and Catholics. While the results are similar as those demonstrated here, we note that increased taxes do not have a statistically significant impact in these alternative models.

[14] See Model 4 of Appendix Table A.11.

[15] See Appendix Table A.11, Model 5. However, in the Online Appendix we also point out that the relationship is somewhat more nuanced. Online Appendix Table OA.9 demonstrates the effects of each individual subsidy, disaggregated from the count measure. In six of eight cases, the individual subsidies have no statistically significant relationship with individual public goods provision. The exceptions are: (1) subsidies to religious colleges and universities, which are negatively associated, and (2) official positions or salaries for clergy, which is positively associated with support for public goods provision.

[16] The other category includes other Christian denominations, Jewish individuals, adherents of Eastern religious, and adherents of other non-Christian religions. Collectively, this category accounts for only about 2 percent of the sample.

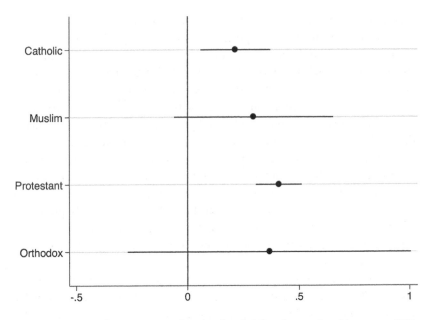

Figure 8.5 Religious denominations and predicted probability of supporting citizen responsibility for public goods provision. Note: Confidence intervals intersecting zero indicate that a relationship is not statistically significant.

religious organization.[17] The results are largely similar to our main results and are shown in Appendix Table A.11, but here we want to briefly highlight the impact of each religious denomination with the aid of Figure 8.5.

We find some support that individuals who identify as being part of Catholic congregations are positively associated with individual public goods provision. This relationship is generally positive and statistically significant.[18] We furthermore find only limited support that Muslims are positively associated with individual public goods provision. We find little

---

[17] The ESS also asked individuals a yes/no question regarding whether they belonged to a religious organization. In order to assess the fairness of our assumption that individuals who answered "not applicable" are not religious adherents, we examined responses to religious denomination against responses to whether or not an individual identified as part of a religious organization. There were no individuals who identified as belonging to a particular religious denomination who also answered "no" to the question of whether they belonged to a religious institution. There were, on the other hand, 14,359 individuals who answered "no" to belonging to a religious institution and who mentioned that the denominational question was "not applicable" to them.

[18] For more detailed discussion of our results and for full regression tables, see Appendix Table A.11.

support that adherents of Orthodox Christianity support individual responsibility for public goods provision. By far, the most robust variable among the individual religious denominations is Protestantism.[19]

Summary and Discussion of Statistical Results

To summarize, the data provide strong support for our first hypothesis, that higher state welfare expenditures are associated with lower likelihoods that individuals support citizen responsibilities for public goods provision. Across all our pertinent statistical models, including the models presented in the Appendix at the end of this book and in the Online Appendix, we find that increases in state expenditure on social protection are associated with a decrease in support for individual public goods provision. The relationship supports the interpretation that citizens feel absolved from personal responsibility for providing public goods when the welfare state is generous. We further find support for the Hypothesis 2, that individuals with higher levels of religiosity are more likely to support individual public goods provision.

Also of interest are the results for our test of Hypothesis 3 conjecturing that high levels of religiosity diminish the negative association between welfare state expenditure and support for citizen responsibility for public goods provision. As we mentioned previously, existing literature suggests two potential outcomes here. The first is that, because the welfare state crowds out the traditional activities of religious institutions, we would expect that the negative association between welfare state expenditure and support for individual responsibility for public goods provision is further amplified among highly religious individuals. The second, however, is that, regardless of the welfare state encroaching on the traditional activities, emphases on charity and selflessness commonly associated with religious theology should have a mitigating impact, among highly religious adherents, on the negative relationship between welfare expenditure and individual public goods provision. The negative and statistically significant impact of the interaction suggests that highly religious individuals mitigate the negative relationship between welfare state spending and individual public goods provision. While highly religious individuals are less likely to support individual responsibility for public goods provision under

---

[19] Our residual "Other" category also has a strong statistically significant and positive relationship. It is difficult to glean much from the observation as it includes several distinct religious denominations and includes only about 2 percent of the sample.

increasing levels of welfare state expenditure, this effect is significantly muted when compared with individuals who are not highly religious. The evidence suggests that, while crowding out does occur, highly religious individuals are somewhat insulated from this impact.

Furthermore, we find evidence that higher levels of taxation are associated with decreased support for individual public goods provision (Hypothesis 4).[20] Interestingly, however, we find little support for Hypothesis 5, that highly religious individuals diminish the negative association between taxation rates and individual public goods provision. We find little support for the proposition that increasing numbers of subsidies to religious organizations decreases support for individual responsibility for public goods provision (Hypothesis 6). This may be at least be partially due to the fact, as we mention later in this chapter, that many individuals are unaware of the extent of those subsidies, to the fact that the subsidies in many countries fall quite short of covering parishes and associations' needs, and in many countries, the religious organizations may have charitable and other activities they want to fund that are not assisted by state subsidies. Finally, when we examined the impact of denominational affiliation, we found that, while Catholics and Muslims showed some association with support for public goods provision, by far the most pronounced and robust relationship occurs with Protestants.

While our quantitative analyses demonstrate these findings using survey data across many European countries, to further our understanding of whether and how the extent of the welfare state affects generosity, and especially the impact on Catholics and Muslims, we turn to our case studies conducted in France, Ireland, Italy, and Turkey.

Case Studies and Interviews

The four countries we studied entered the twenty-first century with somewhat different welfare states. To give our contemporary research some context, we provide a brief survey to establish the historical relationship between church, state, and welfare provision. We then describe the major Catholic and Muslim charities in France, Ireland, Italy and Turkey before moving on to unpack some of the ways in which the welfare state affects the generous and helpful propensities and activities of Catholics and Muslims.

---

[20] As mentioned previously, this relationship is not statistically significant when we isolate Catholics and Muslims.

Historical Context

The Catholic Church has long had a role in providing social welfare and, particularly since the late nineteenth century, has argued forcefully for its freedom to do so. It has also attempted to temper the direction of the provision of social welfare, to stave off socialist and communist movements while protecting workers and the poor. This statement was most pronounced in Pope Leo XIII's *Rerum Novarum* (1891) and in the well-known liberation theology movement that originated with some in the Catholic Church in Latin America (Gutiérrez 1971; Mainwaring and Wilde 1989). In Islam, social welfare has long been provided through institutional means we discussed in Chapter 2, the waqfs or legal modifications thereof, zakat, and other forms of charity. As organized religions, both Catholicism and Islam act on platforms of social responsibility, moderated by the histories and contexts of the states in which their organizations operate. In France, the state took over activities that the Catholic Church and nominally affiliated organizations had been providing during the Third Republic (1870–1940). That situation remains; the Church's charities are legal, but, in contrast to some European countries such as Germany, not central to the delivery of state-funded social welfare. As Manow and Palier observe of France, "Establishing direct state responsibility for the infirm, orphans, and the old aged openly and deliberately challenged the dominance of the Catholic Church in caring for the most destitute" (2009, 151). Eugen Weber famously argued that this and the takeover of education was part of the state's effort to "make peasants into Frenchmen" (1976). Whatever the motive, the state has fundamental responsibility for funding and running social welfare services.

Ireland has a similar trajectory with relatively more room for religious institutions. In the newly independent Ireland of 1922, the state put control of most social services in the hands of religious organizations, though it provided the bulk of the funding.[21] These organizations are predominantly Catholic, with formal or informal ties to the Catholic Church. Initial investments by the state were in public education and child welfare, with pensions and adult healthcare added gradually, until Ireland developed a broad range of social protections that other European states had. Recently, the state has had to step in more actively, due to demographic changes,

---

[21] Ireland was first established as the Irish Free State. The 1937 Constitution disestablished that and led to the declaration of the Republic of Ireland in 1949. The Republic reinforced the Catholic Church's control over the content, provision, and quality of public education (Garvin 2004).

public pressure, institutional child abuse scandals, and changes in the religious behavior of the Irish. It has shifted some social provision to the market; for instance, if one wants and can afford better health insurance, one can buy it privately.

In Italy, the state traditionally has provided rather limited social welfare. After the unification of Italy between 1861 and 1871, the state was dominated by Liberal politicians who preferred to restrain the state's role in social assistance. Borrowing from German Chancellor Otto von Bismarck's example, they established limited, occupation-based social insurance and pension schemes. They left other forms of social assistance to the Catholic Church (Lynch 2009, 98, 103). While the occupations covered have expanded since the 1870s, and new forms of assistance have developed, Italy's system has given birth to the phrase "the poverty of welfare" (Rostagno and Utili 1998). It is based primarily on pension and other benefits for those who have been or are in the formal labor market. "Unemployment, family allowances, and maternity benefits" are low in comparison to other European countries (Lynch 2009, 104; Rostagno and Utili 1998, 8). Much of Italy's social welfare assistance is provided by local and provincial level governments, which is a remnant of the patronage and clientelist systems established by Italian political parties (Lynch 2009, 108–111). Given the marked discrepancies in Italy in the functioning of governments across regions (Putnam 1993; Rhodes, Binder, and Rockman 1996), there are wide discrepancies in coverage and in actual access to services. Education is run by the state.

In Turkey, the state constitutionally defines itself as a social state and is responsible for providing social services for the poor. As part of top-down secularizing reforms in the 1920s after the proclamation of Turkish Republic in 1923, the state took control of properties owned by religious associations. After that, it banned organizing activities on a religious basis. Although religious communities mobilized their followers and established associations and foundations afterward, they never openly affiliated themselves with religion. Legally, they were defined as cultural, social, or economic associations. Since religious foundations had lost their properties to the state, they also lost their capacity to run large-scale charities with their existing investments and capital. This put more of a burden on the state and decreased demands on religious charities. In terms of the state's role in welfare provision, Turkey lags behind many European countries. Turkey did not implement an occupation-based social insurance and pension system until the early 2000s. It then shifted to a universal health-care system and increased state support for those who were not getting pensions. The state provides free education from preschool to college (the government removed tuition for public universities in the early 2010s). While the legal criteria and limits need not concern us here, in each country, secular and religious volunteer organizations and organized religions may also provide charitable services.

Brief Overview of Major Religious Charities
The history of religious-based charities in our four countries has been well covered by other scholars (Göçmen 2014; Isik 2014; Jones 1989; Maguire 2013; Morvaridi 2013; Quine 2002; Sen, Aksular, and Samur 2009; Smith 2003). The Catholic-dominant countries each have one or two large Catholic institutional structures that engage in social welfare activities, and Turkey likewise has one major Catholic organization.[22] The major organizations in Ireland are Cross Care and Society of St. Vincent de Paul; in France *Société Saint Vincent-de-Paul*; in Italy, Caritas Ambrosiana and *Società San Vincenzo de Paoli*; and in Turkey, Caritas Turkey. There are smaller religious-based organizations as well, such as France's *Comité catholique contre la faim et pour le développement – Terre Solidaire* (Catholic Committee against Hunger and for Development-Solidarity of the Earth [CCFD]), which has a specific focus on international development. These Catholic charities are not necessarily organizations governed by the Catholic Church; they may be independent of the Church's authority structure. As for Islamic charitable organizations, Turkey has a number of major culturally based charities, the most prominent of which for our study of Islam is the Gülen movement's Kimse Yok Mu (Is Anybody There?, or KYM), an aid and solidarity association. Although the KYM does not have branches in France, Italy, and Ireland, it does engage in fundraising campaigns in these countries, and these campaigns are supported by volunteers who encourage people to donate to KYM through its website.

In Turkey, because organizing around religion has not been legally permitted since the early Republican era through the time of writing this book, the charity organizations affiliated with different religious communities do not officially use a label that denotes a religious connotation. This, though, has not prevented the formation of several charity organizations associated with different religious communities. These organizations

---

[22] The story is a little complicated in that in Ireland, the state, until recently, ran most of its social welfare programs through the Church (Garvin 2004, 64), and in both France and Italy, many of the major hospitals are run by Catholic organizations, though funded by the state and private insurance companies.

define themselves as charity associations or foundations without explicitly stating their religious nature. Although organizing around religion is not allowed, the state has allowed foreign, non-Muslim religious organizations to operate in Turkey due to its obligations stemming from international agreements.[23]

The major charity organization affiliated with the Catholic Church in Istanbul is Caritas Turkey. It is part of Caritas Internationalis and has a very close relationship with the Bishop's office in Istanbul. Its major mission as humanitarian (IC20). When we conducted the interviews, the largest group benefiting from the charity work of Caritas was refugees, particularly from Iraq. The president of the organization, Rinaldo Marmara, stated that most, if not all, of these refugees were Christians who had left Iraq after the US-led war of 2003. Marmara stated that the reason why most of the beneficiaries were Christians was not because Caritas discriminates against other groups, but because they wanted to avoid the criticism of using charity for missionary work. For this reason, they leave helping Muslim refugees to the state or Islamic charities.[24] Caritas also developed projects for low-income families in Eastern Turkey, focusing more on Christians for the same reason stated above. In addition to Caritas, there are a few hospitals and private schools affiliated with the Catholic Church in Istanbul. There is also an orphanage and a nursing house for the elderly. These associations are under the hierarchy of the Church, but they all have their own separate boards. The laity plays a considerable role in the operation of these charities.

The Islamic-affiliated charity KYM was established in 2002. To be clear, the organization does not refer to religion in its official documents and defines itself as "an international non-profit humanitarian aid and

---

[23] The Treaty of Lausanne (1923) protects the rights of non-Muslim minorities in Turkey. Furthermore, the Turkish government passed new legal amendments in the 2000s to allow international support for non-Muslim minorities in Turkey (Kılınç 2014).

[24] Marmara explained: "Most of our work focuses on Christians. We would love to help all without having any discrimination. However, the sensitivities in state and society lead us to constrain our focus only with Christians, particularly Christian refugees coming from Iraq. The focus is more on Christians. People are concerned that we use humanitarian aid to convert people to Christianity. I can assure you that this is not what we aim in our activities at Caritas. Sure, Caritas is a Christian organization. Sure, we do what we do because we're Christians. Sure, our beliefs motivate us for what we do. However, the target of our charities can be anybody who needs help. Conversion is not a requirement to receive help. But Turkish society does not trust us on this. For this reason, we try our best not to extend our activities to those people that can lead to misunderstandings" (IC20).

development organization."[25] It gained a special consultative status at the United Nations Economic and Social Council (ECOSOC). According to the vice-president of the organization, Levent Eyüboğlu, the organization provides humanitarian relief in five issue areas: educational programs, medical assistance, disaster relief, humanitarian aid, and sustainable development (IM32).[26] By the time of our study, it had a wide presence in Turkey, with 31 branches, and it provides relief in 113 countries (see Figure 8.6 for an example).[27]

In France, the *Société Saint Vincent-de-Paul* (Saint Vincent de Paul, or SVdP) is a prominent Catholic charity, having been founded in 1833 by Frédéric Ozanam, a law student. Challenged to demonstrate his Catholic principles, he and some fellow students set up what remain hallmarks of the organization: home visits to the poor, donations of money or other forms of assistance as needed, addressing the sources of a particular person or family's poverty, and promoting the spiritual development of the volunteers. An organization with a more international focus, *Comité catholique contre la faim et pour le développement – Terre Solidaire*, works to alleviate hunger and promote social and economic development overseas. It is more known by its partial acronym that downplays its Catholic origins, CCFD-Terre Solidaire, and was founded in 1961 as part of the French Church's response to an appeal by the Food and Agricultural Organization, endorsed by Pope John XXIII.[28] Caritas Ambrosiana, in Milan, was created in 1963 by the Archdiocese and is an official office of that diocese. It is related to Caritas di Italia but is a much more extensive organization, which works at local, regional, national, and international levels. The *Società San Vincenzo de Paoli* (Society of St. Vincent de Paul)

---

[25] www.kimseyokmu.org.tr/?p=content&gl=temel_icerik&cl=kurumsal&l=hakkimizda. That website was shut down by the government after the events in Turkey of July 2016. A similar KYM statement is at http://embracerelief.org/wp-content/uploads/2014/10/KYM_IMPACT_STATEMENT1.pdf, accessed Feb. 22, 2018.

[26] Since our interviews with the leaders of the major charities did not follow the regular interview format that we had, we did not count them among the semi-structured interviews. But since we will use their quotations in this book, we assigned them an interview code. For Istanbul, the KYM representative is coded as IM32; France's St. Vincent de Paul, PC27; Caritas Ambrosiana, MC24; Ireland's St. Vincent de Paul, DC29; Cross Care, DC31.

[27] This situation significantly changed when around 2013, the AKP-led government accused the Gülen movement of subversion. The state sent several administrative inspectors to check KYM's financial transactions. In July 2016, after the failed military coup, the government closed down KYM and began judicial investigations.

[28] The leadership of *Action Catholique*, an ancillary organization of the French Church, organized the CCFD.

Figure 8.6 Kimse Yok Mu brochure about activities in Sudan.

evolved in Italy in the 1840s out of the organization founded in France. Currently present throughout Italy, its work is done primarily at the parish level. Ireland has two major Catholic charities, Cross Care, founded by the Archdiocese of Dublin in 1941, and St. Vincent de Paul, founded in 1844, also developing out of the original French organization. St. Vincent de Paul is the largest organized charity in Ireland, and, like Cross Care, its primary focus is on local needs and effectiveness.

Many of the major projects of Catholic charities are government-funded: either by outright awards or through public procurement tender processes, in which the relevant state agency puts out a call for bids. The head of the national office of St. Vincent de Paul in Ireland commented that there's a "whole skill set" to grant-writing (DC29). In Italy, funds also come from a particular income tax (MC24, DC29).[29]

---

[29] The *otto per mille* takes 0.08 percent of a person's income tax and gives it to one of now about a dozen different religions, including the Catholic Church, that have formal agreements with the state, or to the state. Taxpayers can pick which of the religions the

Also noteworthy is the influence of the religious angle. All of the Catholic organizations stressed that a large part of their role is, in the words of Don Roberto Davanzo, the head of Caritas Ambrosiana, to help Christians in their parishes keep alive the spirit and orientation of helping others and to never forget that as Christians, they are to help others (MC24; DC29). They want to get Catholics involved, rather than have them just donate funds. While a cynic might say that's because they've been so crowded out by the state that donating funds is all that's left to them, their understanding of their role does not correspond to conventional welfare state thinking of means-testing or focusing on providing basic material support. A fair bit of the national organization's efforts is directed toward ensuring that the parish-level volunteer groups have the training and other resources they need to do their work, and that when a local group sees a new area of need, they can get help from the national organization to address it. Caritas Ambrosiana sees itself not as a humanitarian organization, but as an organization of the Gospel, with the work of the Gospel as its "fundamental motivation" (MC24). St. Vincent de Paul emphasizes the encounter between people and the learning of others' vulnerabilities. The organization hopes to "make generosity" possible by affecting their volunteers' attitudes and understandings of poverty. "For us, the key thing is the relationship" (DC29).

The relationship between helper and the recipient was also emphasized by the vice-president of KYM. One prominent annual campaign that encourages people-to-people interaction is KYM's *kurban* campaign (Turkish; *qurbani*, Arabic; sacrifice of a livestock animal during the Muslim festival of Eid al-Adha). During Eid al-Adha, the organization not only accepts donations of meat to help the needy, but also recruits volunteers to distribute services in person and to spend time with the recipients (IM32). Most of the time, the volunteers from developed cities in Western Turkey travel to Eastern Turkey to help. In the view of KYM, this practice reduces class-related conflicts and contributes to unity in Turkish society. The representative noted that these activities give people from Eastern and Western Turkey an opportunity to interact (IM32). In the recent years, KYM started international exchanges as well during Eid al-Adha. For example, a volunteer from Paris indicated that he traveled to Pakistan for a KYM campaign in 2007 (PM7). Another program that involved in-person activity was that of medical doctors who provide pro bono medical services in developing countries during their vacation time

funds go to or have the funds go to the state. If they do not pick, the funds automatically go the Catholic Church.

(IM32). By June 2010, KYM had arranged for more than 20,000 cataract patients to be treated in African countries, mostly thanks to the work of the volunteer medical doctors (IM32).

Both Catholic and Muslim leaders emphasized the necessity of state involvement in the resolution of social problems. The Catholic organizations' leaders had a firm view that solving social problems was not their organizations' or the Church's exclusive responsibility. They were not rejecting the idea of helping, but were rejecting the state's efforts to shrink the scope of the welfare state, to abandon what the state had taken over as its responsibilities in earlier decades. For instance, in Milan, Caritas Ambrosiana worked with the city on a city-funded project to house Roma people, but, along with the Archbishop, rejected the city's efforts to shift the entire issue onto the Church: "we'll help, but Roma are not a problem just of the Church" (MC24).

The leaders of the voluntary organizations tended to speak of their work as being complementary to the religious institutions and to the states. For instance, with Caritas Ambrosiana, there are more than 300 parish-level "welcome centers" (*centri di ascolto*, literally "listening centers"), where those having problems often first turn to find immediate assistance. The centers also help people find out what aid is available from state agencies. The centers are, as the director said, the "antennae" of the organization, and from them, the leadership learns more about actual needs and issues. It can then raise those needs and issues with Church leadership and the state. In turn, the Church and the state can suggest a focal area for the organization: the Church through announcing a new charitable initiative, the state through issuing a call for proposals in a new issue area. In Milan, the Archbishop had noticed the sudden impoverishment of local families, due to the recession that started in 2008–9, so in 2010 launched the *fondo familigia lavoro* (working family fund), and Caritas Ambrosiana adopted that as its fundraising campaign that year (MC24). The priest heading up the Paris archdiocese's solidarity office made a similar point (PC22). A volunteer staff member of the regional Ile-de-Paris branch of Secours Catholique noted it cannot "substitute for state services"; what they can do is "follow a family long-term and closely," something that might be harder for the state, as more of a bureaucratic entity, to do (PC9).

KYM representatives made similar points and stated that their role was mostly complementary to the state's welfare policies. As the vice-president Levent Eyüboğlu noted, despite increasing state support for the poor and needy in the 2000s, the state is still far from being sufficient to meet the welfare needs of the Turkish people. There are many people who do not know how to access state resources, and there are also many who abuse the system.

Because of their extensive volunteer networks, KYM was able to identify the genuinely needy (IM32). Eyüboğlu indicated that, because the state helped the needy mostly with material assistance, state support to the poor did not provide long-term solutions. KYM offered educational opportunities to provide a solution that was sustainable. He gave examples of several vocational training centers in Turkey and abroad, funded and run by KYM, that provide the unskilled poor with skills to help them find long-term, better-paying jobs. He noted that in absolute amounts, KYM's support was marginal compared with that of the state, yet he also thought it was providing a more lasting solution for the people that the KYM was able to assist (IM32).

What comes through in interviews with the leaders of the major Catholic charities and regional Catholic charities, as well as with leaders of parish-level charities, is the view that social welfare cannot be provided solely by relying on volunteers and volunteer donations. The volunteers have a wide range of capacities, expertise, and availability that may or may not match the organization's needs. Even at the local level, leaders said they could not always take on someone who wanted to volunteer if the person was not a good fit for the position or role. Further, at the local level, a number of charities have to suspend operations during school holidays, as many of their volunteers are retirees who have grandchildren whom they accompany on vacations. Most individuals are not available to be full-time volunteers. As the leader of Caritas Ambrosiana stated, the drawback of volunteers is that relying on them is less efficient than having regular employees; the volunteers cannot give a lot of time. However, he viewed the volunteers as crucial, because they could "encounter the poor where they are" (MC24).

The large charities are well regarded, so much so that even adherents of other religions, lapsed Catholics, and the nonreligious respond to calls for donations and also volunteer or work as paid staff for them. The charities only ask that volunteers and employees accept the organization's premises and goals; they do not have religious tests for volunteering (MC24, DC26, DC31, PC27).

In Turkey, the major Catholic charity has less engagement with state-sponsored programs due to its affiliation with a minority religion. As the president of Caritas noted, "We do not work much with the state. Recently we worked with the city government for improving our nursing home for the elderly. It is a historical nursing home in a historical setting. The city helped us in updating the building" (IC20). For reasons mentioned earlier, Caritas is a bit restricted in whom they can help. Marmara pointed out that they cannot generate sufficient funds internally for their work in Turkey, explaining, "Most of the time, we work with our European branches to provide the necessary service that we need to do. Caritas offices in Italy and Spain are our main partners for most of the time" (IC20).

Also noting a theme of predominantly operating independently of the state, the KYM representative stated, "Although we have worked with the state in some projects, we are most of the time alone. The state, particularly the city government, sometimes provides us some facilities. However, most of the projects that we conduct are developed and executed by our own organization with little or no state help" (IM32). He added that "we are about to get consultative status at the United Nations Economic and Social Council. Once that is completed, we will be able to voice the needs of the poor better. This status will also give us more recognition and facilitate our charity work." He pointed out that the organization's work is extensive internationally: "Our projects vary from humanitarian aid to Palestinians to sustainable development projects in which we train women to establish their own business from home. We are present in more than 100 countries through various projects, including drilling water wells, establishing schools, providing free health services, and fighting against hunger" (IM32).

The image one gets of the relationship between the major Catholic and Muslim charities and the welfare state is that the former adapt to the structures of the latter, at the same time that the charities actively remind the state of its own obligations to its citizens and to international development.[30] None of the charities wants to revert to a situation in which responsibility for social welfare provision is left to individuals and to charitable organizations, religious or otherwise. They recognize the severe limitations of such a scenario. They see their organizations as facilitating the spiritual development of their volunteers and being able to respond more quickly than the state to nascent social problems. As the next section shows, these views were by and large voiced by parishioners and association members.

Catholics and the State's Responsibility, the Church's Responsibility, and Individuals' Responsibility
We start by considering Catholic interviewees' views on the state's responsibility to help others. To preview, what we find is that their views are varied – even those within the same parish do not espouse a consistent

---

[30] We did not find any evidence of the major charities working collaboratively with charities from other faiths on specific projects; that is not to say they do not, or did not, but that was not the emphasis, particularly at the local level of parishes and associations.

Catholic social welfare-based argument for the state to help those in need. While scholars have written extensively of pre- and post-Vatican II Catholic social welfare doctrine (Berryman 1987; Buchanan and Conway 1996; Fogarty 1957; Gutiérrez 1973; Puggioni 2015; Smith 1991), these doctrines and related analyses appear to have little hold on our parishioners. Indeed, parishioners' comments about the state's responsibility may not differ much from the range of views that likely are held by those less engaged in Catholicism. As we will see below, what is likely different is their views of the Church's and of individuals' roles in complementing the state's social welfare activity. Views of the state's responsibility and its competence undoubtedly also reflected the reality of the times: at the time of interviews, Ireland was in the midst of a massive International Monetary Fund and European Union–organized loan bailout, and the government and major banks' responsibility for the financial problems had been exposed; Italy was in a recession that was compounding its perennial problems of public service delivery; unemployment was high in France; and in Turkey the economic growth rate was the lowest it had been in a decade.

Though a few Catholics did not think the state had a responsibility to provide social welfare (DC12, DC13), a much more frequent refrain was that the state should assist the needy. However, these individuals felt the state may not be well placed to identify needs, nor should it be the only source of assistance. An Italian Catholic in her forties said that "the state has a responsibility to help those in need. If there's a need, then [state intervention] goes well for everyone. But the state can't be aware of the needs of everyone, especially the particularities. The parish priest is the one who knows people in the area and can respond better to specific needs, and is quicker to respond than is the state. Plus, the state in Italy doesn't even do what it's supposed to do." One Ballygall parishioner said of the state's responsibility, "I think so, yeah, definitely, definitely" (DC15). Many thought, as did the above Italian Catholic, that the state has a responsibility but does not do enough: "the state has responsibility to help others, it doesn't do enough for housing in Paris" (PC7). At Santa Maria alla Fontana, a parishioner responded that the state's main responsibility is "social order" and thought the level of assistance provided was "ok," but then, as with many other interviewees, added caveats: she noted regional disparities, that the public debt was too high, yet that there's a lot of poverty in the world, and that "the state should help, not just the Church" (MC1).

Others had complicated responses, noting that the state should exercise leadership in social welfare at the same time that "we are all linked in" and therefore responsible to help others (DC14). Some agreed the state has a responsibility but that it is difficult to know whom they should actually help: "I think it does, yeah, they [the state] had the money to do so, obviously [it is] struggling very hard to cope with all the calls on the public purse because of mismanagement of banks and we've decided to bail out people who invested in Ireland, and they were just speculators ... but then who did they [the state] have the responsibility to? I don't think the government can sort everyone out" (DC16).

Some Catholics tended to differentiate types of responsibilities. Several said the state's responsibility is to be more concerned with "social cohesion" or "social order" (PC4, MC1); another said that "it's not same as the Church's" and noted the "specificity of *laïcité*," and thought the current arrangement on social welfare between the Church and state is a "good compromise" (PC11). An Italian parishioner commented that "the state should have a responsibility, perhaps a bit limited, to help those in need ... ; it should limit itself to helping with material support; it should help materially but not morally" (DC3). Some seemed to think that the Church and individuals should be responsible for helping with immediate needs (MC5), while the state's responsibility was to help people learn how to support themselves. Indeed, Catholic interviewees in all countries had a tendency to see the responsibilities as complementary: as one Milan parishioner stated, the Church helps to identify new forms of poverty and then asks the state to intervene. He seemed to regret the extent to which the responsibility of the Church for helping those in need had "passed to" the state (MC14). While acknowledging that the state still needs to help, one noted that the priest "can be more precise and quicker" (MC15). While a Turkish Catholic felt state programs to Turkish citizens were adequate, she mentioned that the state makes little to no effort to reach new immigrants coming to Turkey. To her, in those situations, the Church community or individuals should fill in (IC3).

Many had a negative view of their state's contribution to social welfare: in response to a question about whether the state has a responsibility to help those in need, an Irish Catholic said, "[A]bsolutely and they do nothing about it. Without the volunteer charities, where would we be? The state does nothing ... It doesn't want to look after disadvantaged people. The state just lines its own pockets" (DC9). Another Ballygall parishioner had an equally dim view of the state: he said it does have a responsibility to help those in need, "but it's failed. Public servants have hijacked the state" (DC10). Another Irish parishioner observed that the state has a responsibility to help those in need, "but it is not managed well, and I don't think the right people are getting help." He noted that salaries for judges are high but the state is lowering the minimum wage (DC2). An Italian Catholic thought the state had a responsibility but that it has a costly infrastructure that doesn't leave enough funds to help the truly needy (MC17). For these Catholics, regardless of how responsible one thinks the state should be for helping those in need, their state has done a poor job of it.

Generally, most Catholic interviewees from Dublin, Istanbul, and Milan thought the state had a responsibility to help those in need and that the state was not living up to its responsibility. An Italian Catholic commented that the state is not helping enough, and it is cutting back on social welfare "with the excuse that it doesn't have any money." She added that she would prefer to give "directly because the state chooses poorly" (MC4). An Irish parishioner was quite negative, even as she was emphatic that the state had a significant responsibility to help the needy: "of course, it's what they should've been doing all along." She commented on the way it seemed that social welfare operated in Ireland: "if you had it [money], you got more ... The total irresponsibility of the state is unbelievable ... It should have a bigger responsibility for the poor in this country" (DC4).

Sometimes parishioners noted it was the state's failure in social welfare that meant the Church's work was all the more important. Mixed in were also comments that the Church was more effective at targeting the needy and getting funds. An Italian Catholic said that the "state has a responsibility to aid others but more happens in the parish" (MC16). Others note the Church filling in for state shortfalls: an Italian Catholic noted that "the [state] social institutions are so underfunded they need private charity to support them" (MC14). Another observed that "the state has a responsibility but doesn't fulfill it. The state doesn't have means to ask for special funds for emergencies, but the Church and priests do" (MC6). A Catholic woman from Istanbul indicated the problems of the welfare system: "the state improved health and social aid recently but I am not sure if they're able to identify the people who are in real need" (IC21). She added that "the local Catholics in Istanbul are doing well but we are in greater need for our immigrant population and the state offers little for them" (IC21). A parishioner at Santa Maria alla Fontana expressed sentiments of many Italian Catholics in the comment that "the state does less than the Church; it is more skeletal; and it loses a lot of money whereas the Church doesn't" (MC18).

Many Catholics thought the state had a responsibility to help those in need but were wary of state welfare being exploited. According to a French parishioner, "yes, in an ideal vision, the state could help others, lots of help would be free" (PC17), and his wife responded, "within limits ... We can't close our eyes to people who have problems, especially on the streets. It would be intolerable if we did. But I don't like people who exploit the system" (PC18). An Irish Catholic also expressed concern about the beneficiaries of state assistance and the tax system: "the state needs to be aware of the needs of different people, but some people who hardly contributed are getting the same as the people who contribute a lot" (DC11). An Istanbul Catholic agreed: "there are some people who abuse the social programs and the state does not do much to prevent this from happening" (IC5).

If individuals thought that the state had a responsibility to help those in need, did they also think that individuals and the Church did? It is important to know, because the crowding-out hypothesis would lead us to surmise that if people thought the state had a significant responsibility to help, then they would not expect the Church or individuals to help. A few Catholics did hold this view. A French parishioner thought the state had more responsibility than the Church and individuals: "[I]t's the state that should do things for people. Bill Gates should pay more taxes ... For St. Augustine, the perfect city doesn't need God. But man isn't perfect. The Catholic Church understands that the secular [*laique*] state is a necessity. The works of the Church aren't sufficient" (PC15). His view was that the Church and its adherents could never replace the state's welfare capacities and that, by virtue of being a state, the state had a responsibility to help the needy. Most Catholics thought that whatever the state responsibility might be, the Church and individuals have a responsibility to help others. As one Irish Catholic said, "individuals have very much so a responsibility. It's a driver in becoming involved." She noted that there are many organizations in Ireland doing "great work" and that "they can only do it with people's help. Who am I to expect other people to do it if I'm not prepared to help?" (DC3). Another noted that the Church has a large responsibility and a "huge amount of ability" to fulfill that responsibility (DC10). One who noted that the state does have a responsibility to help those in need, and to try to figure out who those people and families are, also said that "the onus is on the state or on the Church," then added, "the way the Church really helps is through [St.] Vincent de Paul" (DC24). Another in Dublin commented that one should "do what you can, you can only go as far as people will let you. It boils down to a welcoming parish, we make a point of that here" (DC4).

There was virtually universal agreement among the Catholic interviewees that individuals have a responsibility to help those in need, and that view was not affected by the different kinds of welfare states they were in nor by religious majority or minority status. For example, French Catholics, recognizing that the state has an extensive social welfare system, still said individuals have a responsibility to help others (PC3, PC4, PC8, PC11, PC17, PC18). An Italian Catholic, while noting that the state sometimes falls short in being effective with its resources, said that the "good Christian both pays taxes and makes charitable donations" (MC6). How the welfare state size affected Catholics' views was more along the lines of what one Italian Catholic noted, who said that because the state falls short, private charity is all the more critical (MC14). A Ballygall parishioner thought the state has a responsibility to help, but said that "no matter how much money is there, there still is an onus on people to become involved and help. If you expect governments just to pour out money and the work to be done, you become detached" (DC3). She, like other Catholics, did not see greater state support (if there were such) as absolving individuals from their responsibility to get involved in helping others. Another from Ballygall directed her response toward whether one needed to help the local church, which she strongly differentiated from the Archdiocesan institutions: "Everything has to be funded no matter what it is, whether you feel you have to or you want to give it. Practically, the priests have to live, the church has to be funded. It's a practicality with me. I want to give it anyway. Because I can see the money that we give is put back into the church. I can see it" (DC9). A parishioner in Paris explained that, while the state might pay for basic church building repairs, it doesn't pay salaries, and because the priest is central to providing the Eucharist, which is central to Catholics' spiritual life, everyone in the parish has a duty to aid the parish (PC11).[31] In talking about individual responsibility, a Catholic teacher from Istanbul said that "the state helps the poor but individual responsibility never ends. There is always someone that needs help in some place in the world" (IC13). Many of our Catholics in Istanbul felt themselves responsible to help whenever they were aware of a need (e.g., IC21, IC12, IC8). As one parishioner said, "when you see a person in need, you cannot ignore that, simply thinking that the state will find and help him. In that case, you just help" (IC26).

---

[31] Since the 1905 Law of Separation, as it is known (*Loi concernant la Séparation des Églises et de l'État*), responsibility for construction and repairs of any new buildings rests with the parish. The state pays for essential repairs to pre-1905 church buildings.

Some, nevertheless, voiced the possibility that crowding out by the state does affect people's generosity. An elderly Ballygall parishioner commented that "when the state is helping, people feel exonerated" (DC21). His wife noted that individuals do have a responsibility to help others, no matter what the state does. "If everybody gave a little, it would be much be better" (DC22). The husband added, "If people weren't so greedy, were a little more generous about donations, we'd be a darn sight better, you know?" (DC21).

A slightly different perspective is the role charitable involvement has in fostering a sense of humanity and solidarity. An Irish parishioner observed that, if one just relies on the state to do everything, one becomes "so detached that you don't see what's going on ... it doesn't leave you open for anything ... to listen the word of God, even to people around you and what they're going through." She concluded that, "even if we were floating in money tomorrow you'd still have to get out there and get involved" (DC3). Helping others is viewed as a crucial part of connecting with others and with God. This view was reinforced in a concern expressed by the priest who ran the *Vicariate de Solidarité* (solidarity office) in the Paris archdiocese: he worried that the increasing requirements for expertise in welfare services delivery might squeeze out volunteers. He noted that volunteering, as an expression of generosity, is a crucial part of living one's religion (PC22). A parishioner in Paris seemed to channel his thoughts when she commented of her volunteering that it created a "unity" in her spiritual life, in her "life of faith" (PC13). The vicar stressed that voluntary work "allows Christians to understand what charity is, how to live it" (PC22).

Muslims and the State's Responsibility, the Movement's Responsibility, and Individuals' Responsibility
Interviews with Muslims showed a similar range of views. Like our Catholic respondents, we also saw a weak effect of state welfare policies on their attitudes toward giving and volunteering. We did not observe a direct relationship between welfare policies of the states and giving of Muslim communities in four cities. Although most of the respondents hold the state responsible for providing help to lower socioeconomic classes, they did not seem to change their giving behavior based on whether or not a state supports those in need. They did not mention that welfare policies make them give less but they mentioned that it influences how and where they give. The interviewees do not suggest that the religious organizations should replace the state in providing social and welfare

services. They hold themselves and their organizations responsible to help the poor but see their role as complementary to what the states provide for the people in need.

Virtually all our Muslim interviewees, no matter which country they were in, thought that the state was responsible for helping the poor. They had varying views on whether or not their respective states did a good job of doing so. In justifying state welfare responsibility, many respondents pointed out issues of justice and social order. To a businessman in Paris, for example, "the state should help those who lack basic human needs such as food and shelter. This is important for justice and equality" (PM1). A software engineer in Dublin echoed this point: "for society to have order and peace among its members, the state should support those in need. Otherwise social crisis can become even more costly for both the state and the people in the long run" (DM5). A graduate student in Milan also raised the issue of social cohesion in explaining the reasons why the state should provide social services. To her, "lots of poor people feel abandoned by others. It is only with state support that this feeling can be remedied and social problems can be prevented from emerging" (MM10). The state's role in preventing social divisions was also raised by an Istanbul respondent in his fifties: "the state definitely has a responsibility to help the poor. It is not the poor's fault to be poor. Not everybody is equally lucky. And the state should support those who are less fortunate than others" (IM29).

Muslims' perceptions about the support provided by the states in their respective countries of residence differ. Interviewees judged France as having the most comprehensive welfare policies. People described French welfare policies with positive words (e.g., PM7, PM11, PM14, PM25), mentioning satisfaction with how the welfare benefits are distributed in society. To a Parisian interviewee, as long as the poor know how the system works, the poor are well taken care of by the state (PM11). Almost all of our Muslim respondents appreciated the French welfare system. A Muslim cab driver, for example, stated that "there are many things that you can be critical of in France, but state support for the poor is not one of them. They do a very good job on this" (PM16). A few Muslim business owners that we interviewed were not happy because they had experienced some difficulties in the hiring and firing of employees (PM1, PM7, PM18).

Many respondents in Dublin mentioned the Irish state's support for the poor in positive terms (e.g., DM5, DM10, DM24). However, most of the respondents were also critical of the functioning of the welfare system in Ireland. They did not have the impression that welfare benefits were fairly distributed. Some argued that many people abused the system and used the benefits even though they did not need them (DM10, DM28). Many respondents commented that individuals who exploit the welfare system prevent others more in need from receiving it. As a teacher in her thirties put it, "the state does not have good monitoring mechanisms and unfortunately there are people who abuse this. As a result, sometimes those who need state support may not get it while those who don't can get it" (DM24). A male respondent in his late forties echoes the point: "the state has resources to help the people but those resources are being wasted. The state does not have a good system to make sure that those who need state support get it" (DM8).

Our interviewees in Istanbul and Milan criticized Turkey and Italy, respectively, for falling short on providing social welfare. Although several respondents acknowledged increasing levels of state support for both the lower social classes and the elderly in addition to increasing healthcare benefits for Turkish citizens (e.g., IM2, IM11, IM29), many also raised concerns about the insufficiency of these efforts and injustices in the distribution of the welfare benefits (IM8, IM15, IM28). A respondent in his fifties noted that although the state increased its help for the poor, there are still many elderly, homeless, and poor in impoverished neighborhoods in Istanbul who did not even know that they had the right to get benefits (IM14). A businessman in his fifties thought that "the state should expand the services to a point in which nobody suffers from hunger or poor health conditions. We are very far from that point" (IM21). One respondent complained that there were people around him who abused the system and got welfare benefits even though they did not need them (IM28).

Similarly, many Italian Muslims complained about insufficient government support for the poor and needy. The respondents thought that Italy does not have a strong welfare state structure (MM6, MM8, MM10). A woman in her thirties mentioned the difficult living conditions of several people in her neighborhood and the lack of state support to take care of them (MM11). "State support for the poor is almost zero in Italy. It should not be like this. I have many neighbors in very miserable conditions and there is not much done for them. Only we the neighbors do something" (MM11). To a Turkish immigrant who lived in Italy for a very long time, "the state support for the poor decreased gradually over the last decades. Italy now cannot be considered as a welfare state any more" (MM6).

What do the Muslim respondents think about the responsibility of their own organizations to help the poor? We find that many respondents hold their local associations responsible for helping the poor, though their organizations' abilities to do so varied based on their locations. Where the associations were well established, they had a number of programs aimed at helping the needy that the state may not have been able to reach. Where the associations were much smaller or newer, Muslims focused more on establishing the associations and sustaining them locally, as we discussed in Chapter 7.

In Turkey, Muslim respondents acknowledged increasing state support for the poor, but they also mentioned problems in the system. A female community organizer in Istanbul mentioned several programs that the association organized to decrease poverty, to increase skills of the poor people, to distribute food, and to coordinate with KYM in several social campaigns (IM16). Another respondent said that "in Turkey, the state reformed the health system and resolved health-related issues in recent years. This is great. But we also need to note that the state cannot always do the job perfectly" (IM21). Although the state is seen as a welfare service provider, respondents suggested that there is still much room for charities to fill in the gap left by the state. In the eyes of the interviewees, the biggest gap in the system is the state's failure to identify abusers of the system and those who truly need the support. As the interviewee quoted above said, "the associations and foundations should complement state support [to the poor], because those institutions are close to the people and they can better identify who has need and what kind of need" (IM21). When asked if the state took care of the people who are in need, another respondent said that the state's expanded welfare policies decreased the need for individuals to help the poor (IM7). However, this respondent did not indicate that increasing state support decreased his giving. Instead, he channeled all of his giving to the religious community association: "I give all my charitable contributions to our association, and they are very adept in finding out the real needs in the community" (IM7).

In France, the well-functioning welfare state seemed to have no effect on Muslims' views of their association's responsibility to be generous to the needy. Most directed their giving to their associations, which they expected to help the poor in France and elsewhere. A community leader in Paris mentioned collecting donations for impoverished French neighborhoods and for the victims of a recent flood in Pakistan (PM30). One interviewee felt less responsible to other poor individuals as he did not see them as totally desperate (PM14). A woman in her late fifties concurred: "in France, the state provides lots of health and other services to the poor. If you are not new in the country and if you know how the system works, and if you need state support, you can get it easily in France" (PM11). This seems to be why many Muslims in Paris channeled their giving either to local associations that engage in local assistance programs or to KYM, which helped the needy globally.

In Milan and Dublin, interviewees noted that their associations were not in a position to provide extensive help to those in need. Perhaps more so than interviewees in the other cities, they commented on efforts to help the needy individually. A Milanese respondent noted that "our association surely has a responsibility to help the needy, but we have very limited resources at this point. For this reason, we do not have much to help the needy. But our members themselves are helping the poor individually. They can always contribute to KYM, which specializes on projects for the poor and needy" (MM6). A female respondent in her early thirties in Milan stated that she regularly helped her neighbor who lived in poverty and did not receive any state assistance (MM11). A man in his forties, when asked if the state should help those in need, responded that "the state should have a responsibility to help the people who are poor and needy. If you ask me, if the Italian state does that, I don't think it really does it. To my knowledge, the state has some programs but the requirements are really high" (MM6). He indicated later in the interview that he helps the poor in his neighborhood whenever he thinks someone is in need and not getting much support from others, including the state.

The respondents in Dublin made similar points. One commented, "personally, I do help the poor. I think our association should also be responsible to help the poor and I am sure it will do more once we have more resources" (DM5). Most of the respondents in Ireland found the Irish state's welfare policies sufficient, but they raised concerns about how the state handles social welfare programs. They noted that the failures of the state to provide help in appropriate ways leaves many poor and needy unsupported. There is thus room for private organizations and individuals to fill in. A man in his late thirties stated, "[Y]es, I think the state should support the poor and needy but some people abuse the state support. In Ireland, the state support for the poor has decreased in the recent years. The state is becoming less willing to provide social services. But Irish people themselves are generous and there are some charity organizations which are ready to help" (DM7). A female school teacher in her early thirties mentioned the need for charities to fill the gaps left by the state support (DM9).

The interviewees indicated they had a responsibility to help the poor. In Dublin and Milan, where associations are less engaged in social programs, Muslims seemed to focus a bit more on helping people individually.

A woman in Milan mentioned giving to neighborhood-based efforts to help the poor (MM11), while a woman in her thirties in Dublin mentioned how she organized efforts with other Muslim women, who were not affiliated with the Gülen association, for people in poor neighborhoods in Dublin (DM12). In Istanbul and Paris, respondents tended to talk about helping the needy by way of giving and volunteering in their associations. To a male Istanbul respondent in his fifties, "I do help my relatives and neighbors when I feel that they need. But I do not reserve much money for person-to-person giving. I give the resources I have to my organization and they do the job. I have trust in them that they will use the money in a good way. I also frequently contribute to the KYM campaigns" (IM14). A Paris respondent concurred: "sure, I have a responsibility to help the poor. But our association does it for us. We give out to them and they spend the money based on their needs, which also includes helping the poor" (PM18). In short, the interviews indicate that a relatively effective welfare state does not "crowd out" Muslims' sense that they and their religious associations have a responsibility to help the needy.

Taxes

We asked through our surveys and learned in conversation that most Muslim and Catholic interviewees were unaware of the amount they pay in taxes annually, and did not calculate their giving based on that (since they were not paying attention to it). Most told us they determined their level of financial giving with the discretionary funds they had (more or less some portion of what remained after they paid bills to keep their household afloat) or that they had a target. Many of the interviewees indicated that they were not sure about the tax rates. We do not have quantitative data on tax rates or welfare state size versus our interviewees' charitable donations or other financial giving, nor quantitative data on how much time they spend on charitable activities per week. Yet we have some indication that the size of the welfare state did not affect giving. At the end of the interview, each interviewee was given the option of filling out a survey to collect demographic information and information about their financial giving. On average, Catholics indicated that they give 7.3 percent of income, while Muslims indicated that they give 7.9 percent of income.[32] These averages held across our four countries, indicating that our

---

[32] The response rate to the question about what percentage of income they give annually was 33 percent for Catholics and 40 percent for Muslims.

interviewees' generosity generally was not affected by the size of the welfare state in their countries.

Conclusion: Reflections on Nonstate Social Welfare Provision

We started this chapter by describing an acerbic exchange in 2010 between the city council of Milan and the Milan diocese Archbishop about public housing for Roma people. The Archbishop called on the city to take up its responsibilities; the city replied that if the Church was so concerned about the Roma, it should make available some of its real estate holdings. In the end, it was a civil court that forced the state to provide public housing for some of the Roma who were being evicted from camps on the city's outskirts. The debate highlighted a question about which institutions are responsible, if any, for social welfare provision, and whether state welfare provision crowds out that which might be provided by religious organizations and their adherents. It also highlighted a question about how, when the state retrenches, social welfare might be provided, in part, by mainstream religions.

We found indications from European survey data that a more extensive welfare state reduces the inclination of citizens to feel responsible for spending part of their free time helping others, and that that effect is tempered by religiosity. Our interviews to some extent reinforce those findings: our interviewees, who mostly could be characterized as more religious than the average citizen, thought that individuals, as well as their religious organization and their state, are responsible for providing social welfare. We also found that leaders of major religious charities, as well as local religious adherents, have a more complex view of responsibilities and that they tend to see religion and state efforts as complementary, not competitive. There were concerns over a wasteful, incompetent, or insufficient welfare state, particularly in Italy and Turkey, and views that helping others is an essential part of being Muslim or Catholic, something not displaced by the existence of an extensive welfare state.[33] We also found

---

[33] Some might say that we were interviewing those who remained firm in their faith, despite the welfare state, and that our results do not take into account those who lost their faith precisely because the welfare state expanded and provided services that the religions had previously provided (Gill and Lundsgaarde 2004). Even if that is the case, our findings show that the generosity of the religious is less likely to be crowded out by the welfare state. It is also worth pointing out that in all the work that has been done on the crowding-out thesis, we are among the first to have semi-structured interviews with Catholics and Muslims in Europe and Turkey about whom they think is responsible for providing social welfare.

that despite the common association of "subsidiarity" with Catholicism, Catholics and their charitable institutions have accepted that the state is responsible for universal social welfare provision, that that cannot be provided by individuals or religious organizations alone (Pope Pius XI 1931, paragraph 79). Both Catholics and Muslims see that there is a key role for local-level action by individuals and religious organizations, as even a competent, expansive welfare state may not be able to reach all those needing assistance.

Interestingly, in regard to the extent to which the state is viewed as responsible for social welfare, we did not see differences between inter-viewees in minority or majority status. Those in the religious minority, whether Muslims in Dublin, Milan, or Paris or Catholics in Istanbul, viewed the state they resided in as having some responsibility for providing social welfare. They were not concerned that the state would unfairly help those of the majority religion and discriminate (in social welfare) against those of the minority religion.

There are some caveats to optimism that as the state retrenches in social welfare, or privatizes the delivery of services, religious organizations are suitable substitutes. While the religious charities we discussed do not discriminate against those who do not adhere to their religion, the organizations are not neutral – they have a religious mission, charitable works of which is one such outcome. In contrast, the idea of the welfare state is that it is neutral on religion.

Moreover, while volunteer donations and activities can help, the state "alone can guarantee standards and coverage in social protection for the entire population and is expected to display resolution and flexibility in levying the necessary resources and seeing that they are used to maximum effect" (National Economic Social Council 2005, 39). Coming from a state-appointed social welfare advisory council, such a statement is perhaps not surprising.[34] But it reflects a reality that is often forgotten in the discussion about the crowding out of charity by state-provided social welfare (Gill 2013). In the past, religious organizations in Europe did indeed run welfare services such as orphanages and elder care. Yet the historical record indicates that coverage of the population was sketchy and that it was not until there were massive movements by socialist and labor union

---

[34] Ireland's NESC was established in 1973 to advise the Prime Minister (*Taoiseach*) on economic, social, and environmental policy. The Taoiseach appoints the members, who come from a wide variety of civil society institutions, including employers' and workers' unions; NGOs; or are heads of some government departments.

organizations and women's movements that states began creating broad social welfare programs (Baldwin 1990; Koven and Michel 1990; Pedersen 1993; cf. Haggard and Kaufman 2008). As is currently seen in much of the developing world, where the state does not grant or provide welfare as a universal right, access to social welfare depends on political connections, social status or affiliation, and/or the happenstance of living in an area that is covered by nonstate actors or by a few government programs (Cammett 2014; Cammett and Issar 2010, 417; Cammett and MacClean 2014; Díaz-Cayeros, Estevez, and Magaloni 2016).

Furthermore, churches involved in earlier welfare provision lived off the near equivalent of indentured servitude of nuns and monks, and of the serfs and peasants who tilled their land and paid rents to them. Many of the funds and much of the aid that religious organizations so "freely" gave were derived from exploitation and coercion (Constable 2004). And in many parts of Europe, even in pre-Christianized Europe, religions were supported by the local or regional governing authority, who in turn got the funds from various taxes and other coercive activities. The supply of free labor (nuns, monks) was due to poor economic development as much as to the religious motivation of individuals. When poverty was widespread, the opportunity cost of being a nun or monk was exceedingly low. As societies became wealthier and individuals had more life options, the costs became high, with the result that fewer individuals were willing to provide a life of free labor to their religious organization. This context was one completely lacking in religious freedom. Religions had monopolies on territories. After the Reformation, with the Peace of Westphalia, religions still retained monopolies as the regimes in each country or principality chose one or another religion to be the official religion of the realm (Kaplan 2007). And elsewhere, in the Middle East, the Islamic-law based *waqf* system of public works was inadequate to meet needs. As Kuran states, "there are solid reasons to doubt that the traditional *waqf* system could have served as a vehicle for urban modernization" (2001, 878). Nor have the obligatory "tithing" rituals of zakat and fitr been sufficient to provide broad social welfare or prompt noticeable economic growth.[35]

The larger point is that humanity may not be generous enough on its own to provide enough charity to substitute for state provision that is funded through taxation. If religions were to fully fund hospitals, prisons,

[35] For details on zakat, fitr, and waqfs, see discussions in Chapter 2.

schools, and the like, they would need recourse to taxing authority.[36] The telling example of this is Germany, where all those who are members of one of the religious organizations recognized as a public law corporation (e.g., the Catholic Church) automatically pay an additional 8–9 percent of the amount of their income tax to the recognized religion they are nominal members of. The state collects the funds and then distributes them to the recognized religious organization. With that, the churches have been able to finance an extensive social welfare system (Barker 2000). With more and more people officially withdrawing from the churches in order to avoid the tax, the church welfare systems have less funding, while the state welfare system has not increased commensurately to make up the difference. Nor is there evidence that Germans who have officially left their religious organizations are using their income tax savings to fund charities of their own choosing (Bittschi, Borgloh, and Wigger 2016).

This leads to a related point. While there are suggestions that state-provided welfare "crowds out" religious-based or other welfare, the empirical evidence is mixed. Some find that it does (e.g., Hungerman 2005), others that it does not (e.g., Andreoni 1993; van Oorschot and Arts 2005). Our statistical analyses find that religiosity dampens the effect. Our case studies show that religious activities can be complementary to state activities. Many of the activities of Catholic parishes and Muslim associations in Dublin, Paris, Milan, and Istanbul were geared toward helping individuals figure out how to access state services. Without these efforts of religious (and secular) organizations, state-provided social welfare would be less effective. Many volunteer activities of religious organizations were oriented toward helping individuals find out how to get on a list for subsidized housing, how to register so they would qualify for the equivalent of food stamps, how to get their kids signed up for school, how to compile and fill out a dossier for a residency application, and so forth. Furthermore, nongovernmental charitable organizations can fill in sometimes where the state may not have enough staff to do so and where doing so may be politically controversial. Congregants in our study were particularly oriented toward long-term assistance projects. Many emphasized the

---

[36] This is a complex topic that we cannot fully address here. Certainly, there are debates about the need for a certain level of (now state-provided) social welfare, about required levels of expertise and about regulations that may "crowd out" volunteer efforts, and about the possibility that social welfare is subject to moral hazard. We thank Tony Gill for discussion of these points.

importance of just being with a person over time and helping them figure out how to get back on their feet. Coverage, inevitably, is not universal.

The religious organizations said they did not have the capacity or funds to run entire welfare programs or educational institutions. They had difficulty even finding enough volunteers for their modest programs in the summer months, because the volunteers, mostly retirees or students, went on vacation with their grandchildren. Running a full-service, full-time hospital on volunteer time and funds is out of the question. Instances cited by Davis and Robinson (2012) of social welfare provision by organized religious groups indicate the extent to which success at creating a comprehensive system varies by country, and the sometimes illiberal means by which such groups may do so, and that their ultimate goal may be to restrict the religious liberty of non-coreligionists.

Our findings indicate that one of the key challenges for European states and for the Catholic Church and Muslim organizations is to assess their responsibilities and capacities for social welfare provision. The task cannot merely be off-loaded onto religious organizations or other voluntary organizations, nor monopolized by the state. Further research is needed to identify the opportunities and challenges that nongovernmental entities face in providing public goods.

These important caveats aside, it is clear that religiously affiliated organizations' activities within Islamic associations and Catholic parishes are important providers of public goods in France, Ireland, Italy, and Turkey. They are also major avenues for enabling Muslims and Catholics to express, experience, and live out a vital part of their faith: the teachings on generosity.

9

Conclusion

Religion and Public Goods Provision

One of our Catholic interviewees stated that "you don't have to be Catholic to be charitable" but "I can't separate the two" (PC7).[1] Rather than "separate the two," this book has sought to unpack which aspects of being Catholic, and which aspects of being Muslim, trigger and channel generous behavior, resulting in club and public goods contributions. In a mixed-methods project carried out in Western Europe and Turkey, we have provided some evidence that Catholics tend to respond to prompts and messages of God's grace and the deservedness of the needy, and Muslims tend to respond to a sense of duty to God. The religious communities of both faiths proved important, though not in the way typically expected in behavioral economics and rational choice theory. Members were less guided by community expectations, or monitoring and sanctioning structures of their religious institutions, than by positive feelings for their communities. The communities, for both faiths, were also seen by adherents as critical to their being able to live out their faiths: being able to be active in their communities was a conduit for their generosity, and in turn fostered that generosity. How it worked was slightly different: Catholics saw themselves as manifesting Jesus' love and as "getting back" so much more than they gave from the joy of interaction and helping, Muslims saw themselves as discharging an obligation to God to help others.

Through an examination of how individual beliefs and sense of belonging to a community motivate the faithful to give to their religious organizations, we highlight some micro-foundations of religiously based

---

[1] She was not the only one. A number of our interviewees noted that being generous was a human characteristic, while at the same time noting how it was inextricably tied up in their faith.

public goods provision. Our findings contribute to several literatures. First, we contribute to the literature on social welfare and faith-based initiatives by examining the prosocial motivations of religious communities' members to help others. Our research found that Catholicism and Islam, by inciting specific prosocial motivations, can contribute to the creation of public goods. By doing so, religions can complement the state in providing public goods. We did not test directly for whether religions (and/or other voluntary organizations) could *replace* the welfare state. Our research can only speak to this indirectly, and it does not address the philosophical, political, or moral issues at stake (Cammett and MacLean 2014; Nozick 1974; Singer 2015a). While we show that there is some crowding out by the welfare state and that religiosity mitigates that, people with high degrees of religiosity were still affected by the extensiveness of taxation. They were just affected to a lesser degree than individuals who did not have high degrees of religiosity.[2] Religiosity mitigates the negative impact of the welfare state on generosity, but it does not completely counter it.

Furthermore, we cannot demonstrate the amount of money individuals would contribute in a hypothetical world in which the state no longer taxed its citizens. While more people may contribute to charitable activities and public goods provision, the total revenue collected would quite likely (almost assuredly) be far less than what is collected by the state (Kleven et al. 2011). We have some indicative, though indirect, evidence of this from our experiments. A relatively anemic 21 percent of our experimental subjects voluntarily made a public goods contribution in experiments specifically derived to prime religion, involving a relatively small amount of money. This suggests that, even given relatively small amounts of money, many people may not be particularly generous. It is certainly the case that several of our primes did significantly increase the generosity of Irish Catholics. But imagine asking people to give up voluntarily a substantial percentage of their incomes as in welfare states – we can only speculate what the primes would do in a situation like that. It would be seemingly difficult for mainstream religions to replace the funding levels,

---

[2] For a similar result from research conducted in Germany, see Boyer, Dwenger, and Rincke (2014). One might propose a study of the charitable contributions of those who resigned from the Lutheran or Catholic church in Germany in order not to have 9 percent of their income taken as a tax by the (central) state and given to the churches: did they shift the 9 percent to charities of their choice, or keep the funds? There is little information on this. The one study we know of indicates that they did not (Bittschi, Borgloh, and Wigger 2016).

comprehensiveness, and technical expertise of the state through volunteerism and financial generosity. The modern welfare state has the leverage of coercive powers of taxation.

Second, although we focus on individuals, our study diverges from rational choice perspectives that give weight to individual-level cost/benefit analyses and stress the need for monitoring and sanctioning structures in order to prompt individuals to contribute to collective goods (Berman 2009; Hale 2015). Our work links with research that indicates that religious beliefs have a role in eliciting prosocial behavior (Preston, Ritter, and Hernandez 2010; Warner et al. 2015). We agree that monitoring and sanctioning structures can have a role in public goods provision, but we point out that they may not always be necessary. Some scholars have attributed apparently nonrational helping behavior, in the absence of monitoring and sanctioning mechanisms, to a "warm glow" effect (Andreoni 1990; Imas 2014). Nonrational helping behavior can be explained by the good feelings that the giver gets from helping someone else. We explore this effect: just as students of electoral politics have discovered that individuals vote despite the cost in time and effort outweighing any potential policy benefit (Mueller 2003), we find that Catholics and Muslims may contribute to the works of their parishes and associations for reasons that do not have a direct material benefit. Our case studies shed light on an unacknowledged puzzle of the so-called warm glow literature: what motivates people to help in the first place? How do they know in advance that they will have a "warm glow" feeling from helping? Many of our interviewees noted how surprised they were at what they "got back" from being involved. As a Catholic stated of the people she helped, "they gave more to me than me to them" (MC3). Catholics had not opted to volunteer or give funds in order to feel good; they had volunteered out of other motives, and then found it an emotionally and/or spiritually rewarding experience. The positive affect they had from being engaged with others was one reason they remained involved, but taking the first step had its sources in religious beliefs and in, for many, a sense of caring and responsibility to others. Muslims, in particular, emphasized discharging an obligation to God and that the impact on those who were helped was less significant; Catholics that they were following Jesus' example. Their volunteering to help, whether in a charity or in their religious organization to help it with its day-to-day operations, was purposeful, not merely something to do to fill up time or get out of the house, so to speak. If volunteering were only to occupy time or be with people, the interviewees could have indulged in a hobby, secular club, or team sport.

Specific religious beliefs and the positive feelings of community engagement guide their involvement.

Third, we refine studies of the role of religious beliefs in prosocial behavior and public goods provision. We find that the truism that all religions have a "golden rule" about helping others needs some modification, as it is clear that Catholics and Muslims have different religious beliefs about why they adhere to that "rule" (see Prothero 2010). This makes a difference in how one would activate their social engagement. Our research shows that duty to God activates Muslims, while feelings of love of Jesus activate Catholics. For both, positive affect for the community prompts volunteering and other forms of giving. Further research could investigate the political implications for social welfare provision: when political and civic leaders make calls for religious groups to "help" in some way, they may need to pay attention to the religious composition of their audience.

Fourth, we contribute to the social psychology research on religion and prosociality in several ways. We show the analytical benefits of parsing "religion" into different kinds of beliefs. We show through our experiments that various concepts trigger a range of thoughts and feelings, cautioning that researchers need to be more sensitive to the multiplicity of meanings certain religious terms and constructs may hold for adherents. This was most evident for the term "religion," but also apparent with other belief constructs. We enhanced the study of religion and prosociality by going outside the typical locus of a US university laboratory, instead testing our hypotheses in field settings. We included nonuniversity subjects, thus increasing the external applicability of our findings and the range of life experiences that were (randomly) brought to bear on the different religious primes.

Fifth, and circling back to a question that has preoccupied much literature in the social sciences, we wonder whether some individuals are innately generous or whether they are somehow helping themselves when helping others. Debates about the sources of altruism, and whether it is really altruism, continue. Though our study is not specifically aimed at answering this question, our results have some implications for this ongoing discussion. While it may be impossible to demonstrate definitively whether altruistic actions are truly altruistic or whether they simply fulfill some positive utility for individuals, our study showed that Catholics and Muslims often give and help those far removed their kin group. Even if they receive a "warm glow" from helping others, that feeling is neither a direct nor equivalent compensation for their gift of time and other resources. Further, even if, as some scholars have argued, religion is an evolved adaptation that has enabled humans to cooperate with one another and develop large, lasting communities (Wilson 2002), it is worth asking which particular beliefs and institutions within different religions prompt helping behavior. Our study also tested for whether some religious beliefs can prompt generosity toward those well outside one's own community. We found some evidence of this in our experiments, with Catholics responding to the God's grace and deservedness primes by donating to the public good. In other words, if religion helps develop large-scale cooperation within a large group, it can also have a positive externality of facilitating helping behavior across groups.

There are some limits to the current research. Although the nature of religious beliefs is consistent among followers of a particular religion across countries, we make no claims to have evidence that generalizes to all Catholics or all Muslims. Due to resource limitations, our study was geographically and temporally constrained. We cannot assess here what the full range, globally, is within each religion of understandings of giving and helping. As we have noted in our chapters, context matters (Chaves 2010), even while we have "taken talk seriously" and shown how adherents' understandings of their religious-based generosity frame their actions (Wuthnow 2011). Our study is a first step, and further research needs to be done in other Catholic parishes and Muslim associations to examine the extent to which understandings and framings may vary within each religion depending on sociopolitical and historical context. From this work's baseline, future studies could look for trends in giving and helping patterns within each religion. We are not studying "how much" generosity the specific beliefs and sense of belonging elicit. Yet knowing how Catholics and Muslims conceptualize their generosity is an essential step in understanding how religions affect generosity and public goods provision. This book is a move in that direction.

The question may also arise whether people who are predisposed to be generous self-select into religions; in other words, it could be the case that religions do not make individuals more generous. Instead, generous individuals are more likely to join religions. For several reasons, however, we feel this potential problem of endogeneity does not impact our results. First, many of our Catholic and Muslim interviewees did not "select" into their religion; they were born into it and brought up in it. Granted, as our experiment essays and interviews revealed, some may later have opted out or reduced their involvement. Nevertheless, the experiments showed there was variation in generous behavior among Catholics and Muslims; many participants did not opt to donate any of their participant payment to charity. Being Catholic or Muslim is not synonymous with being generous. As a number of interviewees said, their religion brought out and channeled their generosity; their religion did not have a monopoly on it. Our study was probing not whether religion prompts generosity, but which aspects of each of these two prominent religions prompt, or discourage, generosity. With regard to our experiments, our respondents did not self-select into which randomly assigned experimental prime they received, and so our experimental results likely are not the result of self-selection into religious groups. While our evidence may caution against hypothesizing that the generous select into religion, we must leave that question to further research.

Readers might ask whether differences in understandings of generosity between Catholics and Muslims have an impact on how they give and how much they give. We have not shown in what way these understandings of generosity and their faith make a difference in the amount of funds the interviewees donate. Due to a low response rate to survey questions on financial giving of our interviewees, we do not have systematic data to correlate with the themes that the Muslim and Catholic interviewees stressed.[3] In addition, we are not comparing the religions to see which one is more generous. Generosity is expressed in many forms, such as volunteering or helping one's neighbor, not just as funds donated. Both religions prompt generosity among their adherents. There is a variety of factors that could influence religious-based generosity at a given time and space. Given the very specific conditions of giving in each setting, we hesitate to speculate on the greater or lesser generosity of the adherents of any particular religion. Instead, we have examined whether particular beliefs and institutional structures in Catholicism and in Islam prompt generosity, and we have examined how Catholics and Muslims connect their understandings of their faith and belonging to their generosity. Further research can demonstrate its consequences in terms of how much congregants give of their time and other resources.

Putting It All Together

While some scholars have investigated why members of mainstream religions in wealthy countries do not give more (Smith and Emerson 2008),

---

[3] As noted in Chapter 8, at the end of the interview, each interviewee was given the option of filling out a survey to collect demographic information and information about their financial giving. The response rate to the question about what percentage of income they give annually was 33 percent for Catholics and 40 percent for Muslims. On average, Catholics indicated that they give 7.3 percent of income, while Muslims indicated that they give 7.9 percent of income.

we took up the question posed by the behavioral economics and rational choice literature on mainstream religions, namely, why do members give at all? As we found in analyzing the institutions of Catholicism and Islam, both religions have weak institutional mechanisms for prompting contributions to the collective good, and weak to nonexistent institutional mechanisms for monitoring contributions and sanctioning noncooperation. Given the weak structures, how do the mainstream religions solve the problem of eliciting generosity from their adherents? This mixed-method study, combining field experiments with Catholic and Muslim university students and community members in Dublin and Istanbul, respectively, with case studies in Dublin, Istanbul, Milan, and Paris of a Catholic parish and an Islamic association enables us to see different dimensions of the religious beliefs, and the religious institutions, that may lead Catholics and Muslims to be generous with their resources of time, effort, and funds. Generally, Catholics do not feel or believe that they have a duty to God to help others and to be generous to their organizations. Instead, they think of their giving as inspired by a love for others, by upbringing. We see in the interview findings some correspondence with the experiments, in that Catholics consistently mentioned a love of God and of one's neighbor as reasons for helping others, with some seeing it as a form of God's grace, and many noted it is the responsibility of the Church, of individuals, and of the state to help those in need.[4] The experiments found that Catholics primed with concepts of God's grace or with their religion's teachings about the deservedness of the needy were likely to donate to public goods. In contrast to Catholics, Muslims often link their giving to fulfillment of a duty to God. To Muslims, the act of giving for the sake of God is more important than its beneficial consequences for the recipient. While we did not see this result of duty to God in the experimental behavior, we did see it in the essays on duty to God. That prompt yielded a greater likelihood of Muslims mentioning charity-related topics in their essays, as did the prompts about community expectations, deservedness, and God's grace. Being tied to their community seemed to enhance their sense of responsibility to sustain it.

The religious community plays a significant role in both Catholics' and Muslims' giving. Catholics and Muslims indicated that they derived emotional satisfaction from helping the community. While much research has

---

[4] Had similar interviews been done prior to Vatican II, it is possible participants would have commented frequently on being inspired by a fear of the Church, of the priest, and/or of a nun. This is an observation that several of our Catholic interviewees made (DC13, PC14, PC23).

tended to stress the role of communities in monitoring and sanctioning individuals as a means of compelling "generosity," Catholics' understandings of their religious community do not conform to that model and Muslims' do only slightly, for those who participated in an annual meeting in which they publicly pledged to donate funds to the Islamic association. Catholic institutions, including rituals of giving, have next to no capacity to monitor or sanction those who free-ride on the contributions of others. Muslim institutions are likewise weak at monitoring and sanctioning. Muslims respond to rituals of giving such as zakat and fitr out of a sense of duty to God. Few exhibited awareness of another vehicle for Islamic charity, the waqf, yet many donated to and volunteered in their associations, and helped fund movements that were the contemporary legal framework version of waqfs (*vakıfs* in Turkish). We also saw that prompting Catholics and Muslims to think about the expectations of their respective religious communities led to varied and sometimes negative thoughts and emotions. Our interviews revealed that Catholics and Muslims articulate different faith-based motivations in their contributions to their religious communities, and those motives have less to do with community expectations than with positive affect or a sense of responsibility: for Catholics, to others and the community; for Muslims, to God. In either case, adherents indicated they often responded when asked to help – a finding that is not by any means unique to religious groups (Andreoni and Rao 2011; Frey and Meier 2004). Comments by interviewees and by experiment participants given the community expectation prompt indicate that higher expectations could generate more collective goods production. As one Catholic wrote, "I am keen to engage and bring about a more caring and faith filled society. The apparent lack of expectation frustrates me" (EP656). The hierarchical structure of the Catholic Church may reduce opportunities for being "asked," whereas the more decentralized structure of Islam may increase it, with attendant effects on generosity.

We noticed that for those living as religious minorities, the religious bases for generosity, for club and public goods provision, remained the same, while the target, of necessity, narrowed somewhat. The religious minorities, whether Catholics in Istanbul or Muslims in Dublin, tended to aim most of their volunteering and financial giving at their local religious organization.

While several works have found that belonging to a faith community leads to activities that promote public goods (Putnam and Campbell 2010; Sarkissian 2012), those works have, for mainstream religions, not identified which aspects of the religious beliefs and institutions might create that connection. Applied to religion and public goods provision, we provide an understanding of which aspects of the beliefs and communities of two major faiths, within the contexts of four Catholic parishes and four Islamic associations in Western Europe and Turkey, connect individuals to opportunities. This book has disaggregated the beliefs and their institutions to better understand how and why Catholics and Muslims willingly provide their time and funds to their organizations and to others. The Catholic Church remains a moral force in social and political debates and a spiritual guide to millions. In many European countries, Islam has become the second largest religion, with many actively practicing adherents. In Turkey, Islam is by far the majority religion. How these religions and their adherents approach generosity will have a major impact around the world.

Appendix

Semi-Structured Interview Question List[*]

I'd first like to ask you about your involvement with your religious association. Then I'll ask more questions about your thoughts and feelings about giving, your religion's teachings about giving, your thoughts about the responsibility of the state and your religious organization, and if you've volunteered time or donated other resources to other organizations. I'd like to conclude by learning more about your thoughts on why or when you give to others, and then ask you to fill out a short survey. Remember that you may decline to answer any question, and you may stop the interview at any time.

1. How long have you been attending this church/how long have you belonged to this association?
2. Does your friends, neighbors, and/or relatives attend this church/association?
3. Do you socialize with other church/association members?
4. If so, how often?
5. Do you participate in a lot of church/association activities?
6. What would you say are the teachings of Catholicism/Islam about giving?
7. Does your church/association emphasize those teachings?
8. Did your family emphasize them when you were growing up?
9. Tell me about a typical religious service.
10. How does your church/association ask you to give to it or its causes?

---

[*] This was translated into French, Italian, and Turkish, then each translation was back-translated by a different professional translator into English to check for accuracy of the translation of meaning into each language.

11. What kinds of appeals from your church/association motivate you to give money to your church/association? What kinds are ineffective with you?
12. Who organizes charitable activities in your church/association? (the priest/imam? laity?)
13. Have you heard any sermons in the past three months about charity, giving, or helping others?
14. If so, what do you most remember about them?
15. What were you asked to do?
16. If you give to your church/association, in what ways do you do so?
17. What is the responsibility of individuals to help others in need?
18. What is the responsibility of religious communities to help others in need?
19. What is the responsibility of your church/association to help others in need?
20. Who or what should be the beneficiary of your church/association's charitable activities?
21. Is it correct to say that God requires you to give of your time and money? Do you have a duty to God to do so?
22. When you do give, what's inspiring or guiding you?
23. What does giving make you feel?
24. What happens if you don't give?
25. What is the purpose of helping others?
26. Does the state help people in need in this country? In [name of city]? in other countries?
27. Should it? ("is it the state's responsibility to care for the poor and disadvantaged?" If so, to what extent?) How does it?
28. Does the state do anything to help or encourage charitable donations? Tax deductions for example?
29. Have you given any volunteer time to your church/association in the past six months?
30. If so, could you describe your activity and the amount of time?
31. Have you given any volunteer time to other organizations in the past six months?
32. If so, could you describe your activity and the amount of time?
33. So far, I've asked questions about giving through monetary donations or through volunteer activities. Are there other ways you give of yourself and your resources?
34. Of all the contributions you have ever made, which one gave you the most satisfaction? Why?

35. Of all the things we have spoken about today (or even things we have not), what inspires you to give freely of your time and other resources?
36. Is there anything else I should have asked you about or you would like to add?

Profile of the Interviewees for the Semi-Structured Interviews

Table A.1 *Demographics of Muslim interviewees*

	Muslims in Istanbul	Muslims in Paris	Muslims in Milan	Muslims in Dublin
Total Interviewees	31	31	32	30
Gender				
Female	12	10	8	6
Male	19	21	24	24
Age				
18–24	1	1	4	3
25–36	20	15	18	18
37–55	9	14	7	7
56–70	1	1	0	0
71+	0	0	0	0
Socioeconomic Status				
Lower class	0	3	0	1
Lower middle class	14	10	13	6
Middle class	10	8	8	3
Upper middle class	1	5	7	9
Upper class	2	0	0	1
No response	4	5	4	10

Table A.2 *Demographics of Catholic interviewees*

	Catholics in Istanbul	Catholics in Paris	Catholics in Milan	Catholics in Dublin
Total Number	28	21	21	24
Gender				
Female	9	13	12	16
Male	19	8	9	8
Age				
18–24	0	1	1	0
25–36	9	1	3	1

Table A.2 (*cont.*)

	Catholics in Istanbul	Catholics in Paris	Catholics in Milan	Catholics in Dublin
37–55	10	6	9	9
56–70	8	6	7	10
71+	1	1	1	4
Socioeconomic Status*				
Lower class	0	3	0	0
Lower middle class	11	9	6	22
Middle class	10	3	9	1
Upper middle class	7	1	0	0
Upper class	0	0	0	0
No response	0	5	7	1

Experiment Prompts: Irish Version

Experiment participants were randomly assigned to one of the following seven conditions and given the following general instructions.[1]

General Instructions: *We are very interested in what your thoughts and ideas about the following topic. Take a few minutes thinking about the topic, and then please write or list as much as you feel comfortable with on this topic in the space below. There is no right or wrong response.*

CONDITION 1: Community Expectations

Think about the expectations of your religious community or the religious community you grew up in. Describe what your religious community expects of you. What does that make you think about? How does that make you feel?

CONDITION 2: Similarity

Think about how you are similar to other people. In what ways do the teachings of your religion say that you are similar to other people? Describe how the teachings of your religion suggest that you are similar to others. What does that make you think about? How does that make you feel?

---

[1] The version in Turkish is presented in the Study Codebook in the Online Appendix.

CONDITION 3: Deservedness

Think about people in need who deserve help. What does your religion say about people in need who deserve help? Describe their circumstances. What does that make you think about? How does that make you feel?

CONDITION 4: Duty to God

Think about your duty to God. What does your religion say is your Duty to God? Describe your duty to God. What does that make you think about? How does that make you feel?

CONDITION 5: God's Grace

Think about God's Grace. In what ways does your religion say it means to be filled with God's grace? Describe what things you can do to be filled with God's grace. What does that make you think about? How does that make you feel?

CONDITION 6: General Religion

Think about your religion or the religion you grew up in. Describe your religion or the religion you grew up in. What does that make you think about? How does that make you feel?

CONDITION 7: No Religion Control

Think about the chair and desk you are sitting at. Describe the chair in full detail. Now please describe the desk in full detail. What does that make you think about? How does that make you feel?

Once you have completed writing, please think about what you've written. If you have anything more you would like to add or explain more fully, please do so. If you need more room, feel free to use the back. Otherwise please continue to the second page.

Experiment Results: Raw Regression Coefficients

In the main text of Chapter 3, we present our results as marginal effects in order to aid interpretation of each model's results. Because the marginal effects calculated from logistic regression depend to some degree on values assumed to be taken on by other variables in the model, we present here the raw coefficients from our logistic regressions. Figures 3.1 and 3.2 in the text were derived from information presented in Table A.3. Tables A.4 and A.5 similarly present the full models from which we derived the predicted probabilities for the religiosity variable presented in Figures 3.3 and 3.4 in the text. We also include information about the constant term for each model and model fit statistics.

Table A.3 *Experiment results: raw regression coefficients (primary models)*

Variables	Irish Catholics		Turkish Muslims	
	Model 1 Club Donation	Model 2 Public Goods	Model 3 Club Donation	Model 4 Public Goods
Sample	−1.09***	−0.95***	0.95***	1.77***
	(0.39)	(0.28)	(0.29)	(0.39)
Community expectations	−0.03	0.67	0.03	−0.01
	(0.55)	(0.49)	(0.55)	(0.69)
Similarity	−0.26	0.70	−0.13	−0.24
	(0.59)	(0.50)	(0.57)	(0.72)
Deservedness	0.10	1.00**	0.29	0.39
	(0.54)	(0.48)	(0.53)	(0.65)
Duty to God	0.25	0.96*	−0.55	−0.29
	(0.55)	(0.49)	(0.62)	(0.72)
God's grace	−0.28	1.16**	0.31	0.28
	(0.57)	(0.47)	(0.52)	(0.64)
General religion	0.30	0.41	0.44	0.37
	(0.54)	(0.51)	(0.53)	(0.67)
Constant	−1.35***	−1.24***	−2.11***	−3.15***
	(0.40)	(0.38)	(0.42)	(0.55)
Observations	337	337	352	352
Log likelihood	−145.82	−199.07	−151.78	−107.47
AIC	307.63	414.15	319.56	230.94
BIC	338.19	444.71	350.47	261.85

Standard errors in parentheses; *** $p < 0.01$, ** $p < 0.05$, * $p < 0.1$. AIC, Akaike information criterion; BIC, Bayesian information criterion.

Table A.4 *Raw regression coefficients, Irish Catholics with demographic data*

Variables	Irish Catholics	
	Model 1 Club Donation	Model 2 Public Goods
Religiosity	0.36**	−0.09
	(0.17)	(0.13)
Low socioeconomic	0.27	−0.18
	(0.41)	(0.34)
High socioeconomic	−0.09	−0.35

Table A.4 (*cont.*)

Variables	Irish Catholics	
	Model 1 Club Donation	Model 2 Public Goods
	(0.46)	(0.36)
Married	0.13	−0.21
	(0.45)	(0.36)
High school or less	−0.20	−0.23
	(0.57)	(0.46)
University plus	−0.15	0.05
	(0.38)	(0.31)
Age 25–36	0.07	0.52
	(0.91)	(0.68)
Age 37–55	−0.11	0.53
	(0.74)	(0.55)
Age 56–70	0.23	0.79
	(0.77)	(0.60)
Age 71+	1.33*	0.69
	(0.78)	(0.65)
Gender	0.29	0.00
	(0.33)	(0.27)
Sample	−0.22	−0.66
	(0.68)	(0.50)
Community expectations	0.23	0.67
	(0.61)	(0.50)
Similarity	−0.18	0.77
	(0.66)	(0.52)
Deservedness	0.51	0.91*
	(0.59)	(0.50)
Duty to God	0.42	0.84*
	(0.60)	(0.51)
God's grace	−0.21	1.19**
	(0.62)	(0.48)
General religion	0.61	0.31
	(0.60)	(0.53)
Constant	−3.90***	−1.11
	(1.13)	(0.81)
Observations	326	326
Log likelihood	−133.11	−191.05
AIC	304.22	420.09
BIC	376.18	492.05

Standard errors in parentheses; *** $p < 0.01$, ** $p < 0.05$, * $p < 0.1$.

Table A.5 *Raw regression coefficients, Turkish Muslims with demographic data*

Variables	Turkish Muslims	
	Model 1 Club Donation	Model 2 Public Goods
Religiosity	0.45**	−0.16
	(0.19)	(0.19)
Low socioeconomic	0.21	−0.44
	(0.62)	(0.81)
High socioeconomic	0.33	0.39
	(0.36)	(0.42)
High school or less	0.22	−1.02
	(0.61)	(0.84)
University plus	0.71	−1.00
	(0.63)	(0.85)
Age 25–36	0.30	−0.62
	(1.12)	(0.60)
Age 37–55	0.62	−0.94
	(1.13)	(0.75)
Gender	−0.35	0.22
	(0.39)	(0.43)
Sample	2.15*	–
	(1.13)	
Community expectations	−0.16	0.24
	(0.59)	(0.73)
Similarity	0.01	0.11
	(0.64)	(0.77)
Deservedness	0.10	0.50
	(0.60)	(0.71)
Duty to God	−0.90	−0.44
	(0.75)	(0.82)
God's grace	0.12	0.46
	(0.60)	(0.70)
General religion	0.68	0.50
	(0.60)	(0.74)
Constant	−5.38***	−1.14
	(1.63)	(1.04)
Observations	299	299
Log likelihood	−121.10	−94.43
AIC	274.20	218.87
BIC	333.41	274.38

Standard errors in parentheses; *** $p < 0.01$, ** $p < 0.05$, * $p < 0.1$.

Profile of the Experiment Participants

Table A.6 *Demographics of Turkish Muslim participants*

Total Participants	352
Gender	
Female	172
Male	175
No response	5
Age	
18–24	146
25–36	123
37–55	77
56–70	6
Socioeconomic Status*	
Lower class	6
Lower middle class	23
Middle class	188
Upper middle class	59
Upper class	32
No response	44

Table A.7 *Demographics of Irish Catholic participants*

Total Participants	337
Gender	
Female	215
Male	117
No response	5
Age	
18–24	126
25–36	16
37–55	76
56–70	90
71+	28
No response	1
Socioeconomic Status	
Lower class	11
Lower middle class	50
Middle class	209

Table A.7 (*cont.*)

Upper middle class	63
Upper class	3
No response	1

Mentions of Charity in Content-Coded Essays:
Regression Results

To make our discussion of the qualitative coding results accessible to as broad an audience as possible, we presented our results visually as raw coefficients. Here we present those same results in the format of a conventional regression table

Table A.8 *Experiment prompts and mentions of charity, Irish Catholics and Turkish Muslims*

Variables	Model 1 Irish Catholics	Model 2 Turkish Muslims
Sample	−0.02	0.07
	(0.09)	(0.09)
Community expectations	0.28*	0.35**
	(0.16)	(0.17)
Similarity	0.11	0.10
	(0.16)	(0.17)
Deservedness	1.88***	1.54***
	(0.15)	(0.17)
Duty to God	0.17	0.33**
	(0.16)	(0.17)
God's grace	0.41***	0.45***
	(0.15)	(0.17)
General religion	0.07	0.22
	(0.16)	(0.17)
Constant	0.01	0.02
	(0.11)	(0.12)
Observations	335	351
R-squared	0.40	0.24

Standard errors in parentheses; *** $p < 0.01$, ** $p < 0.05$, * $p < 0.1$.

Full Quantitative Analyses of Content-Coded Experiment Essays: Regression Results

In addition to analyzing the impacts of the prompts on whether participants mentioned concepts related to charity in their essays, we were also interested in the degree to which they mentioned other concepts and topics, as elaborated in Chapters 4 and 5. The discussion in those chapters makes extensive reference to Tables A.9 and A.10, which we present on the next several pages.

Full Hierarchical Model Results of State Expenditures and Individual Responsibility for Public Goods Provision

In Chapter 8, to keep our discussion accessible for a broad readership, we presented only statistically significant predicted probability graphs for our key variables of interest in the main text of the book. Here, however, we present full regression tables for our primary models.

Model 1 of Table A.11 (see after Tables A.9 and A.10) examines the impact of state expenditures on social protection (Figures 8.1 and 8.2 in the book are intended to visually represent the predicted probabilities of Model 1). We find support for the contention of Hypothesis 1 that the higher state welfare expenditures, the less likely individuals are to think they are responsible for spending time helping others, or, more formally, less likely to support citizen responsibility for public goods provision. We see that every percentage point increase in expenditures on social protection as a percentage of gross domestic product is associated with a decreased likelihood of individual public goods provision.[2]

We also find strong support for Hypothesis 2, that higher levels of religiosity will be associated with stronger support for citizen responsibility for public goods provision. In each of our statistical models in Table A.11, each unit increase in an individual's level of religiosity is associated with an increased likelihood of supporting individual responsibility for public

---

[2] Technically, the logit analyses we use suggest that increases in expenditures are associated with a decrease in the predicted log-odds that citizens support citizen responsibility for public goods provision. We use the nomenclature of likelihood throughout the discussion to be reader friendly and not to imply a constant probabilistic relationship. Higher levels of GDP per capita are associated with decreased levels of individual public goods provision in Models 1, 3, and 5, while age has a curvilinear relationship in all five models. Also in all five models, we see that individuals identifying further to the right of the political spectrum are associated with decreased support for the statement that individuals should spend some of their free time helping others.

Table A.9 *Irish Catholics: experiment prompts and mentions of concepts and topics*

Variables	Charity	Norms	Third	Similarity	Rituals	Deservedness	Government	Doctrine	Divine	Disillusioned
Sample	-0.02	0.14	-0.00	0.04	0.41***	0.02	-0.00	0.29**	0.05	0.43***
	(0.09)	(0.12)	(0.03)	(0.05)	(0.13)	(0.07)	(0.01)	(0.12)	(0.08)	(0.09)
Community expectations	0.28*	2.48***	0.06	0.07	0.97***	0.00	-0.00	0.83***	0.26*	0.50***
	(0.16)	(0.22)	(0.05)	(0.09)	(0.23)	(0.12)	(0.01)	(0.21)	(0.14)	(0.15)
Similarity	0.11	0.18	0.09*	1.37***	0.44*	0.02	-0.00	1.11***	0.17	0.16
	(0.16)	(0.22)	(0.05)	(0.09)	(0.23)	(0.12)	(0.01)	(0.21)	(0.14)	(0.15)
Deservedness	1.88***	0.32	0.04	0.02	0.11	0.98***	0.02*	0.36*	0.06	0.19
	(0.15)	(0.21)	(0.05)	(0.08)	(0.22)	(0.11)	(0.01)	(0.20)	(0.14)	(0.15)
Duty to God	0.17	0.20	0.07	0.05	0.90***	0.03	-0.00	1.50***	0.93***	0.37**
	(0.16)	(0.22)	(0.05)	(0.09)	(0.24)	(0.12)	(0.01)	(0.21)	(0.15)	(0.16)
God's grace	0.41**	0.20	0.06	0.06	1.25***	0.02	-0.00	1.06***	0.63***	0.23
	(0.15)	(0.21)	(0.05)	(0.08)	(0.22)	(0.11)	(0.01)	(0.20)	(0.14)	(0.14)
General religion	0.07	1.51***	0.09*	0.04	1.15***	-0.00	0.00	0.55***	0.24*	0.93***
	(0.16)	(0.22)	(0.05)	(0.09)	(0.23)	(0.12)	(0.01)	(0.21)	(0.14)	(0.15)
Constant	0.01	-0.01	0.00	-0.01	-0.15	-0.01	0.00	-0.08	-0.02	-0.16
	(0.11)	(0.16)	(0.04)	(0.06)	(0.16)	(0.08)	(0.01)	(0.15)	(0.10)	(0.11)

Observations	335	335	335	335	335	335	335	335	335	335
R-squared	0.40	0.40	0.01	0.55	0.18	0.28	0.02	0.19	0.16	0.18

Standard errors in parentheses; *** $p<0.01$, ** $p<0.05$, * $p<0.1$.

Key to column labels

- religious norms (Norms)
- third party enforcer (e.g., God watching their behavior) (Third)
- being similar to others (Similarity)
- ritualistic aspects of their religion (Rituals)
- the deservedness of potential recipients of charity (Deservedness)
- the role of government (Government)
- religious doctrine (Doctrine)
- having been inspired by the divine (Divine)
- being disillusioned with their religion (Disillusioned)

Key to row labels

- Sample: whether in the community or student sample
- The seven experiment prompts (six religious concepts plus control)

251

Table A.10 *Turkish Muslims: experiment prompts and mentions of concepts and topics*

Variables	Charity	Norms	Third	Similarity	Rituals	Deservedness	Government	Doctrine	Divine	Disillusioned
Sample	0.07	0.54***	−0.04	0.07	0.56***	0.22***	−0.01	0.27**	0.31***	0.26***
	(0.09)	(0.10)	(0.05)	(0.05)	(0.10)	(0.06)	(0.02)	(0.12)	(0.09)	(0.04)
Community expectations	0.35**	2.27***	0.21**	0.08	0.36**	0.05	0.00	0.58***	0.46***	0.11
	(0.17)	(0.18)	(0.08)	(0.09)	(0.18)	(0.11)	(0.03)	(0.21)	(0.16)	(0.08)
Similarity	0.10	0.02	0.00	0.88***	0.07	−0.00	0.00	0.44**	0.16	0.04
	(0.17)	(0.18)	(0.08)	(0.09)	(0.18)	(0.11)	(0.03)	(0.21)	(0.16)	(0.08)
Deservedness	1.54***	0.09	0.02	0.02	0.30*	0.67***	0.08**	0.53**	−0.03	0.01
	(0.17)	(0.18)	(0.08)	(0.09)	(0.18)	(0.11)	(0.03)	(0.21)	(0.16)	(0.08)
Duty to God	0.33**	−0.05	0.20**	−0.00	1.38***	−0.01	0.00	1.03***	0.95***	0.11
	(0.17)	(0.18)	(0.08)	(0.09)	(0.18)	(0.10)	(0.03)	(0.21)	(0.16)	(0.08)
God's grace	0.45**	−0.00	0.13*	0.02	0.42**	0.03	0.00	0.76***	0.48***	0.03
	(0.17)	(0.18)	(0.08)	(0.09)	(0.17)	(0.10)	(0.03)	(0.21)	(0.16)	(0.07)
General religion	0.22	0.32*	0.16*	−0.00	0.39**	0.02	0.00	0.59***	0.43***	0.35***
	(0.17)	(0.19)	(0.08)	(0.09)	(0.18)	(0.11)	(0.03)	(0.22)	(0.16)	(0.08)
Constant	0.02	−0.05	0.05	−0.02	−0.19	−0.08	0.00	−0.05	0.01	−0.09
	(0.12)	(0.13)	(0.06)	(0.07)	(0.13)	(0.08)	(0.02)	(0.15)	(0.12)	(0.06)

Observations	351	351	351	351	351	351	351	351	351	351
R-squared	0.24	0.45	0.04	0.30	0.25	0.19	0.03	0.09	0.16	0.16

Standard errors in parentheses; *** p < 0.01, ** p < 0.05, * p < 0.1.

Key to column labels

- religious norms (Norms)
- third party enforcer (e.g., God watching their behavior) (Third)
- being similar to others (Similarity)
- ritualistic aspects of their religion (Rituals)
- the deservedness of potential recipients of charity (Deservedness)
- the role of government (Government)
- religious doctrine (Doctrine)
- having been inspired by the divine (Divine)
- being disillusioned with their religion (Disillusioned)

Key to row labels

- Sample: whether in the community or student sample
- The seven experiment prompts (six religious concepts plus control)

Table A.11 *State expenditures and citizen responsibility for public goods provision*

Variables	(Model 1) Social Protection	(Model 2) Taxes	(Model 3) Social Protection/ Highly Religious Interaction	(Model 4) Tax/ Highly Religious Interaction	(Model 5) Subsidies
Country-Level					
Social protection	-0.11***	–	-0.11***	–	–
	(0.03)		(0.03)		
Taxes	–	-0.09**	–	-0.09**	–
		(0.04)		(0.04)	
Subsidies	–	–	–	–	0.01
					(0.06)
Interaction term	–	–	-0.03***	0.02	–
			(0.01)	(0.02)	
GDP per capita	-0.00**	-0.00	-0.00**	-0.00	-0.00**
	(0.00)	(0.00)	(0.00)	(0.00)	(0.00)
Individual-Level					
Age	-5.68***	-5.67***	-6.08***	-6.03***	-3.18**
	(1.44)	(1.44)	(1.42)	(1.46)	(1.59)
Age squared	0.83***	0.83***	0.89***	0.88***	0.48**
	(0.20)	(0.20)	(0.20)	(0.20)	(0.22)
Gender	0.11	0.11	0.06	0.06	0.15
	(0.10)	(0.10)	(0.09)	(0.09)	(0.10)
# in household	-0.01	-0.01	-0.00	-0.00	-0.02
	(0.03)	(0.03)	(0.03)	(0.03)	(0.03)

	(1)	(2)	(3)	(4)	(5)
Education	0.01*	0.01*	0.02*	0.01*	0.00
	(0.01)	(0.01)	(0.01)	(0.01)	(0.01)
Retiree	0.09	0.09	0.09	0.08	0.10
	(0.07)	(0.07)	(0.07)	(0.07)	(0.08)
Household income	0.01	0.01	0.01	0.01	0.01
	(0.01)	(0.01)	(0.01)	(0.01)	(0.01)
Married	0.02	0.02	0.04	0.04	0.01
	(0.06)	(0.06)	(0.06)	(0.06)	(0.07)
Left/right scale	−0.03***	−0.03***	−0.03***	−0.02***	−0.02*
	(0.01)	(0.01)	(0.01)	(0.01)	(0.01)
Religiosity	0.10***	0.10***	–	–	0.11***
	(0.02)	(0.02)			(0.02)
Highly religious	–	–	1.13***	0.50**	–
			(0.22)	(0.21)	
Constant	12.62***	11.53***	13.60***	12.53***	6.96***
	(2.14)	(2.40)	(2.09)	(2.42)	(2.62)
Random-intercept Variance (country)	0.19 (0.05)	0.23 (0.06)	0.19 (0.05)	0.24 (0.06)	0.24 (0.07)
Individuals	26955	27764	26955	27764	16150
Countries	21	22	21	22	21
Log likelihood	−11169.48	−11179.88	−11196.21	−11208.17	−6634.243
AIC	22366.96	22387.77	22422.42	22446.34	13296.49
BIC	22481.79	22503.01	22545.45	22569.81	13404.14

Standard errors in parentheses; *** $p < 0.01$, ** $p < 0.05$, * $p < 0.1$.

255

goods provision.[3] Furthermore, we find support for Hypothesis 3, that highly religious individuals diminish the negative association between welfare state expenditure and support for citizen responsibility for public goods provision. Model 3 (Figure 8.3 in the book demonstrates our primary result visually) assesses the interaction effect between welfare state expenditure and religiosity and their subsequent impact on support for citizen responsibility for public goods provision. The most substantively meaningful variable here is the interaction term between expenditure on social protection and religiosity.[4] The coefficient on the interaction term is statistically significant and negative, indicating that high religiosity mitigates the negative impact of social welfare spending on individual public goods provision. In other words, the steepness of the negative slope in the relationship between welfare provision and public goods support is reduced.[5]

Hypothesis 4 stipulates that the higher the levels of taxation, the lower the likelihood of individuals supporting citizen responsibility for public goods provision. Model 2 of Table A.11 (which Figure 8.4 in the book visually depicts) provides support for this proposition. The model assesses the impact of individual taxes on income, profits, and capital gains on support for citizen responsibility for public goods provision. We see that every percentage point increase in these taxes as a percentage of GDP is associated with a decreased likelihood an individual supports citizen responsibility for public goods provision.[6] On the other hand, Model 4 provides very little support for Hypothesis 5, suggesting that high levels of religiosity diminish the negative association between taxation and support for citizen responsibility for public goods provision. The coefficient on the interaction term of Model 4 is not statistically significant, suggesting

---

[3] We also ran Models 1, 2, and 5 with our isolated and categorical highly religious individuals as opposed to the scaled religiosity measure (Online Appendix, Table OA.7).

[4] Less substantively meaningful are the coefficients on the social protection and highly religious variables in Model 3. The coefficient on total expenditures signifies the impact of each percentage point increase in total expenditures, but only among individuals who are not highly religious. Likewise, the coefficient on "Highly Religious" signifies the impact of high degrees of religiosity if we imagined a hypothetical (and, within contemporary Europe, implausible) scenario where there were no welfare state expenditures.

[5] Due to the greater ease with which our statistical software produces predicted probability graphs for logit models rather than multilevel logit models, Figures 8.1 through 8.4 were run on logit models with clustered standard errors rather than the multilevel models used to conduct our primary analyses. As Online Appendix Table OA.8 demonstrates, the clustered logit models yield very similar results to the hierarchical models used here.

[6] See also discussion in Chapter 8.

that highly religious individuals have similarly diminished support for individual responsibility for public goods provision as their less religious counterparts at increasing levels of social welfare provision.

Model 5 of Table A.11 assesses our sixth hypothesis, stating that higher levels of subsidies to religious organizations should result in lower likelihoods of support among religious adherents for citizen responsibility for public goods provision. The number of different government subsidies has no statistically significant impact on the views of religious individuals that they should spend time helping others.[7]

Full Hierarchical Model Results of State Expenditures and Individual Responsibility for Public Goods Provision, with Religious Denominations

In Figure 8.5 of Chapter 8, we presented a figure depicting the impact of several religious denominations on individuals' support for the idea that they should volunteer some time each week to help others. We utilize that response as a measure of their sense of citizen responsibility for public goods provision to see if state provision of public welfare "crowds out" individuals' inclination to help others directly. Here, we present the full model (Model 1 of Table A.11 examining social protection) from which that figure was derived. We also present several additional models, including our models assessing the impact of taxes, the social protection/high religiosity interaction, the tax/high religiosity interaction, and the number of subsidies.

Table A.12 examines the same models we examine in Table A.11, but here we replace religiosity with categorical variables assessing the religious affiliation of survey respondents. The potential categories include Catholics, Muslims, Protestants, Orthodox, and an "other" category.[8] Each of these categories is assessed against individuals who responded that their

---

[7] We note that the relationship is somewhat more nuanced. Online Appendix Table OA.9 demonstrates the effects of each individual subsidy, disaggregated from the count measure. In six of eight cases, the individual subsidies have no statistically significant relationship with individual public goods provision. The exceptions are: (1) subsidies to religious colleges and universities, which are negatively associated, and (2) official positions or salaries for clergy, which is positively associated with support for public goods provision.

[8] The other category includes other Christian denominations, Jewish individuals, adherents of Eastern religious, and adherents of other non-Christian religions. Collectively, this category accounts for only about 2 percent of the sample.

Table A.12 *State expenditures and citizen responsibility for public goods provision by denomination*

Variables	(Model 1) Social Protection	(Model 2) Taxes	(Model 3) Social Protection/High Religiosity Interaction	(Model 4) Tax/High Religiosity Interaction	(Model 5) Subsidies
Country-Level					
Social protection	−0.11***	–	−0.11***	–	–
	(0.03)		(0.03)		
Taxes	–	−0.07***	–	−0.07***	–
		(0.02)		(0.03)	
Subsidies	–	–	–	–	−0.00
					(0.07)
Interaction term	–	–	−0.03**	−0.01	–
			(0.01)	(0.02)	
GDP per capita	−0.00**	−0.00	−0.00*	−0.00	−0.00**
	(0.00)	(0.00)	(0.00)	(0.00)	(0.00)
Individual-Level					
Age	−5.24***	−5.25***	−4.90***	−4.89***	−5.25***
	(1.71)	(1.70)	(1.60)	(1.60)	(1.70)
Age squared	0.77***	0.77***	0.71***	0.71***	0.77***
	(0.23)	(0.23)	(0.22)	(0.22)	(0.23)
Gender	−0.02	−0.02	0.01	0.01	−0.02
	(0.07)	(0.07)	(0.07)	(0.07)	(0.07)

	(1)	(2)	(3)	(4)	(5)
# in household	0.00	0.01	−0.00	−0.00	0.01
	(0.04)	(0.04)	(0.04)	(0.04)	(0.04)
Education	0.01	0.01	0.01	0.01	0.01
	(0.01)	(0.01)	(0.01)	(0.01)	(0.01)
Retiree	0.09	0.09	0.10	0.10	0.09
	(0.07)	(0.07)	(0.08)	(0.08)	(0.07)
Household income	0.01	0.01	0.01	0.01	0.01
	(0.01)	(0.01)	(0.01)	(0.01)	(0.01)
Married	0.09	0.09	0.10*	0.10*	0.10
	(0.06)	(0.06)	(0.06)	(0.06)	(0.06)
Left/right scale	−0.03***	−0.03***	−0.04***	−0.03***	−0.03***
	(0.01)	(0.01)	(0.01)	(0.01)	(0.01)
Catholic	0.22***	0.21***	0.15*	0.14	0.21***
	(0.08)	(0.08)	(0.09)	(0.09)	(0.08)
Muslim	0.30	0.35*	0.11	0.16	0.34*
	(0.18)	(0.19)	(0.21)	(0.22)	(0.19)
Protestant	0.41***	0.41***	0.35***	0.34***	0.41***
	(0.05)	(0.05)	(0.05)	(0.05)	(0.05)
Orthodox	0.37	0.33	0.25	0.19	0.34
	(0.33)	(0.35)	(0.32)	(0.35)	(0.35)
Other	0.61***	0.61***	0.46***	0.45***	0.61***
	(0.12)	(0.12)	(0.13)	(0.13)	(0.12)
Highly religious	–	–	0.96***	0.51***	–
			(0.27)	(0.20)	
Constant	12.25***	11.21***	11.67***	10.63***	11.12***
	(2.80)	(3.03)	(2.62)	(2.90)	(3.07)

259

Table A.12 (*cont.*)

Variables	(Model 1) Social Protection	(Model 2) Taxes	(Model 3) Social Protection/High Religiosity Interaction	(Model 4) Tax/High Religiosity Interaction	(Model 5) Subsidies
Random-intercept variance	0.14	0.20	0.16	0.22	0.24
(country)	(0.06)	(0.06)	(0.07)	(0.07)	(0.05)
Individuals	22573	23382	22490	23298	23382
Countries	18	19	18	19	19
Log likelihood	−8609.37	−8620.46	−8539.91	−8552.99	−8621.76
AIC	17254.75	17276.92	17119.82	17145.98	17279.52
BIC	17399.19	17421.99	17280.23	17307.1	17424.59

Standard errors in parentheses; *** p < 0.01, ** p < 0.05, * p < 0.1.

religious status was "not applicable," and we take this as meaning these individuals are not members of a religious organization.[9]

We note, first, that our fundamental conclusions regarding the effects of welfare state expenditure, religiosity, taxation rates, and interaction effects remain unaltered in the models including the denominational data. Furthermore, we find some support that individuals who identify as being part of Catholic congregations are positively associated with individual public goods provision. This relationship is positive and statistically significant in three of the five models. It is not statistically significant in the tax interaction model, and it is statistically significant at the 90 percent confidence interval in the social protection interaction model. We furthermore find only limited support that Muslims are positively associated with individual public goods provision. The relationship is only statistically significant at the 90 percent confidence interval in the subsidy and tax models. We find little support that adherents of Orthodox Christianity support individual responsibility for public goods provision. By far, the most robust variable among the individual religious denominations is Protestantism, which is strongly associated with individual public goods provision across all our statistical models.[10]

---

[9] The ESS also asked individuals a yes or no question with regard to whether they belonged to a religious organization. In order to assess the fairness of our assumption that individuals who answered "not applicable" are not religious adherents, we examined responses to religious denomination against responses to whether or not an individual identified as part of a religious organizations. There were no individuals who identified as belonging to a particular religious denomination who also answered "no" to the question of whether they belonged to a religious institution. There were, on the other hand, 14,359 individuals who answered "no" to belonging to a religious institution and who mentioned the denominational question was "not applicable" to them.

[10] Our residual "Other" category also has a strong statistically significant and positive relationship. It is difficult to glean much from the observation, as it includes several distinct religious denominations and includes only about 2 percent of the sample.

References

Abdoun, Karim, Mathilde Chevre, Asthma Al Atayoui, and Abdel Aziz Faïk, eds. 2004. *Histoires de mosquées. Recueil de témoinages.* Schiltigheim: Editions Kalima.

Abrahms, Max. 2008. "What Terrorists Really Want: Terrorist Motives and Counterterrorism Strategy," *International Security* 32/4: 78–105.

Abrams, Dominic, Margaret Wetherell, Sandra Cochrane, Michael Hogg, and John Turner. 1990. "Knowing What to Think by Knowing Who You Are: Self-Categorization and the Nature of Norm Formation, Conformity and Group Polarization," *British Journal of Social Psychology* 29: 97–119.

Ahmed, Ali M. 2009. "Are Religious People More Prosocial? A Quasi-Experimental Study with *Madrasah* Pupils in a Rural Community in India," *Journal for the Scientific Study of Religion* 48/2: 368–374.

Ahmed, Ali, and Mats Hammarstedt. 2011. "The Effect of Subtle Religious Representations on Cooperation," *International Journal of Social Economics* 38/11: 900–910.

Ahn, T. K., Justin Esarey, and John T. Scholz. 2009. "Reputation and Cooperation in Voluntary Exchanges: Comparing Local and Central Institutions," *Journal of Politics* 71/2 (Apr.): 398–413.

Aktipis, Athena. 2016. "Principles of Cooperation across Systems: From Human Sharing to Multicellularity and Cancer," *Evolutionary Applications* 9: 17–36.

Al-Ghazzali, Mohammad. 1966. *The Mysteries of Almsgiving: Ihya-i Ulum al-Din Book 5,* trans. Nabih Amin Faris. Beirut: American University of Beirut.

Alcorta, Candace S., and Richard Sosis. 2013. "Ritual, Religion and Violence: An Evolutionary Perspective." In *Oxford Handbook of Religion and Violence,* edited by Mark Juergensmeyer, Margo Kitts, and Michael Jerryson, 571–596. New York: Oxford University Press.

Alexander, Marcus, and Fotini Christia. 2011. "Context Modularity of Human Altruism," *Science* 334 (Dec. 9): 1392–1394.

Ali, Jan A. 2014. "Zakat and Poverty in Islam." In *Islam and Development: Exploring the Invisible Aid Economy,* edited by Matthew Clarke and David Tittensor, 15–32. Burlington, VT: Ashgate.

Allievi, Stefano. 2003. *Islam Italiano. Viaggio nella seconda religione del paese.* Torino: Einaudi.

Allport, Gordon W., and J. Michael Ross. 1967. "Personal Orientation and Prejudice," *Journal of Personality and Social Psychology* 5: 432–443.

Andreoni, James. 1990. "Impure Altruism and Donations to Public Goods: A Theory of Warm-Glow Giving," *The Economic Journal* 100 (June): 464–477.

Andreoni, James. 1993. "An Experimental Test of the Public-Goods Crowding-Out Hypothesis," *American Economic Review* 83/5 (Dec.): 1317–1327.

Andreoni, James, and A. Abigail Payne. 2003. "Do Government Grants to Private Charities Crowd Out Giving or Fund-Raising?," *American Economic Review* 93/3 (June): 792–812.

Andreoni, James, and Justin Rao. 2011. "The Power of Asking: How Communication Affects Selfishness, Empathy, and Altruism," *Journal of Public Economics* 95: 513–520.

Andreoni, James, Justin Rao, and Hannah Trachtman. 2011. "Avoiding the Ask: A Field Experiment on Altruism, Empathy and Charitable Giving." NBER Working Paper No. 17648, Dec.

Arjomand, Said Amir. 1998. "Philanthropy, the Law, and Public Policy in the Islamic World before the Modern Era." In *Philanthropy in the World's Traditions*, edited by Warren Frederick Ilchman, Stanley Nider Katz, and Edward L. Queen, 109–132. Indianapolis: Indiana University Press.

Arslan, M. 2001. "The Work Ethic Values of Protestant British, Catholic Irish and Muslim Turkish Managers," *Journal of Business Ethics* 31/4 (June): 321–339.

Atia, Mona. 2013. *Building a House in Heaven: Pious Neoliberalism and Islamic Charity in Egypt.* Minneapolis: University of Minnesota Press.

Atran, Scott, and Jeremy Ginges. 2012. "Religious and Sacred Imperatives in Human Conflict," *Science* 336: 855–857.

Atran, Scott, and Joseph Heinrich. 2010. "The Evolution of Religion: How Cognitive By-Products, Adaptive Learning Heuristics, Ritual Displays, and Group Competition Generate Deep Commitments to Prosocial Religions," *Biological Theory* 5/1: 18–30.

Atran, Scott, and Ara Norenzayan. 2004. "Religion's Evolutionary Landscape: Counterintuition, Commitment, Compassion, Communion," *Behavioral and Brain Sciences* 27: 713–770.

Aydın, Mustafa. 2004. "Süleymancılık." In *Modern Türkiye'de Siyasi Düşünce 6: İslamcılık*, edited by Tanıl Bora and Meral Gültekingil, 308–322. İstanbul: İletişim Yayınları.

Bailey, Betty Jane, and J. Martin Bailey. 2003. *Who Are the Christians in the Middle East?* Grand Rapids, MI: William B. Eerdmans.

Baldwin, Peter. 1990. *The Politics of Social Solidarity: Class Bases of the European Welfare State, 1875–1975.* New York: Cambridge University Press.

Bargh, John A. 2006. "What Have We Been Priming All These Years? On the Development, Mechanisms, and Ecology of Nonconscious Social Behavior," *European Journal of Social Psychology* 36/2: 147–168.

Bargh, John A., and Tanya L. Chartrand. 2000. "Studying the Mind in the Middle: A Practical Guide to Priming and Automaticity Research." In *Handbook of Research Methods in Social and Personality Psychology*, edited by Harry T. Reis and Charles Judd, 253–284. New York: Cambridge University Press.

Barker, Christine R. 2000. "Church and State Relationships in German 'Public Benefit' Law," *International Journal of Not-for-Profit Law* 3/2 (Dec.): www.icnl.org/research/journal/vol3iss2/art_1.htm.

Bartkowski, John P., and Helen A. Regis. 2003. *Charitable Choices: Religion, Race, and Poverty in the Post-Welfare Era.* New York: New York University Press.

Basedevant-Gaudemet, Brigitte. 2000. "The Legal Status of Islam in France." In *Islam and European Legal Systems*, edited by Silvio Ferrari and Anthony Bradney, 97–124. Aldershot: Ashgate.

Batson, C. Daniel. 2014. *The Altruism Question: Toward a Social-Psychological Answer.* New York: Taylor & Francis.

Batson, C. Daniel, David A. Lishner, and Eric L. Stocks. 2015. "The Empathy–Altruism Hypothesis." In *The Oxford Handbook of Prosocial Behavior*, edited by David A. Schroeder and William G. Graziano, 259–281. New York: Oxford University Press.

Bean, Lydia. 2014. "Compassionate Conservatives? Evangelicals, Economic Conservatism, and National Identity," *Journal for the Scientific Study of Religion* 53/1: 164–186.

Becker, Gary S. 1976. "Altruism, Egoism and Genetic Fitness: Economics and Sociobiology," *Journal of Economic Literature* 14/3 (Sept.): 817–826.

Bekkers, René, and Theo Schuyt. 2007. "And Who Is Your Neighbor? Explaining Denominational Differences in Charitable Giving and Volunteering in the Netherlands," *Review of Religious Research* 50/1 (Sept.): 74–96.

Bekkers, René, and Pamela Wiepking. 2011. "A Literature Review of Empirical Studies of Philanthropy: Eight Mechanisms That Drive Charitable Giving," *Nonprofit and Voluntary Sector Quarterly* 40/5 (Oct.): 924–973.

Bendor, Jonathan, Roderick Kramer, and Piotr Swistak. 1996. "Cooperation under Uncertainty: What Is New, What Is True, and What Is Important," *American Sociological Review* 61: 333–338.

Benedict XVI, Pope. 2009. *Encyclical Letter Caritas in Veritate of the Supreme Pontiff Benedict XVI.* http://w2.vatican.va/content/benedict-xvi/en/encyclicals/documents/hf_ben-xvi_enc_20090629_caritas-in-veritate.html.

Bennett, Andrew, and Colin Elman. 2006. "Complex Causal Relations and Case Study Methods: The Example of Path Dependence," *Political Analysis* 14: 250–267.

Benthall, Jonathan, and Jérôme Bellion-Jourdan. 2003. *The Charitable Crescent: The Politics of Aid in the Muslim World.* London: I. B. Tauris.

Berger, Peter L. 1974. "Some Second Thoughts on Substantive versus Functional Definitions of Religion," *Journal for the Scientific Study of Religion* 13: 125–133.

Berman, Eli. 2009. *Radical, Religious and Violent: The New Economics of Terrorism.* Cambridge: MIT Press.

Berman, Eli, and David D. Laitin. 2008. "Religion, Terrorism and Public Goods: Testing the Club Model," *Journal of Public Economics* 92/10–11 (Oct.): 1942–1967.

Berry, William D., Matt Golder, and Daniel Milton. 2012. "Improving Tests of Theories Positing Interaction," *The Journal of Politics* 74/3 (July): 653–671.

Berryman, Phillip. 1987. *Liberation Theology: Essential Facts about the Revolutionary Movement in Latin America and Beyond.* Philadelphia: Temple University Press.

Bielefeld, Wolfgang, and William Suhs Cleveland. 2013. "Faith-Based Organizations as Service Providers and Their Relationship to Government," *Nonprofit and Voluntary Sector Quarterly* 42/3: 468–494.

Bittschi, Benjamin, Sarah Borgloh, and Berthold U. Wigger. 2016. "Philanthropy in a Secular Society." Centre for European Economic Research. Discussion Paper 16-021.

Blogowska, Joanna, Catherine Lambert, and Vassilis Saroglou. 2013. "Religious Prosociality and Aggression: It's Real," *Journal for the Scientific Study of Religion* 52/3 (Sept.): 524–536.

Blouin, David D., Robert V. Robinson, and Brian Starks. 2013. "Are Religious People More Compassionate and Does This Matter Politically?," *Politics and Religion* 6: 618–645.

Boix, Carles, and Daniel Posner. 1998. "Social Capital: Explaining Its Origins and Effects on Governmental Performance," *British Journal of Political Science* 28/4: 686–693.

Bonner, Michael, Mine Ener, and Amy Singer, eds. 2003. *Poverty and Charity in Middle Eastern Contexts*. Albany: State University Press of New York.

Borgonovi, Francesca. 2008. "Divided We Stand, United We Fall: Religious Pluralism, Giving, and Volunteering," *American Sociological Review* 73 (Feb.): 105–128.

Bottan, Nicolas L., and Ricardo Perez-Truglia. 2015. "Losing My Religion: The Effects of Religious Scandal on Religious Participation and Charitable Giving," *Journal of Public Economics* 129 (Sept.): 106–119.

Bowers, Jake. 2011. "Making Effects Manifest in Randomized Experiments." In *Cambridge Handbook of Experimental Political Science*, edited by James N. Druckman, Donald P. Green, James H. Kuklinski, and Arthur Lupia, 459–480. New York: Cambridge University Press.

Boyer, Pascal. 1994. *The Naturalness of Religious Ideas: A Cognitive Theory of Religion*. Berkeley: University of California Press.

Boyer, Pierre, Nadja Dweger, and Johannes Rincke. 2014. "Do Taxes Crowd Out Intrinsic Motivation? Field-Experimental Evidence from Germany," Working Paper, Max Planck Institute for Tax Law and Public Finance No. 2014-23.

Brady, Henry E. 2008. "Causation and Explanation in Social Science." In *The Oxford Handbook of Political Methodology*, edited by Janet M. Box-Steffensmeier, Henry E. Brady, and David Collier, 217–270. Oxford: Oxford University Press.

Brady, Henry E., and David Collier, eds. 2004. *Rethinking Social Inquiry: Diverse Tools, Shared Standards*. Lantham, MD: Rowman & Littlefield.

Brady, Henry E., David Collier, and Jason Seawright. 2006. "Toward a Pluralistic Vision of Methodology," *Political Analysis* 14: 353–368.

Brambor, Thomas, William Roberts Clark, and Matt Golder. 2006. "Understanding Interaction Models: Improving Empirical Analyses," *Political Analysis* 14: 63–82.

Brewer, Stephanie M., James J. Jozefowicz, and Robert J. Stonebraker. 2006. "Religious Free Riders: The Impact of Market Share," *Journal for the Scientific Study of Religion* 45/3: 389–396.

Brown, Dorothy M., and Elizabeth McKeown. 2009. *The Poor Belong to Us: Catholic Charities and American Welfare*. Cambridge, MA: Harvard University Press.

Buchanan, Tom, and Martin Conway, eds. 1996. *Political Catholicism in Europe, 1918–1965*. Oxford: Oxford University Press.

Buğra, Ayşe, and Cağlar Keyder. 2006. "The Turkish Welfare Regime in Transformation," *Journal of European Social Policy* 16/3: 211–228.

Buis, Maarten L. 2007. "Predict and Adjust with Logistic Regression." *The Stata Journal* 7/2: 221–226.

Bulbulia, Joseph. 2004. "Religious Costs as Adaptations That Signal Altruistic Intention," *Evolution and Cognition* 10/1: 19–38.

Bulbulia, Joseph, and Richard Sosis. 2011. "Signalling Theory and the Evolution of Religious Cooperation," *Religion* 41/3 (Sept.): 363–388.

Burton-Chellew, Maxwell N., and Stuart A. West. 2013. "Prosocial Preferences Do Not Explain Human Cooperation in Public-Goods Games," *Proceedings of the National Academy of Sciences* 110/1 (Jan. 2): 216–221.

Bush, George W. 2001. *Executive Order: Establishment of White House Office of Faith-Based and Community Initiatives.* Jan. 29, 2001. https://www.gpo.gov/fdsys/pkg/WCPD-2001-02-05/pdf/WCPD-2001-02-05-Pg235.pdf.

Cammett, Melani. 2014. *Compassionate Communalism: Welfare and Sectarianism in Lebanon.* Ithaca: Cornell University Press.

Cammett, Melani, and Sukriti Issar. 2010. "Bricks and Mortar Clientelism: Sectarianism and the Logics of Welfare Allocation in Lebanon," *World Politics* 62/3: 381–421.

Cammett, Melani, and Lauren M. MacClean, eds. 2014. *The Politics of Non-State Welfare.* Ithaca: Cornell University Press.

Candland, Christopher. 2000. "Faith as Social Capital: Religion and Community Development in Southern Asia," *Policy Studies* 33/3–4: 355–374.

Caputo, Richard K. 2009. "Religious Capital and Intergenerational Transmission of Volunteering as Correlates of Civic Engagement," *Nonprofit and Voluntary Sector Quarterly* 38 (Dec.): 983–1002.

Carabain, Christine L., and Ren Bekkers. 2012. "Explaining Differences in Philanthropic Behavior between Christians, Muslims and Hindus in the Netherlands," *Review of Religious Research* 53: 419–440.

Cassanova, José. 1994. *Public Religions in the Modern World.* Chicago: University of Chicago Press.

Catechism of the Catholic Church. 1999. London: Geoffrey Chapman.

Catholic Church. United States Conference of Catholic Bishops. 2006. *Manual of Indulgences: Apostolic Penitentiary.* Washington, DC: United States Conference of Catholic Bishops.

Ceccarini, Luigi. 2005. "Fedeli, secolarizzati, irregolari: i cattolici italiani," *Il Mulino* 5 (Sept.–Oct.): 852–862.

Cesari, Jocelyne. 1994. *Être Musulman en France.* Paris: Karthala.

Charities Aid Foundation (CAF). 2006. *International Comparisons of Charitable Giving.* CAF briefing paper. November. www.cafonline.org.

Chaves, Mark. 2010. "Rain Dances in the Dry Season: Overcoming the Religious Congruence Fallacy," *Journal for the Scientific Study of Religion* 49/1: 1–14.

Chen, Daniel L. 2010. "Club Goods and Group Identity: Evidence from Islamic Resurgence during the Indonesian Financial Crisis," *Journal of Political Economy* 118/2: 300–354.

Cherry, Stephen M. 2014. *Faith, Family, and Filipino American Community Life.* New Brunswick, NJ: Rutgers University Press.

Cherry, Stephen M., and Helen Rose Ebaugh, eds. 2014. *Global Religious Movements across Borders: Sacred Service.* Farnham: Ashgate.

Chwe, Michael Suk-Young. 2001. *Rational Ritual: Culture, Coordination, and Common Knowledge.* Princeton, NJ: Princeton University Press.

Cialdini, Robert B., Stephanie L. Brown, Brian P. Lewis, Carol Luce, and Steven L. Neuberg. 1997. "Reinterpreting the Empathy–Altruism Relationship: When One into One Equals Oneness," *Journal of Personality and Social Psychology* 73/3: 481–494.

Çizakça. Murat. 2001 *A History of Philanthropic Foundations: The Islamic World from the Seventh Century to the Present.* Istanbul: Boğaziçi University Press.

Clark, Janine A. 2004. *Islam, Charity, and Activism: Middle-Class Networks and Social Welfare in Egypt, Jordan, and Yemen.* Bloomington: Indiana University Press.

Clemmons, William P., and Harvey Hester. 1974. *Growth through Groups.* Nashville, TN: B&H Publishing Group.

Cnaan, Ram. 2002. *Invisible Caring Hand: American Congregations and the Provision of Welfare.* New York: New York University Press.

Code of Canon Law. N.d. www.vatican.va/archive/ENG1104/_INDEX.HTM.

Cohen, Adam B. 2009. "Many Forms of Culture," *American Psychologist* 64: 194–204.

Cohen, Adam B., and P. C. Hill. 2007. "Religion as Culture: Religious Individualism and Collectivism among American Catholics, Jews, and Protestants," *Journal of Personality* 75: 709–742.

Cohen, Adam B., and Paul Rozin. 2001. "Religion and the Morality of Mentality," *Journal of Personality and Social Psychology* 81: 697–710.

Cohen, Adam B., J. I. Siegel, and Paul Rozin. 2003. "Faith versus Practice: Different Bases for Religiosity Judgments by Jews and Protestants," *European Journal of Social Psychology* 33: 287–295.

Cohen, Adam B., D. E. Hall, H. G. Koenig, and K. Meador. 2005. "Social versus Individual Motivation: Implications for Normative Definitions of Religious Orientation," *Personality and Social Psychology Review* 9: 48–61.

Cohen, Adam B., A. Malka, Paul Rozin, and L. Cherfas. 2006. "Religion and Unforgivable Offenses," *Journal of Personality* 74: 85–118.

Cohen, Adam B., Gina L. Mazza, Kathryn A. Johnson, Craig K. Enders, Carolyn M. Warner, Michael H. Pasek, and Jonathan E. Cook. 2017. "Theorizing and Measuring Religiosity across Cultures," *Personality and Social Psychology Bulletin* 43: 1724–1736.

Collins, Randall. 2004. *Interaction Ritual Chains.* Princeton, NJ: Princeton University Press.

Constable, Giles. 2004. "Religious Communities, 1024–1215." In *The New Cambridge Medieval History, c. 1024–c. 1215,* vol. 4, edited by David Luscombe and Jonathan Riley-Smith, 335–387. Cambridge: Cambridge University Press.

Conway, Daniel. 1995. "Faith versus Money: Conflicting Views of Stewardship and Fundraising in the Church." In *Cultures of Giving: How Region and Religion Influence Philanthropy,* edited by Charles H. Hamilton and Warren F. Ilchman, 71–78. San Francisco: Jossey-Bass.

Corcoran, Katie E. 2013. "Divine Exchanges: Applying Social Exchange Theory to Religious Behavior," *Rationality and Society* 25/3: 335–369.

Corcoran, Katie E. 2015. "Thinkers *and* Feelers: Emotion and Giving," *Social Science Research* 52 (July): 686–700.

Coriden, James A., and Mark F. Fischer. 2016. *Parish Councils: Pastoral and Finance.* N.p.: Canon Law Society of America.

Cornes, Richard, and Todd Sandler. 1996. *The Theory of Externalities, Public Goods and Club Goods,* 2nd edition. Cambridge: Cambridge University Press.

Cox, James C., and Cary A. Deck. 2006. "When Are Women More Generous than Men?," *Economic Inquiry* 44: 587–598.

Cronk, Lee, and Beth L. Leech. 2012. *Meeting at Grand Central: Understanding the Social and Evolutionary Roots of Cooperation.* Princeton, NJ: Princeton University Press.

Dahlberg, Lena. 2005. "Interaction between Voluntary and Statutory Social Service Provision in Sweden: A Matter of Welfare Pluralism, Substitution or Complementarity?," *Social Policy and Administration* 39/7 (Dec.): 740–763.

Davis, Nancy J., and Robert V. Robinson. 1999. "Religious Cosmologies, Individualism and Politics in Italy," *Journal for the Scientific Study of Religion* 38/3: 339–353.

Davis, Nancy J., and Robert V. Robinson. 2006. "The Egalitarian Face of Islamic Orthodoxy: Support for Islamic Law and Economic Justice in Seven Muslim-Majority Nations," *American Sociological Review* 71/2 (Apr.): 167–190.

Davis, Nancy J., and Robert V. Robinson. 2012. *Claiming Society for God: Religious Movements and Social Welfare*. Bloomington: Indiana University Press.

Dawkins, Richard. 1976/2006. *The Selfish Gene*. Oxford: Oxford University Press.

Deaux, Kay. 1996. "Social Identification." In *Social Psychology: Handbook of Basic Principles*, edited by E. Tory Higgins and Arie W. Kruglanski, 777–798. New York: Guilford.

Decety, Jean, Jason M. Cowell, Kang Lee, Randa Mahasneh, Susan Malcolm-Smith, Bilge Selcuk, and Xinyue Zhou. 2015. "The Negative Association between Religiousness and Children's Altruism across the World," *Current Biology* 25/22: 2951–2955.

Decker, Scott H., and Barrik Van Winkle. 1996. *Life in the Gang: Family, Friends and Violence*. New York: Cambridge University Press.

Den Uyl, Douglas J., and Douglas B. Rasmussen. 1984. *The Philosophic Thought of Ayn Rand*. Urbana: University of Illinois Press.

Dhingra, Pawan H., and Penny Edgell Becker. 2001. "Religious Involvement and Volunteering: Implications for Civil Society," *Sociology of Religion* 62/3: 315–335.

Diamanti, Ilvo, and Luigi Ceccarini. 2007. "Catholics and Politics after the Christian Democrats: The Influential Minority." *Journal of Modern Italian Studies* 12/1: 37–59.

Diefendorf, Barbara A. 2004. *From Penitence to Charity: Pious Women and the Catholic Reformation in Paris*. Oxford: Oxford University Press.

Díaz-Cayeros, Alberto, Federico Estevez, and Beatriz Magaloni. 2016. *The Political Logic of Poverty Relief: Electoral Strategies and Social Policy in Mexico*. New York: Cambridge University Press.

Djupe, Paul A., and Jacob R. Neiheisel. 2012. "How Religious Communities Affect Political Participation among Latinos," *Social Science Quarterly* 93/2 (June): 333–355.

Donahue, Michael J. 1985. "Intrinsic and Extrinsic Religiousness: The Empirical Research," *Journal for the Scientific Study of Religion* 24/4 (Dec.): 418–423.

Dougherty, K., and Andrew L. Whitehead. 2011. "A Place to Belong: Small Group Involvement in Religious Congregations," *Sociology of Religion* 72/1: 91–111.

Durkheim, Émile. 1915. *The Elementary Forms of the Religious Life: A Study in Religious Sociology*, trans. Joseph Ward Swain. London: George Allen & Unwin.

Eastis, Carla M. 1998. "Organizational Diversity and the Production of Social Capital: One of These Groups Is Not like the Other," *American Behavioral Scientist* 42/1 (Sept.): 66–77.

Ebaugh, Helen Rose. 2010. *The Gülen Movement: A Sociological Analysis of a Civic Movement Rooted in Moderate Islam*. Dordrecht: Springer.

Eckstein, Susan. 2001. "Community as Gift-Giving: Collectivistic Roots of Volunteerism," *American Sociological Review* 66 (Dec.): 829–851.

Edlin, Aaron, Andrew Gelman, and Noah Kaplan. 2007. "Voting as a Rational Choice: Why and How People Vote to Improve the Well-Being of Others," *Rationality and Society* 19/3: 293–314.

El Azayem, Gamal Abou, and Zari Heydayat-Diba. 1994. "The Psychological Aspects of Islam: Basic Principles of Islam and Their Psychological Corollary," *International Journal for the Psychology of Religion* 4/1: 41–50.

El-Kazaz, Sarah. 2015. "The AKP and the Gülen: End of a Historic Alliance," *Middle East Brief*, Crown Center for Middle East Studies, Brandeis University, No. 94 (July).

Erdoğan, Recep Tayyip. 2014. "Vakıf Haftası Mesajı," May 5. www.akparti.org.tr/site/haberler/vakif-haftasi-mesaji1/62800#1.

Esposito, John L., and Dalia Mogahed. 2008. *Who Speaks for Islam: What a Billion Muslims Really Think*. New York: Gallup Press.

European Social Survey (ESS). 2004. *European Social Survey Round 2 Data*. Data file edition 3.4. NSD Norwegian Social Science Data Services, Norway – Data Archive and distributor of ESS data.

Fearon, James, and David D. Laitin. 1996. "Explaining Inter-Ethnic Cooperation," *American Political Science Review* 90/4 (Dec.): 715–735.

Feldman, Daniel C. 1984. "The Development and Enforcement of Group Norms," *Academy of Management Review* 9/1: 47–53.

Ferguson, Kristin M. Qiaobing Wu, Donna Spruijt-Metz, and Grace Dyrness. 2007. "Outcomes Evaluation in Faith-Based Social Services: Are We Evaluating Faith Accurately?," *Research on Social Work Practice* 17/2 (Mar.): 264–276.

Ferrari, Silvio. 1999. "State and Religion: The Italian System." Manuscript. www.olir.it/areetematiche/56/documents/Ferrari_Istanbul1999.pdf.

Ferris, J. Stephen, and Edwin G. West. 2003. "Private versus Public Charity: Reassessing Crowding Out from the Supply Side," *Public Choice* 116: 399–417.

Fetzer, Joel S., and J. Christopher Soper. 2005. *Muslims and the State in Britain, France, and Germany*. New York: Cambridge University Press.

Finke, Roger, and Rodney Stark. 1988. "Religious Economies and Sacred Canopies: Religious Mobilization in American Cities, 1906," *American Sociological Review* 53: 41–49.

Fish, Steven M. 2011. *Are Muslims Distinctive? A Look at the Evidence*. New York: Oxford University Press.

Fischer, Robert L. 2008. "In God We Trust – All Others Bring Data: Assessing the State of Research on Faith-Based and Community Programming." Paper presented at the Association for Research on Nonprofit Organizations and Voluntary Action annual conference, Philadelphia, PA, November 20–22, 2008.

Flynn, Kieran. 2006. "Understanding Islam in Ireland," *Islam and Christian-Muslim Relations* 17/2 (Apr.): 223–238.

Flynn, Maureen. 1989. *Sacred Charity: Confraternities and Social Welfare in Spain, 1400–1700*. Ithaca, NY: Cornell University Press.

Fogarty, Michael P. 1957. *Christian Democracy in Western Europe, 1820–1953*. London: Routledge & Kegan Paul.

Foschini, Paolo. 2010. "Tettamanzi: sui rom Palazzo Marino ora rispetti I patti," *Corriere della Sera*, Oct. 8.

Fowler, James H., and Cindy Kam. 2007. "Beyond the Self: Social Identity, Altruism, and Political Participation," *Journal of Politics* 69/3 (Aug.): 813–827.

Fox, Jonathan. 2008. *A World Survey of Religion and State*. Cambridge: Cambridge University Press.

Fox, Jonathan. 2011. "Building Composite Measures of Religion and State," *Interdisciplinary Journal of Research on Religion* 7/8: 1–39.

Fox, Jonathan, and Shmuel Sandler. 2004. *Bringing Religion into International Relations*. New York: Palgrave Macmillan.

Franck, Raphaël, and Laurence R. Iannaccone. 2014. "Religious Decline in the 20th Century West: Testing Alternative Explanations," *Public Choice* 159: 385–414.

Frazee, Charles A. 1983. *Catholics and Sultans: The Church and the Ottoman Empire 1453–1923*. Cambridge: Cambridge University Press.

Frey, Bruno S., and Stephan Meier 2004. "Pro-Social Behavior in a Natural Setting," *Journal of Economic Behavior & Organization* 54: 65–88.

Fridolfsson, C., and I. Elander. 2012. "Faith-Based Organizations and Welfare State Retrenchment in Sweden: Substitute or Complement?," *Politics and Religion* 5/3: 634–654.

Fritz, M. S., and MacKinnon, D.P. 2007. "Requirement Sample Size to Detect the Mediated Effect," *Psychological Science* 18: 233–239.

Galen, Luke W. 2012. "Does Religious Belief Promote Prosociality? A Critical Examination," *Psychological Bulletin* 138: 876–906.

Gamm, Gerald. 1999. *Urban Exodus: Why the Jews Left Boston and the Catholics Stayed*. Cambridge, MA: Harvard University Press.

Garelli, Franco. 2007. "The Public Relevance of the Church and Catholicism in Italy," *Journal of Modern Italian Studies* 12/1 (Mar.): 8–36.

Garvin, Tom. 2004. *Preventing the Future: Why Was Ireland So Poor for So Long?* Dublin: Gill and Macmillan.

Gerring, John. 2004. "What Is a Case Study and What Is It Good For?," *American Political Science Review* 98/2 (May): 341–354.

Gerring, John. 2005. "Causation: A Unified Framework for the Social Sciences," *Journal of Theoretical Politics* 17/2: 163–198.

Gerring, John. 2007. *Case Study Research: Principles and Practices*. New York: Cambridge University Press.

Gill, Anthony J. 1998. *Rendering unto Caesar: The Catholic Church and the State in Latin America*. Chicago: University of Chicago Press.

Gill, Anthony. 2007. *The Political Origins of Religious Liberty*. Cambridge: Cambridge University Press.

Gill, Anthony. 2013. "Religious Liberty and Economic Development: Exploring the Causal Connections," *The Review of Faith and International Affairs* 11/4: 5–23.

Gill, Anthony, and Erik Lundsgaarde. 2004. "State Welfare Spending and Religiosity: A Cross-National Analysis," *Rationality and Society* 16/4: 399–436.

Gillespie, Andra, and Melissa R. Michelson. 2011. "Participant Observation and the Political Scientist: Possibilities, Priorities, and Practicalities," *PS: Political Science & Politics* 44/2 (Apr.): 261–265.

Ginges, Jeremy, Ian Hansen, and Ara Norenzayan. 2009. "Religion and Support for Suicide Attacks," *Psychological Science* 20/2: 224–230.

Gleditsch, Kristian S. 2013. Version 6.0. beta posted November 25, 2013. Originally cited and detailed in Kristian S. Gleditsch, "Expanded Trade and GDP Data," *Journal of Conflict Resolution* 46 (2002): 712–724.

Göçmen, İpek. 2014. "Religion, Politics and Social Assistance in Turkey: The Rise of Religiously Motivated Associations," *Journal of European Social Policy* 24/1: 92–103.

Goertz, Gary. 2006. *Social Science Concepts.* Princeton, NJ: Princeton University Press.

Gomes, Cristina M., and Michael E. McCullough. 2015. "The Effects of Implicit Religious Primes on Dictator Game Allocations: A Preregistered Replication Experiment," *Journal of Experimental Psychology: General* 144/6 (Dec.): e94–e104.

Gorsuch, R. L., and S. E. McPherson, 1989. "Intrinsic/Extrinsic Measurement: I/E-Revisited and Single-Item Scales," *Journal for the Scientific Study of Religion* 28: 348–354.

Gutiérrez, Gustavo. 1973. *A Theology of Liberation: History, Politics, and Salvation,* translated and edited by Sister Caridad Inda and John Eagleson. Ossining, NY: Orbis Books.

Graham, Jesse, and Jonathan Haidt. 2010. "Beyond Beliefs: Religions Bind Individuals into Moral Communities," *Personality and Social Psychology Review* 14/1: 140–150.

Greenberg, Jeff, Sheldon Solomon, and Tom Pyszczynski. 1997. "Terror Management Theory of Self-Esteem and Cultural Worldviews: Empirical Assessments and Conceptual Refinements," *Advances in Experimental Social Psychology* 29: 61–139.

Greif, Avner. 1994. "Cultural Beliefs and the Organization of Society: A Historical and Theoretical Reflection on Collectivist and Individualist Societies," *The Journal of Political Economy* 102/5 (Oct.): 912–950.

Gülen, Fethullah. 2005. "Himmet: Teveccüh, İnfak ve Gayret," Dec. 19. http://www.herkul.org/kirik-testi/himmet-teveccuh-infak-ve-gayret/.

Gutiérrez, Gustavo. 1971. *Teología de la liberación: perspectivas.* Lima: CEP.

Gwin, Carl R., Carol F. Gwin, Charles M. North, and Wafa Hakim Orman. 2009. "Understanding Religious Choice: A Product Attributes Application." Manuscript. https://pdfs.semanticscholar.org/c312/d79667072c9cf0156e64973352d150a3b283.pdf.

Habyarimana, James, Macartan Humphreys, Daniel N. Posner, and Jeremy M. Weinstein. 2007. "Why Does Ethnic Diversity Undermine Public Goods Provision?," *American Political Science Review* 101/4 (Nov.): 709–726.

Hadnes, Myriam, and Heiner Schumacher. 2012. "The Gods Are Watching: An Experimental Study of Religious and Traditional Beliefs in Burkina Faso," *Journal for the Scientific Study of Religion* 51/4 (Dec.): 689–704.

Haggard, Stephan, and Robert R. Kaufman. 2008. *Development, Democracy and the Welfare State: Latin America, East Asia, and Eastern Europe.* Princeton, NJ: Princeton University Press.

Hale, Christopher W. 2015. "Religious Institutions and Civic Engagement: A Test of Religion's Impact on Political Activism in Mexico," *Comparative Politics* 47/2 (Jan.): 211–230.

Haley, Kevin J., and Daniel M. T. Fessler. 2005. "Nobody's Watching?: Subtle Cues Affect Generosity in an Anonymous Economic Game," *Evolution and Human Behavior* 28/3 (May): 245–256.

Hall, Deborah, Adam B. Cohen, Kaitlin K. Meyer, Allison Varley, and Gene A. Brewer, Jr. 2015. "Costly Signaling Increases Trust, Even across Religious Affiliations," *Psychological Science* 26/9: 1368–1376.

Hallaq, Wael. 1999. *A History of Islamic Legal Theories: An Introduction to Sunni Usul al-Fiqh.* New York: Cambridge University Press.

Hancock, Graham. 1989. *Lords of Poverty: The Power, Prestige, and Corruption of the International Aid Business.* New York: Atlantic Monthly Press.

Harper Study Bible Revised Standard Version. 1965. Harold Lindsell, ed. Grand Rapids, MI: Zondervan Bible Publishers.

Harris, Fredrick C. 1999. *Something Within: Religion in African-American Political Activism.* New York: Oxford University Press.

Hassan, Riaz. 2002. *Faithlines: Muslim Conceptions of Islam and Society.* Oxford: Oxford University Press.

Hassner, Ron E. 2009. *War on Sacred Grounds.* Ithaca, NY: Cornell University Press.

Hatemi, Hüseyin, and Kalkan Oğuztürk, B. 2014. *Kişiler Hukuku (Gerçek Kişiler–Tüzel Kişiler.* İstanbul: Vedat Kitapçılık.

Healy, Kieran. 2000. "Embedded Altruism: Blood Collection Regimes and the European Union's Donor Population," *American Journal of Sociology* 105/6 (May): 1633–1657.

Healy, Kieran. 2006. *Last Best Gifts: Altruism and the Market for Human Blood and Organs.* Chicago: University of Chicago Press.

Hechter, Michael. 1987. *Principles of Group Solidarity.* Berkeley: University of California Press.

Helmke, Gretchen, and Steven Levitsky. 2004. "Informal Institutions and Comparative Politics: A Research Agenda," *Perspectives on Politics* 2/4: 725–739.

Hendrick, Joshua D. 2009. "Globalization, Islamic Activism and Passive Revolution in Turkey: The Case of Fethullah Gülen," *Journal of Power* 2/3 (July): 343–368.

Henrich, Joseph, Steven J. Heine, and Ara Norenzayan. 2010. "The Weirdest People in the World?," *Behavioral and Brain Sciences* 2/3 (June): 61–83.

Hennigan, Peter C. 2004. *The Birth of a Legal Institution: The Formation of the Waqf in Third Century A. H. Hanafi Legal Discourse.* Leiden: Brill.

Hill, Peter C., and Kenneth I. Pargament. 2003. "Advances in the Conceptualization and Measurement of Religion and Spirituality: Implications for Physical and Mental Health Research," *American Psychologist* 58: 64–74.

Himes, Kenneth R. 2006. "Vatican II and Contemporary Politics." In *The Catholic Church and the Nation-State: Comparative Perspectives*, edited by Paul Christopher Manuel, Lawrence C. Reardon, and Clyde Wilcox, 15–32. Washington, DC: Georgetown University Press.

Hitchens, Christopher. 2007. *God Is Not Great: How Religion Poisons Everything.* New York: Twelve.

Hoffman, Elizabeth, Kevin McCabe, and Vernon Smith. 1996. "Social Distance and Other-Regarding Behavior in Dictator Games," *American Economic Review* 86/3: 653–660.

Hoge, Dean R. 1994. "Introduction: The Problem of Understanding Church Giving," *Review of Religious Research* 36/2 (Dec.): 101–110.

Hoge, Dean R., and Augustyn Boguslaw. 1997. "Financial Contributions to Catholic Parishes: A Nationwide Study of Determinants," *Review of Religion Research* 39/1: 46–60.

Hovland, Carl I. 1959. "Reconciling Conflicting Results Derived from Experimental and Survey Studies of Attitude Change," *The American Psychologist* 14/1 (Jan.): 8–17.

Hungerman, Daniel M. 2005. "Are Church and State Substitutes? Evidence from the 1996 Welfare Reform," *Journal of Public Economics* 89: 2245–2267.

Hungerman, Daniel M. 2009. "Crowd Out and Diversity," *Journal of Public Economics* 93/5–6: 729–740.

Hungerman, Daniel M. 2013. "Substitution and Stigma: Evidence on Religious Markets from the Catholic Sex Abuse Scandal," *American Economic Journal: Economic Policy* 5/3 (Aug.): 227–253.

Iannaccone, Laurence R. 1988. "A Formal Model of Church and Sect," *American Journal of Sociology* 94: S241–S268.

Iannaccone, Laurence R. 1992. "Sacrifice and Stigma," *Journal of Political Economy* 100/2: 271–291.

Iannaccone, Laurence. 1994. "Why Strict Churches Are Strong," *American Journal of Sociology* 99/5: 1180–1211.

Iannaccone, Laurence. 1998. "Introduction to the Economics of Religion," *Journal of Economic Literature* 36/3 (Sept.): 1482–1484.

Iannacone, Laurence R., and Eli Berman. 2006. "Religious Extremism: The Good, the Bad, and the Deadly," *Public Choice* 128/1–2: 109–129.

Imas, A., 2014. "Working for the "Warm Glow": On the Benefits and Limits of Prosocial Incentives," *Journal of Public Economics* 114: 14–18.

International Monetary Fund. 2015. *Government Finance Statistics*. Washington, DC: International Monetary Fund.

Işık, Damla. 2014. "Vakf as Intent and Practice: Charity and Poor Relief in Turkey," *International Journal of Middle East Studies* 46/2: 307–327.

Iversen, Torben. 2005. *Capitalism, Democracy, and Welfare*. Cambridge: Cambridge University Press.

Jaeggi, Adrian V., Judith M. Burkhart, and Carel P. Van Schaik. 2010. "On the Psychology of Cooperation in Humans and Other Primates: Combining the Natural History and Experimental Evidence of Prosociality," *Philosophical Transactions of the Royal Society* 365: 2723–2734.

Ji, Chang-Ho C., and Yodi Ibrahim. 2007. "Islamic Doctrinal Orthodoxy and Religious Orientations: Scales Development and Validation," *International Journal for the Psychology of Religion* 17: 189–208.

Ji, Chang-Ho C., Yodi Ibrahim, and Soo Dong Kim. 2009. "Islamic Personal Religion and Moral Reasoning in Social Justice and Equality: Evidence from Indonesia College Studies," *International Journal for the Psychology of Religion* 19: 259–274.

Johnson, Kathryn A., and Adam B. Cohen. 2014. "Religious and National Cultures." In *Religion, Personality, and Social Behavior*, edited by Vassilis Saroglou, 338–360. New York: Psychology Press.

Johnson, Kathryn A., Yexin Jessica Li, Adam B. Cohen, and Morris A. Okun. 2013a. "Friends in High Places: The Influence of Authoritarian and Benevolent God-Concepts on Social Attitudes and Behaviors," *Psychology of Religion and Spirituality* 5/1 (Feb.): 15–22.

Johnson, Kathryn A., Morris A. Okun, and Adam B. Cohen. 2013b. "Intrinsic Religiosity and Volunteering during Emerging Adulthood: A Comparison of Mormons with Catholics and Non-Catholic Christians," *Journal for the Scientific Study of Religion* 52: 842–851.

Johnson, Kathryn A., Morris A. Okun and Adam B. Cohen. 2015a. "The Mind of the Lord: Measuring Authoritarian and Benevolent God-Concepts," *Psychology of Religion and Spirituality* 7/3 (Aug.): 227–238.

Johnson, Kathryn A., Rabia Memon, Armeen Alladin, Adam B. Cohen, and Morris A. Okun. 2015b. "Who Helps the Samaritan? The Influence of Religious vs. Secular Primes on Spontaneous Helping of Members of Religious Outgroups," *Journal of Cognition and Culture* 15: 223–237.

Johnson, Kathryn A., Adam B. Cohen, and Morris A. Okun. 2016. "God Is Watching You ... But also Is Watching over You: The Influence of Benevolent God Representations on Secular Volunteerism among Christians," *Psychology of Religion and Spirituality* 8/4 (Nov.): 363–374.

Jones, Colin. 1989. *The Charitable Imperative: Hospitals and Nursing in Ancien Régime and Revolutionary France.* London: Routledge.

Kahl, Sigrun. 2005. "The Religious Roots of Modern Poverty Policy: Catholic, Lutheran, and Reformed Protestant Traditions Compared," *Archives Européenne de Sociologie* 46: 91–126.

Kalyvas, Stathis N. 1996. *The Rise of Christian Democracy in Europe.* Ithaca: Cornell University Press.

Kam, Cindy D., and Robert J. Franzese, Jr. 2007. *Modeling and Interpreting Interactive Hypotheses in Regression Analysis.* Ann Arbor: University of Michigan Press.

Kaplan, Benjamin J. 2007. *Divided by Faith: Religious Conflict and the Practice of Toleration in Early Modern Europe.* Cambridge, MA: Harvard University Press, 2007.

Keenan, Marie. 2012. *Child Sexual Abuse and the Catholic Church.* Oxford: Oxford University Press.

Keister, Lisa A. 2003. "Religion and Wealth: The Role of Religious Affiliation and Participation in Early Adult Asset Accumulation," *Social Forces* 82: 173–205.

Keister, Lisa A. 2007. "Upward Wealth Mobility: Exploring the Roman Catholic Advantage," *Social Forces* 85: 1195–1226.

Keister, Lisa A. 2008. "Conservative Protestants and Wealth: How Religion Perpetuates Asset Poverty," *American Journal of Sociology* 113/5 (Mar.): 1237–1271.

Kılınç, Ramazan. 2007. "Patterns of Interaction between Islam and Liberalism: The Case of the Gülen Movement." In *Muslim World in Transition: Contributions of the Gülen Movement*, edited by İhsan Yılmaz, 118–139. London: Leeds Metropolitan University Press.

Kılınç, Ramazan. 2008. "History, International Norms and Domestic Institutional Change: State-Religion Relations in France and Turkey." PhD dissertation, Department of Political Science, Arizona State University.

Kılınç, Ramazan. 2013. "Muslims and Liberalization: The Case of the Gulen Movement." In *The Muslim World and Politics in Transition*, edited by Greg Barton, Paul Weller, and Ihsan Yilmaz, 82–95. London: Continuum Press.

Kılınç, Ramazan. 2014. "International Pressure, Domestic Politics and Dynamics of Religious Freedom: Evidence from Turkey," *Comparative Politics* 46/2 (Jan.): 127–145.

Kılınç, Ramazan, and Carolyn M. Warner. 2015. "Micro-Foundations of Religion and Public Goods Provision: Belief, Belonging and Giving in Catholicism and Islam," *Politics and Religion* 8/4: 718–744.

Kissane, Bill. 2003. "The Illusion of State Neutrality in a Secularising Ireland," *West European Politics* 26/1 (Jan.): 73–94.

Klaussen, Jytte. 2005. *The Islamic Challenge: Politics and Religion in Western Europe.* Oxford: Oxford University Press.

Kleven, H. J., M. B. Knudsen, C. T. Kreiner, S. Pedersen, and E. Saez. 2011. "Unwilling or Unable to Cheat? Evidence from a Tax Audit Experiment in Denmark," *Econometrica*, 79: 651–692.

Kniss, Fred, and Paul D. Numrich. 2007. *Sacred Assemblies and Civic Engagement: How Religion Matters for America's Newest Immigrants.* New Brunswick, NJ: Rutgers University Press.

Koesel, Karrie J. 2014. *Religion and Authoritarianism: Cooperation, Conflict and the Consequences.* New York: Cambridge University Press.

Koven, Seth, and Sonya Michel. 1990. "Womanly Duties: Maternalist Politics and the Origins of Welfare States in France, Germany, Great Britain, and the United States, 1880-1920," *The American Historical Review* 95/4 (Oct.), 1076–1108.

Kozlowski, Gregory C. 1998. "Religious Authority, Reform, and Philanthropy in the Contemporary Muslim World." In *Philanthropy in the World's Traditions*, edited by Warren F. Ilchman, Stanley N. Katz, and Edward L. Queen II, 279–308. Bloomington: Indiana University Press.

Kuran, Timur. 2001. "The Provision of Public Goods under Islamic Law: Origins, Impact, and Limitations of the *Waqf* System," *Law and Society Review* 35/4: 841–897.

Kuran, Timur. 2003. "Islamic Redistribution through *Zakat*: Historical Record and Modern Realities." In *Poverty and Charity in Middle Eastern Contexts*, edited by Michael Bonner, Mine Ener, and Amy Singer, 275–293. Albany: State University Press of New York.

Kuran, Timur. 2011. *The Long Divergence: How Islamic Law Held Back the Middle East.* Princeton, NJ: Princeton University Press.

Kuran, Timur. 2016. "Legal Roots of Authoritarian Rule in the Middle East: Civic Legacies of the Islamic Waqf," *The American Journal of Comparative Law* 64 (Summer): 841–897.

Kuru, Ahmet T. 2003. "Fetullah Gülen's Search for a Middle Way between Modernity and Muslim Tradition." In *Turkish Islam and the Secular State,* edited by Hakan Yavuz and John L. Esposito, 115–130. Syracuse: Syracuse University Press.

Kuru, Ahmet T. 2005. "Globalization and Diversification of Islamic Movements: Three Turkish Cases," *Political Science Quarterly* 120/ 2 (Summer): 253–274.

Kuru, Ahmet T. 2009. *Secularism and State Policies toward Religion: United States, France and Turkey.* New York: Cambridge University Press.

Kurzban, Robert. 2001. "The Social Psychophysics of Cooperation: Nonverbal Communication in a Public Goods Game," *Journal of Nonverbal Behavior* 25/4: 241–259.

Kurzban, Robert, and Daniel Houser. 2005. "Experiments Investigating Cooperative Types in Humans: A Complement to Evolutionary Theory and Simulations," *Proceedings of the National Academy of Sciences of the United States of America* 102/5: 1803–1807.

Lacey, Jonathan. 2009. "The Gülen Movement in Ireland: Civil Society Engagements of a Turkish Religio-Cultural Movement," *Turkish Studies* 10/2 (June): 295–315.

Landman, Nico, and Wendy Wessels. 2005. "The Visibility of Mosques in Dutch Towns," *Journal of Ethnic and Migration Studies* 31/6 (Nov.): 1125–1140.

Lawler, Edward J. 2001. "An Affect Theory of Social Exchange," *American Journal of Sociology* 107/2: 321–352.

Le Coz, Raymond. 1995. *L'Église d'Orient. Chrétiens d'Irak, d'Iran et de Turquie.* Paris: Les Éditions du Cerf.

Lee, Matthew T., Margaret M. Poloma, and Stephen G. Post. 2012. *The Heart of Religion: Spiritual Empowerment, Benevolence, and the Experience of God's Love.* New York: Oxford University Press.

Leech, Beth L. 2002. "Asking Questions: Techniques for Semistructured Interviews," *PS: Political Science and Politics* 354 (Dec.): 665–668.

Leeson, Peter T. 2014. *Anarchy Unbound: Why Self-Governance Works Better than You Think.* New York: Cambridge University Press.

Leo XIII, Pope. 1891. *Rerum Novarum.* Encyclical of Pope Leo XIII on Capital and Labor. http://w2.vatican.va/content/leo-xiii/en/encyclicals/documents/hf_l-xiii_enc_15051891_rerum-novarum.html.

Lieberman, Evan S. 2005. "Nested Analysis as a Mixed-Method Strategy for Comparative Research," *American Political Science Review* 99/3 (Aug.): 435–452.

Lieberman, Matthew. 2014. *Social: Why Our Brains Are Wired to Connect.* Oxford: Oxford University Press.

Lincoln, Bruce. 2003. *Holy Terrors: Thinking about Religion after September 11.* Chicago: University of Chicago Press.

Lincoln, Ryan, Christopher A. Morrissey, and Peter Mundey. 2008. "Religious Giving: A Comprehensive Review of the Literature." Manuscript, Science of Generosity, University of Notre Dame.

Lindsell, Harold, ed. 1965. *Harper Study Bible*, Revised Standard Version. Grand Rapids, MI: Zondervan Bible Publishers.

Lofland, John, David A. Snow, Leon Anderson, and Lyn H. Lofland. 2005. *Analyzing Social Settings: A Guide to Qualitative Observation and Analysis.* Belmont, CA: ThomsonWadsworth.

Long, Scott J., and Jeremy Freese. 2006. *Regression Models for Categorical Dependent Variables Using Stata*, 2nd edition. College Station, TX: StataCorp LP.

Luttmer, Erzo F. P. 2001. "Group Loyalty and the Taste for Redistribution," *Journal of Political Economy* 109: 500–528.

Lynch, Julia. 2009. "Italy: A Christian Democratic or Clientelist Welfare State?" In *Religion, Class Coalitions, and Welfare States*, edited by Kees van Kersbergen and Philip Manow, 91–118. New York: Cambridge University Press.

Maclean, A. Michael, Lawrence J. Walker, and M. Kyle Matsuba. 2004. "Transcendence and the Moral Self: Identity, Integration, Religion and Moral Life," *Journal for the Scientific Study of Religion* 43/3: 429–437.

Maguire, Moira J. 2013. *Precarious Childhood in Post-Independence Ireland.* Manchester, UK: Manchester University Press.

Mahoney, James. 2007. "Qualitative Methodology and Comparative Politics," *Comparative Political Studies* 40/2 (Feb.): 122–144.

Mainwaring, Scott, and Alexander Wilde. 1989. "The Progressive Church in Latin America: An Interpretation." In *The Progressive Church in Latin America*, edited by Scott Mainwaring and Alexander Wilde. Notre Dame, IN: University of Notre Dame Press.

Makowsky, Michael D. 2011. "A Theory of Liberal Churches," *Mathematical Social Sciences* 61: 41–51.

Manço, Altay. 1997. "Des organizations sociopolitiques comme solidarité Islamique dans l'immigration Turque en Europe," *Les Annales de l'autre Islam* 4: 97–133.

Manow, Philip, and Bruno Palier. 2009. "A Conservative Welfare State Regime without Christian Democracy? The French Etat Providence, 1880–1960." In *Religion, Class Coalitions and Welfare State Regimes*, edited by Kees Van Kersbergen and Philip Manow, 147–175. New York: Cambridge University Press.

Manuel, Paul Christopher, and Margaret MacLeish Mott. 2006. "The Latin European Church: 'Une Messe Est Possible.'" In *The Catholic Church and the Nation-State: Comparative Perspectives*, edited by Paul Christopher Manuel, Lawrence C. Reardon, and Clyde Wilcox, 53–68. Washington, DC: Georgetown University Press.

Maréchal, Brigitte. 2003. "Mosques, Organisations and Leadership." In *Muslims in the Enlarged Europe. Religion and Society*, edited by Brigitte Maréchal, Stefano Allievi, Felice Dassetto, and Jørgen Nielsen, 79–150. Leiden: Brill.

Maréchal, Brigitte, Stefano Allievi, Felice Dassetto, and Jørgen Nielsen, eds. 2003. *Muslims in the Enlarged Europe: Religion and Society*. Leiden: Brill.

Mares, Isabela. 2003. *The Politics of Social Risk: Business and Welfare State Development*. Cambridge: Cambridge University Press.

Mauss, Marcel. 1954/1967. *The Gift: Forms and Functions of Exchange in Archaic Societies*, trans. Ian Cunnison. New York: Norton.

McBride, Michael. 2007. "Club Mormon: Free-Riders, Monitoring, and Exclusion in the LDS Church," *Rationality and Society* 19/4: 395–424.

McBrien, Richard P. 1980. *Catholicism*, vol. 2. Minneapolis, MN: Winston Press.

McChesney, Robert D. 1995. "Charity and Philanthropy in Islam: Institutionalizing the Call to Do Good," Indiana University Center on Philanthropy, Essays on Philanthropy No. 14.

McDermott, Rose. 2013. "The Ten Commandments of Experiments," *PS: Political Science & Politics* 46/3 (July): 608.

McLoughlin, Séan. 2005. "Mosques and the Public Space: Conflict and Cooperation in Bradford," *Journal of Ethnic and Migration Studies* 31/6 (Nov.): 1045–1066.

McNamara, Patrick. 2009. *The Neuroscience of Religious Experience*. Cambridge: Cambridge University Press.

Mervis, Carolyn B., and Eleanor Rosch. 1981. "Categorization of Natural Objects," *Annual Review of Psychology* 32 (Feb.): 89–115.

Messner, Francis, ed. 2015. *Public Funding of Religions in Europe*. Farnham, UK: Ashgate.

Miller, Arthur H., Patricia Gurin, Gerald Gurin, and Oksana Malanchuk. 1981. "Group Consciousness and Political Participation," *American Journal of Political Science* 25/3 (Aug.): 494–511.

Miller, Donald E., and Tetsunao Yamamori. 2007. *Global Pentecostalism: The New Face of Christian Social Engagement*. Berkeley: University of California Press.

Miller, Sharon Louise. 1999. "The Symbolic Meaning of Religious Giving." PhD dissertation, Department of Sociology, University of Notre Dame, Indiana.

Millsap, Roger E. 1997. "Invariance in Measurement and Prediction: Their Relationship in the Single-Factor Case," *Psychological Methods* 2: 248–260.

Millsap, Roger E. 1998. "Group Differences in Regression Intercepts: Implications for Factorial Invariance," *Multivariate Behavioral Research* 33: 403–424.

Misner, Paul. 1991. *Social Catholicism in Europe: From the Onset of Industrialization to the First World War*. New York: Crossroad.

Mitchell, Joshua. 2007. "Religion Is Not a Preference," *The Journal of Politics* 69/2 (May): 351–362.

Moe, Terry. 1980. "A Calculus of Group Membership," *American Journal of Political Science* 24/4: 593–632.

Mollat, Michel. 1986. *The Poor in the Middle Ages: An Essay in Social History*. New Haven, CT: Yale University Press.

Monroe, Kristen Renwick. 1996. *The Heart of Altruism: Perceptions of a Common Humanity*. Princeton, NJ: Princeton University Press.

Mooney, Margarita. 2006. "The Catholic Bishops Conferences of the United States and France," *American Behavioral Scientist* 49/11 (July): 1455–1470.

Morvaridi, Behrooz. 2013. "The Politics of Philanthropy and Welfare Governance: The Case of Turkey," *The European Journal of Development Research*, 25/2: 305–321.

Muchlinski, David. 2014. "Grievances and Opportunities: Religious Violence across Political Regimes," *Politics and Religion* 7/4: 684–705.

Muedini, Fait. 2015. "The Politics between Justice and Development Party (AKP) and the Gülen Movement in Turkey: Issues of Human Rights and Rising Authoritarianism," *Muslim World Journal of Human Rights* 12/1 (June): 99–119.

Mueller, Dennis C. 2003. *Public Choice III*. Cambridge: Cambridge University Press.

National Economic and Social Council. 2005. "The Developmental Welfare State," Working Paper No. 113, May. Dublin: The National Economic and Social Council.

Navaro-Yashin, Yael. 2002. *Faces of the State: Secularism and Public Life in Turkey*. Princeton, NJ: Princeton University Press.

Negri, Augusto Tino, and Silvia Scaranari Introvigne. 2005. *Musulmani in Piemonte: in Moschea, al Lavoro, nel Contesto Sociale*. Milan: Guerini e associati.

Nickerson, David W. 2005. "Scalable Protocols Offer Efficient Design for Field Experiments," *Political Analysis* 13: 233–252.

Norenzayan, Ara. 2013. *Big Gods: How Religion Transformed Cooperation and Conflict*. Princeton, NJ: Princeton University Press.

Norenzayan, Ara, and Azim F. Shariff. 2008. "The Origin and Evolution of Religious Prosociality," *Science* 322 (Oct.): 58–62.

Norris, Pippa, and Ronald Inglehart. 2004. *Sacred and Secular: Religion and Politics Worldwide*. New York: Cambridge University Press.

Nowak, Martin A., and Karl Sigmund. 2005. "Evolution of Indirect Reciprocity." *Nature* 437/27 (Oct.): 1291–1298.

Nozick, Robert. 1974. *Anarchy, State, and Utopia*. New York: Basic Books.

Olson, Mancur. 1965. *The Logic of Collective Action: Public Goods and the Theory of Groups*. Cambridge: Harvard University Press.

O'Reilly, James T., and Margaret S. P. Chalmers. 2014. *The Clergy Sex Abuse Crisis and the Legal Responses*. New York: Oxford University Press.

Ostrom, Elinor. 1990. *Governing the Commons: The Evolution of Institutions for Collective Action*. Cambridge: Cambridge University Press.

Ostrom, Elinor. 2007. "Collective Action Theory," in *The Oxford Handbook of Collective Action*, edited by Carles Boix and Susan Stokes, 186–208. New York: Oxford University Press.

Ottoni-Wilhelm, Mark. 2010, "Giving to Organizations That Help People in Need: Differences across Denominational Identities," *Journal for the Scientific Study of Religion* 49/3: 389–412.

Özgüç, Orhan. 2008. "Islamic Himmah and Christian Charity: An Attempt at Interfaith Dialogue." In *Islam in the Age of Global Challenges: Alternative Perspectives of the Gülen Movement*. Conference Proceedings. Washington, DC: Rumi Forum, 561–582.

Parkinson, Patrick. 2013. "The Smith Lecture 2013. Child Sexual Abuse and the Churches: A Story of Moral Failure?" Manuscript, University of Sydney.

Pedersen, Susan. 1993. *Family, Dependence, and the Origins of the Welfare State: Britain and France, 1914–1945*. Cambridge University Press.

Peifer, Jared. 2007. "Religious Giving as a Response to Community," Center for the Study of Economy and Society Working Paper Series No. 42 (Oct.).

Peifer, Jared L. 2010. "The Economics and Sociology of Religious Giving: Instrumental Rationality or Communal Bonding?," *Social Forces* 88/4 (June): 1569–1594.

Peterson, Christopher, and Martin E. P. Seligman. 2004. *Character Strengths and Virtues: A Classification and Handbook*. New York: Oxford University Press and Washington, DC: American Psychological Association.

Peterson, Nicolas. 1993. "Demand Sharing: Reciprocity and the Pressure for Generosity among Foragers," *American Anthropologist* 95/4: 860–874.

Philpott, Daniel. 2007. "Explaining the Political Ambivalence of Religion," *The American Political Science Review* 101/3 (Aug.): 511.

Pichon, Isabelle, Giulio Boccato, and Vassilis Saroglou. 2007. Nonconscious Influences of Religion on Prosociality: A Priming Study," *European Journal of Social Psychology* 37: 1032–1045.

Pirotta, Laura. 2008. "Il Migrante Turco tra imprenditoria etnica e Organizzazioni Religioise: La Realtà della Città di Como." Doctoral thesis, University of Milan.

Pius XI, Pope. 1931/n.d. *Quadragesimo anno*, referenced at http://w2.vatican.va/content/pius-xi/en/encyclicals/documents/hf_p-xi_enc_19310515_quadragesimo-anno.html.

Pollard, John. 2008. *Catholicism in Modern Italy: Religion, Society and Politics since 1861*. London: Routledge.

Popkin, Samuel J. 1979. *The Rational Peasant: The Political Economy of Rural Society in Vietnam*. Berkeley: University of California Press.

Power, Eleanor A. 2017. "Discerning Devotion: Testing the Signaling Theory of Religion," *Evolution and Human Behavior* 38/1: 82–91.

Preston, Jesse Lee, Ryan S. Ritter, and J. Ivan Hernandez. 2010. "Principles of Religious Prosociality: A Review and Reformulation," *Social and Personality Psychology Compass* 4/8: 574–590.

Prothero, Stephen R., 2010. *God Is Not One: The Eight Rival Religions That Run the World – And Why Their Differences Matter*. New York: HarperOne.

Puggioni, Roberto. 2015. "Roman Catholic Social Thought on Social Justice and Economics: Elements for Debate from Caritas Veritate," *Journal of Catholic Social Thought* 12/1: 109–142.

Putnam, Robert D. 1993. *Making Democracy Work: Civic Traditions in Modern Italy.* Princeton, NJ: Princeton University Press.

Putnam, Robert D., and David Campbell. 2010. *American Grace: How Religion Divides and Unites Us.* New York: Simon & Schuster.

Putnam, Robert D., with Robert Leonardi and Rafaella Nanetti. 1993. *Making Democracy Work: Civic Traditions in Modern Italy.* Princeton, NJ: Princeton University Press.

Pyle, Ralph E. 1998. "Faith and Commitment to the Poor: Theological Orientation and Support for Government Assistance Measures," *Sociology of Religion.* 54/4 (Winter): 385–401.

Queen, Edward L., II. 1996. "The Religious Roots of Philanthropy in the West: Judaism, Christianity and Islam." Bloomington: Indiana University Center on Philanthropy. Working Paper No. 96–4.

Quine, Maria Sophia. *Italy's Social Revolution: Charity and Welfare from Liberalism to Fascism.* Basingstoke: Palgrave, 2002.

Qur'an, The. 2004. Trans. M. A. S. Abdel Haleem. New York: Oxford University Press.

Rabe-Hesketh, Sophia, and Anders Skrondal. 2006. "Multilevel Modelling of Complex Survey Data," *Journal of the Royal Statistical Society* Series A 169, Part 4: 805–827.

Rabe-Hesketh, Sophia, and Anders Skrondal. 2012. *Multilevel and Longitudinal Modeling Using Stata,* vol. 2: *Categorical Responses, Counts, and Survival,* 3rd edition. College Station, TX: StataCorp LP.

Raiya, Hisham Abu, Kenneth I. Pargament, Annette Mahoney, and Catherine Stein. 2008. "A Psychological Measure of Islamic Religiousness: Development and Evidence for Reliability and Validity," *International Journal for the Psychology of Religion* 18: 291–315.

Rand, Ayn. 1957. *Atlas Shrugged.* New York: Random House.

Rand, Ayn. 1961/1964. *The Virtue of Selfishness.* New York: Signet.

Regnerus, Mark D., Christian Smith, and David Sikkink. 1998. "Who Gives to the Poor? The Influence of Religious Tradition and Political Location on the Personal Generosity of Americans toward the Poor," *Journal for the Scientific Study of Religion* 37/3 (Sept.): 481–493.

Reitsma, Jan, Peer Scheepers, and Manfred Te Grotenhuis. 2006. "Dimensions of Individual Religiosity and Charity: Cross-National Effect Differences in European Countries?," *Review of Religious Research* 47/4: 347–362.

Rhodes, R. A. W., Sarah A. Binder, and Bert A. Rockman, eds. 2006. *The Oxford Handbook of Political Institutions.* Oxford: Oxford University Press.

Richerson, Peter J., and Robert Boyd. 1998. "The Evolution of Human Ultra-Sociality." In *Indoctrinability, Ideology, and Warfare: Evolutionary Perspectives,* edited by Irinäus Eibl-Eibisfeldt and Frank Kemp Salter, 71–95. New York: Berghahn Books.

Ritter, Ryan S., and Jesse Lee Preston. 2013. "Representations of Religious Words: Insights for Religious Priming Research," *Journal for the Scientific Study of Religion* 53/3 (Sept.): 494–507.

Roccas, Sonia, and Shalom H. Schwartz. 1997. "Church-State Relations and the Association of Religiosity with Values: A Study of Catholics in Six Countries," *Cross-Cultural Research* 31/4 (Nov.): 356–375.

Roes, Frans L., and Michel Raymond. 2003. "Belief in Moralizing Gods," *Evolution and Human Behavior* 24: 126–135.

Rohlfing, Ingo. 2008. "What You See and What You Get: Pitfalls and Principles of Nested Analysis in Comparative Research," *Comparative Political Studies* 41/11: 1492–1514.

Roodman, David, and Scott Standley. 2006. "Tax Policies to Promote Private Charitable Giving in DAC Countries." Working Paper No. 82, Center for Global Development.

Rostagno, Massimo V., and Francesca Utili. 1998. "The Italian Social Protection System: The Poverty of Welfare," International Monetary Fund Working Paper No. WP/98/74.

Roy, Olivier. 2005. *Globalized Islam: The Search for a New Ummah.* New York: Columbia University Press.

Rozin, Paul. 2003. "Five Potential Principles for Understanding Cultural Differences in Relation to Individual Differences," *Journal of Research in Personality* 37: 273–283.

Rubin, Jared. 2017. *Rulers, Religion and Riches: Why the West Got Rich and the Middle East Did Not.* New York: Cambridge University Press.

Ruiter, Stijn, and Nan Dirk De Graaf. 2006. "National Context, Religiosity, and Volunteering: Results from 53 Countries," *American Sociological Review* 71 (Apr.): 191–210.

Sahlins, Marshall. 1972. *Stone Age Economics.* Chicago: Aldine.

Sakaranaho, Tuula. 2006. *Religious Freedom, Multiculturalism, Islam: Cross-Reading Finland and Ireland.* Leiden: Brill.

Salihoglu, Serhat. 2002. "Welfare State Policies in Turkey," *South-East Europe Review for Labour and Social Affairs* 4: 21–26.

Sarkissian, Ani. 2012. "Religion and Civic Engagement in Muslim Countries," *Journal for the Scientific Study of Religion* 51/4: 607–622.

Sarkissian, Ani. 2015. *The Varieties of Religious Repression: Why Governments Restrict Religion.* New York: Oxford University Press.

Saroglou, Vassilis. 2014. "Introduction: Studying Religion in Personality and Social Psychology." In *Religion, Personality and Social Behavior,* edited by Vassilis Saroglou, 1–28. New York: Psychology Press.

Saroglou, Vassilis, and P. Galand. 2004. "Identities, Values and Religion: A Study of Muslim, Other Immigrant, and Native Belgian Young Adults after the 9/11 Attacks," *Identity* 4: 97–132.

Saroglou, Vassilis, Isabelle Pichon, Laurence Trompette, Marijke Verschueren, and Rebecca Dernelle. 2005. "Prosocial Behavior and Religion: New Evidence Based on Projective Measures and Peer Ratings," *Journal for the Scientific Study of Religion* 44/3 (Sept.): 323–348.

Satow, Kay L. 1975. "Social Approval and Helping," *Journal of Experimental Social Psychology* 11/6: 501–509.

Schaffer, Frederic Charles. 2006. "Ordinary Language Interviewing." In *Interpretation and Method: Empirical Research Methods and the Interpretive Turn,* edited by Dvora Yanow and Peregrine Schwartz-Shea, 150–160. Armonk, NY: M. E. Sharpe.

Scheepers, Peer, and Manfred Te Grotenhuis. 2005. "Who Cares for the Poor? Micro and Macro Determinants for Alleviating Poverty in 15 European Countries," *European Sociological Review* 21/5 (Dec.): 453–465.

Schneider, Helmut, John Krieger, and Azra Bayraktar. 2011. "The Impact of Intrinsic Religiosity on Consumers' Ethical Beliefs: Does It Depend on the Type of Religion? A Comparison of Christian and Moslem Consumers in Germany and Turkey," *Journal of Business Ethics* 102/2 (Aug.): 319–332.

Scott, James C. 2009. *The Art of Not Being Governed*. New Haven, CT: Yale University Press.

Seawright, Jason, and John Gerring. 2008. "Case Selection Techniques in Case Study Research: A Menu of Qualitative and Quantitative Options," *Political Research Quarterly* 61/2 (June): 294–308.

Sen, Mustafa, Arda Deniz Aksular, and Zelal Ozdemir Samur. 2009. "FBOs and Social Exclusion in Turkey." In *Faith-Based Organisations and Social Exclusion in European Cities*, edited by Danielle Dierckx, Jan Vranken, and Wendy Kerstens, 247–281. Leuven, Belgium: Uitgeverij Acco.

Shariff, Azim F., and Ara Norenzayan. 2007. "God Is Watching You: Priming God Concepts Increases Prosocial Behavior in an Anonymous Economic Game." *Psychological Science* 18/9: 803–809.

Shayo, Moses. 2009. "A Model of Social Identity with an Application to Political Economy: Nation, Class, and Redistribution." *American Political Science Review* 103/2 (May): 147–174.

Singer, Amy. 2002. *Constructing Ottoman Beneficence: An Imperial Soup Kitchen in Jerusalem*. Albany: State University of New York Press.

Singer, Amy. 2006. "Soup and Sadaqa: Charity in Islamic Societies." *Historical Research* 79/205: 306–324.

Singer, Peter. 2015a. *Famine, Affluence and Morality*. New York: Oxford University Press.

Singer, Peter. 2015b. *The Most Good You Can Do: How Effective Altruism Is Changing Ideas about Living Ethically*. New Haven, CT: Yale University Press.

Smith, Christian. 1991. *The Emergence of Liberation Theology: Radical Religion and Social Movement Theory*. Chicago: University of Chicago Press.

Smith, Christian. 2003. "Research Note: Religious Participation and Parental Moral Expectations and Supervision of American Youth," *Review of Religious Research* 44/4 (June): 414–424.

Smith, Christian, and Michael O. Emerson. 2008. *Passing the Plate: Why American Christians Don't Give Away More Money*. New York: Oxford University Press.

Smith, Kevin B. 2006. "Representational Altruism: The Wary Cooperator as Authoritative Decision Maker," *American Journal of Political Science* 50/4 (Oct.): 1013–1022.

Smith, Timothy B. *Creating the Welfare State in France, 1880–1940*. Montreal: McGill-Queen's University Press, 2003.

Soetevent, Adriaan R. 2005. "Anonymity in Giving in a Natural Context: A Field Experiment in 30 Churches," *Journal of Public Economics* 89: 2301–2323.

Sosis, Richard. 2003. "Why Aren't We All Hutterites? Costly Signaling Theory and Religion," *Human Nature* 14: 91–127.

Sosis, Richard. 2005. "Does Religion Promote Trust? The Role of Signaling, Reputation, and Punishment," *Interdisciplinary Journal of Research on Religion* 1: 1–30.

Sosis, Richard. 2006. "Religious Behaviors, Badges, and Bans: Signaling Theory and the Evolution of Religion." In *Where God and Science Meet: How Brain and Evolutionary Studies Alter Our Understanding of Religion*, vol. 1: *Evolution, Genes, and the Religious Brain*, edited by Patrick McNamara, 61–86. Westport, CT: Praeger Publishers.

Stanczak, Gregory. 2006. *Engaged Spirituality: Social Change and American Religion*. Newark, NJ: Rutgers University Press.

Stark, Rodney, and William Sims Bainbridge. 1985. *The Future of Religion: Secularization, Revival, and Cult Formation.* Berkeley: University of California Press.

Stark, Rodney, and Roger Finke. 2000. *Acts of Faith: Explaining the Human Side of Religion.* Berkeley: University of California Press.

Stark, Rodney, and Laurence R. Iannaccone. 1994. "A Supply-Side Reinterpretation of the 'Secularization' of Europe," *Journal for the Scientific Study of Religion* 33/3 (Sept.): 230–252.

Starks, Brian, and Christian Smith. 2013. "Unleashing Catholic Generosity: Explaining the Catholic Giving Gap in the United States," University of Notre Dame Institute for Church Life. https://icl.nd.edu/assets/96494/unleashing_catholic_generosity.pdf %22%3Eunleashing_catholic_generosity.pdf.

StataCorp. 2013. "Margins – Marginal Means, Predictive Margins, and Marginal Effects." *Stata Statistical Software: Release 13.* College Station, TX: StataCorp LP. www.stata.com/manuals13/rmargins.pdf.

Stegmueller, Daniel. 2013. "Religion and Redistributive Voting in Western Europe," *Journal of Politics* 75/4 (Oct.): 1064–1076.

Stroope, Samuel. 2012. "Social Networks and Religion: The Role of Congregational Social Embeddedness in Religious Belief and Practice," *Sociology of Religion* 73/3: 273–298.

Sweetser, Thomas P. "The Money Crunch: Why Don't Catholics Give More?," *Chicago Studies* 30 (April): 99–111.

Tajfel, H., and J. C. Turner. 1979. "An Integrative Theory of Intergroup Conflict." In *Social Psychology of Intergroup Relations*, edited by Stephen Worchel and William G. Austin, 33–47. Monterey, CA: Brooks-Cole.

Tcholakian, Hovhannes J. 1998. *L'Eglise Armenienne Catholique en Turquie.* Istanbul: Ohan Matbaacilik.

Thomas, David R. 2006. "A General Inductive Approach for Analyzing Qualitative Evaluation Data," *American Journal of Evaluation* 27/2 (June): 237–246.

Traunmüller, Richard, and Markus Freitag. 2011. "State Support of Religion: Making or Breaking Faith-Based Social Capital?," *Comparative Politics* 43/3 (April): 253–269.

Tropman, John E. 2002. *The Catholic Ethic and the Spirit of Community.* Washington, DC: Georgetown University Press.

Tsai, Lily L. 2007. "Solidary Groups, Informal Accountability, and Local Public Goods Provision in Rural China," *American Political Science Review* 101/2 (May): 355–372.

Tsang, Jo-Ann, Wade C. Rowatt, and Azim Shariff. 2015. "Religion and Prosociality." In *The Oxford Handbook of Prosocial Behavior*, edited by David A. Schroeder and William G. Graziano. Oxford: Oxford University Press.

Tyler, Tom R. 2011. *Why People Cooperate: The Role of Social Motivations* Princeton, NJ: Princeton University Press.

Unruh, Heidi Rolland, and Ronald J. Sider, 2005. *Saving Souls, Serving Society* New York: Oxford University Press.

Utvik, Bjørn Olav. 2006. *The Pious Road to Development: Islamic Economics in Egypt.* London: Hurst.

Van Ingen, Erik, and Tom van der Meer. 2011. "Welfare State Expenditure and Inequalities in Voluntary Association Participation," *Journal of European Social Policy* 21/4 (Oct.): 302–322.

Van Lange, Paul A. M., Jaap W. Ouwerkerk, and Mirjam J. A. Tazelaar. 2002. "How to Overcome the Detrimental Effects of Noise in Social Interaction: The Benefits of Generosity," *Journal of Personality and Social Psychology* 82: 768–780.

Van Oorschot, Wim, and Wil Arts. 2005. "The Social Capital of European Welfare States: The Crowding Out Hypothesis Revisited," *Journal of European Social Policy* 15/1 (Feb.): 5–26.

Van Rompay, Thomas J. L., Dorette J. Vonk, and Marieke L. Fransen. 2009. "The Eye of the Camera: Effects of Security Cameras on Prosocial Behavior," *Environment and Behavior* 41/1: 60–74.

Van Vugt, Mark, Golbert Roberts, and Charlie Hardy. 2007. "Competitive Altruism: Development of Reputation-Based Cooperation in Groups." In *Handbook of Evolutionary Psychology*, edited by R. I. M. Dunbar and Louise Barrett, 531–540. Oxford: Oxford University Press.

Warneken, Felix. 2013. "Young Children Proactively Remedy Unnoticed Accidents," *Cognition* 126 (Jan.): 101–108.

Warneken, Felix, and Michael Tomasello. 2006. "Altruistic Helping in Human Infants and Young Chimpanzees," *Science* 311: 1301–1303.

Warner, Carolyn M. 2000. *Confessions of an Interest Group: The Catholic Church and Political Parties in Europe*. Princeton, NJ: Princeton University Press.

Warner, Carolyn M. 2013. "Charitable Giving Model or Muddle?," *The Review of Faith and International Affairs* 11/4 (Winter): 32–36.

Warner, Carolyn M., and Manfred W. Wenner. 2006. "Religion and the Political Organization of Muslims in Europe," *Perspectives on Politics* 4/3 (Sept.): 457–479.

Warner, Carolyn M., Ramazan Kılınç, Christopher W. Hale, Adam B. Cohen, and Kathryn A. Johnson. 2015. "Religion and Public Goods Provision: Experimental and Interview Evidence from Catholicism and Islam," *Comparative Politics* 47/2 (Jan.): 189–209.

Weafer, John A. 2014. *Thirty-Three Good Men: Celibacy, Obedience and Identity*. Dublin: Columba Press.

Weber, Eugen. 1976. *Peasants into Frenchmen*. Palo Alto, CA: Stanford University Press.

Weber, Max. 1958. *The Protestant Ethic and the Spirit of Capitalism*, trans. Talcott Parsons. New York: Scribner.

Wellman, James K. Jr., Katie E. Corcoran, and Kate Stockly-Meyerdirk. 2014. "'God Is Like a Drug': Explaining Interaction Ritual Chains in American Megachurches," *Sociological Forum* 29/3 (Sept.): 650–672.

Whitehead, Andrew L., 2010. "Financial Commitment within Federations of Small Groups: The Effect of Cell-Based Congregational Structure on Individual Giving," *Journal for the Scientific Study of Religion* 49/4: 640–656.

Whitehead, Andrew L., and Samuel Stroope. 2015. "Small Groups, Contexts, and Civic Engagement: A Multilevel Analysis of United States Congregational Life Survey Data," *Social Science Research* 52: 659–670.

Will, Jeffry A., and John K. Cochran. 1995. "God Helps Those Who Help Themselves? The Effects of Religious Affiliation, Religiosity, and Deservedness on Generosity toward the Poor," *Sociology of Religion* 56/3: 327–338.

Wilson, David Sloan. 2002. *Darwin's Cathedral: Evolution, Religion, and the Nature of Society*. Chicago: University of Chicago Press.

Wilson, David Sloan. 2015. *Does Altruism Exist? Culture, Genes and the Welfare of Others*. New Haven, CT: Yale University Press.

Wilson, David Sloan, and Edward O. Wilson. 2007. "Rethinking the Theoretical Foundation of Sociobiology," *The Quarterly Review of Biology* 82/4 (Dec.): 327–348.

Wuthnow, Robert. 1991. *Acts of Compassion: Caring for Others and Helping Ourselves*. Princeton, NJ: Princeton University Press.

Wuthnow, Robert. 1994. *"I Come Away Stronger": How Small Groups Are Shaping American Religion*. Grand Rapids, MI: William B. Eerdmans.

Wuthnow, Robert J. 2009. *Boundless Faith: The Global Outreach of American Churches*. Berkeley: University of California Press.

Wuthnow, Robert J. 2011. "Taking Talk Seriously: Religious Discourse as Social Practice," *Journal for the Scientific Study of Religion* 50/1 (March): 1–21.

Wuthnow, Robert, and John H. Evans, eds. 2002. *The Quiet Hand of God: Faith-Based Activism and the Public Role of Mainline Protestantism*. Berkeley: University of California Press.

Xygalatas, Dimitris, Panagiotis Mitkidis, Ronald Fischer, Paul Reddish, Joshua Skewes, Armin W. Geertz, Andreas Roepstorff, and Joseph Bulbulia. 2013. "Extreme Rituals Promote Prosociality," *Psychological Science* 24/8: 1602–1605.

Yavuz, M. Hakan. 2003. *Islamic Political Identity in Turkey*. Oxford: Oxford University Press.

Yavuz, M. Hakan. 2013. *Toward an Islamic Enlightenment: The Gülen Movement*. Oxford: Oxford University Press.

Yılmaz, Bahri. 2008. "The Relations of Turkey with the European Union: Candidate Forever?" Center for European Studies, Harvard University Working Paper No. 167.

Yükleyen, Ahmet. 2012. *Localizing Islam in Europe: Turkish Islamic Communities in Germany and the Netherlands*. Syracuse, NY: Syracuse University Press.

Zayas, Farishta G. de. 1960. *The Law and Philosophy of Zakat, the Islamic Welfare System*. Damascus: A. Z. Abbasi.

Index

Index